RAY DAVIES

"Kitts' obvious background in literary and social history offers an entirely new and much needed elevation of the caliber of writing on composers from the rock field whose work is deserving of such a broadening of scope."
—Doug Hinman, Author of *The Kinks: All Day and All of the Night: Day by Day Concerts, Recordings, and Broadcasts, 1964–1997*

"A remarkable history of a genius, deftly told through the art of music. Kitts has taken a difficult man and demonstrated his most effective way of life. *Ray Davies: Not Like Everybody Else* is a truly impassioned work."
—Eric James Abbey, Author of *Garage Rock and its Roots: Musical Rebels and the Drive for Individuality*

"Kitts guides us down memory lane with the fascinating history of the great Ray Davies (with and without the Kinks). Kitts has impeccable musical ears, incredible knowledge, and a keen perception about Mr. Davies, which make this book a must for any Kinks/Ray Davies fan, and a great place to start for those who are less familiar with Davies and the Kinks."
—Bob Putignano, www.SoundsofBlue.com

Ray Davies: Not Like Everybody Else is a critical biography of Ray Davies, with a focus on his music and his times. The book studies Davies' work from the Kinks' first singles through his 2006 solo album, from his rock musicals in the early 1970s to his one-man stage show in the 1990s, and from his films to his autobiography. Based on interviews with his closest associates, as well as studies of the recordings themselves, this book creates the most thorough picture of Davies' work to date.

Thomas M. Kitts, Professor of English and Chair of the Division of English/Speech at St. John's University, New York, is the co-editor of *Living on a Thin Line: Crossing Aesthetic Borders with The Kinks*, the author of *The Theatrical Life of George Henry Boker*, articles on American literature and popular culture, reviews of books, CDs, and performances, and a play, *Gypsies*. He is the book review editor of *Popular Music and Society* and the editor of *The Mid-Atlantic Almanack*.

RAY DAVIES

Not Like Everybody Else

Thomas M. Kitts

Routledge
Taylor & Francis Group

NEW YORK AND LONDON

First published 2008
by Routledge
270 Madison Ave, New York, NY 10016

Simultaneously published in the UK
by Routledge
2 Park Square, Milton Park, Abingdon, Oxon OX14 4RN

Routledge is an imprint of the Taylor & Francis Group, an informa business

© 2008 Taylor & Francis

Typeset in Garamond Three by
RefineCatch Limited, Bungay, Suffolk
Printed and bound in the
United States of America on acid-free paper by
Edwards Brothers, Inc.

Library of Congress Cataloging in Publication Data
A catalog record has been requested for this book

ISBN10: 0–415–97768–1 (hbk)
ISBN10: 0–415–97769–X (pbk)
ISBN10: 0–203–93563–2 (ebk)

ISBN13: 978–0–415–97768–5 (hbk)
ISBN13: 978–0–415–97769–2 (pbk)
ISBN13: 978–0–203–93563–7 (ebk)

For Dylan and Holly
my children

For Michael J. Kraus
my late friend and Kinks colleague

For Doug Hinman
and his inspiring and landmark work on the Kinks

CONTENTS

CONTENTS

FIGURES

PREFACE

In the fall 1964, I bought "You Really Got Me" by the Kinks, my first non-Beatles record. I remember playing and replaying both sides of the 45 on my father's old hi-fi in his basement office, sometimes as he worked. I was riveted. Over the next eighteen months or so, I was moved by other Kinks hits as well, especially "All Day and All of the Night," "A Well Respected Man," and "Dedicated Follower of Fashion." Even as a pre-teen I knew these songs were somehow different. But as suddenly as the Kinks came into my life, they disappeared—what did I then know of union problems and rejected American work visas.

Like many others, I rediscovered the Kinks with "Lola," which led me to *The Kink Kronikles* and then *Everybody's in Show-Biz*. Was this really the same band on both these albums? The same band that produced "You Really Got Me"? Indeed, they were special. A bit quirky, but special. In high school, I played catch-up with the back catalogue, coerced my friends into listening and attending Kinks concerts, and preached the gospel of Ray Davies and the Kinks to anyone who would listen. I was hooked. In college, I was inspired as much by Ray Davies as by Homer, Shakespeare, and Fitzgerald to study literature and major in English.

The Kinks have always been underappreciated, a sort of acquired taste. Many rock listeners and pop music scholars were surprised to see the Kinks listed #5 on *Rolling Stone*'s list of Top Ten Rock Bands of the Century, surpassed by only the Beatles, the Rolling Stones, Nirvana, and Led Zeppelin.[1] Why the surprise? Well, there are at least two explanations. Under the leadership of Ray Davies, the Kinks have intentionally maintained a low profile, especially for pop stars, and, under his restless imagination, they have shifted artistic direction so often that it has been difficult to maintain a steady fan base or for marketers to identify an audience. Just consider that after "Lola's" international success the next four of five Kinks albums were rock musicals.

But it is precisely Ray's unpredictable imagination, his lyrical and musical explorations, his filmic and literary experiments, and his quest for perfection that have endeared him and the Kinks to longtime fans. Of course, he has driven bandmates bonkers and managers to despair. He reworks and re-records songs and seems to endlessly reconsider and change strategies—Ray once quipped that manager Nigel Thomas died rather than take another of his phone calls.[2] Through the years, Davies-inspired delays have resulted in missed opportunities and bad timing. It was not unusual, for instance, for the Kinks to tour in support of an unavailable album.

However, difficult though Davies may be, I have never met anyone associated with the Kinks, either musician or manager, who would not jump at the opportunity to work with him again. I asked drummer Mick Avory about this, "He's a special person. . . . Everyone wants to work with him or be on one of his songs."[3] Davies is indeed one of the greatest songwriters to emerge from the rock era. His and the Kinks' influence was immediate on the Beatles, the Who, and then David Bowie; a few years later on the Sex Pistols, Elvis Costello, the Jam, Bob Geldof, the Romantics, Billy Bragg, and XTC; and into the 1990s and the new century with Yo La Tengo, Blur, Oasis, Ron Sexsmith, Fountains of Wayne, Franz Ferdinand, the Killers, and on and on.

Not Like Everybody Else is a critical biography with its focus on the art of Ray Davies. I consider the life only as it impacts the art. The book studies Davies's work from his first singles with the Kinks through his 2006 solo album, from his rock musicals to his one-man stage show, and from his films to his autobiography. The intent is to arrive at a more complete understanding of the achievement of one of the great songwriters and artists to emerge during the post-World War II era. Hopefully, *Not Like Everybody Else* will bring readers, as it did me in the course of writing, to a more thorough and satisfying appreciation of this remarkable artist.

ACKNOWLEDGMENTS

I must thank many people for their help with this book. I am indebted to Mick Avory, Dave Davies, Peter Quaife, Grenville Collins, Nick Baxter-Moore, Steven Hamelman, Jeff Kitts, Michael Lydon, Stephen Paul Miller, Robert Tomes, Bob Putignano, Dave Emlen, James Martens, Trixie Brunschweiler, Ernie Saill, Gary Burns, Don Cusic, Marianne Spellman, Olga Ruocco, Kevin Gatta, Zak Browne, Carey Fleiner, the Official Kinks Fan Club, Frank Lima, Richard Carlin, Linda Kraus, Tammy Thornton, Thomas Bartoldus, David LeBoeuf, Shawn Rush, René Dellemann, Eric Abbey, Kathleen Vouté MacDonald, Nancy McGeveran, Joseph Trumino, Greg Wilson, Basilio Monteiro, Jaime Rodriguez, Mary Courtney, and Jo Mauro. I especially thank Janice Shaman, whose extraordinary assistance has been greatly appreciated, and all those at Routledge who made this book possible: especially Denny Tek, Chris Bowers, and editor Constance Ditzel.

A special thanks to Doug Hinman, whose thorough discography and day-to-day history on the Kinks made it possible for me to concentrate on interpretation, instead of fact finding.

I greatly appreciate permission to use the photographs of Marianne Spellman, Kevin Reynolds, and Olga Ruocco. Other photos are from the private collection of Michael J. Kraus and the private collection of the author. Photographers from those collections could not be identified despite efforts.

Some of the text in this book first appeared in article form in "Establishing a Sound and Theme" and " '. . . in the grand [and not so grand] tradition': Film, Theatre, and the Triumph of *20th Century Man*" in *Living on a Thin Line*, eds. Kitts and Kraus; and "Think Visual: The Kinks vs. the Music Industry," *Popular Music and Society*, 29.2, 2006.

1

NOT LIKE EVERYBODY ELSE
The shaping of Ray Davies, part I

Just after midnight, on June 6, 1944, the Allied forces undertook one of the greatest risks of World War II when they invaded Normandy. Preparations for the world's largest invasion, dubbed Operation Overlord, were long, well over a year, and confidence was cautious. Certainly, Winston Churchill and Franklin Roosevelt expected success, but they also expected enormous casualties. Before retiring for the evening Clementine Churchill joined her husband in the Map Room where the Prime Minister is reported to have said to her, "Do you realize that by the time you wake up in the morning twenty thousand men may have been killed?"[1]

Operation Overlord proved an overwhelming success as wave after wave of Allied troops pounded the shores of occupied France so that within a month over one million new troops had arrived on the continent with far fewer casualties than expected. Fighting would remain intense over the next several months, but with the success of the invasion and the liberation of Rome on June 5, a spirit of optimism began to take hold in Great Britain, despite renewed German air attacks on England shortly after the invasion. Finally, it had begun to look as though England would emerge victorious.

Raymond Douglas Davies, who would develop into one of the most gifted songwriters of the rock era, was born two weeks after D-Day on June 21, 1944. He was the first son of Fred and Annie Davies, who had previously had six daughters, ranging in age, at the time of Ray's birth, from approximately 6 to 20.[2] The daughters had all been born in the East End, a densely populated working-class stronghold of London. Fred and Annie moved their family to north London in 1939 rather than follow the government's recommendation to evacuate children out of the city because of the threat of Nazi bombers—which, of course, materialized and inflicted large civilian casualties and decimated parts of London and other cities from August 1940 through March 1945.

The Davieses first moved to Huntingdon Road, East Finchley, some five miles outside of central London—"the leafy suburbs" as Ray would quip on occasion. Dave Davies, born three years after Ray, reports that his parents did not feel completely comfortable on Huntingdon Road. The

Davieses were loud and noisy and had frequent family visitors from among their extended families—there were some thirty siblings between Fred and Annie. Most of the children in the area, like those in central London, had been evacuated. After about six months, in January 1940, the family decided to move to a smaller home about a mile and a half away at 6 Denmark Terrace, officially in the postal zone of East Finchley, but just up the road from the center of Muswell Hill in a small area sometimes called Fortis Green after the road that connects East Finchley and Muswell Hill. Money was always tight, the home always overcrowded, but the "leafy suburbs" were refreshing and the early morning smell of baked bread from the nearby bakery comforting.

It is in this north London community and in the post-War years where the artistic sensibility and vision of Ray Davies is rooted. Davies's scope may have widened and deepened through the years, but by the time he left art college in January 1964, his vision was largely established.

The parents and the working-class home

Class consciousness came to the forefront of English daily existence in the late nineteenth century. At that time, according to Asa Briggs, the differences between the residents of London's working-class East End and its upper-class West End began to be pronounced. Not only did the gap in wealth and lifestyles widen in the two communities, but so also did a powerful psychological schism. The result for the working class is that a collective identity developed based on shared experience or what Peter Bailey termed "knowingness," which is, essentially, an awareness of situation.[3] While not all members of the class respond in the same way to the outside world, they remain united in their differentness. For the Davies family and for others, being working class provides social and self-definition as well as a sense of authority in a world in which, until recent times, they had little opportunity.

As a family, the Davieses demonstrated many of the qualities associated with their class. They were practical, resilient, and family oriented. They were necessarily deferent at times and defiant at others, cynical of government bureaucrats and yet patriotic, reserved but capable of rage or elation. They firmly supported the Labour Party and passionately rooted for their favorite sports teams and for England in the World Cup. They enjoyed working-class entertainments like the pre-War music hall, the post-War cinema, the beach at Ramsgate and Southend, and always the pub. A working-class sensibility or "knowingness" is embedded throughout the Ray Davies song catalog from the angst of "You Really Got Me," the satire of "A Well Respected Man," the pride and contentment of "Autumn Almanac," the confusion of "Definite Maybe," and the frustration with his class in "Stand Up Comic."

Solidly working class, Fred Davies, the father, was a fun-loving man and a drinker who chatted up the women in the local pubs and hosted regular Saturday night parties in the family home. Trained as a butcher and later as a gardener, he was nonetheless frequently unemployed. Both his sons, Ray and Dave, recognized their father's shortcomings, and are far more understanding than resentful. After all, Fred included the entire family in his Saturday night parties; he took the family on picnics and to the beach in his black Vauxhall 12—he was one of the first to own a car in the neighborhood—and he supported his sons' ambitions, whether in sports or music. In 1960, when Ray was 16 and Dave 13, Fred arranged their first ever gig at the Clissold Arms, the pub directly across the street from the Davies home and which, because of the brothers' appearance, was honored as one of the first fourteen Britain Pubs in Time in 2006.[4]

While he certainly loved his family, the general response to Fred as a family man is mixed. At times, Dave said, to his mother he could be a "bastard" who would withhold money from her to buy a round at a pub.[5] Others too discussed his shirking of familial responsibility and one interviewee, preferring anonymity, simply referred to him as a "wanker." Fred may have been a bit lazy and selfish, but he was not mean spirited, and Ray has warm memories of going to Arsenal matches with his father, and, after stardom, of sitting at the piano and playing his latest songs for him. "My dad was kind of square, but in a cool way."[6]

In the home Fred yielded authority to his wife Annie. If the mention of Mr. Davies provokes mixed reactions, the response to Mrs. Davies is unequivocal: she was admired by all. She managed the household on funds often scarce and inconsistent and yet she was generous and hospitable. Kinks co-founder Peter Quaife remembers Mrs. Davies's always offering him food, no matter what time of day or no matter how busy she was. "She used to make these incredible egg sandwiches. God they were good! Thick slabs of white bread oozing with butter and a rich fried egg in between. Made a hell of a mess, but oh so satisfying!"[7] Grenville Collins, part of the Kinks' first management team, used to enjoy spending time with Annie: "She was down to earth, very brave, and very tough. I benefited from knowing her," recalls the middle-class Collins. "What she said in the home was law."[8]

Mrs. Davies had a chaotic household to manage. The population of the home might best be described as floating. "It was like a railway station," Dave said of his home, "people in and out and the front door always open."[9] By the time Ray entered St. James Church of England Primary School, in addition to the nuclear family of ten, the small home, three bedrooms upstairs and kitchen and front room downstairs, could include grandparents, sons-in-law, grandchildren, and many aunts, uncles, cousins, who would drop in for an evening or a few days. Because of Mrs. Davies's resourcefulness, neither Ray nor Dave ever remembers lacking food, clothing, or gifts at birthdays and Christmas.

As much as her time was stretched and as much as she relied on her daughters to look after her young sons, Annie oversaw all the details of the home with diligence and protectiveness. When her daughter Peg had an illegitimate child with a French West African, it caused a local scandal, but Mrs. Davies, a fierce defender of her children, comforted daughter and granddaughter and rallied her children on behalf of Jacqueline Michelle, who was teased by neighborhood children and cousins as "Blackie-Jackie." She also confronted a teacher to end her discriminatory treatment of Jackie. A few years later, the ever-watchful mother confronted Mr. Bond, a well-intentioned art teacher who gave a teenage Ray after-school tutoring. With a kind of working-class suspicion of artist types, Mrs. Davies marched down to school and forbade Mr. Bond from working with Ray after school. Bond understood the concern and told Ray that his mother was "a woman of outstanding character."[10]

Although always well intentioned, Mrs. Davies did make mistakes— one which would haunt Dave his entire life. When Dave was sixteen, his girlfriend and perhaps the love of his life, Sue Sheehan, became pregnant. Both Dave and Sue wanted to raise the child together. However, Mrs. Davies and the Sheehans plotted against the young lovers, sending Sue away to have the baby and telling each teen that the other had fallen out of love. The couple would not reunite until 1993 when Dave met his daughter Tracey for the first time and when the former lovers uncovered the scheme that kept them apart. The longing for Sue inspired many of Dave's most poignant compositions: "Funny Face," "Love Me Till the Sun Shines," "Suzannah's Still Alive," "Mindless Child of Motherhood," and "This Man He Weeps Tonight."

Life in the Davies household was always lively, "like being in a Fellini movie," Dave said, "a collage of weird wonderful people, all these big faces, drunk and dancing around the family piano."[11] Despite Annie Davies's best efforts, the home rarely ran smoothly and the family was always a bit different from their neighbors. The Davies's problems were usually more extreme, and their home, even with the era's housing short-age, was more crowded and noisier than the others. There was, to be sure, little privacy for anyone and the overcrowding led to constant rifts among members.

In many ways, the chaos of the home would come to resemble the chaos surrounding the Kinks, who have always been different, always outsiders in the rock world. They did not play Monterey Pop or Woodstock, the major rock festivals of the 1960s, or the Live Aid benefits of the 1980s, and although the Kinks, and Davies in particular, are greatly admired, musicians tend to keep their distance. Marianne Faithful toured with the Kinks in 1964 and recognized something dark about the band. They were "very gothic, creepy and silent. Uptight and fearful of everyone," she said.[12] "Only the mad men in those bands would tolerate us," says Quaife, "like Keith Moon, Brian Jones, the Bonzo Dog Doo Dah Band and the disc jockey Kenny Everett."[13] Chrissie Hynde summed it all when she termed the Kinks, and Ray and Dave specifically, as the Kray twins of rock-and-roll, after London's most notorious gangsters.

At the head of the Kinks chaos has always stood Ray, much as his mother stood at the head of the Davies home—autocratic, stubborn, and proud.

Saturday night parties

The Davies family lived for Saturday nights and the Saturday night parties they hosted. After the pubs closed at 11:00 p.m., Fred would invite his drinking cronies to join his extended family and children's friends for an after-hours party in what would be the family's overcrowed front room, which, in these largely pre-television days, held the family's old upright piano, the most important piece of furniture in the Davies's home, and a 78 r.p.m. wind-up gramophone.

The parties featured plenty of beer and sandwiches and plenty of music and sing-alongs, especially to music-hall numbers with Rene, the most accomplished pianist in the family, on the upright, yielding at times to one of her other sisters, usually Joyce or Gwen. With only the slightest of urgings, Fred, a tap dancer in his younger days, would play his banjo and dance, and Annie a bit more reluctantly would sing, a favorite was "St. Teresa of the Roses," a top-ten UK hit in 1956 for Malcolm Vaughn. Craving attention, Ray remembers his first performance, a pre-school croon of Perry Como's "Temptation." The highlight of the party and the most embarrassing moment for the young Ray and Dave was the father's show-stopping rendition of Cab Calloway's "Minnie the Moocher." Fred, who Ray has referred to as a "closet vaudevillian," would sing and dance about the room and more often than not end his inebriated performance by crashing to the floor.

The influence of these parties on the Kinks, particularly the campy Kinks of the early to mid-1970s, is remarkable. Whether consciously or unconsciously, it seemed as if Ray was trying to recreate the Saturday night parties of his family's home—complete with chaos, beer, and sing-alongs. The band would perform with cases of beer on stage (at least in New York and other tolerant cities), although not much actually got consumed during the performance. Ray might feign drunkenness and spray beer on audiences, slip usually unintentionally, and he might balance a can of beer on his head, a favorite parlor trick, but he was never drunk for a performance. Mick Avory said that Davies "might have a beer or two on the day of a performance," but that "he was never a great guzzler of anything." He went on to say that Ray might take a puff on a joint now and then, but that "we were never a druggie band. We couldn't afford it.

5

Even when the cocaine was rife, no one used it. . . . I've seem more down the golf club."[14]

Like the Saturday night parties, a Kinks concert could be a loose affair, but always within Ray's control. He might engage in a dialogue with the audience, responding perhaps to paper plates flung to the stage with song titles; Dave might talk off microphone with his fans who garnered tickets to be in front of his stage left position, and Ray and Dave might exchange some unbrotherly jibes and sneers. The set would feature a sampling of some un-rock-and-roll songs, resembling music-hall numbers, like "You Are My Sunshine," "Banana Boat," "Baby Face," and others, but omit some of the band's big hits. A certainty was at least one sing-along, not a hip feature in the late 1960s and early 1970s when extended jams and drum solos reflected the sophistication or pretense of the rock performer. Ray might dance, prance, and shimmy around the stage, play the part of a music-hall comedian, and go extended periods without strumming the guitar hung from his neck, which often seemed just another prop. The Kinks could be sloppy in performance, and audiences would leave wondering how to reconcile the clownish performer they had just seen with the introspective composer of "Waterloo Sunset," "Days," "Sitting in My Hotel," "Celluloid Heroes," and others. Like a lively party, the Kinks could be unpredictable, exhilarating, silly, witty, and pointless, all at once—at their best, they were sublime, even sublimely sloppy.

One evening in September 1964, after "You Really Got Me" broke and after a performance at the Silverblades Ice Rink in Streatham, south London, the Kinks and their family and friends celebrated at a local pub. In a private moment Ray asked his father if he were disappointed that his older son had not become a football player. Fred responded with very meaningful encouragement and approval: "Ray, you are doing exactly what I have always wanted to do. Now, let's get pissed."[15]

Sibling rivalry

It is indeed impossible to discuss the Kinks without mentioning sibling rivalry. Certainly, the longstanding tension is real between Ray and Dave or, as journalists frequently refer to them, rock-and-roll's Cain and Abel.[16] Onstage shouting matches and offstage fisticuffs were never publicity stunts. Although frequently juvenile and exacerbating to those working with them, the battles have given rise to some great music. Dave's loud and angry guitar assaults, with spiraling solos, are a fitting counterpoint to Ray's witty lyrics and often vulnerable character portraits and vocal deliveries. Although Ray has performed with several gifted guitarists in his solo career, no other guitarist quite suits Ray like Dave. The music—at its best, forceful, edgy, and elevating—absorbs the tension between the two. Ray explains with a quotation from Orson Welles's *The Third Man*: "Italy has

Figure 1.1 Ray showers the audience with beer in the 1980s. Photo courtesy of Marianne Spellman

had 3,000 years of wars, fighting all the time, and also all the creativity—Michaelangelo [*sic*]. . . . And Switzerland's had 3,000 years of peace, never gets committed, and what has it produced? The cuckoo clock!"[17]

Ray treats the origins of the rivalry humorously in *X-Ray*. Evoking fairy-tales, he talks about his earliest days as being "full of splendour . . . spoiled and mollycoddled to an excessive but wondrous degree, totally befitting the arrival of the first son in a family of girls. . . . Life was simply perfection."[18] Then, on February 3, 1947, David Russell Gordon Davies entered the world, "invading [Ray's] turf."[19] The new son seized attention from his older brother which only increased as Dave turned into a toddler and Ray began school.

As children, Ray and Dave were close only for occasional stretches. At times, they were typical brothers three years apart: best friends and confidants one minute and violent enemies the next. Once, after the brothers saw a French film about an escaped mental patient named Lion, they playfully spoke gibberish to one another for a brief period. Other times, anxious to escape their mother's punishment, they would run to sister Rosie's home only to have Rosie send them back to mom. For most brothers, the physical battles and intense emotional expressions eventually give way to more rational impulses. It is impossible to say why Ray and Dave's rivalry has not subsided, but perhaps it has something to do with Ray's moving out of the Denmark Terrace home at 13 to move in with Rosie, her husband, and son. During the times when most sibling rivalries diffuse themselves, Ray and Dave lived apart, coming together for family functions and music, but not engaged in the daily living experience.

Music brought the brothers together as teenagers and has never let them drift too far apart. When Ray was twenty and Dave seventeen, the Kinks had their first international hit with "You Really Got Me." The long hours together, the pressures to produce hits, and the emphasis on youth and excess in the rock world only seemed to escalate the rivalry, as did the almost usual tension in a rock group between the two key positions of singer and lead guitarist, especially when one feels underappreciated by bandmates, fans, and journalists. In short time, the constant bickering of the pair became an ingrained part of the group's dynamics, work habits, and musical success. It is quite possible that the brothers, consciously or unconsciously, did not try or want to end the rivalry, somehow fearful that it would de-energize the music.

Additionally, Ray's secretiveness has been a constant source of anxiety for Dave. From boyhood, Ray has rarely been open with anyone. "He was very quiet, deep and lonely," says Dave of Ray. "He never shared anything—least of all his mind. And as a little boy I felt completely left out of his life."[20] Ray's most communicative and revealing side has long rested in his songs, but, somewhat paradoxically, screened by his characters, irony, and other subterfuges.

8

Through the years their ambivalence has rarely allowed one brother to say an unequivocally kind word about the other. Replying once to the false and inexhaustible rumor that Jimmy Page played the solo on "You Really Got Me," Ray delivered a backhanded defense of Dave: "My brother Dave hasn't got too much going for him, but to try to take that stuff away from him is bullshit. He invented that guitar sound. I wrote the song, but it wouldn't have been anything without his work."[21] Or consider Dave's praise of Ray's songwriting, particularly "Where Have All the Good Times Gone": "It's such a weird paradox that Ray, who wrote that lovely song, would later become so abusive to me, so cruel and creatively draining. . . . On the one hand he's sensitive enough to understand even the slightest emotion, to feel for the plight and frustration of the underdog, able to offer great insight and compassion. . . . [Yet] he is at times, venomous, spiteful, and completely self-involved. A puzzling dichotomy."[22]

Their relationship is a "puzzling dichotomy." Each considers himself the caretaker of the other and each recalls epiphanic moments in their youth when they realized their protector's role. Ray talks of a recurring nightmare in which Dave slips from his grasp off the side of a cliff. He awoke to see his brother sleeping beside him: "I would always have to protect this interloper, even though I could never quite forgive him for spoiling my solitary but idyllic experience."[23] For his part, Dave tells of pursuing his older brother during one of Ray's sleepwalking experiences in which he thought himself pursued by a tiger: "I realized that night even though I was the younger brother, I would somehow have to fulfil the role of the older one and keep a look-out for him."[24] In large measure, each has looked after the other in time of need. Dave has helped to see Ray through emotional crises and Ray helped to care for Dave after his stroke in 2004. With fitting tragicomic irony, Ray commented, "I cooked really good Italian food for him and his girlfriend. As soon as he started to recover we had an argument and he disappeared."[25]

Both brothers have so long been distrustful of one another that each can only regard the other's actions with suspicion. When Ray hosted a surprise fiftieth birthday party for Dave at the Clissold Arms, Dave believed Ray had ulterior motives, slightly nasty and self-serving. Ray, Dave believed, not only wanted to make himself look generous, but he also wanted to be sure that Dave's age was well known. Dave recalled that for his own fiftieth, Ray opted for semi-seclusion. In 2006, hardly sounding as if the rivalry lost force or ridiculousness, Ray said, "[Dave's] criticisms don't sting any more than they did when he was 5 years old. And basically he hasn't moved on from that point. It's still childish backbiting, but you're talking about a 50-plus-year-old man now. I take it all with a pinch of salt."[26] Curiously, the brothers seem to have few if any shared friends. A friend to one makes one, not quite an enemy, but an object of suspicion to the other.

The absurdity of the rivalry has not been lost on the brothers. From time to time they have been able to poke fun at themselves and their relationship, most notably on the darkly comic "Hatred (A Duet)" from *Phobia* in 1993. On the track, Ray equates the battling brothers to rival nations, religions, and races, but at least the brothers accept their reality: "There's no way that we can agree." After all, they sing, "hatred is the only thing that keeps us together" and "the only thing that lasts forever."

When Ray and Dave create music, however, a remarkably positive and almost telepathic energy emerges. Ray might enter the studio with a rough idea for a song, some chords and a tempo, and the band would jam— rarely would he reveal the lyrics or melody until very late in the process. Dave would frequently veer the jam into the direction Ray had been grasping for. Ray would review the tapes of the session at home and return with a more complete song. "It used to surprise a lot of people who'd see us in the studio," writes Dave, "because we didn't communicate very much. But when you've got that going for you, you don't need to talk. It was very quick, all the good stuff, all the ideas—we always had so many ideas. That psychic bond that Ray and I have had has been really import- ant. But it's nearly destroyed us as well."[27] Ray talked about the telepathy and even spiritual bond of the brothers during his *20th Century Man / Storyteller* shows, adding that the closest he has "ever felt to religion was not [singing] in the church choir on Sunday, but playing with Dave and rehearsing."[28]

It is largely but only somewhat true to think of Ray as the intellect, the calculated, or the head of the Kinks and Dave as the emotion, guts, or heart of the band. Through the years in the Kinks, they have frequently switched roles both on stage and in the studio, and each has proven both controlled and emotive in their solo work—Dave has surprised many by being a tough taskmaster as a band leader. Still, Dave says, "Ray is a genius as far as a lyricist is concerned, but I've always felt I've been the balls part of the band."[29] Very similarly, Ray states, "Dave brings total spontaneity, aggression, immediacy and a unique vocal blend with me. . . . [He] does magic takes, and he stops me from disappearing up my asshole."[30]

The young Ray Davies

Ray Davies was not your ordinary Muswell Hill, working-class boy. He was quiet, aloof, and introspective, an enigma to his father who could relate much more easily to his younger and more boisterous son, who would set off stink bombs and cut school so frequently that he had to erase the zero on one year-end absentee report to reduce the 60 to 6. Fred's relationship with Ray was hardly antagonistic, but it was perhaps distant and strained by a father's inability to comprehend his son. In his

20th Century Man performances, Ray would lift his mug of beer, of which he rarely if ever took more than a sip or two, and proclaim, "My father allowed me to call him 'Dad' after three or four pints of this stuff."[31] While Ray was obviously joking, his quip hints at the disconnect between his father and him—despite their early trips to Arsenal matches. Throughout his career, Ray has sought his father's approval, which he generally received. Ray has never seemed to have a strong sonly impulse to cast off the father: "Most young people rebelled but I wanted to write songs my dad would like," he said.[32]

From an early age Ray, who related more to his mother, took on the features of a Byronic hero: reflective, melancholy, intelligent, independent, and creative. It is an image that publicists and Ray have cultivated for years. The liner notes to *The Kinks Greatest Hits!*, released in America in 1966, describe Davies as "a brooding-faced, long-haired genius. Soft of speech and with cutting eyes. . . . He tries to make that world fit him. Or if not that, shucks that world aside and lives in one all his own." In *X-Ray* Davies refers to himself as a "latter-day Byron."[33] These Byronic traits have long concerned his family. To them, he was too frequently sullen and discontented, spending too much time by himself. He was and still is a notoriously bad sleeper, an insomniac who at least no longer sleepwalks as he did when a child. He did excel at sports, however, where he had some friends, and he did passably in school, better in the arts and English than science and math. No one, including Davies, recalls any traumatic incident, and all seem content to explain that he was born that way. "I came from quite a happy social environment," Ray explains, "but I needed the space. I suppose I was more introvert [*sic*], more difficult to understand."[34]

The two members of the family who best understood the young Ray were his two oldest sisters, Rosie and Rene. Rene, eighteen years older than Ray, was the first to recognize his artistic ability. Married to an abusive husband and living in Canada, Rene and her son Bobby would return to Fortis Green for extended visits. She would bring the latest pop records, bake cakes, and spend time with Ray. She would often crawl into his bed with him during restless nights and she would give Ray impromptu piano lessons. A teacher in Canada, she recognized Ray's talent and appreciated his differentness.

Just prior to his thirteenth birthday, Ray had been nagging his parents about a Spanish guitar in the Les Aldrich Music Shop in Muswell Hill. Rene surprised Ray on his birthday with the guitar. After Rene played a tune on the piano from *Oklahoma!*, her favorite musical and a hit movie in 1955, Ray joined in on guitar. Then Rene, who suffered with heart disease caused by rheumatic fever in childhood, disobeyed doctor's orders for bed rest and went out dancing, one of her favorite activities. Tragedy struck when later that evening Rene collapsed and died on the dance floor at the Lyceum Ballroom in London while the orchestra played a song from

Oklahoma! She was 31. The sensitive Ray was shattered by the loss of not just his sister, but also "a mentor and source of inspiration."[35] He was shocked into silence for about a month.

Rene's funeral and the family's response confused Ray. He couldn't understand how the family could sing maudlin songs, eat sandwiches, and drink beer just after the burial. A profound sadness clutched him, leaving him further disconnected from his family. His Uncle Frank rechristened him "the miserable little bleeder with the long face."[36] By his own admission, Ray said his very presence would turn the most festive occasion solemn, as he "rarely smiled" and "never laughed."[37] It seemed as if the little boy who had once sung "Temptation" had vanished. His behavior, unusual before Rene's death, was becoming of increasing concern to the Davieses. Only Rosie, it seemed, could cut through his silence.

Annie Davies reached the breaking point when she came upon Ray pounding his shins with a hammer. Bruised from playing a football match without shin pads, Ray was trying to strengthen his resistance. It was more innocent that his mother supposed, more a teen's skewed thinking than anything else, but given her son's recent state of mind, her alarm was understandable. A doctor told Mrs. Davies that the bruises on his shin would heal readily enough, but that her son was deeply troubled. The doctor recommended therapy, which in the late 1950s to a very practical, working-class mother must have seemed unsettling and ominous. Always concerned for her children, Mrs. Davies traveled with Ray two days a week to a clinic in Pembridge Villas, Notting Hill Gate. Mr. Davies decided not to accompany his son and wife, perhaps in denial or ashamed.

Not surprisingly, Ray, who has always been distrustful of people, was a reluctant patient in therapy, which may not have benefited him at all. When after some time he failed to identify with the first therapist, a second was assigned to him with a similar lack of success. If therapists found him unresponsive, he found them just as unresponsive as they refused to answer his questions directly. The result of the visits was that he fell behind in his school work and gained a kind of notoriety as a "troubled misfit," one of the "weirdos," and a "loony" whose problem was discussed "in the same shameful whispers as that of the 'queers' who hung around the toilets at the Quadrant bus terminal at the top of Muswell Hill."[38]

During his time in therapy, Mrs. Davies decided that Ray should move out of their chaotic home on Denmark Terrace and in with Rosie and her family on Yeatman Road, Highgate, about a mile away. This was very perceptive and generous of Mrs. Davies, who realized that Ray's best interest was to be with the family member who most related to him and to be where he could have more privacy and more space. While Arthur Anning, Rosie's husband and the inspiration for *Arthur*, could be strict, Ray got along with him and grew close to Rosie's son Terry, who was Ray's approximate age and who worked on some early tours with the

Kinks. During these years, Terry became more of a brother to Ray than Dave while Bobby, Rene's son who stayed behind, became more Dave's brother. Ray was quite content with the Annings, and was devastated when Arthur moved his reluctant sister and nephew to Australia probably in May 1964, prior to the Kinks' major success.

Ray got through these troubled early teen years with the support of his family, particularly Mrs. Davies and the Annings, and with the relief of music and sports. However, bouts of depression have plagued Davies throughout his life, even during seemingly successful periods. In the early spring of 1966, after a string of UK and international hits, there was some talk that Davies needed help and that a temporary stay in a sanatorium might be necessary for the young but fragile and overworked rising star. Manager Robert Wace said that 1965 was "a very bad year for Ray . . . he was very, very unstable."[39] But Wace and co-manager Grenville Collins convinced the family that Ray would be secure under their watch, a duty they assumed diligently. "It is not easy being Ray Davies," one close to him told me. "Under all the brilliance is torture. But without the torture we wouldn't have the great art."[40]

Sports

Sports were very important to the young Ray Davies, especially during his troubled teen years. Through sports Ray was able to interact with others his age, to escape his burdens, to raise his self-esteem, to relieve some self-doubts, and to develop his character, specifically his competitive impulse—which he drew on throughout his career. His father recognized his on-field accomplishments with pride and relief. As in many working-class families, sports brought father and son together to talk and debate, to escape routine, and to dream. As long as Ray was active in sports and cheering for Arsenal, the family's favorite football team and still a passionate interest of Ray and Dave, his father never really believed there was anything seriously wrong with Ray.

Ray excelled at several sports, including track, football, cricket, and boxing. As the incident with the hammer indicates, he took athletic competition very seriously, but never more so than upon his return to William Grimshaw. In early 1960, fifteen-year-old Ray decided to leave school, a decision that was to shape the remainder of his life—but not the way Ray had anticipated. Neither Ray nor Dave liked Grimshaw: "It was a totalitarian system," recalls Ray. "They were preparing factory fodder. I grew up with a fear of being crushed."[41]

Responding to an advertisement in the *London Evening Standard*, Ray took a job in the art department of an engineering magazine in Holborn, central London. He quickly became disillusioned by the boring routine and the lack of creative challenge: "I soon discovered that even though

I had my own office, I was really nothing more than a glorified office boy. . . . I spent most of my time making tea."[42] When asked to demonstrate some creativity, he was provided with inferior paper so as not to waste the good supply. In short time, he left the magazine for other equally unfulfilling jobs.

Frustrated, Ray re-enrolled at William Grimshaw in the fall 1960, returning revitalized. "It was my renaissance as a student—I became sports captain and house captain and we actually won things. I studied art and painting."[43] Indeed, what happened to Davies during his remaining time at Grimshaw would redirect his life. He met Quaife in a music class in the fall 1961 and he came to the attention of Mr. Bond, who gave him extra tutoring for the A-level painting exams and encouraged Davies to attend the Hornsey College of Arts and Crafts in September 1962.

A series of injuries, however, curtailed any promise Davies demonstrated as an athlete. His first serious injury occurred when running as anchor man on a relay team in a district meet. He had just led his team to victory when a protest from an opposing team forced a rerun. Again, Ray's team won, but as Davies sped down the stretch his foot hit a slight bump in the track. A dull pain ran up his spine and down his legs before shooting through his chest and squeezing his heart. Nevertheless he pressed forward, sensing victory and anxious to please his cheering parents. As the race concluded, still in pain, Ray was unable to bend down and untie his shoelaces. Although the pain lingered for some time, he concealed his injury afraid that he would be prohibited from the upcoming football and cricket seasons.

Ray's most serious injury occurred while playing football for Harvey against Faraday, another Grimshaw house. As he leaped for a ball from a corner kick, two defenders tackled Davies who crashed to the ground with his lower back striking the base of the goal post. The pain numbed his entire body and he felt his old track injury aggravated. Although carried off the field, he returned to finish the game, determined not to disappoint his team. The pain, however, lingered for weeks and frightened Davies, who finally realized that he needed treatment. Less than sympathetic, the doctor not only dashed Davies's World Cup dreams and warned him against sports, but he also told him that, in time, he would most likely become disabled. Despite the doctor's counsel, Davies continued to play sports and has throughout his life, and he shows no signs of any disability—even after a severe bullet wound to the leg in a 2004 New Orleans robbery. But after the doctor's visit, Ray envisioned himself transforming into a hunchback, much like the one who worked in Muswell Hill as a gardener, whom the neighborhood children mocked, and who, years later, would inspire one of his most poignant songs, "Autumn Almanac."

Davies's competitive spirit and the will to win are apparent in a story he tells about his race against an accomplished runner in the 220-yard dash in the inter-school competition which placed Grimshaw against more prestigious grammar schools with self-superior youths. As the runners positioned themselves, Davies noticed his chief rival assuming the classic crouch. Davies generally ran from an upright position because of his back problems. However, on this occasion, he was determined not to yield any advantage to his opponent, so he shifted into the standard starting position. As the gun sounded and the racers sprang from their blocks, Davies felt a sharp pain across his back, which gave his rival a huge early lead. Davies pushed himself, but finished a stride behind for second place. "I had mentally brought about my own defeat," he reflected. "I had tried to be orthodox, just like everybody else," perhaps suggesting that the race holds the seed for "I'm Not Like Everybody Else," a favorite among Kinks' listeners, though never a hit single.[44] Throughout his life, Davies has recalled the race, an epiphanic moment for him, particularly when a record label demanded he be more conventional.

The same day also provided an unexpected and humorous moment, which Davies would later draw upon as a performer. At the close of the day, unable to bend after a first-place relay finish, Ray was approached by a young girl on whom he had a crush. While she unlaced his shoes, she told him that the girls had voted him "the boy with the best arse in the school."[45] One of Davies's favorite stage routines, beginning around 1970, has been to turn his back to the audience and invite them to have a look at "the best arse in show-biz."

From a boxing defeat, Davies learned a quick lesson on emotional transference and performance. A very solid schoolboy boxer, Ray advanced in local competitions to an important match against the reigning schoolboy champion of Great Britain, Ronnie Brooks. Ray felt prepared for the fight after some lessons from his brother-in-law Joe Warwick, husband of Dolly and a one-time fighter himself. Brooks, however, proved too tough, physically and mentally, and too well trained. He thrashed Ray, who refused to stay down on the canvas, forcing the referee to stop the fight. "My brain ached for days afterwards," Davies recalled.[46] He realized he was out boxed and outwitted, but was anxious to learn from his defeat. He approached Brooks, who was cordial enough outside the ring, and asked him about strategy. "Well," the young champion revealed, "when I looked at you on the other side, I built up hate for you and I beat you." From the conversation, Ray said he realized that "it's the fanatics who do things in the end. You got to be angry about *something*."[47] More importantly, he learned to draw from his emotions and to project emotions, not necessarily on another person but into a song, an audience, or an imaginary individual. A few short years later, during the recording of "You Really Got Me," he imagined a girl before him and how "every emotion I had was focused on that one image, and nobody could deny me this moment."[48]

Davies's schoolboy boxing success might surprise many who attended a Kinks concert in the early 1970s when Davies merged his music-hall leanings with glam or glitter rock for his campy onstage persona. Effeminate onstage he was anything but offstage. In the fall 1971 at the Ritz Theater in Staten Island, NY, Ray pulled the plug when opening act Yes extended their set in the first of two shows and then booted keyboardist Rick Wakeman on his return backstage.

Sports left Davies with back pains that did not disappear when he left Grimshaw. Throughout his career he has performed in pain. In the mid-1960s, he remembers performing on *Ready Steady Go!* without being able to move, "standing completely bolt upright." Fortunately, the band was miming and he struggled through. "I'm still very restricted," he said in 1994. "I take Panadol. Thank God I don't have to take very strong pills for it any more."[49] Tour and travel plans have long taken Davies's back into consideration. Long rides in a motor vehicle can be painfully uncomfortable and difficult when a performance looms. In May 1998, for instance, rather than drive the approximately three to four hours from Atlantic City to East Hampton, Long Island, for a benefit performance, Ray decided to fly into a local Long Island airport. Unfortunately, with typical Kinks luck, the flight was delayed because of fog and Davies arrived just in time for the performance.

But sports did more than reveal to Davies his strong competitive impulse and his need to win; more importantly, it taught Davies to become self-reliant. Winning, he learned, was within his grasp and would result largely from internal and not external forces. Thus, from sports, he increased his confidence in his own resources and judgments. Such confidence has driven Davies to command all things Kinks and to be an overbearing and over-scrupulous colleague. He records and rerecords tracks endlessly. Quaife recalls being so frustrated by Ray's obsessive reworking of the intro to "Dedicated Follower of Fashion" that he and the other Kinks staged a mutiny and refused to record more takes. According to Quaife, Davies quietly placed the tapes of the song on the studio floor, lit a match, and set fire to them. The band was forced to rerecord what all knew would be a hit.

Davies has called on his competitive impulses and uncanny instincts to provide the Kinks with timely, much needed hits. Around the time of his twentieth birthday, with the Kinks about to be dropped from Pye Records, Davies demanded over the label's objections that the band record and then, when he was not satisfied, rerecord "You Really Got Me." Some six years later, again with the Kinks trying to re-establish themselves in the United States, Davies produced "Lola," another innovative hit. Time after time, Davies has produced a necessary hit single or album by listening to his own creative urges and bucking trends to start new ones.

At a pair of sold-out performances at Queens College, NY, in May 1997, Davies demonstrated his independence, competitiveness, and the long-term significance of his boxing match with Brooks. Anxious to work on another project in England, Davies was not looking forward to the shows. With the Friday night performance barely underway, Davies complained about the quality of the onstage monitors. Then, during a story about the front room of his Fortis Green home, Big Bill Broonzy's "Baby, Please Don't Go," part of the pre-performance soundtrack, burst from the speakers. Davies slammed his copy of *X-Ray* to the stage and walked off. When he returned ten minutes later, he announced that he would not perform *20th Century Man*, but that he would tell some stories and play greatest hits. "That's what you want anyway, isn't it?" he snidely asked. Although they did not see *20th Century Man*, the audience left satisfied. One audience member argued afterwards that Davies's eruption and walk-off were planned—they were not. Davies, however, was not content with the evening. He had satisfied the audience, but in the easiest way—with greatest hits.

Davies was not in much better spirits for the Saturday evening performance, although he did perform *20th Century Man*. He confused accompanist Pete Mathison when he spontaneously left off the climactic end to Act One, a story of a Kinks encounter with the Beatles, and, previously, he had responded crudely to a well-intentioned fan who, when Davies asked rhetorically what an 8-watt amplifier sounded like, called out, "Show us." Davies belligerently told him to "stick your finger up your ass and tell me. Better yet, stick two fingers up your ass and then take a crap. Because that is what it sounded like—shit." Later in Act One, Davies *almost* apologized, explaining that at Kinks shows members of the audience routinely called out, and this fan was just evoking a Kinks concert. The semi-apology was met with some appeasement by a very silent audience.

In Act Two, Davies, for the first time during the two performances, regained his composure for an absolutely inspired performance. He performed the act in its entirety and with what seemed like good cheer and enthusiasm. He gave the show that he intended to perform, not greatest hits, but one which included new and unfamiliar songs. Interestingly, he refused an encore from a very appreciative audience, although he routinely performed encores as part of *20th Century Man*, usually two or three greatest hits. He would leave his mark with this audience on his terms and with integrity, and not with conventional or schmaltzy aids. In this second act, Davies demonstrated all the determination of a boxer behind in a match. He seemed to reimagine the audience as the opponent, which put him in the psychological frame of mind to perform memorably.

2

SOMETHING BETTER BEGINNING

The shaping of Ray Davies, part II

Music was pervasive in the Davies household. The sisters played the piano, the dad the banjo, all sang and danced, and the gramophone constantly spun music from a wide spectrum of pop selected by family members representing a broad range of ages and tastes. As a result, Ray absorbed the jazzy pop of Judy Garland, Kay Starr, Frank Sinatra, and Nat King Cole, the croonings of Bing Crosby and Perry Como, the booming voice of Ethel Merman and the operatic tenor of Mario Lanza, the light pop of the Andrew Sisters and Doris Day, the musicals of Rodgers and Hammerstein, the sentimental and patriotic spirit of Vera Lynn, the emotional timbres of Johnnie Ray, the husband–wife team of vocalist Mary Ford and guitar wizard Les Paul, the big band sound of the Ted Heath Orchestra, trad by the Chris Barber Band, skiffle by Lonnie Donegan, and big band vocalist Al Bowlly, a favorite of Fred Davies. The family's country favorites included Chet Atkins, Slim Whitman, Conway Twitty, and Hank Williams, who Davies said "was the first singer who struck a chord with me."[1]

It was on this gramophone that Ray first heard his early guitar heroes: Duane Eddy, Charlie Christian, Tal Farlow, Johnny and the Hurricanes, and James Burton, who played on Ricky Nelson's records. The Davies sisters played the latest rock-and-roll records by Bill Haley and the Comets, Elvis, and Little Richard, the swing-doo-wop of the Crew Cuts' "Sh-Boom," and Phil Spector's and his Teddy Bear's "To Know Him Is To Love Him." That front-room gramophone provided Davies an incredibly comprehensive schooling in pop music.

Davies, like so many other future English rock artists, was deeply influenced by the music hall, which he heard not in the theater, like his parents, but in movies through the Old Mother Riley films, over the wireless and later television through *Hancock's Half-Hour*, and in pubs and family sing-alongs. On Saturday evenings, Ray and Dave would sometimes slip out of their home to sit beneath the window of the Clissold Arms to listen to sing-alongs. The music hall through its lilting and simple melodies and its satire and stories brought laughter, hope, and feelings of working-class solidarity while relieving anxiety and grief. Virtually every Davies family event featured sing-alongs, whether Saturday night parties or funerals.

It is remarkable how these varied pop sounds from his childhood home found their way into the music of the Davies brothers and the Kinks. Ray, for example, croons on "No Return" from the Kinks' *Something Else* (1966) and later on "That Old Black Magic" from *Storyteller* (1998). The influence of Rodgers and Hammerstein and the Broadway musical can be felt in "Oklahoma U.S.A." from *Muswell Hillbillies* (1971), "Here Comes Flash" and other tracks on *Preservation Acts I* and *2* (1973, 1974). Davies draws on trad jazz for "Unreal Reality" from *Everybody's in Show-Biz* (1972), the big band sound for "Come Dancing" (1983), the blues for "A Gallon of Gas" from *Low Budget* (1979), country for "Muswell Hillbilly" (1971) and "The Informer" from *Phobia* (1993), and 1950s rock-and-roll for "Ducks on the Wall" from *Soap Opera* (1974) and "The Last Assembly" from *Schoolboys in Disgrace* (1975). Such a list, a tribute to Davies's and the Kinks' diverse catalog, can go on and on.

In a surprising moment on stage in Kaukauna, Wisconsin, on June 5, 1993, Davies demonstrated just how thoroughly he has absorbed these early influences when he paid tribute to country great Conway Twitty, who had suddenly died earlier that day from a burst stomach aneurysm. Drummer Bob Henrit remembers: "The night . . . we had been chatting away in the trailer that [Twitty] had just died. Then, on stage, from nowhere, Ray went be-ring [*imitating opening notes of Twitty's 'It's Only Make Believe'*] . . . Jim [Rodford, bassist] and I looked at each other, and we actually came in exactly where we were expected to come in. It was miraculous! You could have heard a pin drop. I'm not sure if everybody out there knew that Conway Twitty had died, and even really cared, but it was such a moment for the rest of us."[2] Interviewer Michael Kraus, who was in the audience that night, assumed the song had been rehearsed. Henrit said that he and the others had played it in other bands, but never in the Kinks. His closing words on the performance are significant, "But you know, once [the song's] in there, it tends to be in there."

Since his *20th Century Man / Storyteller* tours of the 1990s and his solo tours of the 2000s, Davies has carefully selected the pre- and post-performance music, most, if not all of which, could have been played on the gramophone in his family's front room. The selections open a window onto Davies's musical youth and earliest influences. Consider the following sample: Hank Williams's "You're Cheatin' Heart" and "Honky Tonk Blues," Chuck Berry's "Reelin' and Rockin' " and "Memphis" (Dave's favorite Berry song), George Formby's "When I'm Cleaning Windows," Sinatra's "Under My Skin," Bill Broonzy's "Hey, Hey, Baby" and "Baby Please Don't Go," Johnny Cash's "Big River," Patsy Cline's "Honky Tonk Merry Go Round," the Everly Brothers' "Wake-up Little Susie," "Leaning on a Lampost" from the musical *Me and My Girl*, an instrumental by Chet Atkins, and since Hurricane Katrina in 2005 and Davies's residence in New Orleans prior to the storm, at least one or two old New Orleans jazz numbers, a boogie-woogie piano jam, and a classic zydeco recording. In the lobbies of select theaters during *20th Century Man*, Davies posted photographs of music-hall performers like Max Miller (one of his father's favorites), Billy Cotton, Max Wall, Dan Leno, H. Campbell, and Johnny Danvers.

In the Davies home, family members were expected to not just listen to music, but to make music as well. While Ray first learned to play piano from his sisters, the first instrument he received was a ukulele, which he earned after an emergency visit to the dentist after a bad fall. It would be on the guitar, however, that Ray starred, first taking lessons with sister Peg's husband, Mike Picker, an Irishman who studied classical guitar. Ray would meet in Mike and Peg's small Muswell Hill flat to listen and then imitate the records of Buddy Holly and Merle Haggard, for example, with Ray singing and strumming rhythm and Mike playing lead. Sometimes they would record themselves on Mike's tape recorder. In time, Dave joined the pair.

Ray found the guitar an outlet for his increasing anxieties and troubled moods. Both he and Dave recall the cacophonous and jarring combinations of chords he would produce. "I picked up the guitar and went off into dreamworld with it."[3] He taped one such experiment, which Dave recalls: "This old instrumental is the most terrifying thing you've ever heard. It's a horrifying, discordant set of shrieks from the guitar. Some of the harmonies that should be picked out with fingers, he played with his thumb. The result is fantastic."[4]

Unknown to most rock music listeners, Ray has developed into a first-rate guitarist. Yet neither with the Kinks nor in his solo work has he displayed his ability, yielding lead roles to Dave or others and sometimes barely playing rhythm onstage with the Kinks. Bob Henrit, who joined the Kinks in 1984, commented on the brothers' jams: "I was amazed what the pair of them, Ray and Dave, could actually do." Ray especially surprised him: "He can do Chuck Berry solos and things better than Chuck Berry can do them. You know those very jazzy things that Chuck Berry used to do . . . Ray does them better. . . . I mean, he's a great guitarist. I was going to say he's a great rhythm guitarist, but he's just a great guitarist."[5] While Ray has been known to dictate lead guitar lines to his brother and others, there seems to be no explanation for his reluctance to showcase his own ability. Peter Quaife struggled for an explanation, "Ray is probably one of the best guitarists around, but he liked to keep it under wraps because Ray is Ray," which is to say that for inexplicable reasons Davies just prefers to keep some things, actually a lot of things, secret.[6]

Sometime in late 1960, however, Ray demonstrated his ability in public when he and Dave began to perform together in local pubs like the

Clissold Arms, the Stag, and the Victoria, occasionally using the name of the Kelly Brothers, after their paternal grandmother's maiden name. Plugged into a 30-watt Watkins Dominator amplifier, which Ray received for his fifteenth birthday, Ray would play lead and Dave rhythm during a short set of instrumentals which included songs like "Sweet Sue," "Sweet Georgia Brown," something perhaps from Chet Atkins, and an original instrumental "South," which evolved into "Tired of Waiting for You." "It was easy to work with Dave when we started," Ray says, "because we had a lot of records we liked in common, Bo Diddley and blues—John Lee Hooker, Big Bill Broonzy . . . It was fun to sit down and play."[7]

About a year later, in the fall of 1961, Peter Quaife joined the brothers. Quaife, who began playing guitar as therapy for a badly injured hand which he had impaled on a spike in a garbage dump, first teamed with Davies after a music class at William Grimshaw. Quaife tells the story: "At the time I had just started playing guitar and I was no good. . . . [Mr. Wainwright] said, 'bring your guitar next week.' Then Ray put his hand up and said he played guitar and I was surprised because I didn't know. The following week we brought along our guitars. I think I played a Duane Eddy number. Then Ray picked up a guitar and played this Spanish piece which was REALLY impressive. I remember thinking, 'I wish I could play that!' "[8] Mr. Wainwright suggested the pair form a band and play at a school dance. Dave, who Quaife knew from his raucous reputation but not as Ray's brother, joined them along with John Start on drums.

Pete, whose father owned a small grocery, lived a few blocks apart from the Davieses with the Davies and Quaife homes and the school forming points on a triangle about a mile and one-half from one another. The four students got together for rehearsals and played together on and off for the next two years. In the early performances the quartet played almost exclusively instrumentals, songs of the Ventures or UK imitators the Shadows. A set list might include "Wheels," "Apache," "Perfidia," "Riders in the Sky," and "Walk Don't Run," which Davies may have first heard on a Chet Atkins record in 1957, well before the massive international hit for the Ventures in 1960.

The foursome did consider a vocalist, a fellow student at Grimshaw and the Elvis Presley of Muswell Hill, none other than Rod Stewart. But Stewart, strong-willed and stubborn, would have never worked out with the Kinks as he and Ray would have been locked into an endless battle for control. "He was on the football team," recalls Quaife, "and he and Ray were both very competitive and hated each other."[9] At first, vocal leads were shared by Dave and Ray, and only after much encouragement did Ray become the dominant lead vocalist.

As the band developed, different influences inspired them. Ray began listening to more and more American blues and rhythm-and-blues—Lead

Belly, Howlin' Wolf, Slim Harpo, Chuck Berry, and, after watching his performance on *This Wonderful World* through Granada Television, Big Bill Broonzy, "the first blues guitarist we picked up on. We used to try to copy what he played."[10] At art college Davies discovered Sonny Boy Williamson at Fairfield Halls: "I was 18 and didn't care that this man was old enough to be my grandfather—the music was the important thing."[11] Additionally, most likely in the very early 1960s, the brothers saw Bert Stein's *Jazz on a Summer's Day*, which featured performances of the 1958 Newport Jazz Festival. The brothers were especially taken with Berry's rendition of "Sweet Little Sixteen" and Jimmy Guiffre and Gerry Mulligan's rendition of "Train on a River," which Dave says formed the inspiration for "You Really Got Me," though neither song seems to resemble the other.[12]

As with most bands, these early years were very exciting. The boys were developing rapidly as musicians and discovering and incorporating new influences and sounds. After Ray and Pete left Grimshaw, they remained in the band, billing themselves as the Pete Quaife Quartet or Dave Davies Quartet, named after whichever musician got the gig. When the venue did not permit a drummer, they became a trio, performing regularly in the fall of 1962 as the Ray Davies Trio at the El Toro Coffee Bar in Muswell Hill and as the Ray Davies Quartet at the Railway Tavern in Crouch End. It was from September 1962 to December 1963, when Ray attended art college, that his world dramatically widened and the artist began to form.

Art college and film

In the fall of 1962, after finishing William Grimshaw, Davies and Quaife entered Hornsey College of Arts and Crafts, about three miles from the center of Muswell Hill.[13] Always concerned about her older son, Mrs. Davies was very pleased. "Me mum," Dave says, "was desperate that Ray would not end up doing a mundane everyday job, and she encouraged him to get a better education."[14]

Art college not only kept Davies out of the work force, but it also gave him the opportunity to explore different art forms and to find his identity—a process which would be ongoing for decades. His frenetic schedule, crammed with activity, included painting in his course work, playing football two days a week at a local club, performing solo on campus and in different band combinations off campus, studying acting in weekend classes, watching and making films, and socializing. In an enjoyable way, his loyalties were divided between music, football, art, and film.

Ray got along well with his instructors at art college and he appreciated their tutoring and lectures—at least when he attended and was not worn out from his other activities, specifically a late night gig. One of his instructors, Freddie Crookes, noted something that everyone associated with Ray has been saying ever since: "I can remember him being a very lively, animated person. There was almost *too* much going on. . . . He had a lively mind. He seemed to get on with the other students, but there was possibly a bit of friction because he was very independent. He was quite a strong person. He went his own way."[15] For years, Davies's restless personality and artistic vision has frustrated those around him. He routinely begins one project, moves on to another, returns to a previous project, then on to something new, and back again. It was especially frustrating to the original Kinks when in the late 1990s Davies contacted them about reuniting. Hopes were high, but as quickly as Davies mentioned the reunion, he seemed to forget about it. After more than a year passed, he raised the possibility again, but after several meetings with Dave, Avory, and others, terms could not be agreed.

At Hornsey, Ray began to consider filmmaking as a potential pursuit, but the curriculum, however, offered few opportunities for film study. Davies and fellow student Paul O'Dell therefore organized a film society and collaborated on several eight-millimeter films, which Davies found exciting: "Anything else at art school seemed dull in comparison."[16] At one point, Davies met with a college official to request that Hornsey develop a department of film studies. It was a bold initiative for the shy Davies, and the official swiftly rejected his recommendation, informing him that the curriculum was being revised to emphasize the commercial arts over the fine arts. As a result of the meeting, Davies would transfer out of Hornsey the following fall. "Film, my next love to sport, was rapidly taking over as a genuine creative option," he recalls.[17] Unfortunately, Davies's time at Hornsey is marked in part by tragedy when O'Dell committed suicide. The startling blow took Ray some time to recover and only rarely and only briefly has he discussed the tragedy. Again, it was art, sports, and music that proved therapeutic.

Davies's interest in film and filmmaking was not surprising. Since childhood, he had been going regularly to the cinema, which by the end of World War II had replaced the music hall as the main theatrical entertainment for the working class. Just about every week Davies would see a film. The whole family might take the short stroll to the local cinemas, either the Ritz or the Odeon, where sister Joyce worked as an usherette, or Ray might accompany sister Rosie either with a date or providing cover as she secretly met a suitor. Ray once joked that he saw several movies multiple times that way.

At art college Ray began to explore a range of films. He watched documentaries like Robert Flaherty's *Man of Aran* and epic masterpieces like Akira Kurosawa's *The Seven Samurai*, which led him to other foreign filmmakers like Polanski, Truffaut, Fellini, Bergman, and Eisenstein. Films were seizing Davies's imagination: "My notebooks were full of thumbnail sketches of faces and camera angles in the style of Eisenstein rather than studies in the style of John Bratby, Mondrian or Piero della Francesca."[18] He began to notice how the story, the cinematography, the protagonist, the acting, the photography, all coalesced into a totality to stir his emotions, his intellect, and his imagination. "I was not just being entertained, I was being educated and artistically motivated by the images I saw on the screen."[19] More than most others, Davies as a music producer seeks totality, especially shaping albums towards a unified effect and vision.

Davies's interest in film developed during the peak period of the British New Wave or Kitchen-Sink cinema. In the early to mid-1950s, a powerful concentration of working-class voices emerged in literary works, the like of which Britain had not seen before. By the late 1950s, the rage, frustration, and alienation of these "angry young men" found its way onto the screen in one film adaptation after the other: *Look Back in Anger* (directed by Tony Richardson, 1959, play by John Osborne); *Room at the Top* (Jack Clayton, 1959, novel by John Braine); *Saturday Night and Sunday Morning* (Karel Reisz, 1960, novel by Alan Sillitoe); *A Taste of Honey* (Richardson, 1961, play by Shelagh Delaney); *A Kind of Loving* (John Schlesinger, 1962, novel by Stan Barstow); *The Loneliness of the Long Distance Runner* (Richardson, 1962, novel by Sillitoe); *This Sporting Life* (Lindsay Anderson, 1963, novel by David Storey); and *Billy Liar* (Schlesinger, 1963, novel by Keith Waterhouse).

The works of the "angry young men" serve as a kind of prologue to the 1960s, making the working class not only objects of curiosity and sympathy, but also chic. By the swinging sixties, it was sylish for the upper classes to slum with the working class, a trend John Lennon ridiculed in November 1963 in his introduction to "Twist and Shout" at the Prince of Wales Theatre, a televised Royal Command Performance: "Would the people in the cheaper seats clap your hands, and the rest of you, if you'll just rattle your jewelry." In actuality, the "angry young men" opened the way for rock music and artists like the Beatles, Rolling Stones, and Kinks.

In "Where Are They Now?" (1973), Davies references several "angry young men" (Barstow, Osborne, Waterhouse, and Sillitoe) and their creations like Arthur Seaton from *Saturday Night and Sunday Morning*, Jimmy Porter from *Look Back in Anger*, and Joe Lampton from *Room at the Top*. Through the years, the kitchen-sink vision has found its way into many of Davies's songs: "A Well Respected Man," "Dead End Street," "Autumn Almanac," "Slum Kids," and many more. In "This Is Where I Belong," the singer repeats the lesson that so many film protagonists, like Lampton and Frank Machin (*Sporting Life*), must learn: "I won't search for a house upon a hill . . . for this is where I belong." Davies, however, has resisted being tied too closely to the movement. "I never knowingly sat down and said I'm going to write kitchen-sink music. . . . I just wrote about normal everyday people, their hopes and fears."[20]

24

But what is particularly interesting about Davies is the depth with which the arts studied at college have shaped his approach to songwriting and music making and provided him with a vocabulary for explaining his artistry. In his songs, Davies creates characters and presents them in revealing but usually mundane moments, a technique, at least in part, developed directly through art school assignments:

> I think it goes back to when I was an art student. I used to go out sketching for the day. Everybody had a project for that week to do. For my project, I honed in on people in parks, people I saw in railway stations sitting down and waiting for their trains, looking worried, looking happy, people in love—a single person with a backdrop, with the world rushing forward. It was just finding a person in that moment in their life almost like a still photographer who finds somebody and snaps him, and says, "That's the moment." I found them alive, or whatever, and I could grab that moment and write about it. That's maybe the way I started in my formative years as an artist, if you like, and it went on to my songwriting.[21]

Davies separates himself from many pop songwriters in that he does not solely depict an emotional moment, but instead creates a narrative with a more complex character placed in a context or "with a backdrop," as he puts it. He achieves the full effect in many memorable ballads: "Young and Innocent Days," "Oklahoma U.S.A.," "Art Lover," "Don't Forget to Dance," and the neglected "Killer's Eyes," which is not only about the killer but also the singer's confusion.

As Davies has said, his songs are created from a dramatic perspective, one from which he still finds exciting to write. "Even back to 'Waterloo Sunset.' There's a plot with two people, and a bit of a sub-plot, this guy is on his own, something has happened, maybe his girlfriend has left him, and he sees two people together and says 'Wouldn't it be nice to be like them' . . . that's what that song's about. And that's the good thing about songwriting—you're the composer, the artist, the film director, the publisher, everything."[22] Indeed, Davies's songs do seem like brief plays or short films in which he uses his authorial control to create a screen behind which he can camouflage his own anxieties and opinions without being overtly confessional or didactic. "I've always enjoyed writing to a different character," he has also said. "It allows me to say what I think is true. . . . I still write character songs today and sort of cast myself as an actor in them."[23]

This creative strategy informs just about the entire Davies catalog, including *X-Ray*, his "unauthorized autobiography"; small masterpieces in addition to "Waterloo Sunset" like "Sunny Afternoon," "Dead End

Figure 2.1 Ray in the 1970s

Street," "Lola," and "Holiday in Waikiki"; incisive social commentaries like "A Well Respected Man," "Dedicated Follower of Fashion," and "Definite Maybe"; and entire albums from *Village Green Preservation Society* through *Other People's Lives*. His approach has also led Davies to develop especially effective stage pieces and to develop himself into one of rock's great performers. On stage, for instance, he will transform himself into the repentant drunkard for "Alcohol," the down-on-his-luck toff in "Low Budget," or, most recently, the comedian in "Stand Up Comic." Although there are more subtle shifts throughout the set, Davies, for these songs, will go well over the top with often hilarious results.

Davies sees himself as an *auteur* in that his musical concerns and vision supersede that of all others. In the studio, his approach is like that of the meticulous Brian Wilson, who explores many possibilities until the recording results in a definitive version, one that lives up to what has been conceived in his imagination—though Wilson imagines more aurally and Davies more visually. It is the opposite approach of Bob Dylan, who records quickly and who considers songs essentially dynamic and protean, wonderfully subject to reinterpretation depending on time, place, and mood. Davies, like Wilson, seems to relish the quest for a perfect composition and recording. "The standard he keeps up is always good," says Avory. "Sometimes he takes too long, but he gets there in the end. Eventually he gets what he wants."[24] That may be the case, but keyboardist John Gosling had had enough during the *Misfits* sessions and quit the Kinks when Davies called for take 64 of the mediocre "Get Up."[25] Often Davies delays albums with the differences between earlier and later versions frequently indecipherable to even those who worked on them. Although the majority of songs Davies composed for *Other People's Lives* were completed and initially recorded by 1998 and performed in concert by 2000, the album went unreleased until 2006.

Actual filmmaking has never been far from Davies's mind. Long frugal, he surprised his family and friends when after early financial success with the Kinks he purchased a very expensive Ariflex camera, 16 mm, which could make professional quality motion pictures. He began making films for potentially large audiences as early as 1966 with the promo for "Dead End Street," which fused slapstick, dark humor, and social commentary with a decided silent film influence and which showed on the continent but was banned by the BBC. Although he included stills in the "Dead End Street" promo and he composed some incisive songs about photographs for *The Kinks Are the Village Green Preservation Society* ("Picture Book" and "People Take Pictures of Each Other"), Davies has never been much interested in photography. "I don't think that Ray ever took any photographs," recalls Mick Avory.[26] In 1967, Davies proclaimed, "I'm really a frustrated filmmaker."[27]

In 1983 Davies decided to fulfill his longtime ambition when he began writing, composing, and directing *Return to Waterloo*, a sixty-minute film which aired to mostly positive reviews on British television in November 1984 and then in select US theaters. Released twenty years after "You Really Got Me," the film captures the anxiety, frustration, and dissatisfaction of contemporary suburban life in England, and lives out an oath Davies made in 1964: "In 1984 I shall be fighting what I fight now. The same kind of petty authority and pocket-sized tyrants I resent now will be around in 1984."[28] In 1990, Davies began filming *Weird Nightmare: A Tribute to Charles Mingus*, a documentary on the jazz musician which aired on Channel 4 TV in the UK in June 1993. In the skillful documentary, Davies interviews members of Mingus's family and jazz and rock musicians (Don Alias, Elvis Costello, Henry Threadgill, Keith Richards, among others), while cleverly using the visual and sonic imagery of New York City's subway system, specifically the elevated tracks from which Mingus sometimes drew inspiration.

It was in art college where Davies not only developed his interest in film, but more importantly his artistic consciousness. "When I was at art school as a student, what I got out of it was colour, expression. Now I find you turn out a bad song for the same reason you turn out a bad painting—insincerity."[29] Art college kept Davies out of a deadend job, gave him time and freedom to develop his musical abilities, and shaped his artistic sensibility—benefits shared by so many rock artists of the British Invasion era: John Lennon, Keith Richards, Eric Clapton, Jeff Beck, Jimmy Page, Peter Townshend, Syd Barrett, Brian Ferry, Brian Eno, David Bowie, and on and on. As a result of the art college experience, British rock musicians in the 1960s began to think of themselves as artists and not merely as pop musicians and tunesmiths. The effect was an increasingly innovative and adventurous music with artists' responding and challenging one another in a highly charged atmosphere. As Davies said and what many of the rock musicians above could have said, "Without the bridge of art college, I don't think the rest would have happened. I wouldn't have done music."[30]

Music during art college and the birth of the Kinks

The year 1963 was a pivotal one in the history of rock-and-roll. Working-class culture, youth culture, art school attitudes, and "angry young men" arrogance, all converged into a powerful entity that began to take over the UK. At the forefront of the new era were the Beatles with a series of number ones: "Please Please Me," "From Me to You," "She Loves You," and "I Want to Hold Your Hand." Here was a group of working-class lads, not middle class and not public-school trained, yet they wrote and played their own music with an excitement and magnetism that attracted all England. Soon middle-class and upper-middle youths wanted to be part of the scene, which, until then, they had experienced only vicariously in the kitchen-sink films. The swinging sixties were underway.

In late 1962 Ray Davies started to direct his energies towards music. At a Hornsey College Christmas dance on December 15, he sought the advice of the legendary Alexis Korner whose Blues Incorporated were the featured performers. Korner recommended the art school student to his manager and the future manager and producer of the Yardbirds, Giorgio Gomelsky, who, within a week, arranged for Ray to sit in with the Dave

Hunt Rhythm and Blues Band at the Piccadilly Jazz Club in Soho. Davies may have been pleased and even flattered to be jamming with Hunt's professional musicians, but he was awestruck and inspired by the supporting act—the Rollin' Stones (as they then presented themselves). Hunt dismissed the Stones as a mere skiffle group, but Ray saw passionate musicians his own age playing the music he loved. The PA may have distorted the sound and muddied the barely audible vocals, but the energy and excitement were sensational. "I think that was the best I've ever seen 'em play," says Davies, "Really!"[31] In the young Stones, Davies saw possibilities, possibilities that would have to wait but would never again be far from his mind.

Less than a couple of weeks later, on New Year's Eve, the Ray Davies Quartet opened for Cyril Stapleton & His All-Star Orchestra at the Lyceum Ballroom in central London, the same ballroom in which Rene Davies collapsed and died some five and one-half years earlier after presenting her brother with the guitar he had longed for. It was a big gig for the teens and loaded with nuance and implication for the Davies brothers particularly. It is impossible to say the kind of complex emotions that ran through the brothers that evening, but certainly Ray was aware of the prestige of the gig, of the shifting currents in pop music, of the promise implicit in any new year, and of Rene's spirit and her influence on his musical pursuits. That evening Davies began to consider a career in music.

Within a few days of the Lyceum gig, Ray accepted an offer to become the permanent guitarist for the Dave Hunt Band, a perfect fit for Hunt. Davies was not only a talented guitarist who could play different types of music including trad jazz, blues, and more, but he was also young—and young faces were taking over the pop music scene. In addition to Ray on guitar, Hunt's seven-piece band featured the leader on trombone, Hamilton King on vocals, a saxophonist, pianist, bassist, and drummer, who on occasion was Charlie Watts before he joined the Stones in mid-January 1963. For approximately the next six weeks and while continuing his studies at Hornsey, Davies played three nights a week with Hunt, which brother Dave described as "a kind of jazz-influenced pre-R&B group."[32] The band provided a brief but important apprenticeship for Ray, who experienced the inner workings of a band, the dynamics of a rapidly changing musical scene, and the excitement and frustrations of professional musicians. "We had good nights and bad nights," Ray recalled. "One night there were literally no people there, so we had to take turns going into the audience and clapping ourselves. One of my fondest memories of the time was when it was my turn to be the audience."[33]

Shortly after leaving Hunt, Davies joined Hunt's former lead singer in the Hamilton King Band, sometimes called the Blues Messengers or the R & B Group, which, as the name suggests, sought to benefit from the booming trend in rhythm-and-blues. The lineup featured King, a large man with high-pitched vocals and harmonica, Ray on guitar, Dave Ambrose on bass, Peter Bardens on piano, and an unidentified drummer. Bardens, who would go on to success in Camel and a series of progressive New Age solo albums, recalled Davies as not only a very good guitarist but also a very good showman who would play his guitar behind his head, roll on the ground, and kick his legs in the air.[34] Ray remained with King until June when the band began to fall apart. King struggled on for another year with only limited success.

Throughout his tenure with Hunt and King, Davies played with the Quartet or the Ramrods as they were known since a name change that spring. His commitment, however, was less than total, and he often looked down on his less experienced brother and friends. Yet Dave kept the band alive and was rapidly developing as a guitarist, which Ray noticed as he began to see the band's potential, especially in the wake of the Beatles' success. But Ray was still contemplating a career in film. He decided to leave Hornsey at the end of the spring semester and to study film at the Central School of Art & Design in September. He missed the application deadline, however, and had to register for the fall semester at the Croydon School of Art, where he would bide his time until he could procure a grant for Central.

In July 1963, the Ramrods lost their drummer, when upon graduation from Grimshaw, John Start lost his desire to be a musician. Start wanted to pursue other interests, like weekend boat racing, prior to beginning work as a surveyor. He remained a casual friend of Pete, but he never saw Ray or Dave again. The Ramrods were forced to rely on pick-up drummers for a series of gigs at US Air Force bases backing Rick Wayne or "Mr. Southern England," a black body builder. With the strange logic that would so often characterize the decisions of the Kinks, the Davies brothers decided that Quaife was responsible for the drummer's replacement since he was the one who drafted Start, a Quaife family friend, into the band. Quaife recruited Mickey Willet, a competent drummer with professional experience who some three years earlier with Tommy Bruce & the Bruisers had a #3 hit with "Ain't Misbehavin'."

In September 1963, the Ramrods changed their image and their name, after Dave's suggestion. They took the Boll-Weevils from a B-side of rebellious rocker Eddie Cochran and dropped the cardigans and matching shirts financed by Start's father for black stage attire. More importantly, at this time, they met then vocalist Robert Wace and his manager Grenville Collins, who were on the hunt for a backing band to support Wace for a series of society gigs. After being put in contact with Willet through a friend, the pair decided to attend a Boll-Weevils' rehearsal at Muswell Hill's Athenaeum Ballroom. While Wace would hardly be a vocalist the Boll-Weevils would recruit, they agreed to back him, correctly believing that they would gain a few extra gigs as well as exposure to different audiences. Wace's career as a singer would be short-lived, but he and Collins would be part of the band's management team until 1971.

Wace and Collins were like alien figures to the Boll-Weevils. They were middle-class, public-school types, or as Wace once said, "we came from that high society background."[35] They were an unlikely match for the rowdy working-class Boll-Weevils. Wace and Collins were both tall, dressed dapperly, spoke with posh accents, and had a craving for show business. Wace, who thought of himself as a bit of a ladies' man, wanted to sing and Collins wanted to manage. About the same age as Ray, Collins worked in the stock market and Wace as a sales representative in his father's manufacturing company. The band had never had any intimate dealings with anyone from their class and backgrounds, and they regarded the pair with awed skepticism and humor, often targeting them with crude jokes as if in a music-hall skit, where the working classes often got the better of the upper classes. "They used to make me laugh," says Avory. "It was just their way. Their public school way."[36] In his *20th Century Man* performances, Ray mocked the accent and demeanor of Wace and Collins with hilarious results.

To prepare them for the society gigs, Collins and Wace advanced the Boll-Weevils for new stage outfits (pink tab-collar shirts and blue corduroy trousers) and a 30-watt amplifier. The Boll-Weevils generally opened the set with songs like "Got Love If You Want It," "Johnny B. Goode," "Route 66," "Little Queenie," "Bo Diddley," "Poison Ivy," and extended rave-ups like "Smokestack Lightning" and "Money (That's What I Want"). Dave sang lead more at that time than in years to come. Wace would then take the stage and in his public-school accent deliver four or five songs like Buddy Holly's "It's So Easy," "Rave On," "Peggy Sue," and "Think It Over," or more recent hits like Trini Lopez's "If I Had a Hammer," Freddie & the Dreamers' "I'm Telling You Now," Billy J. Kramer's "Bad To Me," Gerry & the Pacemakers' "I Like It," and the Isley Brothers' "Twist and Shout," made popular by the Beatles during the summer of 1963. Wace said he lacked confidence to perform any longer than a half an hour or so and only to his limited audiences. "He wasn't a bad vocalist," says Dave with a little sarcasm, "kind of a mixture of Noel Coward and Buddy Holly, cute in a silly way."[37] The Boll-Weevils mostly enjoyed the high-society type dances and debutante balls, where they were regarded as quaint, authentic working-class curiosities complete with cockney accents and all.

After a month, Wace's aspirations as a vocalist grinded to a halt when he decided to join the Boll-Weevils on stage in London's tough East End, the original home of the Davies's family. The working-class audience booed and laughed at the pretense of the posh, un-rock-and-roll vocalist. "I had a few tomatoes and cabbages thrown at me, and that rather soured me on [performing]," which, by this time, according to Wace, he was starting to find "rather demeaning actually."[38] It must be noted, however, that Wace did have good musical judgment, which Davies tapped into until the manager's departure in 1971. "Ray trusted Robert Wace," says Collins with support from Avory and others. "Wace would go to his home and Robert would be like an editor. Robert would say something like 'rearrange the middle,' very gentle suggestions. Robert couldn't write, but he could make suggestions to Ray."[39] Dave was saddened by the eventual departure of Wace and Collins, after which his brother became more controlling and "meaner and more selfish."[40] Although the pair made managerial mistakes, they always had the band's best interest at heart.

Within no more than two weeks of the East End incident, Ray formally asked Collins to manage the Boll-Weevils as they drove down Fortis Green Road late one night after a gig. After they pulled in front of the Davies home, Collins walked Ray to the home's waist-high front gate, which Davies closed between them. He looked deeply into the stockbroker's eyes: "There's going to be a lot of trouble before this is over."[41] It was a peculiarly foreboding and dramatic statement from a promising young performer to his new manager. Collins was understandably confused, but he would feel the full implications of Ray's premonitions over the next seven years. Wace, with his singing career wisely behind, joined Collins as co-manager.

In late November, the band underwent their fourth name change of 1963 when they rechristened themselves the Ravens. Thought to be more commercial, the name was inspired by the Roger Corman horror movie based loosely on Edgar Allan Poe's poem. Despite holding the moniker for less than two months, it is their most well-known pre-Kinks billing and the name Dave Davies used at times for his backing band in the mid-1990s. Shortly after becoming the Ravens, the managers requested that the band fire Mickey Willet.[42] With a hit single behind him from a previous band, Willet had become a nuisance for Wace and Collins, challenging them on the details of bookings and payments to the band. While the inexperienced and younger managers no doubt felt threatened by Willet, the clashes probably resulted more from misunderstanding and miscommunication than intentional deception. But, in truth, Willet was never a good fit for the band in image, musicianship, or personality, which is not to say that he was incompetent or difficult for the other musicians. He was just different. He was a few years older, clean cut, and more professional in an aging style, one that belonged to the late 1950s or early 1960s. He admitted that he felt an outsider among his bandmates.

With a replacement drummer, probably Johnny Bremner, the Ravens continued their schedule and Wace and Collins continued to hawk demos and songs to record companies and publishers, an effort begun in October. The Ravens were rejected by Parlophone, EMI, and Decca Records, which also rejected the Beatles, but there was some interest in the smaller Pye label, which led to a contract in early 1964.

A significant meeting in late November would affect Ray Davies and the Kinks for years to come. While trying to sell original songs to Kassner Music, a publishing company, Robert Wace met Larry Page, a music veteran with experience in performing, managing, and publishing. Page was tempted enough by the demos to see the Ravens in rehearsal and impressed enough to sign them to Kassner and offer to help the fledgling management team. Wace and Collins agreed to give the strong-willed music entrepreneur 10 percent of the band's earnings for help in procuring a record contract and advice on stage presentation, material, and business matters. The three managers and Kassner Music evolved into a complex entanglement that took years of litigation to sort out.

Page was asked to leave in September 1965 after a disastrous Kinks summer tour of America, only to return as manager from July 1984 until April 1989. There has never been any love lost between Page and the other managers. "They were both dandies," says Page of Wace and Collins, "each about six foot six and when you spoke to them they'd stand there in their £500 pinstripe suits, bouncing on the balls on their feet. They weren't managing. They were investing. I controlled the band and all they did was take their share. They had no knowledge whatsoever of the music business, so whatever I told them to do, they did."[43] Just as bluntly, Wace says that Page was little more than an "opportunist" who "was never the manager of the group, although he may like to think himself as one."[44] With all the uncertainty and hecticness of those pre- and early Kinks days it is impossible for anyone to say who did what.

In late December, the band decided on still another name change. They wanted something more contemporary than the Ravens. There are several versions as to how they derived the Kinks.[45] As Doug Hinman notes, several people, but no band members, have been credited for suggesting the moniker: booking agent Arthur Howes (whom Dave credits), Kinks' first photographer Bruce Fleming, an anonymous friend of Robert Wace, and Larry Page (whom Ray credits and Hinman finds the most probable). According to Ray, the band and Page were in a pub when one patron noticed Ray's orange tie, Quaife's and Dave's fake-leather capes, and all of their "kinky" boots, which resembled those worn by the Cathy Gale character in the popular British TV series *The Avengers*. Another patron referred to the young musicians as "kinks," and according to Ray, Page suggested the name based on the comment. "Larry's eyes were glowing with excitement," recalls Ray. A few days later he showed the band mock-up art work. "*Kinks*," Page said. "It's short—five letters. You'll be bottom of the bill, so you need something that will stand out."[46] The band reluctantly approved the gimmicky name.

However, before they unveiled the name at the end of January 1964, they needed a permanent drummer. One of the managers contacted Mick Avory, who posted an advertisement in the January 25 issue of *Melody*

Maker: "Drummer. Young, good kit, read, seeks pro-R&B groups, MOL 4615." After his audition, Avory was invited to join the band, although he hardly looked kinky—in fact, he had just had a haircut and, to Ray, looked very much like a boy scout. The lineup for the Kinks was set, but not before Avory asked a question, "Why do you have three managers?" Ray explained innocently, "That's the way it evolved . . . we didn't ask for three managers."[47] In a few short months, the Kinks would make their impact on the world music scene.

3

YOU REALLY GOT ME

Finding a sound and a theme

On New Year's Day 1964, Ray Davies met with Freddie Crookes, a counselor and department head at Croydon School of Art, to discuss whether or not he should return to school for the spring semester or pursue a career in music. The practical-minded Crookes advised Davies to finish the current semester, which ended in about two weeks, and then try music for six months. If music did not work out, Davies could always return to college in the fall. Following Crookes's advice, Davies put the Kinks into full drive—overdrive, in fact. Within one week, the Kinks signed with Arthur Howes, who promoted several tours for the Beatles and who agreed to place the band on a package tour with the Dave Clark Five; within two weeks, the Kinks raced into the studio to record demos for the consideration of Pye Records;[1] within three weeks, they signed with Pye and recorded with producer Shel Talmy;[2] within four weeks they recruited Mick Avory, their drummer for the next twenty years, and, on February 7, they released "Long Tall Sally," their first single, which they promoted on *Ready Steady Go!* Ideas, musical and business, were tossed around, including one which encouraged Ray to write songs. The push was on to make the Kinks a player on the explosive musical scene.

One idea that did not stick had to do with image. Larry Page was particularly troubled by the gap in Ray's front teeth. Before his appearance on *Ready Steady Go!* Page explained to Davies in his East End cockney, "They'll never let you on the box with railings like that, cock. I've fixed you up an appointment with a dentist. He'll sort you out."[3] Davies dutifully reported to the dentist and was prepared for the procedure—until he heard the drill revving. When he asked for details, he discovered that the dentist planned to cut away his two front teeth and replace them with caps. Davies leaped from the chair and called Page and Collins, who compromised and allowed their potential star to wear temporary caps for the show. The result was that Davies appeared on British national television with, as he says, "the largest front teeth since Bugs Bunny." Davies decided to keep his natural teeth, and rock journalists were afforded a forever reference to the famous gapped-tooth grin.

The Kinks' first single

The flurry of activity, however, did not climax with a hit. Arthur Howes had recommended "Long Tall Sally" to the Kinks after he had seen the Beatles perform the Little Richard number in Paris on January 16. The Beatles had not yet recorded it, and Howes thought he would do the Kinks a favor and give them the lead on a potential hit. The Kinks quickly worked out an arrangement, which they had no opportunity to try before a live audience, and recorded it on January 20, along with five other songs, including what would be their second single. Although they had several other Little Richard covers in their set list, "Long Tall Sally" was not the right song for them. Their almost Merseybeat arrangement zapped the energy from the song, and although Ray delivered a solid harmonica solo, his vocals lacked the necessary fire and punch of either Little Richard or Paul McCartney, whose performance led to a #1 EP that June. At this point in the Kinks' career, the song might have been better delivered by Dave who might have sung with more abandonment.

Despite an aggressive campaign by Kinks' management, which besides the television appearance, included a half-page, front-cover advertisement in the *New Musical Express*, "Long Tall Sally" reached only #42 on the *Melody Maker* charts, where it lasted just one week before disappearing into oblivion. While the Kinks may have been excited about its chart appearance, the position was almost certainly manipulated and had little to do with the television appearance. Grenville Collins explains, "Whatever success it had was hyped—we probably had shipped an excessive number of records to make the charts, but the records were never purchased."[4] The record did garner some positive reviews, but one suggested that the B-side, "I Took My Baby Home," a Davies original, should have been the A-side.[5]

On March 28, the Kinks embarked on their first major package tour with headliners the Dave Clark Five, the Hollies, and others. The Kinks would perform an approximately twelve-minute set of four songs drawn from "Long Tall Sally," "Bo Diddley," "Smokestack Lightning," "Too Much Monkey Business," "Tutti-Frutti," "Beautiful Delilah," "Got Love If You Want It," "Talkin' Bout You," "Bye Bye Johnny," "Louie Louie," and the originals "You Still Want Me" and the recently composed "You Really Got Me." The tour lasted until May 14 with the Kinks experiencing their shares of highs and lows as typical of new acts. There was the excitement and fun of being on the road and in a tour bus with other young musicians, of imagining oneself a pop star, and of sometimes hearing enthusiastic responses to their music, but then there were also the disappointment and frustration of unenthusiastic responses to the music, of endless advice from the more experienced, of tiredness resulting from poor sleeping conditions, and, at one point, of being demoted to the opening slot of the bill.

Toward the end of the tour, on April 25, the Kinks premiered their new stage attire: heavy red hunting jackets, black riding trousers, frilly shirts, and boots. Designed and custom-fitted by Berman's and Nathan's, the pre-eminent theatrical costumiers in London, the outfits, specifically the over-powering red jackets, gave the Kinks a Dickensian look, as if they were to spend an afternoon on a Victorian country estate. Their new appearance defied logic. The outfits were neither historically accurate, nor compatible with their working-class origins and attitudes, nor stage friendly—they were "so thick that you could hardly breathe in them let alone drum," recalls Avory.[6] Yet, oddly enough, the outfits worked just as the Beatles' collarless jackets of 1963. The band felt unique and more professional, and they had an identifiable look. "Lo and behold," Ray reports somewhat mystified, "we looked like us." An early champion of the band who would later induct them into the Rock and Roll Hall of Fame, Graham Nash of the Hollies boosted their confidence when they appeared with their new look for the first time: "Now you look like the Kinks."[7] Fans too approved. One fan, a teenager at the time, said, "The ruffles were right up my street. The clothing made them stand out . . . very sexy." This fan also makes clear that the concept of the Kinks as a working-class band was irrelevant to everyone at the time: "I didn't think of them as working class, just as the band from up the street."[8] The Kinks performed regularly in the hunting jackets until late 1965, even in the Australian heat, which left them, according to Ray, "exhausted and dehydrated at the end of each concert."[9]

On April 17, while on the Dave Clark tour and a week before premiering their new outfits, the Kinks released their second single, "You Still Want Me," a Davies original but derivative of the Merseybeat sound and no more or less catchy or forgettable than probably dozens of other singles released that week—with little investment, record labels would typically let fly a series of singles with the hope that one or more would strike big. But despite the full-page advertisement in the *New Musical Express* (*NME*), paid by Kinks' management, "You Still Want Me" went nowhere and generated no interest.

The Kinks' management team was not ready to quit, however. A day after the package tour ended, the Kinks set out for a fully-packed schedule of club and ballroom dates, many in the north where they had been well received. Whether they realized it or not, the Kinks had hopped on the rock-and-roll merry-go-round of recording, promotion, and touring, followed by more recording, promotion, and touring. Significantly, on the beginning leg of the tour, May 19 in Sheffield, Ray met Rasa Didzpetris, whom he would marry in December 1964 and have two daughters (Louisa, born May 23, 1965, and Victoria, born December 25, 1968) before their breakup in June 1973. Rasa's distinct background vocals contributed to the uniqueness of many early Kinks tracks, including "Waterloo Sunset," "Autumn Almanac," and "Days."

Figure 3.1 The Kinks in their Dickensian stage outfits in 1964: (L–R) Quaife, Avory, Dave, and Ray

"You Really Got Me"

On August 2, 1964, two days before the release of "You Really Got Me," the Kinks met the Beatles, whom they were to precede immediately on stage in Bournemouth, in the south of England. John Lennon, who had quickly developed into a master competitor, decided to intimidate this unproven act and to keep them aware of their proper place. As Ray tells the story and as other Kinks and Grenville Collins confirm, Lennon approached Ray as he prepared to step on stage.[10] He asked about Ray's Fender Telecaster guitar and then brashly adjusted one of its controls before condescendingly brushing some dandruff off the shoulders of Ray's red hunting jacket. Then, as Lennon peeked at the crowd through the curtains, Ray, with nervous innocence, said, "It's our turn. You're on after us." Lennon, in his deep northern accent, replied, "With the Beatles, laddie, nobody gets a turn. You're just there to keep the crowd occupied until we go on." Duly intimidated, Davies took the stage but not before Lennon added something else: "Well, lads, if you get stuck and run out of songs to play, we'll lend you some of ours"—most bands opening for the Fab Four did include a Beatles song to minimize the screams for the headliners. As the Kinks played, calls for John, Paul, George, and Ringo rained upon them. Ray's competitive furnace, however, began to heat up. Recalling his schoolboy defeats in track and boxing, he decided to change the set list, replacing "Got Love If You Want It" with their single in waiting, "You Really Got Me." The song had been well received for several weeks now, and if the Kinks were going to lose this audience, they would do so with their own material and on their own terms. Dave turned up the volume on his amp, blasted the ragged chords, and within seconds the crowd applauded and screamed for the Kinks. It was a proud moment for the band, one none has forgotten. During the Beatles set, which Ray watched admiringly from just off the side of the stage, he heard someone call for the Kinks. Lennon responded with a comment into the microphone which Ray could not grasp, but for a few moments, on one evening, the Kinks threatened to upstage the Beatles. "It was as if we had taken the first round off the Beatles," said Ray. The following week when the Kinks were again to support the Beatles, they were shifted away from the headliners and, instead, closed the first half of the show.

For the Beatles, the memory of Bournemouth lingered past the following week. In April 1965 at the *NME* Poll Winners' Concert in London, broadcast over the next two weeks by ITV television, the Kinks had to follow the Beatles, as the Beatles had to leave early for another booking and the Kinks were late in arriving from Denmark. It was an unenviable position no matter what the reasons, but especially disastrous as the Beatles played inspiredly. As they left the stage, a panicky Collins caught Lennon, "John, we can't follow that." Lennon responded, "There's your payback for Bournemouth."[11] The Kinks could muster little energy and their performance before a crowd of 10,000 was described as "particularly disappointing," "bad vocally and musically," and "undeniably diabolical."[12] Round two to the Beatles.

The Kinks' path to that *NME* concert began on August 4, 1964, with the release of "You Really Got Me." Although audiences had responded enthusiastically to the song since the Dave Clark tour, record executives thought it too loud and crude, lacking in melody, and too far removed from the harmonies and smooth rhythms of the popular Merseybeat sound—one executive, according to Ray, compared Dave's guitar to a "barking dog."[13] Pye Records would have preferred the Kinks to record something else for their third and, most likely, final single. But with two failed efforts behind them and their career in jeopardy, the Kinks insisted on "You Really Got Me," and to anger executives further, the barely twenty-year-old, unproven lead singer and composer demanded to re-record the song because the production on the first recording dissatisfied the band. Pye only yielded to Davies because Larry Page, the representative of Kassner Music assigned to the Kinks, threatened to withhold the mechanical license to the song. Pye agreed to allow the Kinks to re-record "You Really Got Me," but at the band's expense—costs were assumed by Wace and Collins. Then, having fulfilled its end of a three-single contract with the Kinks, the company could release the band from the label.

However, the success of "You Really Got Me" was sudden and sweeping. Entering the *Melody Maker* charts in the August 15 issue, "You Really Got Me" reached #1 on September 19 before exiting the charts twelve weeks after its debut. American success was similarly dramatic. Appearing for the first time on the *Billboard* charts on September 26, the record, released on Reprise, remained for fifteen weeks, including five weeks in the top-ten. Davies's stubborn commitment to his song and the Kinks' re-recording had paid off.

The record of "You Really Got Me" was very different from the song Davies conceived in the front room of his Muswell Hill home. Initially, he considered the song a tribute to his favorite blues artists, especially Big Bill Broonzy. In *20th Century Man / Storyteller*, Davies performed the song as conceived: slow, bluesy, hypnotic and certainly effective, but hardly innovative. Two contributions reshaped the song. First, Ray's plunky piano chords were transformed into raw power chords when Dave transposed them for his guitar, which, filtered through his tiny, green Elpico amplifier with its slashed speakers, sounded maybe not loud but harsh. Immediately, the brothers recognized that they had something significant.[14] "It was as if something magical had descended upon us in the modest little room," says Dave.[15]

The second development occurred later when the Kinks were on tour. Arthur Howes felt concerned about the Kinks' stage act. He called in Hal Carter, who had polished the acts of many British performers, but ones of a different type and era than the Kinks. Most of Carter's suggestions were conventional and hackneyed: he suggested the inclusion of more pop rather than blues arrangements, more movement from band members, and even some dance routines. Carter, predictably, met resistance, and one day, during another stressful rehearsal, Graham Nash interceded on behalf of the Kinks, restoring any self-confidence Carter might have stripped away. "Leave the boys alone," Nash told Carter. "They have nothing to do with what you're to do with. They got their own thing, and it's strong. Don't destroy it."[16] Carter, about ten years older than Ray, did not intimidate the Kinks, who pulled pranks on him and teased him relentlessly, mocking his cross-eyed appearance and upturned nose, his affected accent, and his accomplishments with Billy Fury. Yet the Kinks actually liked Carter as they recognized his good intentions, and perhaps too, they with Carter, the Hollies, and the other bands were united in their dislike of the arrogant Dave Clark, who was more businessman than musician.[17]

Significantly, Davies did follow at least one of Carter's recommendations when the performing consultant suggested that he personalize "You Really Got Me" by opening the song with a girl's name or a reference to a girl. Davies agreed and settled on "girl." With that one-word addition the song assumed a definable content (one with which teens could easily relate), an increased urgency and sexuality that matched the forceful sound of Dave's guitar, and a focus to the intensity of the speaker's obsession. Interestingly, Carter said he only suggested it because he initially criticized the song and saw Ray's disappointed look. "If he hadn't have reacted with such a long face I probably wouldn't have said anything."[18]

Of course, the charts also influenced the transformation of "You Really Got Me" from slow blues to out-and-out rocker. Davies took note as the Swinging Blue Jeans and Rolling Stones scored huge hits early in 1964 with covers, respectively, of "Hippy Hippy Shake" and "Not Fade Away," and, as the Kinks went into the studio in mid-July to re-record "You Really Got Me," the Animals held #1 with a rave-up of the American folk song "House of the Rising Sun," which would be toppled the following week by the Stones' cover of "It's All Over Now." And, on the July 10 *Ready Steady Go!*, Manfred Mann performed their cover of "Do Wah Diddy Diddy," a soon-to-be #1 written by the Brill Building team of Ellie Greenwich and Jeff Barry. Ray believed that the Kinks were certainly at least as good as these bands, and he wanted not merely to match but to surpass their achievements—which meant he needed a smash with an original song, one more rhythm-and-blues or rave-up rather than blues or ballad.

To create this original, Dave Marsh believes that Davies turned to the Kingsmen's "Louie Louie." He claims, in fact, that not only "You Really Got Me" but also "All Day and All of the Night" and the Who's "I Can't Explain" were "blatantly based" and "borrowed, to put it kindly," from "Louie Louie."[19] The influence, however, seems more indirect than direct, and certainly not blatant—despite manager Larry Page's recommendation to Ray that he write a song like "Louie Louie." For as Ray, who denies the direct influence, says credibly, "Larry was always asking me to write lots of songs like lots of different things, whatever was successful."[20] Both hits are similar in their "gaps and silences" and burstings of chords, and the Kinks did perform "Louie Louie" on stage, both before and after the creation of "You Really Got Me." If he had "blatantly based" his song on the former hit, Davies, who has long been sensitive to charges of borrowing, would have never included "Louie Louie" on the set list after composing "You Really Got Me," and he certainly would never have recorded the song for the *Kink-Size* EP released in late November. Given the nature of artistic creation and the role of the unconscious, it is impossible to measure the influence of "Louie Louie" on the Kinks' breakthrough track, but clearly it is not as substantial as Marsh asserts. To confuse matters further, consider the comments of singer Dave Berry, who had a few UK and continental hits in the mid-1960s and who reviewed "You Really Got Me" for *Melody Maker* without knowing the title or group: "Great! The Kingsmen? It sounds like them from the intro. . . . On second thoughts,

I'd say it was British." Then in a remark that "said it all" for Ray, "I like these records that sound as if they've gone into a recording studio and done what they wanted to on the spot."[21]

At the time of the re-recording, Davies may not have comprehended what he and the Kinks were creating with "You Really Got Me," but he knew that he had something special and that he was writing about frustration and obsession. "Those thumping chords started playing down my headphones and in the first row of my imaginary audience I saw a girl. Every emotion I had was focused on that one image, and nobody could deny me in this moment."[22] On page, the sparse lyrics seem unimpressive, but the limited vocabulary works with Dave's slashing staccato power chords, tight but frayed, and session drummer Bobby Graham's pounding rhythms to reveal a speaker whose obsession and frustration with a girl has limited his ability to function and driven him into neurosis: "You got me so I don't know what I'm doing . . . You got me so I can't sleep at night."[23] Ray delivers the story through escalating and fading vocals and at the 1:15 mark breaks down in delirium, depicted in Dave's frenzied guitar solo of sputtering, clipped notes. The singer's fit passes with the end of the solo, and the speaker, after a pause, recovers his external appearance of normalcy when he resumes singing. In live performances, the Kinks frequently extend the song to include Davies's re-singing the lyrics, but in a higher pitched voice, even more pleading and more vulnerable, more revealing of the speaker's fragility.

The importance of Dave's guitar on "You Really Got Me" cannot be overstated. As Ray has said, "If Dave never plays another note, his performance on 'You Really Got Me' will always give him a special place among guitar players. The sound was created in our parents' living room and ended up being copied by nearly every rock guitar player in the world."[24] Dave's guitar cannot only be interpreted as a replication of the neurotic mind, but also as an expression of teenage angst, lust, and the youthful impulse to rebel. "The song came out of a working-class environment," Dave said, "people fighting for something."[25] Dave's expression of victimization (real or imagined) at all the social, political, and cultural forces that stifle uniqueness, mirrors not just teenage angst but also working-class angst and the neurotic/psychotic mind (which is not to say that youth and working class are psychotic, although they may often feel driven to neurosis). "Violent tension," says Ray, "is the essence of a lot of our early sounds—aggression and rebellion against an establishment that wasn't on our side."[26]

The influence of "You Really Got Me" was immediate. The record was barely released when the Who, then the High Numbers, included an instrumental version of the song as part of their live set. Peter Townshend wrote "I Can't Explain," a Who favorite and a top-ten UK hit, based on "You Really Got Me." "I wrote 'I Can't Explain' specifically to get a deal with Shel Talmy," Townshend said. "I listened to 'You Really Got Me,' which I thought was a terrific record and a fantastic song at the time. Ray's early use of key changes was just brilliant."[27] More directly, in a 1971 *Rolling Stone* interview, Townshend admitted, "['I Can't Explain'] can't be beat for straightforward Kink copying. It seems to be about the frustration of a young person who is so incoherent and uneducated that he can't state his case to the bourgeois intellectual"[28]—a statement that implicitly refutes Marsh's later claim about "Louie Louie's" overarching influence. The distorted and riveting power chords of "You Really Got Me" have served as a seed for hard rock, garage, punk, and heavy metal, re-articulated by Black Sabbath, the Clash, Metallica, and a host of others, and the song itself has been covered by over seventy-five artists, including Mott the Hoople, the Buddy Miles Express, Robert Palmer, and Van Halen, who had a top-forty hit with their release in 1978. "I heard it when I was at school and it really blew me away," says Mike Rutherford of Genesis. "I'd never heard a riff like it. It's still one of the greatest riffs of all time."[29]

The Kinks' first album

In late August 1964, with "You Really Got Me" soaring in the UK charts, Pye Records rushed the Kinks into the studio and gave them about a week to record an album. *Kinks*, released in October 1964, represents a kind of hodgepodge of pop styles of the day: Chuck Berry and Bo Diddley rockers ("Beautiful Delilah," "Too Much Monkey Business," "Cadillac"), rhythm-and-blues covers ("Long Tall Shorty"), blues classics ("Got Love If You Want It"), Merseybeat ("Just Can't Go to Sleep"), electric folk ("I've Been Driving on Bald Mountain"), novelty ("I Took My Baby Home"), and the hit "You Really Got Me." The album reveals a competent, energetic, and assured young band in need of focus—which, before long, they would find under Davies's leadership. However, given the era of its release with its emphasis on singles not albums, *Kinks* remains a success, at least in how it responds to the perennial youthful craving for excitement and energy and expressions of alienation, angst, and sexuality. In a sense, *Kinks* and rock music respond to Jimmy Porter's outburst in *Look Back in Anger*, the kitchen-sink drama and film: "Damn you, damn both of you, damn them all. . . . Oh, heavens, how I long for a little ordinary human enthusiasm. Just enthusiasm—that's all."[30] What *Kinks* lacks in consistent originality, it compensates for in "human enthusiasm," youthful bravado, or as Jon Savage calls it, "gusto."[31] On the band's ordinary cover of "Long Tall Shorty," for instance, Dave sings with a conviction and arrogance, a passion and certitude, that characterizes much of the British Invasion blues. "They call me Long Tall Shorty / Because I know what love is all about," sneers a seventeen-year-old Dave with aplomb on American television's *Shindig!*

43

On another level, however, *Kinks* indicates that a significant new song-writer might be forthcoming. Davies composed almost half of the fourteen songs on the UK release, which is about all anyone thought marketable. The concept of the singer-songwriter or band as self-contained unit was not yet fully established. It was only in July 1964 that the Beatles released *A Hard Day's Night*, their third album and first with all original compositions—their first two albums feature slightly more than half originals. On the first two albums of the Rolling Stones, the second released about the same time as *Kinks*, only five of the twenty-four tracks are originals. For *Kinks*, Davies composed a catchy melody for "Just Can't Go to Sleep," turned a concise and humorous lyric on "I Took My Baby Home," and reached mature accomplishment on "You Really Got Me" and "Stop Your Sobbing," the merit of which would not be fully recognized until Chrissie Hynde and the Pretenders scored a hit with it in 1979 and further established the Kinks' credibility with New Wave audiences.

Probably inspired by Davies's encounter in July 1964 with an old girl-friend, "Stop Your Sobbing" is darkly humorous. The singer, who seeks a swift, gentlemanly break, tries to stop the relentless and, for him, irritating tears of his soon-to-be former lover. But all his commands and gentle coaxing fail, as does his babyish prattle through pursed lips in the bridge: "Each little tear . . . / Makes, makes-a-me want [*sic*] / To take you in my arms and tell you to stop all your sobbing." The song ends with the situation unresolved and the singer frustrated. Of some historical note, the neatly uncluttered track fills in gaps with some *oohs* from Ray's future wife Rasa, who makes her debut with the Kinks.

The marketing of pop stars has long been crass, manipulative, and frequently demeaning to fans and musicians alike—and, certainly, the Kinks like most young bands were exploited. Producer Shel Talmy recommended that, for *Kinks*, the band record "Bald Headed Woman" and "I've Been Driving on Bald Mountain," a couple of American folk songs sung by Odetta. What the band did not realize and what they did not discover until the album's release was that since the songs were in the public domain, Talmy with minimum effort could claim composition credit and thus receive songwriting and publishing royalties. "They were my perks, a way for me to get in on the publishing royalties. They were just folk things I adapted—old PD (public domain) folk songs,"[32] said an unapologetic Talmy, a solid producer and engineer, known for creating a hardworking but comfortable atmosphere in the studio, who, as Davies said, was never overbearing or too dominant, but instead let "the record take place."[33] By record industry standards, Talmy did nothing unusual or unethical. "I found out that this was quite a common scam," said Dave.[34] Generally considered the weakest tracks on the album, neither song was ever played by the Kinks before or since the recording sessions. Just a few months later, Talmy had the Sneakers record "Bald Headed Woman" as the B-side of "Just Can't Go to Sleep," the Davies song, and the Who record "Bald Mountain" as the flip side of "I Can't Explain."

The cover of *Kinks* features the four band members, hands crossed just below the waist in their hunting jackets, the title in bold red letters outlined with white, and all bathed in a fiery glow. It is effective art work, more so than the cover for the American release, which loses the red tint and places the band's name and revised album title (*You Really Got Me*) in a white backdrop isolating both from the photograph. The identical liner notes, however, launched a gimmick that embarrassed Davies and the others: the **K** Kampaign. "The letter **K** has been sadly neglected in the English language for centuries," begins the notes. "The Kinks, when they are knot making records or doing one-knight stands, are kampaigning to restore the **K** to its rightful and knoble place . . ." Conceived by Grenville Collins, Robert Wace, and Brian Sommerville, a former journalist turned publicist whose clients had included the Beatles, the **K** campaign reached its nadir with the release of the 1965 EP, *Kwyet Kinks*, which marked the initial release of "A Well Respected Man." Years later, Sommerville admitted that the **K** campaign was a "silly idea . . . just more grist for the mill."[35] Collins, however, was more defensive, but humorously so: "The **K** controversy served its purpose. The **K** thing is easy to criticize in hindsight, but it worked." Referencing *The Sunshine Boys*, Collins continued, "Remember the Walter Matthau and George Burns' movie? Matthau says that 'a **K** is funny.' He's right. There is something intrinsically funny about a **K**. And we had two of them!"[36] To Davies, a former art school student and admirer of musicians and songwriters like Big Bill Broonzy and Hank Williams, the frivolity of the **K** campaign was offensive and embarrassing. Peter Quaife said the "**K** thing . . . was something someone thought up and decided to shove another load for us to carry on our backs! I began to hate the letter **K**!"[37]

Just under the introduction to the **K** campaign, Sommerville profiled each of the Kinks. Adapted from the Beatles, the marketing strategy was intended for fans to identify with individual members, so as to feel a stake in their success, and, most importantly, to support that member by purchasing the band's recordings and concert tickets. The profiles, while not necessarily inaccurate, are more like caricatures. Ray, for instance, is the stubborn artist who "composes, listens to what other [*sic*] have to say about his compositions and then they record what he originally wrote!" Sommerville, who had no idea how prophetic those words were, continued, "he has definate [*sic*] ideas of his own about almost everything and enjoys the occasional sulk." The many grammatical and typographical errors throughout the notes suggest that not only the recording but also the packaging of *Kinks* was rushed. Dave's entry, which includes a comma splice and dangling modifier, portrays him as cute and fun-loving: "Dave who is Ray's brother, is 17 . . . Although the youngest Kink, no girl

45

passes unnoticed when he's around." Peter Quaife was depicted as the Kinks' George Harrison, "the quiet one," "a Mod" who "enjoys horse-riding," indeed, a favorite activity of his youth. Pete may have been over-shadowed in volume by Dave, but he was quick to demonstrate his wit. In 1964, captured on *Kinks: BBC Sessions,* he tells deejay Brian Matthew that the group plans to grow their eyebrows long! If Pete is depicted as the Kinks' George, Mick is the Ringo of *A Hard Day's Night* (released in the summer 1964): "Even without his drums he never stops drumming. In fact, you could say he is kinky about drumming." As an entity, the Kinks are "perfectionists," artistically rebellious, and "a sleeve-writers [*sic*] nightmare" as they insist on musical changes until release—again, more prophetic than, at that time, accurate.

For the most part, Sommerville was very accomplished at what he did and, like Hal Carter before him, had to tolerate the Kinks' almost relentless teasing of him. Sommerville had a number of tricks to generate publicity for the band. In 1965, in Manchester, for instance, he hired young fans to break police barriers as soon as the Kinks emerged from the building after the concert. To minimize damage and injury, he informed the local police of his plot, and to gain as much publicity as possible, he convinced the national press to be at the sight. "We actually got national coverage from that," says Collins. "We sold many records because of this."[38]

Kinks sold very well, remaining on the UK charts for almost six months, peaking at #4, and maintaining a position on the US charts as *You Really Got Me* for over six months, reaching #29. However, before the album was completed, all associated with the Kinks knew that they needed a follow-up single to "You Really Got Me," one that would be similar in sound so as to fortify the group's identity. During the sessions for *Kinks,* Davies introduced another song, an old instrumental that he and Dave had played years earlier called "South," now retitled "Tired of Waiting for You," the brilliance of which all immediately recognized. Fearful the song's revenue-producing potential would be lost if the song were buried on an album, and yet recognizing that "Tired" was not the appropriate follow-up to "You Really Got Me," all agreed to withhold the recording for a more auspicious moment. The strategy worked well. Released in early 1965, "Tired" became a #1 hit.

"All Day and All of the Night"

In the fall of 1964, Davies needed to compose a follow-up to "You Really Got Me." As he would time and time again, he rose to the occasion and wrote "All Day and All of the Night" as music publisher Edward Kassner prevented him from leaving the piano. Unlike and because of "You Really Got Me," "All Day" developed swiftly. "I started thumping out chords—it was really easy. A few days later . . . we routined 'All Day and All of the

Night' at rehearsals [and] recorded it the next day."[39] Dave noticed a different atmosphere in the studio from when they recorded "You Really Got Me": "The frowns of derision and sarcastic scowls had now turned to smiles of approval and looks of admiration."[40] Released in the UK in late October and in the US in mid-December, "All Day" peaked at #2 in the UK by late November and #7 in the US by February.

"All Day" was the classic follow-up for which record companies yearn. It resembled its predecessor without being imitative. Like "You Really Got Me," "All Day" features an aggressive guitar riff jaggedly distorted; a frantic, sputtering guitar solo; and an obsessive speaker. Yet "All Day's" riff is slightly more complex, the key changes perhaps more subtle, and the singer more menacing. "All Day" represents the ultimate embodiment of the Kinks' hard-rock, power-chord style, a style they would continue to explore, although "All Day's" achievement would remain unsurpassed. On stage, Davies has consistently introduced the song as "my personal favorite."

After "All Day's" release, composer Burt Bacharach, reviewing singles, called the song "neurotic." At first Davies was puzzled; then he agreed: "It's youthful, obsessive and sexually possessive . . . a *very* neurotic song."[41] As with "You Really Got Me," Davies does indeed depict the obsessive, neurotic state, but the possessiveness of this speaker marks a shift, one that indicates external destruction and not just self-destruction. This subtle shift makes for a more terrifying song, full of foreboding cymbal and chord crashes. In "You Really Got Me," the singer's neurosis is apparent with his opening words and staccato rhythm, but in "All Day" the singer conceals his neurosis, perhaps even psychosis, more effectively by beginning more rationally: Davies's singer says he cannot be content unless his "girl" is with him at all times. Certainly, listeners may suspect neurosis, but these opening lines could lead conceivably to a statement of love, exaggerated by innocence—which is, of course, conventional in pop songs. The extremity of the opening lines of "You Really Got Me" closes such possibilities, pop hyperbole notwithstanding.

The psychic state of the singer is soon revealed when we hear the second verse when the depth of the singer's obsession goes beyond the routine hyperbole of a pop love song. His bald, unsentimental, and numerous references to eternity signal danger: *last for ever, all day and night time, never, all of the time, all day and all of the night*. Similarly, he commands that she surrender to him with the imperative: "leave me never." Just before the guitar solo, the speaker shouts, almost indecipherably, "Get 'em off," a colloquial British vulgarism usually launched at a passing woman exhorting her to remove her undergarments. It is obviously a more intimidating, if sophomoric command than the "Oh, no!" which precedes the solo in "You Really Got Me." In "All Day," the solo again spews forth a series of clipped notes, but this time reflective of an even more depraved mind orbiting out of control.

The singer in "You Really Got Me" is obsessed, frustrated, but somewhat reserved, even timid next to the singer of "All Day." In live performances with lines re-sung in an elevated voice, the speaker becomes more vulnerable and perhaps pitiable. However, in "All Day," the singer is not only obsessed and frustrated, but also determined and possessive, aggressive rather than timid; and while in concert Davies uses the same elevating voice as he does in "You Really Got Me," it produces a different effect. Instead of voicing vulnerability, the singer confirms his dementia, earlier indicated by his obsession, by the guitar solo, and by crashing cymbals that fill the song. The speaker might be a prototype for the more direct and controlled singer in the Police's "Every Breath You Take," in which the speaker threatens to stalk his former lover "every single day." Sting's singer has alienated or tried to alienate himself from his internal voice of moral authority. Davies's singers in both recordings are in the process of accomplishing that alienation, with the speaker in "All Day" about to complete it. In short, we are listening to minds disintegrating into madness.

"Tired of Waiting for You" and a world tour

When "All Day and All of the Night" slipped in the charts, Pye called for the release of "Tired of Waiting for You." However, something was missing from the August recording. In late December with "All Day" having fallen in the three previous weeks from #8, #16, to #20, Dave was rushed into the studio to add his distinctive sliding barre chords to the record, which would then connect the ballad to its hard-rocking predecessors, thereby at once unifying and diversifying the Kinks sound. It was a master stroke. By February 1965, the Kinks had their second #1 UK hit, and by late April their highest ever showing on the US charts, #6, a position matched only by "Come Dancing" in 1983.

"Tired of Waiting for You" is a love song, although an ambiguous one, like so many of the love songs Davies would write. Unlike the lyrics to his two previous hits, however, the words to "Tired" did not come easily. He read through his notebooks and found some inspiration in a poem about waiting for success, but it did not seem quite right. With no lyrics, he delayed his vocal track one day, faking a sore throat. He was no more prepared the following day, but he had to sing something. Suddenly, as he stepped to the microphone and listened to the backing track with its vibrating bass and the background vocals of Dave, Pete, and Rasa (the inspiration for the song), the lyrics came to him: "I sang the first words that came into my head," he said.[42] The result was the creation of a scene implicit with the frustrations of love along with recognition of love's rewards. But Davies was not satisfied with his ability to improvise, albeit an improvisation developed after much contemplation. Instead, he felt he had lost control of the entire situation—the recording, the song, and his creativity.

48

Like the singers of "You Really Got Me" and "All Day and All of the Night," the singer of "Tired" reveals frustration, but, unlike those singers, not obsession, possessiveness, neurosis, or psychosis. Previously "a lonely soul," the singer appreciates the relationship, and reminds his love that her life is certainly her own and that she "can do" as she likes. Trying to remain rational and unemotional, he only asks for a single favor—that she not keep him waiting. Of course, the nature of that favor is obscure; perhaps he is referring to commitment, sex, or simply relief from her quotidian tardiness. At the time of the recording, Rasa lived with her parents and attended Catholic secondary school, a situation that necessitated trysts, one of which led to Ray's spraining an ankle as he scaled a wall. Ultimately, however, the occasion for the song or the specific favor is unimportant as the song concerns itself with the drama of the confrontation and the singer's repression of his emotions and anxieties, which the long vowels in the lyrics, functioning like an elongated sigh, help him to release at least somewhat calmly: "So tired, tired of waiting, tired of waiting for you . . . I was a lonely soul . . . But you keep me waiting."

The singer's anxiety and the song's tension are underscored through the clean production of Talmy, which emphasizes Quaife's fat, pumping bass lines threatening to explode, and Dave's guitars, one featuring the rising and falling power chords sliding through the song and signifying the escalating and subsiding tension of the scene and the other with its rumblings and distortions, adding as Dave said, "a more cutting emotional edge," reflective of the singer's struggle to conceal his anger.[43] But there is no frenzied guitar solo and, except for an occasional gravelly vocal line, the speaker retains his composure throughout his complaint. The drama in this common scene—a lover trying to voice a complaint without its escalating into a fight—has, in part, led to the song's enduring appeal. The song has been covered by artists such as Elvis Costello (1986), Green Day (1994), and Dwight Yoakam (1997), and by Joey Ramone at a Kinks tribute show in what might have been Joey's last public performance.[44] Dave Davies said that he and Ramone had agreed to work together.[45]

On January 16, 1965, the day after the UK release of "Tired of Waiting for You," the Kinks embarked on a rapid-fire, one-month world tour that would take them to Australia, New Zealand, Singapore, Hong Kong, and New York for a stream of concerts, interviews, tapings, and promotional appearances. It was an eye-opening experience for the still provincial north Londoners. On a refueling stop in a Moscow airport, wisecracking Pete Quaife found himself escorted back onboard at gunpoint when he asked a Soviet guard about recently ousted leader Nikita Khrushchev: "Is baldy still running the country?"

On another refueling stop in Vietnam, the band's plane was escorted by American jet-fighters in and out of the airport. Nerve-racked Ray remembers looking out the window and seeing what must have been skirmishes below. On takeoff, he accepted a valium from a nearby passenger. Other stopovers and events were if not less dramatic at least less frightening. In Bombay, a sleepless Ray awoke at sunrise to hear the chantings of native fishermen, an experience, he says, that reached into his soul to inspire the innovative "See My Friends." In Australia, he and Dave had an emotional meeting with their sister Rosie, cousin Terry, and brother-in-law Arthur Anning. The tour concluded in New York where the band filmed two segments for *Hullabaloo*, a variety show marketed to the youth, during which they encountered their first union problems when they initially refused to join the American Federation of Television & Recording Artists (AFTRA). While in New York, the band visited local nightclubs, like the Peppermint Lounge and the Copa Club, and while they did see Ornette Colman perform, they were dissuaded from visiting Harlem. All in all, despite some expected negative reviews and articles in the "adult" press, particularly in Australia, the tour was very successful and largely incident free with the Kinks performing to large, enthusiastic crowds.

Kinda Kinks

When the band touched down in London on February 14, "Tired of Waiting for You" was #1 on the *Melody Maker* charts. Within six months, the Kinks had scored three international hits with a distinct sound and they were talked about in the same breath as the Beatles. The afternoon after their return and after Ray's morning visit to a specialist for treatment of his swollen foot from an insect bite in Hong Kong, they were hurried into the studio to record an album to capitalize on the success of "Tired." They had three days to complete the LP, slated for a March 5 release, and Pye expected the deadline to be met. This time the album featured ten Davies originals (one co-written with Dave) and two covers (a weak "Dancing in the Street" and the bluesy "Naggin' " sung by Dave with the same swagger he drew on for "Long Tall Shorty"). On the whole, the ten originals on *Kinda Kinks* surpass in quality and artistic maturity the originals on *Kinks*. Several are very strong, including "Something Better Beginning," which captures the drama, excitement, and doubt of new love; "Nothin' in the World Can Stop Me Worryin' about That Girl" and "So Long" (derivative perhaps of Woody Guthrie and Hank Williams), which reveal a more intro-spective composer; and "Got My Feet on the Ground," an assertive rave-up.

The songs, however, fail to achieve their potential through the rushed arrangements and production which left little opportunity for reconsider-ations or re-recordings. Davies desperately wanted to re-record his vocal on "You Shouldn't Be Sad," for instance, but Talmy refused, citing the dead-line. "Shel's revenge," Davies called the producer's response, alluding to his own insistence on re-recording "You Really Got Me" and unintention-ally showing up the producer. Davies remains bitter about the recording of *Kinda Kinks*: "The whole album suffered from slovenly, callous disregard for our music. Listening to some of the mistakes made my toes curl, and will do so for the rest of my life." The Kinks, he realized, had become a trendy commodity. "It was as though everyone around us was cashing in, making as much money as possible before we lost the golden touch."[46]

With another sloppy sleeve—Jimmy Anderson's "Naggin' " was mistitled and composing credits incorrect—*Kinda Kinks* was released on March 5 in the UK and by April peaked at #3 on the album charts, the highest position for an album in the Kinks' thirty-plus album history. However, the chart life of *Kinda Kinks* was brief, at ten weeks less than half that of the 23-week span of *Kinks*. "It would have stayed there longer," comments Davies, "but for the good taste of our fans, who must have realized that while the songs showed promise, the record was a disaster."[47] Marketing strategists for the US dictated that *Kinda Kinks* be withheld and, instead, called for the release of *Kink-Size* in mid-March, an assemblage of tracks released previously in the UK with two featured US hits, "All Day and All of the Night" and "Tired of Waiting for You." The strategy worked as *Kink-Size* held the charts for over seven months with a peak position of #13. *Kinda Kinks*, released in the US in mid-August, fared poorly without a new hit single and held the charts for just nine weeks peaking at #60. But in 1965, the money and prestige lay in singles.

"Ev'rybody's Gonna Be Happy" and "Set Me Free"

Prior to Christmas 1964, the Kinks recorded the follow-up to "Tired of Waiting for You." With "Ev'rybody's Gonna Be Happy," Davies's artistic adventurousness emerged in the studio, an adventurousness that in years to come would irritate and frustrate record companies, marketing departments, promoters, fans, and fellow Kinks. He composed "Ev'rybody's Gonna Be Happy" in the jazzy soul style of the Earl Van Dyke Trio, a band the Kinks toured with and admired. By Kinks standards, however, the record flopped, reaching only #20 in the UK and going unreleased by Reprise as an A-side in the US.

While Ray was disappointed with the relative failure of "Ev'rybody's Gonna Be Happy," he was more upset by the reaction surrounding the record. "You've lost that Kinks sound," they told him. "To this day I've no idea what they meant by that."[48] Davies's comment is suspicious. Surely he knew the reference was to songs of frustration, not happiness, with loud, chunky chords, raw and frayed. But, on the other hand, he never expected the Kinks to be about one sound. Just prior to the time of recording the single, he commented: "Being a Kink is an art, only I'm dabbling in sounds, not pictures."[49] "Ev'rybody's Gonna Be Happy" represents a "dabbling," perhaps not as artistically successful as Davies's later experiments in country, music hall, rock theatre, or stage musicals, but the record signaled that Davies and the Kinks would not allow themselves to be so easily codified. A rarity in the Kinks catalog, "Ev'rybody's Gonna Be Happy" is driven by the rhythm section of Quaife's funky bass line, which inspired the song, and Avory's uncharacteristically busy drumming. "It's like a Motown sort of sound," says Avory. "In retrospect, it should not have been a single, but it was something different to do. I quite enjoyed that because it suited my style."[50]

Yielding to external pressures for a hit, Davies wrote "Set Me Free" in the Kinks' established style. Similar to "Waiting for You," the ballad features slashing power chords and a neurotic singer who pleads to be set free from the binds of love—on *Shindig!* the Kinks performed the song on a set of large rocks, insinuating a sentence of hard labor. But the top-ten UK hit made Ray, as he says in *X-Ray*, feel like a hack, "a whore," for he had "to contrive and target an audience rather than write from an inward, subconscious flow."[51] In 1965, some three months after its release, Ray said, "I'm ashamed of that song. I can stand to hear and even sing most of the songs I've written night after night, but not that one. It's built around pure idiot harmonies that have been used in thousands of songs."[52] Dave is not nearly so harsh about the record, agreeing that it was "contrived" with Ray's voice "uncomfortably high in places," but he also finds it "quite charming."[53] Of course, Pye, Kassner, and management loved it, considering "Set Me Free" the most commercial song Davies had written to date.

In recent years it seems as if Davies has reassessed "Set Me Free." On *To the Bone* in 1996, the Kinks play a more bluesy arrangement which far surpasses the original. The track opens with Dave's loud, distorted power chords followed by his solo, which plays off the melody, before giving way to Ray's now more assured vocals that have more of an edge than falsetto. Although it cannot be said with certainty, Ray's reconsideration of "Set Me Free" may have begun after he completed *X-Ray* and while preparing the stage version of his "unauthorized autobiography," at which time he may have realized that the song did spring from his subconscious. In the historical context established in *20th Century Man / Storyteller*, "Set Me Free" seems to be less about male–female relationships as it is about an artist imprisoned by the demands of pop stardom. When he wrote the song in the early spring of 1965, Davies was under relentless pressure to produce hits, to write album tracks, to tour, and to promote. He was also a newlywed and an expectant father, and he was not yet twenty-one!

Sound and theme

With the late May 1965 release and ten-top UK success of "Set Me Free," the Kinks had solidified a unique sound and theme, one that would resurface throughout their career in various permutations and variations. While only one dimension of the Kinks' style, the sound, sometimes neglected for whole albums, has accounted for some of their finest and most expansive moments: "I Need You" (1965), which to Avory "sounded like 'You Really Got Me' backwards,"[54] "Till the End of the Day" (1965), "Brainwashed" (1969), "Top of the Pops" (1970), "Sleepwalker" (1977), "Permanent Waves" (1978), "Destroyer" (1981), "Labour of Love" (1983), "Wall of Fire" (1993), and "Drift Away" (1993), among others.

The Kinks made particularly effective use of the sound on "The Hard Way," one of the high points on *Schoolboys in Disgrace* (1975), a concept album connected with *Preservation Acts 1* and *2* through its anti-hero Flash. "The Hard Way," the final song in a three-song sequence concerning Flash's expulsion from school, is loosely based on Dave's caning and expulsion from Grimshaw after he and his girlfriend Sue cut school for a morning rendezvous. In "I'm in Disgrace," Flash is distraught over his girlfriend's pregnancy, and in "Headmaster," he asks for sympathy. The psychotic Headmaster responds in "The Hard Way," which like "You Really Got Me" and "All Day and All of the Night" is driven by a riff developed from power chords and the theme of frustration.

The Headmaster regards Flash as he no doubt regards all his students, as part of an inferior breed, "born to waste" as "factory fodder."[55] For Flash and for Davies, the Headmaster represents the voice of the state, inculcating students with their defined role in the culture. At Grimshaw Secondary Modern School (one of many schools established for students who did not perform well on the Eleven Plus examination[56]), both Ray and Dave received the message that they were to "be a slave to a lathe," as Ray sings on "Second Hand Car Spiv." Instead, they found escape through music. Flash heard a similar message—about being "fit" only to sweep streets— and found his escape through crime. Davies has said that "The Hard Way" has "the most social significance on the record . . . based on friends' visits to the Youth Employment Officer and the way they were pushed into jobs they did not want. By the age of seventeen some of them were sad people, already bitter, regretting not having worked harder at school or developed skills."[57] As a symbol of authority, the Headmaster treats Flash with the same disdain and arrogance as management treats factory workers like Davies's friends or like Arthur Seaton in *Saturday Night and Sunday Morning.*

The Headmaster is not only tyrannical and scornful, but also duplicitous and perverse. He finds a psychosexual pleasure in browbeating Flash, who in "Headmaster," the preceding track, asks for forgiveness in the tones of a schoolboy, but not unlike an unfaithful lover. Flash confesses to being "a naughty boy" and having "dishonoured" the Headmaster. Flash asks for "one more chance" and pleads for the Headmaster not to tell his friends that he "bent over." Flash's extreme concern for secrecy is more common in one sexually manipulated and violated than a child hit by his schoolmaster, which for many youths can be a badge of honor.

If the Headmaster does not, in fact, sexually abuse Flash, he does find psychosexual enjoyment in the act of scolding. His response is filled with double entendre, beginning with the title of "The Hard Way," and including the contrasting tones of the Headmaster's voice from deep, forced masculinity (opening lines) to effeminate enunciation (closing lines), to a lascivious, gleeful quaking on "killer's touch," one of a pair of suspicious phrasings about the boy's intellect requiring a "killer's touch," which could refer to a direct act of oppression or aggression, perhaps sexual.

Another of the Headmaster's questions is similarly perplexing. He wonders why the boy does not "cooperate" and then warns Flash that if he continues to "sit there and vegetate" he will end up "illiterate." The implication behind "cooperate" could be sexual, with the reference to literacy masking the innuendo, but the reference to "sit there and vegetate" is even more ambiguous, with "vegetate" possibly suggesting a veiled pass or sexual jealousy. The problem is that Flash has not "vegetate[d]," but has been too active with his girlfriend. In concert, Davies has substituted the more heavy-handed "masturbate" for "vegetate," which he delivers with a cracking voice on *One for the Road* (1980) and which more clearly reveals the mindset of the Headmaster.

Dave's guitar mirrors the Headmaster's sexual aggression. The chords slash through the song, adding to the tension of the scene, and the two solos, a sputtering but controlled repetition of notes at different octaves, suggest a sexual duality while the second solo, which ends the song, turns almost melodic and ends on its highest note, suggesting some kind of fulfillment, perhaps sexual or psychosexual.

The final verse, just before the second solo, is delivered in different tones, fatherly rebuke and motherly tenderness, with the repetition of "hard way," which occurs several times, approximating not only the caning but also the sexual act or sexual posturing. In concert, Davies has performed the song with academic black gown and a grotesque, long-nosed mask, suggestive of a phallic, and emphasizing the Headmaster's sexual decadence and the humor of the song, dark though it be. The humor develops from the scene (an innocent but sexually experienced schoolboy entrapped by a corrupt, salivating, but esteemed Headmaster) and is maintained since the consummation of the Headmaster's desires is unseen and probably only psychosexual.

The Kinks retool the band's power sound and theme of frustration and neurosis for comic effect in "State of Confusion," video and title track from their 1983 album. The song opens with Dave's familiar chord slashing, on which organist Ian Gibbons lays a thin, haunting strain, followed by a belligerent guitar riff, and then Ray's tormented scream, which signals the beginning of the drama. This opening might be from a soundtrack of a spoof of a B-movie horror film. In the video, the protagonist pop star appears trapped in a recording booth, frustrated by slipping headphones and, a few moments later, by a self-operating console board.

The scene shifts to the star's home, presumably the next morning, where his frustration continues. The words and visual imagery present a catalog of domestic frustration, many caused by technological malfunctions: flooded basements, woodworm in the attic, collapsed ceiling, defective tumble dryer, broken television, deficient video, inaccessible computer, unclosable window, unremovable bottle cap, ultra-sharp razor, and faulty milk carton. The pop star feels himself victimized by modern technology and gadgetry, including cars, washing machines, leaky roofs, tape recorders, and more. The anti-hero struggles en route to work, where, in Chaplinesque scenes, human traffic and speed thwart attempts to enter a phone booth and automobile traffic makes crossing a street perilous and time consuming. That Davies devotes eight lyrical lines to crossing a street magnifies the anti-hero's frustration and lengthy passing of time. At work, filming a video or television show, the frustration continues as cue cards become difficult to locate and the strap slips from his guitar as encroaching cameras invade the protagonist and stifle his performance, stripping it of naturalness, for in this high-tech filming, improvised movement or instinctive gesture is unworkable. Davies may be commenting on the intrusive nature of technology on creativity and performance, but he is also spoofing his own infamous klutziness and discomfort with modern gadgetry. He did not drive a car until the mid-1980s.

In the lyrics, but left undepicted in the video, the protagonist loses his girl who "couldn't stand the boredom when the video broke down." Like the filming scene in the video, the implication is that people are being victimized by gadgetry. Here, the relationship lasts only as long as the technology is available to divert the couple's attention from each other. The couple seems as unfeeling as the technology around them; each is capable of replacing or discarding the other as easily as a worn-out appliance. For Davies, here and elsewhere, the proliferation of technology has numbed human emotion, leaving people in a perpetual state of psycho-emotional-political confusion. The *State* in the song's title carries multiple associations, all appropriate to the song and video: the psychic *state* of a person, the government or *state* promoting a consumerist culture, or the *state* of pop music in which the video protagonist finds himself entrapped—all these *states* to Davies have become impersonal and dehumanized in the age of hyper-technology, an age he has described as "a mechanical nightmare" ("20th Century Man").

The song and video have different endings with different implications. In the song the protagonist lies awake troubled by financial considerations, unable to find refuge in the dream world of sleep. He is forced to conclude that there can be "no escape" from the contemporary world's ubiquitous state of confusion. The video, however, closes with a sense of triumph. The star arrives for a performance; struggles to exit his minuscule dressing room (like the recording and phone booths, images of entrapment entered unsuspectingly); bumps into an ironing board; bangs his horizontally hung guitar on the door frame; and reaches the stage with an untied shoe, unplugged guitar, and his band well into performance. However, as the song and video end to enthusiastic applause, the star leaps with outstretched legs and the frame freezes at the top of the leap, an image of spontaneous energy suggesting that the anti-hero has overcome, at least temporarily, contemporary burdens and technological limitations through his art. Such leaps, not so incidentally, are a regular feature of Davies's showmanship, furthering the autobiographical interpretation of the video. The video should not be interpreted as incompatible with the lyrics, which imply ongoing frustration relieved only by sleep, or as a forced happy ending for the MTV audience, but rather as an extension—not contradiction—of the lyrics, which with the video suggest that relief can be found more significantly in the process of creation and artistic performance. That both video and song are humorous makes such an extension suitable and plausible—although the humor remains dark.

Of course, the song itself is an extension of a riff and theme developed and permutated from "You Really Got Me" and "All Day and All of the Night," through humorous treatments in "Sleepwalker" and "Permanent Waves," to its fullest comic expression in "State of Confusion." Thus, by August 1964, the Kinks had created a sound and a theme that they would revisit and reshape for over the next three decades. Even more significantly, those loud distorted guitar chords had an immediate impact on the direction of rock music and rock guitarists.

4

A WELL RESPECTED MAN
Satirist, ironist, and social commentator

The year 1965 should have been an exciting and rewarding one for the Kinks. They were in the midst of a string of international hits, they were sought after for television appearances, they toured the world, and they created a unique sound with their own music. They were ranked with the Rolling Stones, both only second to the Beatles. Yet despite continued hits, 1965 turned disastrous. Few connected with the Kinks believed that they would survive the year as a unit. Exhaustion, forced togetherness, fragile personalities, pressure, too many managers and contracts, and America, all took their toll on the band.

In 1965, most in the music business considered the peak period of earning power for a band or pop star to be brief, perhaps a couple of years at best. Therefore, the Kinks were ushered from studio to tour to promotional appearances with little if any break between cycles. At the end of March 1965, the Kinks broke down. Ray collapsed on stage during a performance in Scotland with signs of pneumonia; Dave suffered from bronchitis; and, Pete, while in the men's room of the Odeon Cinema in Muswell Hill, fainted resulting in stitches and a concussion. For ten days, from March 26 through April 3, the Kinks machine grinded to a halt—but not completely. Pete still managed an interview and Ray and Dave spent a few hours recording demos. The exhilaration and adrenalin produced from the initial excitement of hit records was fizzling. But any sustained break was not in sight.

The stress intensified the tensions within the band. Beginning in early 1964 and then increasingly after the success of "You Really Got Me," the four Kinks found themselves together for long stretches of time in the cramped spaces of vans, buses, shared hotel rooms, studios, and dressing rooms where they would be forced to wait sometimes hours between arrival and performance. This would tax the strongest of friendships, and the Kinks were more musical partners than friends or even brothers in Ray and Dave's case. Furthermore, Ray, the musical leader, was frequently aloof, moody, or just reticent, hardly qualities of a solid road captain. For his part Dave could be nasty, confrontational, and explosive, finding a usual victim in the good-natured, quiet Avory, who as the only non co-founder and as a south Londoner was an easier target than the others. Quaife, a schoolboy friend, could not be so easily intimidated by either Dave or Ray and often tried to serve as a peacekeeper between Dave and Avory and the battling brothers.

Despite the turmoil within the band, Grenville Collins notes that "all divisions melted away when the Kinks were confronted by external opposition . . . they would become a pack of wolves."[1] And no one, promoters or star, could escape the wrath of the Kinks, as English pop star Bobby Shafto found out one evening in the fall of 1964. Avory tells the story:

> We used to get this girl to come along and do a rave. . . . She would do a little striptease and we'd all play tambourines. The only available room was the one Bobby Shafto was in. He came in and made a fuss. He started doing the star bit, so we had a little kafuffle with him. Nothing terrible. We just put him in his place.[2]

Collins then had to contend with Shafto's screaming and tearful manager: "Those disgusting, filthy, animalistic creatures have just beaten up my star."[3] On another tour, Ray had to be locked in his dressing room to be kept from attacking Joe Cocker, and in June 1972, backstage during a shoot for *Top of the Pops*, Davies had words with Noddy Holder and members of Slade, resulting in Ray's splashing a pint of beer over bassist Jim Lea's head.

Cardiff

The internal battling, however, climaxed on May 19 at the Capitol Theatre in Cardiff, Wales, where the Kinks were performing with the Yardbirds during their Jeff Beck era. On the previous evening, in Somerset, Dave returned from a post-show party and physically assaulted Avory who defended himself by blackening both Dave's eyes. The punch-up did not end the squabble and the bickering took center stage at Cardiff. Wearing sunglasses, Dave barked insults and obscenities at Avory throughout the opening song, "You Really Got Me," whose title suddenly assumed a post-fight significance. As the band broke into Chuck Berry's "Beautiful Delilah," Dave kicked over Avory's drums. Avory erupted and clubbed the guitarist with his high-hat, opening Dave's head and knocking him to the floor. Avory, believing he might have killed his bandmate, fled from the theater to escape police. Dave had to be hospitalized and received sixteen stitches to close his wound. The police investigated but were placated, at least initially, by Kinks' management who explained that something had gone wrong with a special effect. The band returned to London where Dave spent ten days recuperating in the home of his sister Joyce and Avory hid out in journalist Keith Altham's house in Surrey.

It looked as though the Kinks would be searching for a new drummer. Five days after the Cardiff incident Ray went into the studio to create demos for songs that Kassner planned to place with other artists, including Peggy Lee who recorded "I Go to Sleep" and Dave Berry who had a European hit with "This Strange Effect." Accompanying Ray on the demos was probably Quaife and drummer Mitch Mitchell, future member of the Jimi Hendrix Experience and then a member of Riot Squad, who had performed with the Kinks in Cardiff and other stops on their most recent tour. Mitchell hoped to replace Avory, but the change was unnecessary. It is curious to speculate how Mitchell, a busier and more explosive drummer than the more restrained Avory, might have reshaped the sound of the Kinks—given, of course, the freedom. To quell rumors of his departure and to appease the police who were now considering charges against Avory of grievous bodily harm, Avory provided an explanation to the press:

> [We] had worked out a routine for "You Really Got Me" [and] as the song reaches its height, Dave is leaping around and ends by whirling his guitar round his head and pretending to throw it to the audience. It was then that my 18-inch crash cymbal was knocked over and fell on him. It's untrue that we had rowed and are going to break up. It was just an unfortunate incident. The whole thing worked out fine the night before in Taunton.[4]

Larry Page summoned the band to his office to convince them to continue. After further damage control, on June 17, the Kinks departed for their first American tour with Page, road manager Sam Curtis, and occasional visits from Edward Kassner. Surprisingly, neither Wace nor Collins accompanied the band. "I never understood why Robert and Grenville stayed in England," wonders Dave, "when this was potentially one of our most crucial career moves."[5]

Collins, however, contends that there was no need to accompany the band. There was other Kinks business to be conducted in London, including preparations for the release of "See My Friends" in late July, and, besides, the band, Wace and Collins believed, were in good hands with Curtis, "an imposing figure who would keep them in line."[6] Avory agrees with Collins. "They could operate better being in the office; you know, chasing record companies and doing their business."[7]

America

The Kinks were hardly a cohesive unit as they trudged off to conquer America. Ray was dejected over leaving his wife and less than one-month-old daughter, and Dave and Mick could not so easily put the recent past behind them. "The band was in disarray," says Mick. "Everything was going pear-shaped. We shouldn't have actually gone." From beginning to end of the tour, nothing seemed to completely work, and the band could never regain an esprit de corps. "I hated every moment," says Avory.[8] While the opening gigs were exciting and well received, the band was disappointed in New York to see themselves listed on the marquee as "The Kings" and stressed in Philadelphia to see Page jailed briefly for not paying a local tax demanded by a union official.

The tension only mounted as the Kinks traveled into the Midwest where, on the following night, they performed on a makeshift stage in Peoria, Illinois, in front of a capacity crowd of 700, much smaller than they were led to expect. Frightening, however, was their redneck chauffer, who Davies sings of in "Americana," a song composed for *20th Century Man*. The "punk from a B-movie" pretended to telephone Elvis and "waved the six gun around menacingly" while mocking the Kinks. Not only was the tour not gaining needed momentum, but more serious problems also lay ahead.

Things started to turn ugly when, on June 25, the Kinks pulled into Reno, Nevada. Ticket sales were slight and the promoter, Betty Kaye Productions, gave the Kinks half the scheduled payment for the performance with the balance to be paid on the following evening at the Sacramento concert, which Betty Kaye was also promoting and where receipts were expected to be higher. The Kinks were uncooperative. They played half time or about twenty minutes in Reno, angering the promoter. In Sacramento, Davies requested the balance of the Reno payment, which Kaye refused, arguing and later winning the point legally, that the Kinks only played half the scheduled time. The Kinks were infuriated when they took the stage in Sacramento, and, according to Page, played only "You Really Got Me" for the duration of their 45-minute set—which is unlikely, however. Sam Curtis says they played a lengthy version of the hit, but not for forty-five minutes, and neither Quaife nor Avory remember the supposed one-song concert.[9]

On July 4 at San Francisco's Cow Palace, the Kinks and Kaye had still another dispute. With the arena less the one-quarter filled, the promoter offered the band a check instead of the prescribed cash. The Kinks refused to perform. Kaye had had enough with the English toughs and lodged a formal complaint with the American Federation of Musicians, which would not be the only complaint unions would receive. Two days previous to the Cow Palace, as the Kinks prepared for a performance on Dick Clark's new weekday afternoon television show, they had a run-in with an official from the American Federation of Television & Radio Artists (AFTRA). The circumstances are not entirely clear, but apparently Ray punched the official. "I remember doing this television spot," recalls Davies, "and this guy kept going on at me: 'When the commies overrun Britain, you're really going to want to come here, aren't you?' I just turned around and hit him, about three times. I later found out he was a union official."[10] In "Americana," Ray adds that Dave not only refused to sign a necessary form, but that he also told the official to "fuck off." The official responded, "You're never gonna work in America again." As a result of the confrontations with Kaye and union officials, the American Federation of Musicians (AFM) withheld necessary works permits for the Kinks until 1969, in effect banning the Kinks from America for four crucial years. It is probable that the AFM sought to make an example of some young English musicians who, the union believed, were taking work from Americans. The Beatles were too popular to harass and the Stones, despite their rebellious image, were generally cooperative with officials and promoters. The Kinks, however, were unruly and hardly cooperative, thus an easy target.

By the time the Kinks arrived on the West Coast, they were living the Henry James story in reverse: America was crushing the innocent Europeans. America had become an "evil place" for Davies,[11] not the land of opportunity and enchantment that he had envisioned from songs and movies. But the Kinks and their relatively inexperienced management team were unprepared for America, especially xenophobic attitudes and the power of unions. Furthermore, Davies and the Kinks were becoming more and more irritated with Larry Page, who they felt was neglecting his duties to scout new bands for Kassner Music and Denmark Productions, the company Page had founded with Kassner. Page alienated the Kinks when he signed on to become Sonny and Cher's English representative, bragging, "I'll be the first back to England with their song: 'I Got You Babe.' "[12] In fairness to Page, he did nothing unethical and, in fact, hawked Davies songs to American artists, including Sonny and Cher who recorded "I Go to Sleep" as did Peggy Lee. Additionally, the Kinks, particularly Ray and Dave, could be nightmarish for a manager. "The thing you have to remember about the Kinks," said Robert Wace, "is that until 1967 they weren't even house-trained."[13]

But the Kinks felt neglected and, finally, abandoned when on the morning of July 4, Page failed to meet them for the flight from Los Angeles to San Francisco. On the previous evening during which he had to persuade Davies to take the Hollywood Bowl stage, Page had informed three of the four Kinks, but not their mercurial leader, that he would be retuning to England and that he had arranged for tour details to be executed by Sam Curtis and Don Zacharlini, a successful owner of a chain of laundromats.[14] Ray was dissatisfied and called an impromptu meeting in the airport where the Kinks resolved to remove Page from their management team. "He left us high and dry," remembers Avory.[15] "Of course I didn't leave them in the lurch," Page replies. "I left Sam Curtis there; I left the publisher there; I left the agent there. They were *very* well looked after. Sam Curtis was a very efficient roadie."[16] It would not be so easy to remove Page.

Lawsuits

On September 2, 1965, Wace and Collins, through attorney Michael Simkins, served papers on Page and Kassner to terminate the contract between Boscobel Productions, Wace and Collin's company, and Denmark Productions, ending, in effect, Page's involvement with the Kinks. Less than a week later, Denmark replied that it had no intention of ending the contract which gave it some managerial responsibilities and 10 percent of the Kinks' income. Simkins argued that all contracts signed by the Kinks were null and void since at the time of signing, Dave, according to British law, was in his "infancy." Boscobel planned to re-sign the band with a clause prohibiting subcontracting of management responsibilities.

At the same time, Simkins informed Davies that he had no binding agreement with Edward Kassner and was therefore free to assign his songs to other publishers. After meeting publisher Freddy Beinstock, a client of Simkins, Davies signed a five-year agreement with Beinstock's Belinda Music, which, in a year, would allow Davies to set up his own publishing companies at which time Davies's affiliation would shift to Carlin Ltd., another Beanstock company. For the UK rights, Davies created Davray (not referencing his brother but formed from *Dav*ies + *Ray*mond) and, for the US rights, Mondavies (Ray*mond* + *Davies*). This was the greatest blow to Kassner and Page as the earnings from co-managing and advising were slight compared to the publishing royalties, but the managerial responsibilities provided access to Davies and his songs. At one time, Kassner had tried to secure Davies by offering the composer £40 a week for life in exchange for all future songs. Davies refused, noting that the publisher, a Nazi concentration camp survivor, had "a completely empty look in his eyes . . . a look from hell . . . all feelings for the rest of humanity had been squeezed out of him."[17] With his prize songwriter about to skip, Kassner appealed again to Davies and again was unsuccessful. Kassner then registered the upcoming Kinks single "Till the End of the Day" with the Performing Right Society, hoping to halt its release, but Pye released the record a week ahead of schedule to avoid injunctions.

Interestingly, at this point, those close to Davies were concerned that he had "dried up" as a songwriter as his production had declined from what had been a steady year-long stream of songs. Wace arranged for an inspirational meeting for Ray with Mort Shuman, who, with Doc Pomus, wrote classics for the Drifters and Elvis such as "Save the Last Dance for Me," "This Magic Moment," "Little Sister," and "Viva Las Vegas," among others. Shuman reported that Ray would be fine after a little rest.

Kassner, however, would not go away so easily, and lawsuits, which would take the rest of the decade to sort out, were underway. Kassner Music and Denmark Productions sued Davies, Belinda, Pye, and Boscobel regarding publishing rights, and, Denmark sued Boscobel on the breach of contract over managerial participation. The later suit came to trial in the late spring 1967 when Judge John Widgery discounted the notion of "infancy" believing that the Kinks were mature enough in 1964 to sign contracts. However, the trial turned in Boscobel's favor with Ray's testimony against Page and his actions while on the American tour. Thus, the contract between Boscobel and Denmark was legally terminated.

The case involving publishing rights would linger until October 1970 with an out-of-court settlement with Davies and the Kinks' management worn down by Kassner's legal threats and wranglings. Davies, in effect, decided to cut his losses, settling with Kassner "for a small lump sum, and a reduction in royalties due [him] as a writer of all those early hits."[18] But Davies found it a relief to put the dispute behind him. The contracts the Kinks signed in 1964 and 1965 while decidedly not favorable to them were little different from the contracts of other young artists. Pye, for instance, had a series of five one-year options which they exercised without increased royalty rates. Suspicious of Pye's accounting and anxious to renegotiate the contract, Grenville Collins pursued the label's chief executive Louis Benjamin, who finally told him, "Look, Grenville, if I pay them any more they will be making more money than me."[19] Of course, when the Kinks signed with Pye, their management had little if any experience and the Kinks were, like pop artists of any era, just anxious to be on the scene. Additionally, the financial stakes in 1964 were not what they would be by 1968, the first year that album sales surpassed singles sales. As Collins puts it, "At this time, the music business was developing into a music industry."[20] Most bands, even with hit records, earned their income through live performances.

"A Well Respected Man"

In late July 1965, Davies returned from America disappointed and stressed. Neither the gigs, America, nor Page had lived up to expectations. Realizing that Davies needed a holiday, Wace and Collins sent Ray, Rasa, and their infant daughter to the Imperial Hotel, a plush resort on England's southern coast in Torquay. Davies felt like an outsider in a milieu with palm-court orchestras, health spas, and high tea, and, to avoid the snobbery of the other guests, rarely left his room. "They knew I was in a rock and roll band." One afternoon, while on the seaside promenade, an upper-class guest invited Davies to join in a foursome for golf. Davies declined and immediately checked himself and his family out of the hotel. "They tried to make me one of them saying, 'Come on, play golf with me.' I took an instant dislike to them because the establishment draws you in and makes you one of them and that's as far as you can go. You can't break out. People like Lennon realized that."[21] What may have been a simple golf invitation incited Davies's working-class pride and resentment, as he believed the invitation resulted only from his celebrity. Davies may have heeded a warning from kitchen-sink films like *Room at the Top*, in which Joe Lampton loses his identity and freedom by rejecting his uncle's advice to "Stick to your own people."

With increasing clarity, Davies realized that he and the Kinks were a valuable commodity. Everyone wanted a piece of the revenue-producing pop stars and everyone wanted to be seen with them—even those who would have snubbed them just months earlier. As a result of the incident at Torquay, the tour of America, and business of making music, Davies's songwriting took a new direction. "I decided I was gonna use words more, and *say* things."[22] The result was satire and a folkish strain that would remain steadfast in the Kinks catalog.

Davies's first satire was inspired directly by Torquay while drawing on the upper-class mannerisms of Collins and Wace, whom the Kinks labeled "Bob the snob"; by Davies's observations at the debutante gigs and social parties the Kinks once played; and by Bob Dylan, whose influence was ubiquitous by this time and who expanded the thematic and musical range of top-forty radio in 1965. By the end of that summer, Dylan had scored five top-ten records in the UK: "The Times They Are A-Changin'" (#9, March), "Subterranean Homesick Blues" (#9, April), "Mr. Tambourine Man" (#1, July for the Byrds), "All I Really Want to Do" (#4, August for the Byrds) and "Like a Rolling Stone" (#4, August). Reports circulated that the Kinks rehearsed Dylan's "Absolutely Sweet Marie" and "Most Likely You Go Your Way and I'll Go Mine" for their stage show, which is unlikely especially since the source proved to be a mischievous Mick Avory interview.[23] Certainly, however, Davies did call Dylan and Picasso "two giants of twentieth-century art."[24]

Yet despite the commercial success of Dylan and other protest songs— Barry McGuire's "Eve of Destruction" hit #3 in the UK in September 1965—Pye refused to release "A Well Respected Man" as a single. No doubt the label wanted a record in the same vein as the Kinks' earlier hits. On July 30, the Kinks released the groundbreaking "See My Friends," which fared better than "Ev'rybody's Gonna Be Happy" but reached only a modest #11 in the UK and flopped completely in the US. Pye then compromised and released "A Well Respected Man" on *Kwyet Kinks*, an EP. On the airplay and strength of "A Well Respected Man," *Kwyet Kinks* turned into an astonishingly large seller, reaching #1 on the EP charts. For a time, Ray considered releasing a series of satirical EPs, but LPs and single commitments interfered. Recognizing the appeal of "A Well Respected Man," Reprise released the song as a single in the US, where it rose to #13. In addition, the label featured the song on the Kinks' fourth American LP, *Kinkdom*, a collection of tracks from the EP, various A- and B-sides, and tracks previously unreleased in America. As with *Kink-Size*, released in March 1965 in the US, no new recording was necessary. Although

Kinkdom remained on the charts for four months, it barely cracked the top-fifty. The liner notes describe Kinkdom as a land where "inhabitants . . . have to go dancing every night except Monday . . . a land so wild, so fantastic, so far out that about it even Rand is scared to tell McNally." Although Davies's lyrical range had expanded, the quality of Kinks' liner notes had not.

"A Well Respected Man" not only introduces Davies the satirist/social commentator and ironist—although Davies is far more direct in songs than listeners often realize—but it also establishes the prototype for Davies satires. Over the next three years Davies would write a series of songs which focused on an individual and exposed the foibles of England's class structure. From an artistic perspective, the best of which include "Dedicated Follower of Fashion," "Dandy," and "Sunny Afternoon," with "Mister Pleasant" (a major hit on the continent) and "Tin Soldier Man" only marginally successful and "Plastic Man," a failure. All draw from folkish rhythms with the better songs developing from characterization and humor rather than bitterness. At the extremes, there is "Sunny Afternoon," the richest in characterization and subtle, dark humor, while at the other end is "Plastic Man," a clichéd portrait with little humor or surprise.

While Davies may have been influenced by Dylan and the folk music of the time, he was influenced even more by the British music hall. "For years and years, I denied it. . . . I think that's because music hall is, in rock and roll terms, quite an uncool thing to be associated with. . . . Whereas the blues is. But music hall was undeniably an important influence. And I'd put someone like [English comic singer and banjo-ukulele player] George Formby right up there with [American bluesman] Bill Broonzy. I feel they're connected in some way—albeit through me. Some of the acoustic guitar stuff I do resonates with the George Formby style."[25] Davies folk rhythms in songs like "A Well Respected Man," "Dedicated Follower of Fashion," "Dandy," and "Sunny Afternoon," are decidedly English and music hall, as are the *oom pah* tuba in "Tin Soldier Man," the cheerful piano of "Mister Pleasant" (played by Nicky Hopkins), and the sing-along insistence in all the above songs—sing-alongs were intrinsic to the music hall and its communal spirit. Consider the following, written in 1976:

> If we British have any folk songs at all these are they. Listen to a pub or coach outing sing-song anywhere in the British Isles and you'll hear teenagers singing Music Hall songs that are often over a hundred years out.[26]

The British music hall and American vaudeville both employed the variety-show format, which included the low humor of slapstick skits, stand-up comedy, trite love songs, and, generally, escapist entertainment that found its audience in the working classes. However, many routines, especially in the music hall, feature satire and caricatures of upper-class types which reinforced working-class solidarity, working-class pride, and a sense of shared knowledge or "knowingness." They may have been exploited but they refused to be defeated: "Don't let the bastards grind you down," says Arthur Seaton in Alan Sillitoe's *Saturday Night and Sunday Morning*. It was important, however, that the mocking of the upper class and the attack on class structure not be overwhelmed by bitterness and cynicism. It had to be kept somewhat light and humorous, or as V. C. Clinton-Baddeley states, like "the rude boy attacking pomposity with a pea-shooter."[27]

While the satire might be a bit more edged than the music hall and Dave's electric guitar lines rock, "A Well Respected Man" could easily have been performed in the music hall. Through caricature, mimicry, and double entendre, the song attacks the hypocrisy of a seemingly virtuous upper-class gentleman consumed by greed, lust, and selfishness; it features a simple melody, folkish rhythms, an almost *oom pah pah* bass line, and a rollicking sing-along chorus with its upsweeping "And he's oh so good . . . oh so fine . . . oh so healthy . . ."—even the tinny sound of the recording, emanating especially from Avory's drums, contributes to the music-hall feel. Of course, at the time of its release, few young English listeners and even fewer American listeners would have understood the song's indebtedness to the music hall.

As "A Well Respected Man" opens, Davies gently strums a chord, pauses, and describes the visible routine of his subject's life, which includes a seemingly solid work ethic based on consistency and "punctuality" and, as we hear at the end of the chorus, acting "conservatively." The satire through verse one and the chorus is subtle, but unmistakable. In the second stanza Davies deepens and clarifies his attack on ingrained middle-class pretense and morality when he attacks the protagonist's mother, who attends meetings on foreign trade but is more interested in seducing young men, perhaps the wait staff, with cash, and the father, who remains home to seduce the maid. At the song's conclusion, his mother, who knows the best about "matrimonial stakes" and the importance of appearance and status will find him a suitable mate. With each successive verse, Davies clarifies the irony of the chorus, which begs a smirk and a sing-along in the best sense of music-hall "knowingness."

The third verse is the song's most interesting as Davies turns not bitter, but darkly and scatologically humorous with homoerotic and decadent images. We hear that the protagonist "likes his own back yard" and "his fags the best," and then, suggestive of absurd smugness, that "his own sweat smells the best." Davies has denied that the first images were intended to convey the closet homosexuality of the protagonist: "I had naively meant a fag to be either slang for cigarette or, at worst, that the well-respected man had been at public school, where [he performed] the most humiliating tasks."[28] Authorial intent aside, the references to "backyard" and "fag" have homosexual implications and conjure images of exclusive English public schools where homosexuality was not uncommon for boys lonely and isolated from their families and young women. Davies joked in *20th Century Man* of Wace's and Collins's public school days: "One up the bum, no harm done." For the "well respected man" such proclivities need to be concealed just as much as his greed for his "father's loot," which he will grab when "pater passes."

In the final verse, Davies reveals his growing vocal confidence as he turns actor and mimics the posh accent of his character, especially with references to "stocks," "shares," and the "regatta," significantly not rugby or football. This marks a major step forward in Davies's development as a singer-performer. Never a vocalist with incredible range, Davies, from this point forward, more than compensates by finding appropriate phrasings, tonal shifts, and inflections, to deliver songs in convincing and emphatic ways. As Davies grew more comfortable with himself as singer-performer, he began to write more in the first person, assuming the identity of his protagonists.

By turning to his English roots, gaining confidence in his ability to write lyrics, and experimenting with vocal stylings, "A Well Respected Man" marks a major progression in Davies's artistic maturation.

"Dedicated Follower of Fashion"

Like "A Well Respected Man," Davies's next satire was also inspired by an actual incident. Just before Christmas 1965, Davies hosted a party in his new semi-detached. One of the guests, a fashion designer, raved about the latest trend: "I got pissed off with him. I said you don't have to be anything. You decide what you want to be, and you just walk down the street and if you're good, the world will change as you walk past. . . . I wanted it to be up to the individual to create his own fashion. Anyway, I had a fight with him, a terrible brawl. I kicked him, I kicked his girlfriend up the arse. It was awful, there was blood. I was grovelling in the gutter with him—it was sad."[29] The next day Davies vented his anger more productively, and he wrote "Dedicated Follower of Fashion."

More comfortable with the folk and satirical dimension of the Kinks sound after the EP and the American success of "A Well Respected Man," Pye recognized the hit potential of "Dedicated Follower of Fashion." The recording sessions were stressful, however. With Davies more assertive than ever, he sought a sound that was only vaguely defined in his imagination. He had difficulty especially with the intro. After multiple experiments and takes, the other Kinks staged a mutiny, refusing to play the song again. They had confidence in the song and found Ray's little tinkerings tedious. According to Pete Quaife, Davies took the master tapes, dropped them to the studio floor, and set them on fire, thereby forcing the band to replay the number. Eventually, Davies got his intro and, at least, a passable recording, though he would remain unsatisfied.

By April, the Kinks had a #2 hit on the UK charts, but in the US the record barely cracked the top-forty, peaking at #36. It is difficult to account for the lack of American success. The references to specific locations in London were probably not a determinant; Carnaby Street was internationally known, and, in 1966, two years after the Beatles appeared on *Ed Sullivan* and one year before the Summer of Love, American youths were still at least somewhat Anglomaniacal. The most likely explanation is that because they could not secure American work visas the Kinks could not promote the single. Of course, the song itself advances another possible explanation—put simply, the fickleness of pop culture.

As with "Well Respected Man," "Dedicated Follower of Fashion" has its roots in the music hall. But in "Dedicated Follower," Davies again shows development, in much the way "All Day and All of the Night" marked an improvement over "You Really Got Me." In "Dedicated Follower," the caricature is more developed, the satire and imagery is even funnier ("frilly nylon panties," "the Carnabetian army"), Davies's vocals more actorly, and the refrain of the chorus infectious: "With 'A Dedicated Follower of Fashion' such a hit, people started coming up to me in the street and singing the chorus in my face: 'Oh yes he is . . . oh yes he is.' "[30]

Much of the humor in "Dedicated Follower" results from the mock heroic imagery and tone. The record begins with heavily overdubbed electric guitar and bass pounding out chords that connect the song to earlier hits and sound almost like a bell summoning the Carnabetians. Then, to the accompaniment of what he called his "weedy" sounding acoustic guitar,[31] Ray introduces his foppish protagonist who is on a quest for "the latest fads and trends" and to "buy the best." Davies mocks the "fickle" protagonist-quester by comparing him to a flower and then a butterfly who "flits from shop to shop" and who wears polka dots one week and stripes the next. The "Carnabetian army" is, of course, on an elusive quest, which Davies underscores through the song's circular imagery, an effect which demonstrates further development for the songwriter. Consider the following:

- The song begins and ends with the pounding acoustic and bass guitar chords, suggesting the always ongoing quest to remain fashionable.
- The protagonist's clothes are "never square."
- The fop's world is "built," not *on*, but "*round* discotheques and parties."
- Sarcastically, the singer refers to the fop's "little *rounds round* the boutiques of London town."

In many ways for Davies, the protagonist of "Dedicated Follower" represents an archetypal figure of the 1960s, an era for which Davies is hardly nostalgic. Davies saw the breakdown of social barriers, the radical fashion shifts, the drug culture, the self-righteousness of the protest movements, all as at least somewhat artificial or, as he once referred to the 1960s, "a total lie" and "a con."[32] In a sense, the fop, like many of the participants, is trendy, shallow, and only superficially daring and "dedicated" to a cause which he pursues with all the fervor of a religious pilgrim.

A promo film for "Dedicated Follower" was shot by Davies's friend and art-school tutor Barry Fantoni, an established illustrator and jazz musician who was soon to play a pivotal role in the development of *Private Eye*, the satirical magazine. In the film, which may not have been used at the time, Fantoni mocks the young serious-minded shoppers who, in their quest for the hip, stalk Carnaby Street in crazed dress and carry unusual objects, the shoppers' frivolousness contrasting with glimpses of older, hardened Londoners, who limp along in drab clothes. The Kinks pop in and out of boutiques, and in one of the film's wittiest moments, Fantoni inserts a series of stills featuring the band and then models in hackneyed hands-on-hips poses, smug smiles, and defiant stares, intended to send up the absurdity and artificiality of the fashion world.

Interestingly, the promo reveals a camp undercurrent taking shape in the Kinks, one that had been forming as early as "See My Friends," but one that would not assert itself until 1970 with "Lola" and only find its fullest expression around the time of *Everybody's in Show-Biz* (1972) and continuing through *Soap Opera* (1975), at which point camp gradually declined as a Kinks inspiration. While an overarching term, camp is frequently associated with gay subculture and with excess, artifice, and silliness—all features of the music hall, where cross-dressing was common. Indeed, Old Mother Riley (mentioned in "Village Green Preservation Society") was created and played on stage and in film by a male, Arthur Lucan.

At first, Dave was most comfortable with camp as it was an outlet for his often outlandish behavior and dress, which at one time featured his wearing briefs over his trousers. "I loved the theatrics and flamboyance of that period, the style and fun. I grew really long sideburns [and] dressed to shock. Always looking for attention."[33] Dave's shifting guises, however, were not dictated by designers, but by his own impulses. Once from a women's hat shop, he purchased the "silliest item" available, a purple and pink stripped floppy hat, which he wore everywhere—on stage, on television, and in photo shoots, seizing every opportunity, as he said, "to camp it up in public." Ray could appear effeminate with his sometimes limp-wrist posturing on stage, his supposed homosexual references in "See My Friends," "Well Respected Man," and now "Dedicated Follower," and a certainly campy 1967 UK television performance of "Autumn Almanac." But in the mid-1960s Ray tended to be more reserved, brooding, and even depressed, while Dave was more free-spirited and adventurous, enjoying the pop star's life while Ray, married with children, was consumed by the legal entanglements and pressure to produce hits. Ray expressed at least some envy for Dave's lifestyle in "Two Sisters," with contrasting sisters serving as stand-ins for the brothers, and in "Dandy," an album track for the Kinks but a #5 hit in the US for Herman's Hermits, in which the singer at once chastises and celebrates a womanizer.

In addition to the film, the advertisement for "Dedicated Follower," which appeared on the front page of the March 4 *NME*, could also be considered camp. The illustration, conceived and executed by Ray, featured the Kinks in Carnaby Street attire appearing as *fin-de-siècle* decadents. Dave, drawn with large collar, kipper tie, striped jacket, slit eyes, and half frown, slumps in a fashionably jaded and dissipated posture—an appropriate portrait for one living the sex, drugs, and rock-and-roll lifestyle. Behind Dave, on his right, stands Mick Avory. Dressed in black and partially slumped, the drummer seems reserved and withdrawn, but his half-grin, closed eyes, and raised eyebrows suggest he is more worn than innocent. Pete stands erect in side profile in the portrait's center. With pointed nose, defiant glare, and hair well-coiffured, he seems arrogant, but the large **K** on his turtleneck, referencing the **K** Kampaign, gives him an air of the ridiculous.

Ray's self-portrait is haunting. He stares straight ahead through empty, almost squinted eyes, darkly encircled. His well-sculptured nose and tightly closed lips indicate firmness and moral rectitude, forming a visual warning. Tightly clad in a kind of floral print turtleneck, horribly designed, Davies appears to be suffocating as the shirt climbs to the very top of his neck. Not dissipated but exhausted with worry, he looks disheartened and imprisoned by the demands on his pop star's life. It is an eerie self-portrait, which seems wholly without irony.

Mental overload

As "Dedicated Follower" climbed the charts, Davies experienced a breakdown, "a mental overload," he called it, one which had been gaining momentum and rising to the surface since Cardiff.[34] By March 1966, it had been eighteen months since "You Really Got Me" broke and Davies stepped on the pop treadmill of composing, recording, performing, touring, interviewing, and battling internal and external band conflicts, and now lawsuits. He was stressed and exhausted, physically and mentally broken, and consigned to bed rest. "I was a zombie," he said. "I went to sleep and I woke up a week later with a moustache."[35] During his scheduled recuperation, which was to last from the beginning of the second week in March until the middle of the second week in April, Davies received visits from his family and from Barry Fantoni and Jimmy Marvel, a very supportive school friend. The family visits were not always comforting, however. Annie Davies was very concerned about her son and thought perhaps he would be better cared for in a sanatorium—Collins convinced her otherwise. Arguments often broke out, especially between Gwen and Rasa, with at least one quarrel leading to the sister's bloodying the wife's nose. Ray tried to remain calm by listening to Frank Sinatra records, reading a book on arranging by Glen Miller, and sneaking out to the sites of his boyhood adventures and athletic heroics. He reported "overwhelming fits of paranoia," all, he added with characteristic irony, "totally justified."[36]

Surprisingly, Kinks activities were not suspended during Ray's recuperation. The band kept a scheduled ten-day tour of Belgium and France with stand-in Mark Grace, a local friend in the Cockneys who at least looked similar to Ray and who knew all the material. While a press release announced the substitution, it is doubtful if many concertgoers heard of or realized the star's absence. Astute fans, however, would have recognized that the Kinks' leader had somehow transformed into a left-handed guitarist. Obviously, the tour was very uncomfortable for the remaining Kinks, who were compelled by management into playing the dates. There were, however, lighter moments. At a taping for a television show, a desperate Collins harassed the cameraman to avoid close-ups of Mark, who had been instructed to perform with head down, and at one concert as Dave knelt for a solo, a confused fan informed him that the lead singer was an imposter, causing Dave to burst into laughter as the fan left the theater. These lighter moments aside, the tour was a disaster and struck at the self-integrity of the Kinks. Dave reported that he only managed the tour by being "totally stoned the whole time."[37]

One morning, with the tour underway, Ray seethed as the tension escalated between him and publicist Brian Sommerville. Never enthusiastic about gimmicky publicity, Ray was outraged when in late February Sommerville scheduled the Kinks for a promotional appearance at, of all things, the opening of a new boutique. Davies felt exploited, misunderstood, and, worse, disrespected as an artist—hadn't Sommerville listened to "Dedicated Follower"? Then, with Davies recuperating, Sommerville suggested that the press have access to the singer's sick bed. Ray refused, and Sommerville chided his client for being selfish and unprofessional. In dramatic fashion, the former track star raced approximately six miles from his north London home to Sommerville's office in central London. Crashing through the door, Davies threw a wild punch which Sommerville dodged only to strike his chin on a chair. Davies dashed from the office, ducking in and out of doorways, with the police following in what Davies called "a Keystone-cops-style-chase."[38] Of all places, Ray ran to Edward Kassner's office, his former publisher and now adversary. Thankfully, someone called Robert Wace, who arrived on the scene with a doctor. Explaining to the police that Davies was suffering from "nervous exhaustion caused by a physical breakdown," the doctor escorted Davies home.[39] Sommerville's days with the Kinks ended, and the Kinks signed on with

Allan MacDougall's Project Publicity, with the Kinks account assigned to partner Frank Smyth, who would become a friend of Davies until Smyth's death in 1997 and the inspiration for the song "Storyteller" (1998).

Face to Face and "Sunny Afternoon"

Despite the breakdown, Ray was in the midst of one of his most productive periods. During a flurry of activity, especially in April, Davies wrote many new songs, including most of the material for *Face to Face*, which was recorded mostly that spring and scheduled for a summer release, but delayed until the fall because of discussions with Pye and Reprise. Generally, *Face to Face* is regarded as the Kinks' first significant album, although Davies demonstrated an interest in creating specifically for the long form with *The Kinks Kontroversy*, released in the UK in the fall 1965 and in the US in the spring 1966.[40] Perhaps inspired by Dylan's breakthrough album of 1965, *Bringing It All Back Home*, which began rock's shift from the single to the album, Davies sequenced a series of five love songs on *Kontroversy's* original side 1 in which the singer proclaims his love ("Ring the Bells") and then moves from desperate longing ("Gotta Get the First Plane Home"), anticipation ("When I See That Girl of Mine"), self-acceptance and invitation ("I Am Free" by Dave), to finally the ecstasy of love fulfilled in "Till the End of the Day."

But 1966 was dominated by satires—half of the fourteen tracks on *Face to Face* are satirical: "Dandy," "Session Man," "Rainy Day in June," "A House in the Country," "Holiday in Waikiki," "Most Exclusive Residence for Sale," and "Sunny Afternoon." As Mick Avory notes, "Sunny Afternoon," the album's featured hit, marks another "milestone" in Davies's songwriting, one which pointed the way to "Waterloo Sunset" and then *Village Green Preservation Society*.[41] If we think of "You Really Got Me," "All Day and All of the Night," and "Tired of Waiting for You," as Davies and the Kinks' first great triumvirate of hits, a second triumvirate can be formed from "A Well Respected Man," "Dedicated Follower of Fashion," and "Sunny Afternoon," all are folkish and satirical, and each, like the songs in the first group, is fully accomplished but demonstrates artistic growth.

"Sunny Afternoon" is Davies's ironic masterpiece. Like the other songs in the satirical triumvirate, "Sunny Afternoon" is heavily influenced by the music hall in its rhythms, melody, arrangement, humor, characterization, and working-class perspective, as well as the addition of Nicky Hopkins on piano with, as Davies said, its " 'good-time,' music-hall feel."[42] Unlike the others, however, "Sunny Afternoon" is performed in the first person, with Davies assuming the voice of a down-on-his-luck aristocrat. By giving voice to his protagonist, Davies gives full play to his irony, satire, and ambivalence.

"Sunny Afternoon" opens with a descending chord pattern and bass line establishing an ominous tone, one immediately undercut by the entrance of the vocals, which Davies delivers in a posh accent, sounding especially whiny and nasally from a bout with hay fever. The aristocrat complains of his dire circumstances: he is behind in his taxes; the government has seized much of his property, including his yacht; and his girlfriend has stolen his car to return to her parents with tales of debauchery and abuse. The profligate seeks the listeners' pity and assistance, pleading for them to "help me, help me sail away." He asks for reasons to remain, but all he has left are an ice-cold beer, his "stately home," and "this sunny afternoon."

Of course, the largely youthful and working-class audience laughs at the aristocrat, without scorning or despising him—67 percent of the English population considered themselves working class in 1966. In fact, in a double irony, listeners sympathize with him, if only to an extent, even though he lives in a lavish home while they must persevere with a housing shortage, even though only one-half of their homes had refrigerators, and even though they would have been fortunate to ever own a car let alone a yacht.[43] On the one hand, however, the audience and the aristocrat share common problems with governmental bureaucracy, taxes, and love, and both find refuge in a beer. More to the point, however, the poor bleeder's whining, cowardice, and helplessness make the audience feel superior and self-reliant, evoking their working-class pride and sense of survival. There seems to be no class solidarity to support the effete and once pampered aristocrat whose despair and self-pity are so exaggerated and so self-indulgent that a working-class listener could be moved to both laughter and pity. Davies's attitude toward his protagonist is the same as what he and the other Kinks felt toward the upper-society types for whom they played debutante balls and society functions in pre-recording days, and, at least in the beginning, toward Collins and Wace, which is to say, an odd mixture of curiosity, resentment, fondness, and mockery.

Davies began writing "Sunny Afternoon" to protest the Labour government's new tax code, which took direct aim at the wealthy, particularly nouveau riche rock stars. At just about the same time, George Harrison wrote and recorded "Taxman" (recorded mid-April 1966, released as the opening track on *Revolver*, August 5, 1966), his vituperative attack on both Labour and Conservative parties, singling out then Prime Minister Harold Wilson, Labour, and future prime minister Edward Heath, then Conservative leader, and protesting the 95 percent income tax imposed on those in the top bracket, where the four Beatles found themselves—"There's one for you nineteen for me," sings Harrison's tax collector. Although in "Sunny Afternoon," "big fat momma" embodies the government with the "squeeze" referring to the tax bite, Davies's attack is mild, if at all noticed, as protagonist and tale dominate the song. Davies admitted that he could not write a protest against the government with the Labour Party in power. Since his youth, he had been indoctrinated with the politics of Labour, which, he believed, championed the working class against the wicked forces of the elitist Conservative Party. To side against Labour would be to betray his class. Certainly, Davies was wealthy—at least on paper—and he had traveled the world as an international celebrity experiencing things beyond the realm of possibility for his former classmates at Grimshaw, but he could not abandon his roots to oppose Labour and thereby side with the upper classes. In a country where class identification is so important, Davies's class dilemma and ambivalence would haunt him to the point where he would begin to see himself as classless. "Sunny Afternoon" is born out of his struggle with class identification.

"Sunny Afternoon" was a huge summertime hit in England, remaining at #2 on the *Melody Maker* charts for just about all July, while on the *NME* charts it reached #1, knocking off the Beatles' "Paperback Writer," a source of euphoria to the competitive Davies. "To my great delight we knocked the Beatles off number 1. They'd been there for just a week— that's one of the joys of my life."[44] No doubt Davies recalled the day the Kinks had upstaged the Beatles in Bournemouth and the day the Beatles returned the favor at the *NME* Awards. To be clear, Davies has always been a fan as well as a competitor of the Beatles. In years to come he would introduce the Kinks' rendition of "Twist and Shout," usually during an encore, with, "Motown meets the Beatles. It doesn't get any better than that."

"Sunny Afternoon" was released at a fortuitous time. The summer was especially hot in England, and English and especially working-class pride were high as the football team would go on to win the World Cup. Both events helped the song. "I gambled on it being a very hot summer," Davies said, "and the longer the sun stayed out, the more records we would sell."[45] The sluggish voice of the aristocrat, the music-hall tempo, and the sing-along refrain of "in the summertime," gave the record an effective summertime feel.

"Sunny Afternoon" did not have the same impact on America. Released in the third week of July, it steadily climbed the charts to become a moderate hit, reaching, on October 1, #14, a position which a Kinks single would not surpass in America until four years later with "Lola." Most importantly, perhaps, "Sunny Afternoon" elevated Davies into the top tier of young songwriters. Curiously, in 2006, with England in the middle of a hot summer and making a run for the World Cup, Razorlight, a young London-based band with a lead singer from Muswell Hill, asked Davies to join them for a new recording of "Sunny Afternoon." As of this writing, the recording has not been released. It is probable that Davies was not satisfied with the recording.[46]

Figure 4.1 Ray in front of his Fortis Green home in 1967. Courtesy of Olga Ruocco

"Dead End Street"

Although the Kinks would release the extraordinary album, *Face to Face* on October 28 in the UK, Pye did not think any of the songs suitable as follow-up singles to "Sunny Afternoon." So, a week before the album's release, the Kinks found themselves in Pye Studios recording "Dead End Street," their fall single and another Kinks classic. Begun in the spring when Davies was emerging from his breakdown, "Dead End Street" was completed only prior to the recording session. Besides Ray's working-class identity, the song was inspired by a biography Davies had been reading and by the disaster in Aberfan, Wales. The Al Capone biography led Davies to contemplate the similarities between Depression America and post-World War II England, milieus that produced folk heroes like Capone and the Kray Brothers. On the day the Kinks recorded "Dead End Street," a waste depository from a coal mine in Aberfan collapsed and its contents slid down a mountain side destroying twenty houses, a farm, and a school, killing 144 persons, including 116 children between the ages of 7 and 10. "Dead End Street" responds to a culture of upper-class indifference and governmental insensitivity that allowed the storage of colliery waste above a working-class school and compounded the tragedy with an insensitive response in which the National Coal Board was ordered to compensate families only £500 per child, an amount reduced after money was raised for the families from a publicly subscribed disaster fund. Turning increasingly cynical, Davies infuses "Dead End Street" with working-class angst, pride, tenacity, and "knowingness."

"Dead End Street" and "Sunny Afternoon" form bookends. Both songs begin with threatening bass lines, employ first-person singers and two-verse, two-chorus structures, invite audience sing-alongs or in "Dead End Street," shout-alongs, and both draw very strongly from the music-hall tradition. "Sunny Afternoon," however, voices the dissent of a decadent aristocrat, frustrated by taxes which have ruined his "life of luxury," while "Dead End Street" expresses the indignity of a couple unemployed, who cannot afford the rent or a decent meal. Both songs, from opposite points on the class spectrum, address what could be called the false optimism in Britain of the 1960s. On the surface, England seemed prosperous: wages kept ahead of inflation, new car ownership continued to increase, new appliances were becoming common, and almost 50 percent of the population had private telephones[47]—on the opening track on *Face to Face*, Davies gives humorous treatment to the problems of shared phone lines on "Party Line," an obscure reference to most urban Americans by 1966. "Sunny Afternoon" and "Dead End Street," however, suggest that not all have shared in the general prosperity, and "Dead End Street," in particular, speaks for those so shut out as to be threatened with homelessness. The song resonated in 1966 Britain, reaching #6 on the charts, but it did not receive much attention in America where the nation was becoming consumed by the tensions over Vietnam and race.

"Dead End Street" with its metaphoric title and choral shouts is an anthem for the poor. A greedy landlord sends a rent collector who pounds on the door of an unemployed couple who suffer through "cold and frosty" mornings with little heat, a cracked ceiling, a leaky sink, and little food—instead of the traditional Sunday working-class meal of roast beef, they eat bread and honey. Yes, the imagery may be heavy handed and may sentimentalize the couple, but the angst and communal spirit in the defiant shouts of "dead end" and "yeah" along with the song's close drown out the sentimentality. In the final forty-five seconds, John Matthews, hired only minutes before the take, plays a bluesy trombone solo full of resignation, but not sorrowful so much as carefree, while in the background lead vocals fade, shouts of "yeah" turn to whispers, hands clap rhythmically, and Ray's piano sounds a lighthearted riff. The overall effect, which Jon Savage called a "reeling, carnival fade-out,"[48] recalls a splashy conclusion to a number from a music hall, West End or Broadway musical with choral shouts fading into a soft shoe. But the implication here is that the spirit of the working class will not be broken and that despite continued hardship and unfair governmental actions, the working class will endure and even enjoy.

Dave Davies, who has rarely failed to include the song in his solo performances, considers "Dead End Street" one of the most significant songs in the Kinks' canon:

> "Dead End Street" was the epitome, to me, of what the Kinks were all about. A song full of character, pathos, yet containing an underlying sense of hope. Reflecting a fondness for the past but at the same time expressing a determination and yearning for change. Anguished voices calling to a heartless world. A world where the plight of the ordinary person mattered little.[49]

The "fondness for the past" is signaled strongly in the echoes of the music hall at the song's conclusion.

The Kinks wanted to do something different to promote "Dead End Street." Tired of the hackneyed lip-sync performance on *Top of the Pops*, Davies drew on his interest in film and his college experiences with Paul O'Dell to develop a promotional film, which Davies expected to air on British television. The film, which picks up on the music-hall elements, opens to the song's ominous intro with the Kinks as pallbearers carrying a coffin through the city streets and into the home of an apparent widow, a role Ray doubles in with crooked wig and snarled toes. The camera then breaks to a bleak city street on a wintry afternoon and a succession of photographs expressing working-class poverty, misery, perseverance, and pride. The stillness of the slides is haunting, especially in its contrast with the motion of the storyline.

When the film returns to the widow, we see the pallbearers pressing shoes onto her feet. Again, the camera cuts away for a second series of slides similar to the first. Meanwhile, the widow must be careful to elude her vigilant landlord, a kind of silent-screen villain. A short, grotesque figure with a bushy mustache and oversized bowler, he picks his nose as he tries to eavesdrop on the events inside the home before deciding to wait the widow out with his assistant played by Dave. Throughout the promo, the exaggerated acting and melodramatic close-ups are stylized on the silent film—silent films would influence later Kinks videos as well, including "State of Confusion" and "Lost and Found." As the promo moves toward its conclusion, the pallbearers exit with the coffin while presumably the widow remains in the home. After continuing their journey for a time, the pallbearers pause for a cigarette break, during which the supposed corpse forces the lid off the coffin and escapes down the street. Although sympathetic to the widow and although working class themselves, the pallbearers have a corpse to deliver, so, resembling Keystone Kops, they give chase. The promo continues in fast motion as the smiling husband, dressed in pajamas and nightcap, races away, leaping and clicking his heals as the film fades.

The *Dead End Street* promo is a bold fusion of slapstick and social commentary. The song's music and lyrics keep both elements in balance, prohibiting one from dominating the other. The ending, which might seem either silly or overly optimistic, actually retains the balance. Yes, the husband and presumably his wife find escape from bill collectors and working-class drudgery and suffering, but it took daring, incredible resourcefulness, and savvy manipulation of the system and the cultural oppressors. Clearly, the triumph of the couple is unusual. Most working class will remain frozen in their social condition, metaphorically expressed through the stillness of the film's photographs. Unfortunately, after its screening, this remarkable three-and-one-half-minute film was banned by the BBC for being distasteful. With minimal controversy, the BBC could allude to the darkly humorous treatment of widows, pallbearers, coffins, and corpses. Perhaps, however, Davies surmised the true reason for the ban: "It showed slums and poverty and so they wouldn't run it. I guess they prefer films about running around in parks, jumping over chairs."[50]

Shel Talmy departs

"Dead End Street" was also significant in that it effectively ended the Kinks' Shel Talmy era, which had begun in January 1964. Talmy's work on "Dead End Street" struck the Kinks as complacent and disengaged. When Davies requested a re-recording of the song, Talmy refused, proclaiming the last take a hit as he exited the studio. The Kinks, however, did not follow Talmy and re-recorded the song with Davies as producer. Among changes, Davies dropped the organ with its "whirligig fairground effect"[51] and replaced the cheerful French horns with the trombone played by Matthews, who was immediately recruited while on break from a gig at a nearby pub. The next morning Davies played Talmy the new recording, but the producer failed to distinguish it from his own very different work. Nothing was said, and Pye released Davies's production crediting Talmy as producer. When Talmy's contract with the Kinks expired a few months later in the spring of 1967 and after repeating a similar scene with "Waterloo Sunset," Talmy and the Kinks parted amicably.

On balance, Talmy's work with the Kinks served both well. Robert Wace's assertion that the Kinks never respected Talmy seems highly improbable.[52] Despite the near disaster with "You Really Got Me" and despite his two "compositions" or "perks," as Talmy termed his writing contributions to *Kinks*, the producer was enthusiastic and respectful of the Kinks' music. Dave spoke of his work on the re-recording of "You Really Got Me": "He understood what we wanted now, and allowed the music to come through more naturally."[53] Certainly, Talmy must be credited for capturing the raunch and distorted guitar of the early Kinks sound and for supporting the band's early experiments, like "See My Friends"—

although he did not want to release "Ev'rybody's Gonna Be Happy." The Kinks and Talmy had a courteous and professional relationship, which is saying a lot considering, at this time, the band's frequently strained relationship with managers, publishers, promoters, publicists, and Pye. "I can't even remember any cross words being exchanged in the studio . . . essentially the guys were terrific, and low key," says Talmy.[54] The Kinks and Davies, in particular, simply outgrew Talmy. By the end of the producer's contract, Ray was anxious to branch out and experiment with the band's music.

Satirical technique

By the end of 1966, Davies had established the foundation of his satirical agenda, both in theme and in technique, at least in song. Throughout his career, he would write about the effects of class consciousness and the faulty vision of the Welfare State on English culture and life. The concerns of "Dead End Street" have been widened and deepened in *Arthur* (1969), *Muswell Hillbillies* (1971), *Preservation Acts 1* and *2* (1973, 1974), several songs on *Low Budget* (1979), and *Think Visual* (1986), as well as in his film *Return to Waterloo* (1984), his stage show (*20th Century Man / Storyteller*, first performed in 1995), his collection of short stories *Waterloo Sunset* (1997), and his solo album *Other People's Lives* (2006)—no Kinks album, Davies film, or book has been without some satire or social commentary since "Well Respected Man." But the fullest expression of Davies's irony and view of global corporate control is his "unauthorized autobiography" *X-Ray* (1994).

While his rhythms, melodies, specifics, and perspective render his song-satires unique, his best ones, whether acoustic, folkish or rock, tend to employ the following rather conventional techniques:

- *First-person point of view* from a defined, if not fully developed character, like the fallen aristocrats of "Sunny Afternoon" and "End of the Season"; the working-class patriot of "Victoria"; the punk teen of "Father Christmas," perhaps the only Marxist Christmas carol; or "Definite Maybe," an underrated track from *State of Confusion*, about a frustrated, rather ordinary citizen who has been classified as deceased by the state.
- *Humor.* Like most satirists, Davies is most effective when presenting humorous characters or caricatures and comic scenes. But he is frequently dark ("Skin and Bone," "Black Messiah," "A Little Bit of Abuse"), sexual ("When I Turn Off the Living Room Light," "Lola," "Ducks on the Wall"), and sarcastic ("Brainwashed," "Prince of the Punks," "Stand Up Comic"). His humor undercuts any sentimentality and bitterness.
- *Irony and incongruity.* In his lyrics and music, Davies uses irony to

demonstrate the world's fundamental incongruity, as in the closing section of "Dead End Street" or the cheerful, carousel-like melody of "The Moneygoround"; to illustrate the state's betrayal of the working class in "Victoria," *Muswell Hillbillies*, or "Shepherds of the Nation"; to emphasize the hypocrisy of self-importance and complacency in "Shangri-la" or the chorus of "Well Respected Man."

- *Specificity.* Davies is most effective when working with particulars, when referencing Waikiki ("Holiday in Waikiki"), "lavatories" ("Shangri-La"), "scrum" ("End of the Season"), or "L.B.W." ("Cricket"). Not only do the details add to the humor of the song, but they also ground the song in a specific time, place, and culture.

Like most satirists, Davies is far less effective when he is blunt, humorless, and non-specific. Songs like "Plastic Man," "Pressure," "Repetition," and "Aggravation" may present Davies's view on the stress, monotony, and loss of individuality in postmodern life, but they lack the richness, subtlety, and wit of songs like "Sunny Afternoon," "Victoria," and "Holiday in Waikiki." The weaker songs lack defined characters and voice and tend to whine in their directness. In "Aggravation," for instance, Davies sings, "Who needs it? The aggravation the daily goddamn hassle / It's a bummer, who gives a damn? / Bumper to bumper in the traffic jam."

Davies's satirical vision emanates from his love and intense pride in being English—and specifically English, not British. He is passionate about what he sees as England's cultural demise, which began, he claims in "New World," with World War II and continued under a steady stream of politicians, shortsighted and selfish, Conservative and Labour—which makes aligning Davies with a political party slippery. Consider his *Melody Maker* interview of April 1966:

> I hope England doesn't change. . . . I hope we don't get swallowed
> up by America and Europe. I'm really proud of being English. . . .
> I don't care if a bloke votes Labour or Conservative as long as he
> appreciates what we've got here. We have so much that is great,
> compared with other countries, and people just don't realize it.
> *I want to keep writing very English songs.*[55]

(italics mine)

Davies has remained true to his mission. He chronicles such things as the destruction of village greens and thatched cottages and the movement to a more sanitized suburban culture, where parking lots replace dance halls, where sterile apartment complexes replace "sleazy" but vibrant urban districts, and where corporations buy out local breweries and produce less flavorful and unique blends in favor of mass quantities. Such cultural shifts, Davies notes, benefit the corporate structures and upper classes while destroying freedoms and traditions that instilled, in everyone, a sense of Englishness but sustained, in particular, the working class. Davies's politics may be vague, even flexible, but always they revolve around concerns for individual freedoms and opportunities, which he sees as too often thwarted.

Despite his cynicism and perhaps paranoia about governments and global conglomerates, Davies, like most satirists, is ultimately hopeful. His best songs find inspiration in working-class individuals—their endurance, resourcefulness, rejuvenation, joyfulness, and sometimes, their capitulation. Ultimately, therefore, Davies's politics, satire, and irony are grounded in a sensibility more Romantic than political.

5

WATERLOO SUNSET
The Romantic imagination of Ray Davies

Ray and Rasa Davies saw in 1967 at the Davies's annual New Year's Eve party at the Queen Alexandra, a small pub located right next to the family's Denmark Terrace home. As Big Ben chimed and Londoners sang "Auld Lang Syne," the overcrowded Alexandra broke into "Sunny Afternoon." It was a proud moment for Davies, who would frequently premiere his songs to his father on the family's upright piano.

Davies and the Kinks had much to celebrate that New Year's Eve. At that moment, "Dead End Street" was riding the UK singles charts at #6; three weeks earlier *Face to Face* had reached #8 on the *Melody Maker* album charts; and that November *The Kinks Greatest Hits!* climbed to #9 on the US charts at the front end of an astonishing 64-week run—no other Kinks album would match that position and streak. If these feats were not enough, the football-crazed Davieses also celebrated England's victory in the World Cup, the final game of which the Kinks watched on London television causing them to arrive two hours late for a gig in Devon and giving them only ten minutes to perform before a midnight curfew and 6,000 booing fans.

In general, however, 1966 proved that Davies and the band could not only withstand but also triumph over adversity. Ray had overcome his emotional struggles in the spring, and the band was undeterred despite the cancellation of an American tour when the application for work permits was rejected and despite the draining legal battle between Boscobel (Kassner, Page) and Denmark (Wace, Collins), which would lead to the first trial in the late spring 1967, with Ray and Dave testifying. Furthermore, after a June 3 gig in northwest England, Peter Quaife and roadie Jonah Jones were seriously injured in a car crash, with Quaife's fracturing several bones in his left foot and sustaining a concussion and injuries to his head which required stitches, while Jones suffered even more serious injuries to his pelvis and head after being thrown through the windshield. Both required lengthy stays in a north of England hospital, during which time families, friends, and band members made the long journey from London for visits—all except Ray, which especially embittered Quaife. With Quaife sidelined for what was thought to be a few weeks and with management anxious for the band to tour and record, John Dalton was hired as the temporary bassist. In September, Quaife, while recuperating in Denmark under the care of girlfriend Annette Paustian and her family, upset Davies when he resigned from the Kinks. By mid-November, however, Quaife returned and Dalton went back to his day job as a coalman. But it would never be the same for Quaife and the Kinks again. As the bassist says, the return marked the "beginning of the end" for him and the band.[1] Still, after three tumultuous years of exhilaration, disappointment, and mayhem, the Kinks could celebrate New Year's 1967 as "rock and roll survivors," as Davies would sing a few years later on *Preservation Act 1*.

Without America

Failure to obtain the necessary work visas for America proved to be seren-dipitous for Davies and the Kinks. Without having to tour the massive US, the Kinks could slow down the rock-and-roll treadmill and compose, rehearse, and record at a more relaxed pace, while Ray was able to spend more time with his wife and daughter and both Quaife and Dave had time to marry and begin families. The music reflected the more relaxed Kinks. The hard-rocking Kinks of "You Really Got Me" and "All Day and All of the Night" may have been present on stage, but were absent from the studio. In a sense, Ray rejected America just as America had rejected him. His influences and inspirations for the next several years would be predominantly English and English folk traditions—until the New Orleans sounding *Muswell Hillbillies* in 1971. "If we had stayed in America," Davies says, "I wouldn't have had the nice roll of English songs."[2]

With "A Well Respected Man" in the fall of 1965, Davies began to focus on English culture and its outdated class structures, but by 1967, his songs turned more pensive, more reflective, and more personal—although he would construct a screen to conceal himself from the listener. The results in 1967 were three extraordinary singles ("Waterloo Sunset," "Death of a Clown," and "Autumn Almanac") and a masterful album, *Something Else*. Although released as a Dave Davies single, "Death of a Clown" is to all intents and purposes a Kinks record. Ray produced the single and is cred-ited as co-writer; Quaife and Avory play on the record and Rasa provides backup vocals; and the track appears on *Something Else*. In a melancholy mood, Dave wrote the song in the front room of the Davies Fortis Green home on the old upright at least in part as a response to his recent mar-riage. "I messed around with various tunes, pondering my marriage, my days as a raver," he wrote. "I felt my life was like a circus performer's. I was always expected to be the life and soul of the party, whether at clubs, pubs or whatever."[3] The single reached #3 in the UK.

In America, these records went largely unnoticed. Although *The Greatest Hits* still held the charts a year after its release, Reprise may have tried to regain momentum for the Kinks with the release of *The Live Kinks*, a hapless recording from an April concert in Scotland. Marred by poor sound and screaming fans, the album seemed anachronistic during the Summer of Love with the rise of the album and rock's consideration of more serious themes.[4] *The Live Kinks* might have been more timely in 1966 when the Stones released a very similar live set, *got Live if you want it!* So much had changed in a year. Interestingly, the Kinks had been approached to play the Monterey International Pop Festival that June, but without the necessary visas their appearance would have been impossible. The festival, which introduced America to Jimi Hendrix and the Who and the world to Janis Joplin, might have redirected the fate of the Kinks as well.

The Romantic Davies

If Davies the satirist emerged in 1966, Davies the Romantic emerged in 1967 when by retreating into English culture, he unconsciously tapped into the English Romantic tradition and found his strongest artistic impulse, one that would inform the bulk of Davies's work to the extent that Michael Kraus has argued that Davies's "work is best understood and appreciated as an extension of the English Romantic art tradition,"[5] and Ross Wetzsteon has said that Davies is "such a 'dedicated follower' of Wordsworth that he could be called the greatest rock star of the 19th century."[6] Davies has commented himself on his Romantic image: "They expect me to be this wandering poet walking around Hampstead Heath with a notebook and a scarf round my neck looking like William Blake."[7] Ironically, Davies is frequently seen in a blazer and scarf, and he certainly keeps notebooks and diaries. If Davies does not cultivate his Romantic image, he at the very least relishes it. In "London Song" from *Storyteller* (1998), he catalogs "great Londoners" beginning with William Blake.

English Romanticism blossomed in the late eighteenth century and early nineteenth century when poets like Blake, Wordsworth, Coleridge, Shelley, Keats, and Byron responded to the artistic conservatism of the Neoclassicists of the just previous age, authors like John Dryden, Alexander Pope, and Samuel Johnson. While Romanticism is a somewhat amorphous term, these early Romantics were preoccupied with themes and issues which have come to preoccupy Davies and other rock-and-rollers. Consider the following:

- a strong faith in the individual and in uncorrupted human goodness;
- a faith in intuition, instinct, and impulse as superior to reason, rationalism, and tradition and a corresponding trust in passion as a justified reaction;

- an insistence on individual liberty and individual expression, reflected in a preoccupation with common lives, common struggles, and ordinary language; an obsession with removing imposed boundaries, and sympathy for the neglected and disenfranchised;
- an obsession with the self, the inner life, and the need for personal rather than communal definition;
- a distrust and cynicism toward cultural institutions;
- a preference for nature over civilization, with nature as a source of human restoration and a reflection of the inner world of the self;
- an understanding of the significance of dreams;
- a willingness to experiment with new forms and media;
- an interest in the faraway, the gothic, orient, or even demonic, for instance.

Writing in 1959, David Perkins wrote that "we are still living in the comet's tale of the early nineteenth century." Perkins may have been discussing poetry, but he could have been talking about rock-and-roll. The contemporary poet, he wrote, had an almost desperate need to create a new technical means to express "certain urgent notions, impressions and way of feeling which had not previously been exploited in poetry." The poet, he argued, and the rock performer, I add, had to embody "the image of the discoverer, a man isolated in some difficult exploration or quest."[8] In poetry, there have been technical explorations from Wordsworth through Whitman and Ginsberg, mirrored in rock by, among other developments, the guitar explorations of Chuck Berry through Jimi Hendrix and Jimmy Page. Clearly, though, Perkins is referencing the Romantic preoccupation with transcending boundaries, which Perry Meisel sees as the key link between rock and Romanticism.[9]

"Waterloo Sunset"

In the spring 1967, Davies tapped into his burgeoning Romantic impulse for "Waterloo Sunset," his single greatest song as well as his highest achievement as a producer. Bob Geldof, leader of the Boomtown Rats and activist, said that "you have to take that [song] out of the context of simply being the Kinks and you have to put it into great songs that will always exist in the pop pantheon, and 'Waterloo Sunset' is top five, no question."[10] Davies, who has referred to the song as his *Hamlet*, conceived "Waterloo Sunset" as a commentary on the decline of the once dominant Merseybeat sound.[11] "I wanted to write a song about a Liverpool sunset," explains Davies, "because of the death of Merseybeat. . . . Then I thought, I'm a Londoner, why all the tributes to Liverpool?"[12] The song was not complete when Ray, as he would frequently at this time, previewed an early version of the song to the recently married Dave in his new home in

85

Cockfosters, about a ten-minute drive from their childhood home in Fortis Green. Encouraged by the friendship of Rasa and Dave's wife Lisbet, the brothers were fairly close then—closer than they had been before or would be since. After hearing the draft of "Waterloo Sunset," Dave knew immediately that they had something special. With Ray on piano and Dave on guitar, the pair began improvising vocal harmonies around the chorus. It was one of those magical moments, which Ray would later define as spiritual in *20th Century Man*, when the brothers set aside all their differences and petty squabbles and connected through music. Both were exhilarated. "In fact," writes Dave of the rough piece, "if it had been recorded then and there with just a piano and acoustic guitar it would have been perfect."[13] Ray raced home and wrote the bridge: "Every day I look at the world from my window."

The Kinks entered the studio in mid-March to lay down the backing tracks with Shel Talmy as producer and Nicky Hopkins, a favorite of Talmy and the band, on piano. But the session did not feel right to Davies, who was especially anxious about his most personal song to date, although neither Talmy nor anyone else had heard the completed lyrics, which Davies was still shaping at the time of the session. At this time, the relationship between Talmy and the Kinks was cordial but strained. Since at least *Face to Face*, Davies was anxious to produce the Kinks himself, but he had to wait for Talmy's contract to expire, which it would sometime in the first half of 1967 when producer and band parted amicably. In many ways, *Something Else* was a transition album, partially produced by Talmy and Davies, although it is now impossible to say who is responsible for what. The UK release cited no production credit, but the US release credited Shel Talmy Productions. Certainly, by the September recording of "Autumn Almanac," Ray was in control of the Kinks sessions, where he would remain.

Davies had ideas on how to produce "Waterloo Sunset" in particular and the Kinks more generally, but he was reluctant to share the ideas with Talmy, fearful the producer would use them in his work with competitors like the Who, Small Faces, Easybeats, and Manfred Mann, among others. Davies decided to do with "Waterloo Sunset" what he had done with "Dead End Street," i.e., record the song surreptitiously. He told Talmy that he wanted to experiment with an album cut. In early April, Davies entered Pye Studios to re-record the backing track with Quaife on bass, Avory on drums, and himself on acoustic guitar, omitting the piano almost entirely except for his own brief striking of a chord at the very end. About a week later Dave added his electric guitar with its clipped intro, brief solo similarly clipped and playing off the melody, and some intermittent power chords. The lyrics were still not finished: "I went home and polished up the lyrics until they became like a pebble which had been rounded off by the sea until it was perfectly smooth."[14] After another week or so, Ray brought in Dave, Quaife, and Rasa for the magnificent and complex backing vocals, which are more integral to the song than "backing" suggests, remaining almost continuous from the second line forward. The recording process went almost effortlessly with everyone happily complying with Ray's overall vision while contributing ideas of their own. Quaife recalls the session: "The entire studio was fidgeting with a case of giggly jitters as each track was finished. Everyone was concentrating fully on the recording as it progressed. It got to the stage where nobody could do anything wrong—no matter what was suggested it went on the recording."[15] Quaife goes on to say that he suggested the *ooh, la, la*'s above the verses.

Finally, Ray had only to add his lead vocals. But he was nervous and self-conscious about the intensely personal lyrics, which he had yet to share with anyone. "I thought the others would burst out laughing when they heard me sing. It was like an extract from a diary nobody was allowed to read."[16] With the Kinks and Rasa watching, he stepped to the microphone and nailed his vocals on the first take. And no one laughed. Clearly, they recognized that they were part of something special. "When we had finished," Quaife reports, "we went home and, strangely, didn't say a word to anyone! We *knew* that we had a hit on our hands and we were content with that" (italics his).[17]

All that was left was the mix, especially crucial to a record but especially here because of the complex vocal arrangements. Again, it went smoothly. Realizing how important this recording was to Davies, engineer Alan MacKenzie invited Davies to operate the faders on the console board. The recording process, which Doug Hinman estimates took a total of ten hours, was completed.[18] "There's no memory of that song that isn't a pleasure," said Davies.[19] "The perfect recording of the perfect record," says Quaife.[20]

Increasingly, the studio began to serve Davies as a means of escape from mounting pressures, a place he could step into and control. At the time of "Waterloo Sunset," Davies was trying to reconcile three very different self-identities: the pop star, the litigant in a major court case, and the suburban husband and father. As a star, he could be self-indulgent and egotistical, but stressed by the continuous demands for product; as a litigant, he was preparing for a very stressful and complicated legal battle; and as a husband and father, he found pleasure and relaxation, but sometimes felt the demands kept him from his work. In one role or another, Davies felt trapped, a feeling revealed in several songs from the era. In "Two Sisters," from *Something Else*, Davies contrasts the lives of sisters Priscilla, a frustrated suburban housewife, and Sybilla, a swinging London single—stand-ins for Ray and the pre-married Dave. Told largely from Priscilla's perspective, "Two Sisters" contrasts the "drudgery of being wed" with single life in a "luxury flat," but concludes that Priscilla is "better off than the wayward lass that her sister had been." However, "Mister

Pleasant," written shortly after "Two Sisters," ridicules the comforts, complacency, and dishonesty of suburban life. On "Session Man," Davies criticizes session musicians who themselves become "a chord progression . . . not paid to think just play" with "no favors done." It is quite possible to interpret the song as self-critical, with Davies's expressing his self-disdain with acquiescing to the demands of labels, producers, publicists, and other components of the rock-and-roll machinery.

At the time of "Waterloo Sunset," Davies felt himself "the lost soul who was desperately insecure and looking for friendship which would not turn into some kind of betrayal and end up hurting me."[21] The singer is a fragile, perhaps lonely personality who has overcome despair through a Romantic concept: he turns to nature. He places himself in a privileged position, overlooking, literally and figuratively, the bustling London scene beneath him, with "a dirty old river," bright taxi lights, and "people so busy . . . swarming like flies round Waterloo Underground." The singer detaches himself from the frenzy behind a window, fending off Byronic brooding (which Davies was prone to) as signaled by the opening and recurring descending bass line, and finds contentment—the kind of contentment that Davies longed for at the time. As long as the singer can "gaze at Waterloo sunset" he is "in paradise."

Here as elsewhere for Davies, the sun is a central image of healing. In "Lazy Old Sun" from *Something Else*, he calls the sun his "one reality" and pleads with the sun to "shine [his] way" and "kiss [him] with one ray of light," while in "Lavender Hill" he needs the sun "to saturate [him] with love." In "Drift Away" from *Phobia*, the singer internalizes the sunshine and escapes "tension everywhere" and "the smell of fear" by drifting away to his "island in the sun, imaginary paradise, perfection." For Davies, the sun offers security, contentment ("Sitting in the Midday Sun," for example) and hope ("After the Fall"), while its absence reflects disharmony and tension ("Rainy Day in June," "There's a Change in the Weather," "Stormy Sky"). The sun and storm imagery may be conventional, but Davies gives it freshness through context and melody. Olga Ruocco, who explores Davies's use of weather imagery, notes, in what might be an odd coincidence, that his very name suggests a beam of sunlight and that he was born on June 21, the zenith of the sun's path.[22] Nowhere, however, is the image of the sun more stunning than in "Waterloo Sunset."

To create "Waterloo Sunset" Davies withdrew into a Wordsworthian moment of serenity to rely on what the early Romantic called a "spontaneous overflow of powerful feelings [that] takes its origin from emotion recollected in tranquillity."[23] Specifically, Davies recalled a childhood hospitalization in the Waterloo area:

I was in a hospital, at St. Thomas, for an operation when I was a kid. I nearly died. I had a tracheotomy and the balloon burst.

I was attached to a machine and I had a nightmare and pulled all the things out of my arms. Then two or three or four days later I couldn't speak because of the operation. Two nurses wheeled me out on to the balcony, where I could see the River Thames. It was just a very poetic moment for me.[24]

In many ways, the child is father both to the man and to the song.[25] The singer, like Davies the child, is comfortable in his solitude, finding peace within and emphasizing that he needs "no friends"—even as he watches young lovers Terry and Julie escape London into a world of a couple where they can "feel safe and sound."[26] In "Waterloo Sunset," the singer regains childhood peace and what has been called the "lost domain," or the Romantic longing for a place "real or imagined, known for a brief time and then lost," a kind "of prelapsarian world of innocence and love before the fall into the more confused world of adulthood, fame, or lost love."[27] For perhaps only the duration of the sunset or the song, the singer reclaims Eden.

"Waterloo Sunset" achieves a Romantic transcendence through the lyrics with their delicate and melodic delivery, through the musical tension between the descending bass line and Dave's occasional power chords against Ray's acoustic guitar and Dave's lead lines, and through the backing vocals, which soar, cross, and play off each other to create a texture that becomes celestial, hymnal, and even celebratory, reflective of a mind able to rise above "the din of towns and cities" and find "sensations sweet" and "tranquil restoration."[28] In tonal effect, "Waterloo Sunset" captures the same fleeting serenity that Wordsworth's speakers find in "Lines Composed above Westminster Bridge," "It is a Beauteous Evening," and "Composed by the side of Grasmere Lake."

"Waterloo Sunset" is an elevated and exalted pop song, a sublime accomplishment. Released in the UK on May 5, 1967, the single held #2 on the *Melody Maker* charts for three consecutive weeks, unable to unseat "All You Need Is Love," the Beatles' Summer-of-Love keynote. Released in the US on July 26, "Waterloo Sunset" had absolutely no chart impact, flopping at a lowly #141 in *Cash Box*—the failure resulting most likely from the Kinks' exclusion from the US, the lack of record label support, and the declining interest among American youths in Englishness. During the Summer of Love, young Americans were more interested in images of San Francisco and Flower Power than London, its undergrounds, and Waterloo sunsets. In 1997, "Waterloo Sunset" reappeared on the UK charts when Cathy Dennis's recording reached #11. However, for all the song's magnificence, it has been recorded by only about two dozen mostly minor artists, excepting David Bowie.[29] It is probable that the song has been victimized by Davies's remarkable production, which many might believe unsurpassable.

Figure 5.1 Ray in the early 1970s

"Autumn Almanac"

The Kinks' next single took Davies's quest for the lost domain in a slightly different direction. Again, he draws inspiration from his childhood and, again, from a time when his health was threatened. After a track and then football injury, Davies was informed by a doctor that he could end up

90

disabled. Obviously troubled, the young Davies would take some hope from a hunchbacked neighborhood gardener who accepted his disfigurement and seemed to be living a fulfilled life. As an adult being pulled by conflicting identities, he thought of Charlie and found, as he did in the Waterloo sunset, some comfort:

> [Charlie] tended the garden with loving care, and as the seasons changed he swept up the dead leaves and prepared the garden for the next life cycle. Watching him always made me feel optimistic about the future; that there was always a better day coming. As a child he had symbolized everything that I feared. Now I was a man, he could not only be my friend, but share in my accomplishments. . . . I looked at Charlie as he endured his predicament and felt at one with him.[30]

Charlie functions in much the same way for Davies as many of Wordsworth's poetic characters function for Wordsworth, which is to say, they remind the poet of the necessity of a simple existence without the controls and hypocrisies of institutions. In "The Solitary Reaper," for instance, the reaper works in the field and sings in a "voice so thrilling" that it inspires a poem and brings comfort to the weary traveler, while in "Cumberland Beggar," the beggar, who lives "in the eye of Nature" (l. 197) and is the bane of statesmen, serves to remind villagers of "past deeds and offices of charity else unremembered" (ll. 90–1), "keeps alive the kindly mood in hearts," and "compels [them] to acts of love" (ll. 91–2, 99–100). On *Muswell Hillbillies*, Davies celebrates his Uncle Son who lived a simple, ordinary life, who demonstrated kindness and tenderness to the young and depressed Davies. For *20th Century Man*, Davies returned to Charlie again for "X-Ray," a song about the importance of seeing beyond the superficial.

Charlie, like the singer in "Waterloo Sunset," is content to remain on the fringe of post-World War II English consumerist culture, finding contentment in the garden, in the seasonal cycles, in his working solitude, and in traditional working-class culture. As with most Romantic heroes, the further removed from a culture's institutions, the more fulfilled the individual. In "Autumn Almanac's" richly sensual opening lines, the singer immerses himself in the early morning crispness and with senses fully awakened, he sees, smells, hears, and feels "the dew-soaked hedge," the caterpillar, the cracking dawn, the breeze, the yellow leaves, and the sweep of his rake. Davies's use of alliteration (". . . creeps a crawly caterpillar," "the breeze blows leaves," and "autumn almanac") interlocks the natural images and indicates the singer's connectedness to them. Andy Partridge points out the "woodiness" of the song: "Everything sounds like sticks and branches." The founder member and chief songwriter of XTC continues, "I wish I had written that song. I'll probably spend my life trying to. It's such a huge ghost; my entire songwriting career has been trying to exorcise it."[31]

The singer embraces the life-affirming images and events of the season, even its difficult cold weather periods when he hides indoors with friends, tea, and currant buns, and looks forward to his "football on a Saturday" and "roast beef on Sunday," typical working-class fall rituals, and a holiday in the working-class resort town of Blackpool on England's northwest coast and very different from Ray and Rasa's post-American tour holiday in the plush Imperial Hotel in Torquay on England's southern coast. In the short story "Afternoon Tea" in *Waterloo Sunset*, one character finds that it was not so much the smell of the tea or the taste of the cake but "the familiarity of the ritual that calmed him . . . the chance to stop in an ever-changing world and consider the moment"—which is what the gardener experiences.[32]

Without being superficial or slight, the singer in "Autumn Almanac" is Davies's quintessential yea-sayer. He is guided by nature or his almanac, which makes tolerable his deformity and "poor rheumatic back," a detail and self-referent indicative of Davies's desire for similar deep contentment.[33] But Davies's restlessness could never bring him the contentment of his singer, who proclaims that he will always "stay here if I live to be ninety-nine." Then, in a curious line, he sings that "I can't get away because it's calling me," followed by backing vocals of "come on home, come on home." But the singer has gone nowhere and demonstrates no need to search, whereas the composer has. Davies's unconscious may have usurped his creation at this point, as for all his travels and residences in New York and Ireland, for example, Davies has throughout his life maintained a home in north London, minutes from his childhood home, where he still frequents neighboring pubs. Yet, in life, it is doubtful that Davies can maintain the singer's prolonged chant of *yes*, as he does at the end of the song, first triumphantly and surrounded by a merry chorus of *la-las*, *ba-bas*, and *ohs*, and, finally, at the conclusion, three times, in a note of quiet contentment.

The singer, like the singer of "Waterloo Sunset" and other Davies characters, is capable of existing in what Keats called "negative capability"— that is, dwelling with "uncertainties . . . without any irritable reaching after fact & reason."[34] In actuality, living in negative capability has largely eluded the restless Davies. As one anonymous former intimate of Davies told me, "Under all the brilliance is torture. . . . If the demons that own Ray Davies settled down, there would not be the clever lyrics."[35] For Camille Paglia, the Romantic archetypes of "energy, passion, rebellion, and demonism" thrive in the music and lifestyles of rock musicians.[36] Interestingly, Davies began *20th Century Man* with an ironic but somewhat sinister gleam in his eye: "Tonight I read from the Black Book . . . the tormented ravings of a sex-crazed rock 'n' roller."

Yet the negative capability of the singer in "Autumn Almanac" leads us to consider his song as a kind of suburban pastoral or a proletarian pastoral. Although associated more with the Elizabethans and Neoclassics, pastorals were written by Blake and then Wordsworth who used the form, as Harold Toliver states, "in his praise of simplicity and distrust of urban life" and to "reconceive the tension between society and nature," which is what Davies does in "Autumn Almanac."[37] By necessity, the protagonist of a pastoral is simple, wise, and visionary, like Davies's singer, for the pastoral "assumes that natural men are purer and less vicious than cultivated men" and hold "a special sympathy" with nature.[38] The pastoral and "Autumn Almanac," as well as "Waterloo Sunset," turn from the distractions and corruptions of urban culture to find a more meaningful and contented existence through nature. Thus, in its implicit condemnation of urban culture, the pastoral, for Davies, voices the concerns of the working class and points out an escape from the dead-end street, which, as Davies's catalog suggests, is not so easily accomplished.

Drawing from English folk traditions for its melody and the music hall for its *oom pah* rhythm, "Autumn Almanac" is hardly straight ahead rock-and-roll, and yet with Ray's distorted acoustic chords, Dave's punctuating electric guitar, and the falsetto harmonies of Dave, Pete, and Rasa, it is all Kinks. One BBC commentator told Davies that for years to come, "Autumn Almanac" would be a standard for brass bands[39]—it hasn't happened yet. Released appropriately in mid-October 1967, "Autumn Almanac" exited the UK charts just as appropriately at the onset of winter after peaking at #5. Released in late November in the US, the record failed to chart, perhaps perceived as out of time with rock's psychedelic movement, its protest songs, and the country's widening generation gap. A cheerful song about a contented, middle-aged English gardener who liked football and roast beef dinners, performed by a band many thought of as finished, might not have played well on American radio. As Bernard Gendron notes, "The rock 'n' roll record cannot function for them as an alien object."[40] Yet despite its US chart failing, American Kinks fans have long considered it a favorite.

Dreams

While the singers of "Waterloo Sunset" and "Autumn Almanac" find contentment on the fringe of society and comfort within themselves and their solitude, most of Davies's singers seek a desperate escape through the imagination or dreams—some sixty of his songs mention dreams. On "David Watts," the opening track of *Something Else*, the "dull and simple" singer dreams of being the best athlete and the smartest, most popular student. In "Oklahoma U.S.A.," the protagonist escapes her dreary existence to be "far away" and in the arms of Errol Flynn, and in "Predictable,"

93

the singer sits at work, contemplates his monotonous life, and dreams of "far away places." "Some people like to live with dreams," says Davies. "I know that I do, it's the only way one can sort of get by."[41] Some singers escape to an imagined past that may or may not have existed. The singer of "Victoria," for instance, longs for the croquet lawns, village greens, and morality of the nineteenth century, while the singer of "Yours Truly, Confused N10" laments the deterioration of his north London neighborhood and evokes Shakespearean England as he longs for "that green and pleasant land . . . that throne of kings, that sceptred isle set in a silver sea."[42]

Davies's dreamers frequently want to escape themselves as much as their surroundings, often yearning for self-annihilation. The singer of "Dreams" from the soundtrack of *Percy* asks not be awakened from his daze as he fantasizes about being "far away" and living inside his dreams, while the singer of "Fancy," which after "See My Friends" represents Davies's second foray into the exotic sounds of India, creates an impenetrable world in his imagination. On several songs, the desire for self-annihilation recalls the opium dreams of Coleridge and Thomas de Quincey. In companion pieces "Lavender Hill" and "Misty Water," Davies creates mystical landscapes, one dark and one light. After recording "Lavender Hill" in August 1967 and "Misty Water" in May 1968, the composer-producer decided against releasing the tracks, yet both found their way onto the US-only release *The Great Lost Kinks Album*, a late January 1973 compilation released by Reprise without the Kinks' knowledge, which included a failed UK single ("Plastic Man"), B-sides, and unused tracks—the release of which Davies was only made aware of upon receipt of a copy sent to him by a concerned American fan. Although the Kinks were then signed to RCA and had released *Everybody's in Show-Biz* the previous August, Reprise believed that having rejected the *Percy* soundtrack that it could release a post-contract collection. To write the liner notes, Reprise contracted John Mendelssohn, once a Kinks supporter, but at this point embittered, some say, at Davies for not producing his band Christopher Milk. Mendelssohn's liner notes were scathing, attacking Davies as "bitchily egocentric," his once brilliant songwriting as "greatly dimmed," and condemns the Kinks' RCA release. Davies was enraged when he first saw the sloppily manufactured album, which did not feature writing credits on several songs and which was sent to him only by an American fan. After litigation, the album was pulled from circulation around 1975 and never reissued. Despite Davies's reaction, *The Great Lost Kinks Album* is a favorite among Kinks fans, for although it is an uneven record, it contains some rare gems, some of which, like "Rosemary Rose," "Misty Water," and "Lavender Hill," would never be officially released in the US again. "Lavender Hill" and "Where Did the Spring Go?" have never been granted an official Kinks release anywhere after *The Great Lost Kinks Album*, which only held the charts for five weeks and peaked at #145.

In both "Misty Water" and "Lavender Hill," the singers seek escape into a mystical Eden, a nature of paradisal forgetfulness, not far removed from classical mythology's lotus-eaters or Coleridge's opium dreams. In both songs, Davies negates restoration and privileges dreams and even death, any world apart from actuality. In "Lavender Hill," the speaker longs for paradise, a land of the imagination, one he can enter and not leave. "I want to walk eternity into a land of make believe," the song begins. The imagery, pure fairy-tale and lost domain, is the singer's attempt to find self-oblivion through either song or imagination. He desires that "the clouds roll over me," "the sun shine down on me," and the "sun saturate me with love," as he enters the soft pastel-colored hill where he will "live on sugar and milk" as birds "sing sweet melodies" and "daffodils . . . sway in the breeze." But these saccharine images are undercut by the held chords of the Mellotron of either Ray or Nicky Hopkins, which bind the singer to the earth despite the breeze "whispering Lavender Hill for me."

In "Misty Water," the almost unbearably sweet images of "Lavender Hill" shift to dark shadows and hidden recesses. The singer's escape quest leads him to an unnamed location near the town of Straight and Narrow, ironic how the "dark and misty place" should be so near a town whose name suggests virtue and respectability, almost a reference back to "Well Respected Man." All the residents except Anne Maria and her daughters are afraid of the nearby haze and mist, which encourage an allegorical reading about the fear of self-adventure and the preference for social codes. To a fast rock-and-roll rhythm, the singer exclaims with almost childhood excitement that "I like misty water / I like fog and haze," lines which conclude the song in a rollicking incantation and serve the speaker like alcohol, the mythological lotus, or de Quincey's opium to obliterate straight-and-narrow reality.

"I Go to Sleep"

But more powerful than either of these is "I Go to Sleep," which Davies wrote as Rasa was in a Muswell Hill hospital giving birth to their first daughter while Ray waited nervously in his parents' front room, tinkering on the piano. What emerged in "I Go to Sleep" is one of Davies's strongest statements about longing, love, dreams, and annihilation as the responsibilities of fatherhood and an impending American tour weighed on the then not yet 21-year-old. The next day Davies recorded a demo of the song, which went officially unreleased until a CD reissue of *Kinda Kinks* in 1998. Soon after the demo session, however, Peggy Lee released "I Go to Sleep" as a single and Cher recorded it on her debut solo album in 1965. Later, in 1981, Chrissie Hynde and the Pretenders scored a top-ten UK hit with the song.

Yet the definitive recording remains the Kinks' demo, which features only the composer accompanying himself on piano. A slow, hauntingly raw recording, the demo is meditative, even brooding as the tormented speaker longs for a reunion with his lover in the oblivion of dreams and sleep. The melancholy of the singer vibrates through the minor key of the piano chords and the melody which strains for a lilt, never fully achieved, as the singer looks up from his pillow, imagines her presence, and then seeks a more powerful representation of her in the world of sleep: "I go to sleep, sleep, and imagine that you're there with me"—a line consuming six of the fourteen lines. The line's wistfulness is punctuated by two delicate and ominous high notes after the first *sleep* and then one note after the second.

In "I Go to Sleep," the singer tries to create a private world, a lost domain which seals his lover and him from the external world. His effort is reflected in the structure of the lyrics. Eight of the fourteen lines begin with *I* and, for a ninth, *I* follows only *when*. The enclosure is complete when thirteen of the lines end with *me* with the only other line ending with *die*. It is a sparse world of the couple without the Edenic images of "Lavender Hill" or the anesthetizing images of "Misty Water," yet the negation of the external world suggests self or, here, couple annihilation with *sleep* substituting for perhaps an unconscious desire for death. To the Romantic consciousness, death has long been a great seductress. In "Ode to a Nightingale," Keats writes, "I have been half in love with easeful death," and in "Why Did I Laugh Tonight? No Voice Will Tell," the poet acknowledges the intensity of verse, fame, and beauty, but says that "death [is] intenser—Death is Life's high meed." The underlying sadness in "I Go to Sleep," as well as in "Lavender Hill," "Misty Water," and later in "Celluloid Heroes," results from this attraction to death and the surrendering of self.

Tropical paradises

Davies also treats this theme of escape humorously. In "Apeman" and "In a Foreign Land," his singer-characters want to flee faceless bureaucracies, Gauguin style. "Apeman," a Kinks classic, sung by Ray in calypso—a style he first used with great ironic effect on "I'm on an Island"—was released in late 1970 and went on to become a top-ten hit in the UK, Australia, Canada, and several European countries, but only scored #45 on *Billboard*'s US single charts. "Apeman" is Davies at his ironic best. The problem for the singer is not that the contemporary world has *dehumanized* him, but rather that it has *humanized* him. He wants to run away from honking horns, inflation, and the threat of nuclear war to distant shores where he and his Jane can take off their clothes, live in the jungle, and "sit in a tree and eat bananas all day." The singer's wish is ultimately unfulfilled, emphasized by the track's position on *Lola versus Powerman and the Moneygoround*, where it is sandwiched between "Rats" and "Powerman," songs about oppressive forces.

On "In a Foreign Land" from *Misfits*, however, the singer completes his escape to a tropical island. Fed up with bills and taxes, this once well-respected man grabs as much of his money as he can, bids a sardonic farewell to the "champagne and caviar set" and the "rich man's daughters," and dashes to a land of bananas and sand, where his new career goal is to "slum and drink all the rum [he] can get," proclaiming triumphantly that he has "finally made the grade." A jubilant rocker rarely performed by the Kinks, "In a Foreign Land" features, as *Misfits* does throughout, some of Ray's finest actorly vocals, and, on this track only, bass guitar by John Dalton who effectively anchors the song while following Ray's vocal inflections and tonal shifts. The song was recorded in July 1976 during the early sessions for *Sleepwalker*, but it was wisely judged not a sonic or thematic fit for their Arista debut.

What connects most of Davies's characters is a Romantic sensibility that starts with the composer himself. A piece of Davies seems to be in most of his characters. At their core is a strong impulse to resist conforming, to resist yielding individual authority to forces that seek to commodify the individual. Davies's characters are often eccentric, brooding, angst-ridden, disillusioned, restless, and self-absorbed. Through various means they try to escape from themselves, whether through nature ("Autumn Almanac," "Waterloo Sunset"), or other means, usually temporary and ultimately unfulfilling: daydreams ("Some Mother's Son," "Predictable"), films ("Celluloid Heroes," "Video Shop"), creativity ("The Contenders," "Working in the Factory"), sleep often unsettled ("Too Much on My Mind," "Sleepless Night," "Still Searching"), movement ("Misfits," "In a Foreign Land," "Run Away"), or a desire for self-annihilation ("I Go to Sleep," "Lavender Hill"). Some rail against the culture ("20th Century Man") and some wage one-man wars ("Here Come the People in Grey," the suburban vigilante in "Over the Edge"). Most tend to be solitary figures who, as Davies sings in "Still Searching," are "wandering nomad[s]" still searching for their dreams.

The rebel Lola

Davies's most successful and conscious rebel is Lola, the subject of the smash international hit and, with the exception of "You Really Got Me," the band's most important single, or as Doug Hinman says, a "career-saving" record,[43] which brought the Kinks renewed stature in England, regained relevance in the States, and a lucrative contract with RCA.

Davies has provided several stories about the inspiration for "Lola." One has Robert Wace, after a long night of dancing, leaving the club supposedly with a woman when, in the light of daybreak, Davies noticed the stubble on the "woman's" face. According to Davies, Wace was too drunk to care.[44] On another occasion, Ray altered the story but kept the same ending. On a date one evening with Andy Warhol discovery Candy Darling, Davies detected the increasing stubble on the drag queen's face.[45] Later, he denied the date with Candy and simply said they were out to dinner and he knew "it was a drag act."[46] Still, yet again, Davies said "Lola" chronicles his own experience dancing with a transvestite in the Castelle Club in Paris.[47] During his *20th Century Man / Storyteller* tour, Davies usually introduced "Lola" very simply: "Here's a song about a real transvestite."

While the single seems to tell a story about a young innocent's escape from the clutches of a determined transvestite, "Lola" nevertheless makes a politically charged statement signaled both by the context of the album on which it appears and in the context of Davies's past and future work. On *Lola versus Powerman and the Moneygoround, Part One* (there is no part two), Lola, implicitly, fights off forces of exploitation and corruption by resisting conformity and creating an alternative reality in London, the epicenter of Powerman's power. Unlike the protagonist in "Apeman," who can only dream of escape, Lola thrives with a self-indulgent authority among the soulless power brokers of "Powerman," "Rats," "Money-goround," "Top of the Pops," and "Denmark Street." "It's a mixed up, muddled up, shook up world except for Lola," who remains vibrant, self-assured, and independent, unlike the confused, tentative singer. Lola embodies the album's final statement, towards which the Contender strives: "Got to be free to do what I want."

The setting for "Lola" registers a protest. Set in a tacky Soho club, which Davies establishes with just two details (champagne that tastes like "Coca-Cola" or "cherry cola" and "electric candlelight"—pure kitsch!), "Lola" is about passion, moral and sexual confusion, and lush sleaze. In "Lola"—setting, music, and character—a strong life impulse throbs, one that those in power try to repress, in part, by sterilizing settings. In "Come Dancing" the local dance hall is transformed into a bowling alley and in "Welcome to Sleazy Town," inspired by Cleveland's downtown "revitalization," the "Corporation" destroys a once "bouncy . . . hot . . . alive" scene for "motorways and shopping malls." For Davies, music is in danger of becoming as sterile and economically driven as the landscape— consider "Denmark Street" and the title track from *Think Visual*. Davies counters this with the music and vocals of "Lola," which shifts from a seeming folk ballad to a hard-driving, rock anthem sung in an intention-ally strained voice even though Davies realized recreating such a vocal in performance night after night would be stressful.

In "Lola," Davies taps into the energy of a rich history in England and Europe of cross-dressing both for subversive purposes and for fun. Natalie Zemon Davis documents several transvestite riots, particularly between the mid-fifteenth and mid-nineteenth centuries.[48] On one occasion, in the middle of the eighteenth century, men disguised as women destroyed tollbooths and turnpike gates at the Gloucestershire border to the sound of shouts and drumming, and in 1812 General Ludd's Wives, two weavers dressed as women, led hundreds in the destruction of steam looms and the burning of a factory in Stockport. Certainly, the purpose of dressing as women was not sexual, but besides providing effective and accessible disguises, it had the effect of liberating rioters from conventional behaviors. Lola is, of course, liberated, but "she" also begins, at the very least, to subvert or liberate the sexual identity of the song's narrator.

Throughout modern Europe, male cross-dressing was sanctioned during carnivals, masquerades, and plays, and was considered a device to release pent-up licentiousness and to clarify the cultural structure even while reversing its codes. But such sanctioned gender-bending also suggested alternative behaviors—in much the same way, again, as Lola's cross-dressing works on the singer and as Davies's onstage feminizing, particularly during the early 1970s, challenges notions of male sexuality and identity among the Kinks' audience. Curiously, in *Don Juan*, Lord Byron raises issues of sexual ambiguity and confusion through his own Lolah, who had "an accent rather rough" not unlike Davies's Lola with her "dark brown voice," and who desires to share a bed with Don Juana, actually Don Juan in cross-dress (Canto the Sixth, XLIV). The success of "Lola" and the emergence of England's glitter or glam rock movement in 1971, which began to peak the following year with the emergence of Gary Glitter and David Bowie's *Ziggy Stardust*, led the Kinks into a glitter rock excursion.

Through "Lola," Davies expresses the Romantic credo for self-expression, individualism, and anti-authoritarianism. Davies and his singer admire Lola's certitude, independence, and energy, although both stop short of Coleridge's proclamation in *Table-Talk* that "a great mind must be androgynous." Gender-bending is liberating for both Lola and the singer, much as it is for husband and wife in the less accomplished "Out of the Wardrobe" in which after some dozen years of marriage first husband and then, after initial panic, wife begin to cross-dress and end up with the "best of both worlds" and "in a state of elation."

"I'm Not Like Everybody Else"

In "I'm Not Like Everybody Else," however, Davies makes his most direct expression of individualism. A classic to Kinks fans, but little known outside Kinkdom, "I'm Not Like Everybody Else" was initially released as the B-side to "Sunny Afternoon," resurrected for *The Great Lost Kinks Album*, included on various compilations through the years, and re-recorded live in its now definitive version for *To the Bone*. One of only a handful of songs that both Ray and Dave feature in their solo live sets, it served as Ray's opener throughout most of 2006 and was featured in the Kinks' last performance to date, June 15, 1996 as headliners at the Norwegian Wood Music Festival in Oslo. When he conceived the chest-thumping anthem probably in late 1965, Davies was trying to establish himself as a songwriter apart from the Kinks. He tried to interest Eric Burdon and the Animals, who, in 1965, had three top-ten UK hits with "Don't Let Me Be Misunderstood," "We Gotta Get Out of This Place," and "It's My Life"—none written by the band. It seemed like a good fit, but the Animals rejected the offer.

In its initial version recorded in January 1966, "I'm Not Like Everybody Else" is an angry young man's rant, not unlike one by Jimmy Porter or Arthur Seaton in *Look Back in Anger* and *Saturday Night and Sunday Morning*. At the time of the session, Ray was twenty-one and Dave, who took lead vocals, not yet nineteen. "I won't take all of the hand-me downs," sneers Dave as the song opens, nor will "I take it all lying down," he continues. His abrasive guitar lines, complementing the sneer, play off Quaife's thumping bass line, which erupts at times in a flurry of notes. Angst-ridden and defiant, the song threatens more than proclaims that the singer is not like everybody else. The result, however, is a one-dimensional pro-test from an "angry young man," that grows somewhat tedious by its conclusion at 3:29, lacking the tension of the 1996 version which takes on new meaning and depth.

Ray's introduction to the song on *To the Bone* is revealing: "This was a song that was a B-side, but I like this song very much. . . . It kind of sums up everything that we're about, the Kinks. Because everybody's expecting us to do wonderful things and we mess it all up usually." "I'm Not Like Everybody Else" retains its resistant posture, but now incorporates tested awareness, vulnerability, and humor. Ray, on lead vocals, is more reflective than angry, but still defiant, stubbornly individualistic, and ultimately triumphant. The song begins in a slower time and builds to its closing crescendo almost six never tedious minutes later with an audience chanting along to the chorus. Not only are the vocals more revealing and subtle, but so also is Dave's guitar, which in several breaks reveals a wider emotional range, at times melodic and tender, and at other times piercing, harried, and soaring. The song builds to an emotionally triumphant conclusion and perhaps for singer and chanting audience a cathartic release.

Davies, however, recognized the paradox of the song: "It's the typical line to come from somebody who is like everybody else. It's the most ordinary sort of predictable person 'cause they all think that. Don't they?"[49] This is one of the central dilemmas in rock culture, where dif-ferentness and counterculture values are articulated in a music and fashion often imitated and recycled to appeal to the largest possible audience. While giving full voice to this dilemma, the live "I'm Not Like Everybody

100

Else" also addresses the struggle of self-identity and self-assurance through the following binary oppositions:

- the singer's defiant statement of individuality and his pledge to his lover to "do anything that you want me to;"
- sneering vocals and vulnerable vocals;
- individual voice of the singer and mob chanting of the audience;
- slow rhythmic opening and hard-rocking conclusion;
- melodic guitar solo and piercing guitar solo;
- Bob Henrit's pounding drums, Dave's rumbling, distorted guitar chords and Ray's sometimes tender vocals.

These oppositions create the suspense and tension that the original recording lacks, and thus recreate a deeper emotional experience, one driven by perseverance and commitment. From the early 1960s through the middle 1990s, Davies's artistic and personal restlessness has led the Kinks through shifting styles of music and presentation, which have often angered bandmates, managers, record labels, and alienated fans. "The Kinks are like no other band," says Dave. "We've managed to draw from so many different influences and sometimes it's worked and sometimes it hasn't. . . . I think that's probably why we never really reached the great success of the Stones or the Who. Because I think a lot of times record companies really didn't know what to do with the Kinks."[50] In a very real way the song reflects the tension within the Kinks, specifically the battling brothers, and Davies himself, but it is the battling and the need for expression that has produced the great music.

Above all, it is a Romantic preoccupation with self and self-expression that has driven Davies, a sensibility that has led him to experiment with different forms and inspirations from the raga rock of "See My Friends," a 1965 UK hit, to *20th Century Man*, his one-man stage show over thirty years later. However, in 1968, Davies's Romantic impulse would find full expression in *The Kinks Are the Village Green Preservation Society*, for many, perhaps including Davies, the Kinks' masterpiece.

6

THE VILLAGE GREEN
PRESERVATION SOCIETY
Time, place, and identity

Despite in many ways a positive artistic and commercial 1967 with a first-rate album in *Something Else*, three brilliant top-five UK singles ("Waterloo Sunset," "Autumn Almanac" and Dave's "Death of a Clown"), and the recording of other tracks that would find their way on to *The Kinks Are the Village Green Preservation Society* (hereafter *Village Green*), the Kinks were largely absent from the counterculture conversation—although they had received very positive coverage in both the March and December issues of *Crawdaddy!*, a hip American underground publication. Allen Klein, the Kinks' US business manager since July 1966, planned a brief American tour in late 1967, which fell through when even with Klein's clout the Kinks could not secure recommendations for work visas from the American Federation of Musicians. Apparently, a shady promoter in Texas took advantage of the Kinks' absence and used American impostors for a few dates.

The rise of the album

Rock music experienced a major transition in 1967 and 1968. With the counterculture movement galvanized by antiwar protests in the United States and anti-American protests in England and throughout Europe, rock musicians found themselves in positions of cultural authority, which most embraced and found inspiring, if not inflating. Like never before, rock musicians became spokespersons for the generation and felt impelled to make grand statements politically, culturally, and aesthetically. The album soon became the medium of expression for rock musicians, who were anxious to be done with the pressures and restrictions of manufacturing the all-important hit single. "You put yourself on the line every three months or so," said Keith Richards, "and therefore it had to be distinctive or else."[1] By 1968, when albums outsold singles for the first time in the United States, young people considered rock music a transformative force that could, if not save the world, at least save individuals. In 1970, on "Rock and Roll" from the Velvet Underground's *Loaded*, the generally dark and skeptical Lou Reed could sing with authority that Jenny's life was "saved by rock and roll."

The rise of the album, concurrent with the escalating political power of the young, began in 1965 with not coincidentally Bob Dylan, the uncomfortable voice of his generation. In March, Dylan released *Bringing It All Back Home*, which immediately raised the expectations for the album and signaled the very competitive dynamic beginning to operate in the rock music world. Dylan, with his one side electric and one side acoustic album, announced that he was reclaiming rock-and-roll, bringing it back home from England and firing it with more rawness and lyrical majesty—a point not lost on John Lennon and Ray Davies, especially. In August, Dylan struck again with the international sensation "Like a Rolling Stone," a six-minute single and the opening track on *Highway 61 Revisited*.

Perhaps like no time before or since, in the mid- to late 1960s rock musicians listened to each other, anxious to respond and outdo the other. In December 1965, the Beatles responded to Dylan with their first album masterpiece, *Rubber Soul*. Brian Wilson listened: "*Rubber Soul* is a complete statement, damn it, and I want to make a complete statement, too!"[2] Wilson labored for months—much to the consternation of fellow band members, record label executives, and accountants—and emerged on May 16, 1966, with *Pet Sounds*, which sent shock waves around the rock world, if not in sales at least to musicians. But Dylan, as if to counter, released *Blonde on Blonde* on the very same day, and, in August, the Beatles released *Revolver*, which they had contemplated titling *Freewheelin' Beatles*, mimicking the title of Dylan's second album. Wilson returned to the studio to work on the more ambitious *Smile*, "a teenage symphony to God"[3] and, ultimately, the most influential album *never* to be released—i.e., until Wilson returned to the studio to complete and re-record the album in 2004. "Oh, it was incredible," said Davies. "The Beatles were waiting for the next Kinks album, while the Who were waiting for the next Beatles record. It was a very exciting time. There was even more anticipation among the artists than the fans."[4]

The atmosphere for the serious rock musician was highly charged, competitive but largely appreciative if not always friendly. In the spring 1966 Dylan, while on tour in England, caught up with Keith Richards. "I could have written 'Satisfaction,'" Dylan told the Stones guitarist, "but [you and Jagger] couldn't have written 'Tambourine Man.'" In a *Rolling Stone* interview Jagger agreed, but retorted that Dylan could not have *sung* "Satisfaction."[5] The two went on to become friends with Jagger's sitting in on some early sessions for Dylan's *Blood on the Tracks* (1975), and, in the mid-1990s, the Stones performed "Like a Rolling Stone," released on *Stripped* (1995), with Dylan seemingly responding with performances of "Brown Sugar" in 2002, perhaps proving that he might have been able to sing a convincing "Satisfaction." As Davies said looking back on the rivalry of the era, "Townshend was very competitive. . . . Paul McCartney was one of the most competitive people I've ever met. Lennon wasn't. He just thought everyone else was shit."[6]

After the release of *Revolver*, Ray Davies was invited by *Disc and Music Echo* to be a guest reviewer. While Davies spoke favorably of several tracks, including "I'm Only Sleeping" ("a most beautiful song"), "Good Day Sunshine" ("This'll be a giant"), and "Here There Everywhere" ("It's nice—like one instrument with the voice and the guitar merging"), he could be scathing, citing "Eleanor Rigby" as a song "out to please music teachers in primary school." His competitive edge surfaces in several comments. After calling "Yellow Submarine" "a load of rubbish," Davies says, "I take the mickey out of myself on the piano and play stuff like this," and, referring to the Indian sound on Harrison's "Love You To" (*sic*), "This sort of song I was doing two years ago," referencing "See My Friends," and, as if to soften the jab, "now I'm doing what the Beatles were doing two years ago."[7]

Such competitiveness along with the cultural authority granted the rock musician by the audience and the proliferation of free-form FM radio in the US prodded the rock artist to be more assertive creatively. But the transition to the album begun by Dylan in March 1965 with *Bringing It All Back Home* was completed with the June 1967 release of the Beatles' *Sgt. Pepper's Lonely Hearts Club Band*. The music was innovative and bold, carefully crafted and produced, modern and melodic, and its presentation and packaging were elaborately conceived and executed as if to declare the importance of the disc inside. The cover was designed by Peter Blake, a fine artist, not the usual graphic artist or illustrator, and the gatefold, used for the first time, included song lyrics, another first, and, highly unusual, no single supported the album. *Sgt. Pepper's* influence has been immense. In *Rolling Stone*'s December 2003 list of the top "500 Greatest Albums of All Time," the top five albums were released between 1965 and 1967: *Sgt. Pepper's* #1, *Pet Sounds* #2, *Revolver* #3, *Highway 61 Revisited* #4, *Rubber Soul* #5, and, at #9, *Blonde on Blonde*.

Despite the ongoing war in Vietnam, the Summer of Love was a decidedly optimistic time for youth culture. There was the sense that "Flower Power," a term coined by Beat poet Allen Ginsberg two years earlier, would prevail. At the Monterey International Pop Festival, June 16–18, organizers John Phillips of the Mamas and Papas and Lou Adler, manager and record producer, vowed that the festival would "shower the country with waves of ecstasy and purification" through "music, love and flowers."[8] Then a week after Monterey, some 400 million viewers from some two dozen countries tuned in to *Our World*, the first live international satellite broadcast, to watch the Beatles, dressed in flower-power regalia, premiere their new single, "All You Need Is Love." Surrounded

TIME, PLACE, AND IDENTITY

and accompanied by friends and pop rivals Mick Jagger, Keith Richards, Graham Nash, Keith Moon, Marianne Faithful, and many others—but no Kinks. The Beatles gave voice to the Summer of Love's collectivist spirit, its innocence and optimism, its confidence and moral authority, and all the exhilaration that comes with feeling a part of a positive historical turning point.

1968

But all changed in 1968. The year got off to a shocking start when at the end of January the North Vietnamese launched the Tet Offensive, a massive assault on the American military. The brutality of the fighting, broadcasted on television, stunned the world. The war was clearly escalating, not winding down as many had hoped. While opposition to the war may have grown substantially after the Tet Offensive, Summer of Love optimism and flower-power innocence were crushed in its wake, now appearing empty and frivolous. Throughout Europe, the war aroused anti-American feelings especially in young people, who took to the streets to protest America's moral bankruptcy. On March 17, some 80,000 protesters tried to storm the American Embassy in London's Grosvenor Square, leading to hundreds of arrests and some ninety police injuries. Mick Jagger was present and wrote "Street Fighting Man" in response.

A month later, racial tensions escalated in England when Enoch Powell, Conservative Party Member of Parliament, delivered a speech in his home town of Birmingham expressing fear at the staggering growth of the non-white population in England. Through its immigration policies, he saw England as "a nation busily engaged in heaping up its own funeral pyre. . . . I seem to see the 'River Tiber foaming with much blood.' "[9] The supporters of Powell were primed for his message. Anxious about the radical assault they had witnessed on all kinds of social and political issues launched by the young, women, and minorities and frightened that the race riots of America would soon come to Britain, they rallied in support of Powell while others rallied in opposition, and Asians and West Indians walked in fear. Many, besides Powell, believed they were living through the collapse of western culture and its once sustaining traditions and comforting morality.

At this time, the politics of serious rock music were by necessity countercultural—for both sales and credibility. Rock musicians were expected to support specific rallies and appear at festivals and hip venues like Bill Graham's Fillmore, east and west. Negotiating a precarious balance of being both friend and god, musicians were simultaneously leaders and rank-and-file members of a community, which, perhaps above all, valued individualism and liberty. Grace Slick of the Jefferson Airplane explains the dichotomy: "I felt like a princess in a benign court—one without thrones or crowns," and quickly adds, "The audience was just more of 'us.' The performers were just more of 'us.' "[10] The status and artistry accorded the rock star led to lyrical sophistication and musical experimentation, which often led to transcendent results, as in the Velvet Underground and Cream, but just as frequently to bombast and banal jams, as also in the Velvet Underground and Cream.

At the Eleventh Hour

The Kinks seemed hopelessly outdated, especially with the release of *The Live Kinks* in August 1967 in the US and *Live at Kelvin Hall*, same album different title, in January 1968 in the UK. *Something Else*, released in the US in January 1968, restored some credibility to the band, but it received only minimal although important underground press, charting at only #153. Also in January, branching out from the Kinks and looking to establish himself further as a songwriter, Davies worked on songs for the BBC's *At the Eleventh Hour*, a variety show with satire and music for which Davies accepted a commission to write a song a week for ten weeks, beginning with the December 30 show. Davies wrote satires on current news items, many culled from his local paper the *Hornsey Journal*. He followed a rigid schedule, with his song submitted by Thursday, recorded on Friday, and aired on Saturday. The short-lived satirical series ran for only ten weeks, but its distinctive English humor and satire deepened Davies's retreat into his own English composing sensibility, indirectly furthering what would be *Village Green*. Song titles are somewhat revealing: "You Can't Give More Than You Have" (known also as "He Spent More Than He Had"), "If Christmas Day Could Last Forever," "We're Backing Britain," "Poor Old Intellectual Sadie," "Could Be You're Getting Old," "Just a Poor Country Girl," "The Man Who Conned Dinner from the Ritz," "Did You See His Name?" and "This Is What the World Is All About." All were sung by Jeannie Lamb who was backed by an orchestra and the Mitchell Singers; unfortunately none of the performances have been preserved and none of any demos Davies may have recorded have been released.

The one song familiar to Kinks fans, "Did You See His Name?," sharpens the desire for the others. Rerecorded by the Kinks in May but unreleased until *Kink Kronikles* in 1972, "Did You See His Name?" is one of many barely noticed gems in the Kinks catalog. The straight-ahead rocker tells of a man who "stole a tin of beans" and then had his name and picture published in the local paper, which led to his humiliation, loss of job, and suicide. The sentimental story works because of the neutral tone of the storyteller who asks rather simply "did you see his name?," the rocking rhythm which neutralizes the sentimentality and emphasizes the satire on the often unnecessary public humiliations and unsympathetic ways of journalism, gossip, and judicial systems.

Ray enjoyed the recognition and the challenge of the assignment and accepted a similar commission in late 1968. Beginning in January 1969, he wrote one satirical love song a week for six weeks for *Where Was Spring*, a BBC series produced by Ned Sherrin, who became a friend of Davies and perhaps the "prominent queen" in "Top of the Pops" on *Lola versus the Powerman*. The six songs, recorded by the Kinks, complemented the show's script. Two of the songs, "Where Did the Spring Go?" and "When I Turn Off the Living Room Light," found their way on to the infamous *Great Lost Kinks Album*.

"Wonderboy"

In March 1968, the Kinks entered the studio to record their spring single. A commercial disaster, "Wonderboy" went nowhere, reaching only #28 on the *NME* charts and failing to chart in *Melody Maker* or the US. The song provoked strong reactions. It has been cited as the favorite Kinks record of John Lennon, who demanded that one of his favorite King's Road restaurants play the song over and over while he lunched. It is conceivable that Lennon had "Wonderboy" in mind when he wrote "Beautiful Boy (Darling Boy)." On the other hand, Pete Quaife loathed the record. " 'Wonderboy' was horrible," he says. "It sounded like Herman's Hermits wanking. Jesus, it was bad. I hated it. I remember recording it and doing the la-la-las and just thinking, 'What kind of bloody prissy sissy nonsense are we doing? We're the guys that made "You Really Got Me," for Chrissakes!' "[11]

"Wonderboy" was released when Rasa was barely pregnant with their second daughter: "Maybe I wanted a boy," said Ray. His further comments are insightful: "What the song is about is looking at a child for the first time and wondering what's going to happen in its life. . . . On paper, as it's written, it's one of my favourite songs."[12] The weakness of the record lies more with Davies the producer rather than Davies the composer. The lyrics hesitate in their joy and optimism, more pensive and cautionary than the melody and production suggest. In the liner notes to *Kink Kronikles*, John Mendelsohn called the record "one of the most irresistible of the Kinks' popcorn singles"—and the melody is indeed gleeful and infectious—and the *Record Mirror*, referring to the lyrics as "charmingly sophisticated," coined a new phrase to define the record, one that thankfully didn't stick, "philosophy pop."[13] However, the lyrics, directed at the newborn, are darkly Romantic, privileging the dream world over actuality. In the opening lines, the singer directs the infant to "turn your sorrow into wonder" and to "dream alone, don't sigh, don't groan, life is only what you wonder," with, later, *wonder* transforming to *conjure*. The song concludes with the thrice repeated "life is lonely," with the delivery fading as the singer apparently drifts into a dream world prodded as Quaife's bass roars and vibrates. The production of the song is pure bubblegum with any intended irony, which could have worked, insufficiently signaled and thus lost. The problem is not with the lead vocal delivery or the melody, but with the effete and campy *la-las* and *ahs* that run throughout the song above the lead vocals, and the snappy, sparkling acoustic guitar fills, which sound like a harpsichord, underneath the melody. The gleefulness of the arrangement overwhelms the uncertainty and sophistication of the lyrics. Quaife's bass tries unsuccessfully to ground the song with its slow pulsating beat, but can only hint at some of the doubt in the lyrics.

With the release of *Live at Kelvin Hall* in January and now "Wonderboy," the Kinks' UK status was sinking fast. The band itself seemed unfocused. Quaife's dissension was escalating, Ray was working outside the band, Pye was toying with the idea of Dave's solo career, and the troublesome lawsuit between Denmark and Boscobel was coming up on appeal. To promote "Wonderboy," the Kinks accepted a slot on an unimpressive package tour of England, perhaps the only option open to them. Along with the Herd, which featured a young Peter Frampton and a #5 hit at the time with "I Don't Want Our Lovin' to Die," and the Tremeloes with their January top-ten "Suddenly You Love Me," the Kinks labored through the three-week April tour. It was 1964 all over again, except this time the Kinks were not the exciting young upstarts. Dave termed the Herd the " 'new faces' of '68" with the Kinks as "the 'old faces' of '66."[14]

It was an uncomfortable, at times humiliating tour for the Kinks. "Everyone was panicking," Ray said, "because 'Wonderboy' wasn't sounding like a hit record. Among the management and the agent, Danny [Betesch], there was definitely a sense that the band wouldn't go on for much longer. I remember Danny came backstage when the record flopped and said, 'Well, you've had a good run. You've enjoyed it.' As if it was all over for us."[15] Under rehearsed and with little enthusiasm, the Kinks delivered mostly hits in two perfunctory performances a night to sometimes small crowds. "It was a chore, very dull, boring and straightforward," says Quaife.[16]

With death coming quickly to "Wonderboy," Pye wanted to capitalize on the tour, and, with about ten dates left, released two EPs: *Dave Davies Hits*, featuring last year's "Death of a Clown," and *The Kinks*, featuring four tracks from *Something Else*. Both sold very poorly. *Dave Davies Hits* represented the ongoing but halfhearted attempt to develop Dave as a solo artist should the Kinks dissolve, which now seemed imminent. Pye's efforts on Dave's behalf had begun the previous July with the release of "Death of a Clown." After the single became a smash, a press release announced that a Dave Davies solo LP, which never materialized, would be released in September. Later, tentative plans for a

February and March 1968 solo European tour were arranged and then canceled, although the previous fall Dave had lip-synched "Death of a Clown" on European television and in August on England's *Top of the Pops*, where with acute irony he was introduced as "Ray Davies" by host Alan Freeman. After Dave's subsequent singles, "Susannah's Still Alive" (November 1967) and "Lincoln County" (August 1968), failed to chart, his solo career was put on hold.

Uncomfortable Kink

By early 1968, Peter Quaife was no longer a comfortable Kink. Ever since his return from his injury in the fall 1966, Quaife felt increasingly marginalized. The management team and Pye, he believed, were pandering to Ray at the expense of the group. "I don't really blame Ray, I blame the managers for putting thoughts into his head, telling him he could do this and he could do that, without giving any regard to other members of the group."[17] It was especially painful to Quaife, a co-founder of the group and a schoolmate of Ray's. In the studio, he began to feel more and more like a session player, and in business decisions, he found himself out of the loop. At one point, Quaife said that no one would respond to his questions about the group's finances and that the accountants were prohibited from talking to him.

In late January, Quaife arrived at a one-off gig at the Lanchester College of Technology, Coventry. The always mischievous bassist dropped a hint in the press that his broken wrist resulted from a scuffle with a bandmate when, in fact, the injury happened in a household accident. The injury did not bother Quaife much, but it did "bother Ray mightily," says the bassist. Yet because of the increasing tension within the band, Ray had to repress his anger at Pete. "I must admit," says Quaife, "it gave me great pleasure to see Ray's anguished expression and listen to his vacant cries of false empathy!"[18]

Quaife's contentment as a Kink did not improve with the April tour. In May, the Kinks began recording during the week and playing gigs on weekends. It is during one of these sessions, May 27 perhaps, that the legendary story of Quaife's "Daze" rebellion occurs, a story that Ray featured in *20th Century Man* and *Storyteller*. Davies worked hard to perfect the sound for "Days," a very personal song and the Kinks' important follow-up to "Wonderboy." Quaife, however, was less than attentive. "In those days . . . we put on the bass/drums and all the rest of it and then we were 'required' to stay there until the entire recording was finished, which could sometimes take three days; [my] input was about five minutes!" Quaife resented having to "sit in the studio like good little boys and wait until everything had been put on, mixed down, and finished, which meant after a while it became colossally boring."[19] At one point, Ray reports that

Figure 6.1 Ray Davies in the mid-1970s

Quaife handed him the box that would hold the master tape, and substituted the word *Daze* for *Days*.

Davies did not recognize Quaife's frustration or his humor, admitting
that "my work had become too precious to me."[20] Quaife changes one

110

detail in the story, but the spirit is essentially the same: "what I was doing was doodling. I was drawing this little man . . . and Ray saw it and got really upset! That I was doodling instead [of] listening to the damn music. He started making a big fuss about it and the usual cods, and I went 'Fuck it, Ray, I'm out of here,' and I just walked out, Rasa came running after me."[21] Pete adds that the figure he was drawing was himself. The tension did not disappear by that weekend. "But the first time I ever really fell out with Pete was when he wrote 'Daze' on the tape box of 'Days.' "[22] On Saturday morning, the Kinks boarded a plane for Dublin for an evening gig. Yet upon landing, one Kink was missing: Quaife. Unnoticed, he had snuck off after boarding. Grenville Collins phoned Rasa, who tracked Pete down and got him on a later flight, too late, however, for the gig in Wicklow, which had to be canceled. "He left us in the lurch," a still bitter Collins says years later.[23] By this time, if it wasn't clear already, Quaife's days as a Kink were drawing to a close.

Depressing tours

The following week the Kinks embarked on a two-week tour of Sweden to generate some needed income. Expecting to play rock festivals, the Kinks discovered only upon arrival that they had been booked into outdoor public parks—another low point. "Those Swedish 'folk parks' were so depressing," recalls Dave, "parents strolling around with kids licking ice-lollies alongside genuine fans and party revellers. . . . It was a horrible, soulless experience."[24] Again, the Kinks played a string of hits and nothing recorded after the year-old "Waterloo Sunset."

That fall, even as the Kinks were finishing their greatest album, they had another similar experience when for quick cash they played some north England cabaret dates, performing twenty- to thirty-minute sets of hits in front of dinner crowds. "The cabaret audiences dressed up in evening clothes," recalls Ray, "and gambled in an upstairs room, using cash instead of chips. Then they ate potato chips [french fries] and scampi when they went downstairs to watch the cabaret. . . . we played too loud for both the audience and the management. On one notable occasion Dave played the opening of 'All Day and All of the Night' so loudly that the scampi and chips on a nearby table were blown off by the reverberations from the amplifier."[25] Dave survived the disastrous tour in much the same way he endured the Ray-less, imposter tour of France and Belgium. This time, though, he turned to alcohol. "Some nights I'd finish a whole bottle of Scotch before going on stage. The shows were only twenty minutes, and I thought I could easily manage that while drunk."[26] The Kinks were on the sidelines during 1968, one of rock's most exciting years and one of the world's most tumultuous.

111

One case resolved

If Quaife's discontent and the string of poor gigs in 1968 were not difficult enough for the band, the Kinks also had to endure the ongoing legal battles with Larry Page and Eddie Kassner. Page's appeal of Judge Widgery's decision that justified Wace and Collins's termination of Boscobel's contract with Denmark came before the Court of Appeals from March 25 through April 1 and then again from May 1 through 3, before the verdict on June 28, 1968—Mick Avory was the only Kink to testify this time. While the three deciding justices, Winn, Harman, and Salmon, did not uphold the details and reasoning of Judge Widgery's decision, the outcome remained the same. The court ordered only the repayment of unpaid commissions for the period from June 30 to September 14, 1965, at which time the contract was terminated by Boscobel, and rejected Denmark's claim to 10 percent of the Kinks' earnings from September 1965 to the present. Judge Salmon was especially sensitive to Page, who had, the justice said, to deal with "a group of highly temperamental, jealous, and spoilt adolescents."[27] However, he continued, he could not legally award a percentage to Denmark, who would have been entitled to a larger sum had Page sued instead for damages. Dissatisfied, Page again appealed, but on October 9 the Appeals Committee of the House of Lords rejected his application. The lawsuit involving management was finally over, after three years of controversy. However, Davies's publishing royalties would remain frozen in escrow for another two years until the lawsuit with Kassner Music would be resolved.

A team again

In mid-June, the Kinks submitted some fifteen tracks to Reprise for their latest US release, tentatively titled *Four More Respected Gentleman*, a reference to the three-year-old US hit "Well Respected Man," which would have only further cemented the Kinks' American image as a dried-up oldies band. The album was to include three tracks that would find their way on to *Village Green*, some that would be released on *Kink Kronikles*, and some on *The Great Lost Kinks Album*. Perhaps not entirely pleased, Reprise demonstrated no enthusiasm for *Respected Gentleman* and dropped all plans for the album after hearing of *Village Green*.

The same day as the Court of Appeals announced its decision in favor of Boscobel, Pye released "Days," the Kinks' summertime single. Ray had wanted to rework the recording, but Pye was understandably impatient. The Kinks had not released a single since the failed "Wonderboy," and they had not had a hit since "Autumn Almanac" peaked the previous November. Keith Moon of the Who, guest reviewer for *Melody Maker*, commented perceptively on "Days," referencing the song's personal nature, the sparse production, and either its timelessness or outdatedness, which no one was sure of at the time: "Memoirs of Ray Davies. . . . This sounds very much like a demo with Ray on acoustic guitar. . . . Sounds pretty much dated, like one of those songs Pete [Townshend] keeps under his sink."[28] Unknowingly, Moon summarized the unreleased work the Kinks had been doing over the past year, which would find its way out in the coming months on one version or the other of *Village Green*. Importantly, "Days" peaked at #10 on the *Melody Maker* charts and slightly lower on other charts—not surprising, it failed to chart in the US. While not a monster UK success, the chart positioning gave the Kinks a much needed boost.

Still, even with the better than modest success of "Days," the Kinks' future was very much in doubt. Throughout the past year the Kinks had done much recording, but no one quite knew what the tracks would be used for. At one point, there was talk of a Ray Davies solo album. After the release of "Days," however, the Kinks rallied. Whether to complete what they thought would be their final album or whether to give themselves a new start might be uncertain, but surely they were intent on completing the type of album that they wanted. Surprisingly, they regained their team spirit, and all the Kinks recall those sessions with fondness. "Yeah that was quite a band effort," Avory recalls. "We rehearsed all the songs thoroughly and got the right sounds and feels. Then it was worked on so the structure of it was quite good."[29] In an interview at the time, Dave was excited by the new work. "It's the best thing we've ever done," he said.[30] Quaife again felt a significant contributor. "Ray lightened up a bit. He listened to all of our ideas—at least during the recordings and rehearsals." The harmony was only short-lived, however. "After the album was done, he went back to being Ray."[31]

At the end of July with the Kinks on a two-week break, Ray, Rasa pregnant with their second daughter, and three-year-old daughter Louisa moved from their semi-detached in north London to "a manorial mock Tudor mansion," a large home in the suburbs of Borehamwood, Hertford-shire.[32] Convinced by two of his sisters that he deserved a more luxurious living space, Ray was never really comfortable there: "The night we moved in, I decided that the house was not suited to myself and my young family." The house had all kinds of problems including "old solid-fuel central heating which made clanging noises, and a large paneled dining room that was riddled with woodworm and dry rot." Furthermore, it was not as convenient for the other members of the Kinks who had to travel to Borehamwood for rehearsals. Quaife recalls taking the underground to High Barnet to meet Dave who would drive him to what the bassist sarcastically called the "mansion."[33] In some ways, the Kinks were removed from their north London roots. Some fifteen months later, Ray and his family moved back to East Finchley into his former semi-detached, which now included an extension. Davies's parents still lived just down the road, a very short walk away.

As if things weren't hectic enough, the summer of 1968 saw Ray and Dave announce a new production company intended to develop new talent in a nurturing environment—the same principle upon which the Beatles founded Apple two years later. However, with no immediately forthcoming distribution deal it would not be until September 1974 when Konk would release its first album, Claire Hamill's *Stage Door Johnnies*, which failed to chart in either the US or UK, where it was released in January 1975. During a BBC broadcast in which Hamill filled in on backing vocals for the Kinks, Ray introduced her as "a lady who's going to be a star in 1975; I know because I'm going to make her a star."

For the span of a few weeks in the summer of 1968, life within the Kinks was good with a new found camaraderie, at least in the studio, and new ideas. One misunderstood, sometimes ridiculed concept was Ray's announced plans for a Kinks pantomime to be staged in the Midlands during the Christmas season. Pantomimes, very traditional British Christmas entertainments, are generally based on nursery tales with stock characters and songs. It is entirely possible, given the characters to emerge on *Village Green*, to visualize a pantomime featuring Johnny Thunder, the Phenomenal Cat, and Walter, although Monica, given her prostitution, might be omitted from the family entertainment. Certainly, a pantomime is in keeping with Davies's restless imagination, his interest in preserving English culture, and his interest in Dylan Thomas's *Under Milk Wood*.

Village Green Preservation Society

While the pantomime did not come together, *Village Green* did, but not before much debate and change of mind as to tracks and track listings. Pye announced the release date of the twelve-track album as September 27. An advanced copy was sent to Keith Altham, a journalist and supporter of the Kinks, especially helpful during the Cardiff incident, who wrote a glowing review in the *NME*: "This is Mr. D's personal musical museum," and says the title track "could well have been a single, and even a No. 1 single."[34] Pye quoted the review in ads for the album. However, with the album close to British production, Davies decided to halt the release, at least in the UK. It was too late to stop release in several countries, including Sweden, Norway, France, and New Zealand.

Ray argued for a specially priced double album of twenty tracks, but Pye refused and compromised with a fifteen-track release. Davies took the Kinks back to the studio to record at least two additional tracks, "Last of the Steam-Powered Trains" and "Big Sky," both of which now seem indispensable to the concept of *Village Green*. At the same time, the band may have also recorded "All of My Friends Were There," also added to the new *Village Green*, along with "Sitting by the Riverside" and "Animal Farm." Dropped were "Mr. Songbird" and "Days," which peaked three months before on the singles charts. While the changes made for a decidedly stronger album, the November 22 UK release date was not favorable. The Kinks had to compete for Christmas sales with the Beatles' white album, released the same day, and the Stones' *Beggars Banquet*, released a couple of weeks later. Pye did little promotion and seemed anxious to just get the record out and over with—especially before Davies changed his mind again. The Kinks, it seems, resigned themselves to *Village Green*'s limited appeal and poor sales. Davies did few interviews and the Kinks did not tour in support of the album.

Not surprisingly, *Village Green* went largely unnoticed, charting neither in the UK nor in the US where it was released in early February 1969. However, in the US, Mo Ostin, president of Reprise, loved the record and was anxious for the Kinks to tour America—which suddenly looked like a possibility. But perhaps more importantly, *Village Green* increased the cult status of the Kinks and their artistic idiosyncrasy. Yes, they were out of time, but, to however small a following, wonderfully out of time. Increased validation, which had begun with *Crawdaddy!*, now came boldly from reviews in the *Village Voice* and *Rolling Stone*, whose review, not published until June, was written by Kinks champion Paul Williams of *Crawdaddy!* In perhaps the most influential review ever written about the Kinks, Williams hailed the genius of Ray Davies who "makes statements" and "says the sort of stuff that makes you delighted just to know that someone would say stuff like that . . . only genius could hit me so directly, destroy me and rebuild so completely." While *genius* was affixed to Davies's name as early as 1966 on the certified gold *The Kinks Greatest Hits!*—"a genius living in London . . . a brooding-faced, long-haired genius"—Williams now gave the term credibility with the result that it would be affixed to Davies's name with seeming permanence. Just as significantly, the review authenticates the cult following developing around the Kinks: "Maybe there's some sort of real bond between Kinks-lovers the world over. I mean it's not just some rock group. It's more like a taste for fine wines from a certain valley, a devotion to a particular breed of cocker spaniel. . . . We're a select few, no doubt, so we may as well love each other and stick together." Kinks devotees did not read any irony in the review, and indeed none was intended. Even during the arena years in the late 1970s and early 1980s, the core of Kinks fans familiar with the entire body of work was small, but very durable and tolerable, following Davies through various musical shifts, sloppy and misrepresentative stage performances, and many inconsistencies. "If you are [into the Kinks]," Williams closes his review, "brother, I love you. We've got to stick together."

Village Green represents Davies at the pinnacle of his Romanticism, incorporating all the major preoccupations of the traditional Romantic conscious as outlined in the previous chapter. The album alternates between the Byronic brooding voice of the sensitive artist struggling on the margins of an unappreciative culture and the contented Wordsworthian voice uplifted through nature and friendship and the very act of creation and speculation. However, Davies's Romanticism was not in keeping with the dark and almost demonic urges which had developed in rock music as a result of the chaos of 1968 and led to smash hits like the Stones' "Jumpin' Jack Flash" and the Crazy World of Arthur Brown's "Fire," and the guitar assaults of Hendrix and Clapton. Davies's Romanticism was far less confrontational and more escapist.

Under Milk Wood: time and place

The initial inspiration for *Village Green* came from *Under Milk Wood*, the classic 1953 radio play by Dylan Thomas, a leading neo-Romantic. In *Milk Wood*, Thomas creates a small seacoast town in Wales, and peoples it with dozens of defiant eccentrics like, among many others, Dai Bread, the bigamist baker and his contented wives; Lord Cut-Glass and his sixty-six working clocks; Willy Nilly, the mailman who reveals the contents of letters as he delivers them; and unmarried Polly Garter who delights in caring for her many illegitimate children and the direct inspiration for the Kinks' "Polly," the B-side to "Wonderboy" but left off *Village Green*. Davies had hoped to transform *Under Milk Wood*, subtitled *A Play for Voices*, into a musical, perhaps a pantomime, or at least an album. "I wanted [*Village Green*] to be *Under Milk Wood*, something like that, but I never got the chance to do it because we had to make albums."[35]

Although *Village Green* may not be the *Under Milk Wood* adaptation Davies had first hoped for, the album certainly reveals the play's influence. Davies creates his own marginalized and whimsical characters, and shares Thomas's yearning for withdrawal from a world of conformity and his obsession with time. Davies approached the album more like a director than a record producer. As Quaife said, "He was saying 'imagine what it was like in an English village' and he wanted all those characters to portray that, so when he explained it to us we all understood and we went into the studio and had a thoroughly good time."[36]

Besides the characters, it is easy to see what attracted Davies to *Under Milk Wood*. Published in 1954, the text included Thomas's original plot outline, which he abandoned but which offers insight into the themes and characters of Thomas as well as Davies. Thomas's town of Llareggub is to be cordoned off and declared an "insane area," since no asylum could hold its eccentric population. The citizens protest and litigation follows. However, when the prosecutor delivers his closing argument and presents his vision of the ideal town, the citizens of Llareggub withdraw their appeal and beg that the original order be enforced. The desire for isolation from an authoritative bureaucratic culture reflects Davies's desire to escape from his sometimes hopelessly complex world of recording, touring, in-band conflict, litigation, bans, shortsighted managers, and greedy record executives and song publishers. With 1960s rock music and radicalism becoming increasingly international, Davies was becoming increasingly private. "I wanted to be Walt Disney," says Davies. " 'Village Green' meant nothing to me except in my fantasy. It was my ideal place, a protected place. It's a fantasy world that I can retreat to. . . . It was my own Wizard of Oz land."[37] Thus *Village Green* becomes an extended treatment of Davies's dream theme, of escaping the world and himself and entering an idealized world with a reconstructed self-identity.

Thomas structures *Milk Wood* around the passing of a typical day with the sparse action beginning in the pre-dawn hours and ending late that night. Both *Milk Wood* and *Village Green* are obsessed with the passing of time. What was said about Thomas could just as well have been said about Davies: "that our birth is the beginning of our death, is the main theme with which Thomas struggles continually."[38] Consider songs early and late of Davies: "Where Have All the Good Times Gone" (1965) and "Run Away from Time" (2006). Every song on *Village Green* reveals an acute awareness of time. Characters seek to preserve both distant and recent artifacts and moments ("Village Green Preservation Society," "Picture Book," "People Take Pictures of Each Other"); others long for a cultural or personal past of at least perceived peacefulness and innocence ("Animal Farm," "Village Green"); some recall past personal glory ("Last of the Steam-Powered Trains") and others try to deny or to slow time ("Johnny Thunder," "Sitting by the Riverside," "Wicked Anabella"); some escape time through obsession ("Starstruck," "Phenomenal Cat," "Monica") and some through reminiscence and nostalgia ("Do You Remember Walter," "All My Friends Were There") or contemplation, yearning for understanding ("Big Sky"). Through this central theme of time, Davies explores identity, spirituality, and the importance of place.

Preservation and place

To construct his mythical place, his "Daviesland" as termed in a Reprise promo campaign but first used on the liner notes to *Something Else*, the Kinks open the *Village Green* with what Davies has called "the national anthem of the album." But "Village Green Preservation Society" is an uncharacteristic anthem, more whimsical than solemn, more unpredictable than staid, and more ironic than direct. Indeed, the first listed item to be preserved is Donald Duck, which is hardly English and hardly countercultural. Asked the significance of the reference, Davies replied simply, "I like Donald Duck,"[39] which he demonstrated in a performance of *Storyteller* in Peekskill, New York, during the spring of 1997 when he expertly

117

mimicked the voices of Donald Duck and several other cartoon characters like Tweety Bird and Sylvester. In the next line, the Preservation Society pledges itself to the salvation of Desperate Dan, another comic-strip character popular among English youth especially in the 1950s and 1960s, but a Scottish cartoon creation.

The Preservation catalog could have been assembled by friends over drinks, humorously debating what most needs to be saved or placed in private worlds. In fact, Davies said the list was inspired after ordering a pint from the "wood" at a pub in rural Devon, only to be told that the draught now comes from pressurized metal kegs. "I notice the difference," commented Davies. "Some wouldn't. But it doesn't get you in the legs anymore."[40] In times of world upheaval and professional and personal confusion, Davies's unpretentious catalog reveals a longing for the warmth and stability of home, community, and country. There are references to enjoyable foods (jams, custard pie), well-ordered domesticity (Tudor houses, china cups, antique tables, Mrs. Mopp—a detergent), family entertainments (vaudeville, Old Mother Riley), wholesome heroes (Sherlock Holmes), wicked but clearly defined and distant villains (Fu Manchu, Moriarty, Dracula), traditional virtues (virginity), and patriotism (George Cross), while rejecting the bureaucratic vision behind post-war English architecture: "We are the Office Block Persecution Affinity" and "We are the Skyscraper Condemnation Affiliate."

The seemingly disparate items on Davies's list coalesce in the tranquil image of the village green, which summarizes the singer's yearnings and withdrawal from contemporary culture, reflected in the only somewhat affirmative chorus: "Protecting the old ways . . . Preserving the new ways . . . What more can we do?" Significantly, however, in the context of the song, with its gentle acoustic guitar runs in the intro to the vocal harmonies, inviting sing-along melody, and the warm images, the question suggests that Davies is operating with the negative capability of Keats— the ability to dwell with "uncertainties . . . without any irritable reaching after fact & reason."[41]

As Davies has indicated, "Village Green Preservation Society" sounds the album's keynote, which might be put this way: the only escape from the burden of time and life is through the imagination and the creative process. "I was searching and a bit lost," Davies said of the period around *Village Green*.[42] The album represents his quest for certainty, which he finds in the studio. Thus the album for Davies and listeners results "in a momentary stay against confusion," to use Robert Frost's definition of poetry. Outside the studio, Davies was embroiled in all kinds of personal and professional distractions, demands, and uncertainties. Still today, the studio might be Davies's only safety zone.

In fact, *Village Green*, album and place, represents a safe haven not only for Davies and his imagination but also for those extensions of his psyche, i.e., his characters, and perhaps for listeners who might themselves feel out of place and time. Everything in *Village Green*, music and ideas, develops from the characters and their awareness of time and their own mortality. As Ken Rayes says, "In this album, Davies and The Kinks seek to preserve their past as a means to preserve personal meaning and significance, as a way to maintain a sense of order and cultural stability."[43] Joseph Marotta goes further, arguing that Davies's characters are on a quest to recover a lost domain, a period of real or imagined bliss, defined more fully by Jack J. Boies:

> The lost domain is a beautiful, visionary land, visited or witnessed for a brief time by a fictional character and then lost to him. . . . But the tragedy for the fictional character is that . . . he can never return. . . . What all successful lost-domain stories do is project to the reader a mood of such penetrating *nostalgia* that it can no longer be clearly communicated through that word. It is an overpowering excitement combined with a knife-sharp bittersweet yearning, containing all of the urgency of sexuality but at the same time, often wholly divorced from the sensation of physical desire. It is a feeling that most people have had vividly in dreams. . . . There is a sense of fulfillment of all heart's yearnings.[44]

In the intensity of the experience and the longing for its recovery, the lost domain can be closely linked with not only childhood but also an imagined return to Eden. The speaker in Dylan Thomas's "Fern Hill," for instance, recreates the childhood bliss of life on a farm through golden and green images, "holy streams," and "Adam and maiden." However, as happens to those in quest of the lost domain, an inescapable adult awareness of time interferes: "Time held me green and dying / Though I sang in my chains like the sea."

Davies expresses a similar sensibility in *X-Ray*:

> The early days in my little kingdom were full of splendour. The flowers of summer had reached full bloom. The birds sang in orchestrated harmony and echoed my own contentment: I was spoiled and mollycoddled to an excessive but wondrous degree. . . . Life was simply perfection.[45]

As in "Fern Hill" and *X-Ray*, the characters of *Village Green* seek to regain Eden and, in their brief but ultimately impossible recovery, the album derives its emotional depth with its vacillations between joy and sorrow, contentment and disappointment, and tranquility and torment.

Transformation

To recapture the lost domain and to escape the "chains" of time, the characters of *Village Green* devise similar but nuanced strategies to create alternative worlds and to evade introspection. For some, the attempt and escape are all consuming while others seek more of a quick respite from personal and cultural anxiety and uncertainty. In addition to the characters, there is a controlling consciousness to *Village Green*, an overarching voice which comments, speculates, and philosophizes in tones which can be solemn and playful, but always sympathetic to the characters.

In one group are characters who seek self-annihilation through transformation, psychological and actual. Their escapes represent a complete rejection of their cultures and their selves, past and present—characters like Johnny Thunder, Phenomenal Cat, the protagonist of "Starstruck," and the singers of "Sitting by the Riverside," "Monica," and "People Take Pictures of Each Other." These characters have much in common with earlier Davies creations from "I Go to Sleep," "David Watts," and "Lavender Hill," and later ones from "Oklahoma U.S.A.," "Celluloid Heroes," and "Drift Away." On *Village Green*, Davies employs exotic rhythms, unusual instruments and arrangements, and wordless childlike choruses to suggest their retreat to another world, one without responsibilities and burdens and associated with the lost domain of carefree childhood.

Johnny Thunder, for instance, appears at first to be an impenetrable individualist on a stated quest to avoid conformity. However, if we look closely at Johnny, his restless movement is a strategy to evade responsibility to himself and others ("Johnny Thunder don't need no one . . . speaks for no one"), as he has transformed himself into the object he rides, the "thunder and lightning" of presumably his motorcycle. Johnny Rogan notes Thunder's glamorous mythological power before quickly adding that he is "never developed as a flesh and blood character," which is the very point of the song and Johnny's self-annihilation.[46] He may have escaped conformity but at the expense of his human spirit. As signaled by the chorus of *ba-bas*, Johnny has created a perpetual childhood, complete with a mother figure who prays for him. Similarly, the singer of "Sitting by the Riverside" finds peace in his withdrawal to the riverside, where the psychedelic swirls and vibrations of the keyboards, particularly the Mellotron, reflect his spiraling out of himself and into a wine-induced state where he feels "it is heaven to be like a willow tree."

"Phenomenal Cat" is a kind of dark fairy-tale. Despite the fanciful protagonist, the gentle melody, inviting Mellotron-generated flute, and the repetition of "fum-fum[s]," diddle-um-di[s]," and "la-la[s]" sung in a voice resembling *The Wizard of Oz* munchkins, the song tells of a cat who on his travels finds the secret of life, which he does not disclose, but instead assumes a life of stasis in which he sits in a tree and eats "his way through eternity." Was the secret so numbing?

In "Monica" and "Starstruck," the protagonists avoid the self-reflection brought on by the privacy of the night by losing themselves in activity, actual and imaginary, and focusing themselves on lamplights, midnights, nightly shadows, city lights, stars, club life, and dreamed love. In "Monica," a song more about the singer than the prostitute of the title, Davies borrows a Dylan Thomas technique in which Thomas recharges stock phrases by changing a word. Thus, in "Fern Hill," for instance, Adam and Eve becomes "Adam and Maiden," and in "Monica," morning to midnight becomes "morning to moonshine." While the singer claims ownership over Monica ("I shall die if I should lose Monica"), it is clear from the context of the album that he possesses Monica only in his fantasy world, one conveyed through the calypso rhythm of the song. Yet, strangely enough, "Monica" is the closest track to being a love song on the album. In "Starstruck," the failed American single from *Village Green*, the protagonist is most likely a groupie "starstruck" on both the song's singer and the night-life, which the singer warns will inevitably lead to her destruction. The woman has companions in other Davies songs of crushed female innocence like "Little Miss Queen of Darkness," "Polly," and "Big Black Smoke."

Immersed in the past

A second group of characters immerse themselves in their pasts, and through an intensely nostalgic vision and selective memory try to regain their lost domain. But the singers in the following songs have only limited success: "Do You Remember Walter," "Last of the Steam-Powered Trains," "Animal Farm," and "Village Green." The overriding emotion in "Do You Remember Walter" is bitterness, in "Animal Farm" longing, in "Village Green" regret, and in "Steam-Powered Train" a forced pride yields to confusion and disillusionment.

However, the singers in "All of My Friends Were There" and "Wicked Annabella" draw on the past for comfort and inspiration in much the same way Davies the songwriter does with "Steam-Powered Train" when he constructs the song around an old chugging blues riff from Howlin' Wolf's "Smokestack Lightnin'," a song performed regularly by the early Kinks and ideally suited for a song about a retired train. In a sense, these three songs illustrate Ralph Waldo Emerson's concept of a usable and inspiring past, one not ossified in preservation.[47]

"Wicked Annabella" is a dark but playful fairy-tale in which the singer warns children of staying up past their bedtime. Hideous Annabella lives in "perpetual midnight," mixes brews, burns souls with her eyes, and with her "little demons," preys on those children who avoid sleep. The ominous drum intro, the vibrating bass and reverberation, Dave's shuddering power riff, and his understated vocals, create an atmosphere of good-humored horror that Dave has turned into a highlight of his solo tours beginning in 1997—the Kinks never performed the song on stage. Like "Phenomenal Cat" and "Steam-Powered Train," "Wicked Annabella" could have played well in the pantomime or on the children's album that *Village Green* was rumored to be in the weeks before its release.

In "Do You Remember Walter," the singer longs for the innocence and boyish adventurousness of a youth spent with his best friend Walter, with whom he has promised to "fight the world so we'd be free." But the singer feels betrayed by Walter, who discarded his youthful idealism to become probably "fat and married and always home in bed by half-past eight." The narrator is bitter, wishing he and Walter had kept their plan to "buy a boat and sail away to sea." Realizing the time for Johnny Thunder escapism has passed, the singer rejects the present and retreats into his memory where the past is alive: "People often change, but memories of people can remain." In "Walter," the singer is angry, frustrated, and bitter over what he perceives to be his betrayal by Walter and time. His assault on his childhood companion and the present is signaled by Avory's machine-gun drums, the driving bass of Quaife and the piano of probably Ray, and Dave's distorted guitar rumblings.

The singer's immersion into his nostalgic vision is not much different from that of the singer of "Animal Farm," who escapes the "big and wild and half insane" present in which "dreams often fade and die in the bad, bad world" for his memories of his life on a farm, where he coexisted with animals and lived in rustic simplicity. In "Animal Farm," the singer ends each verse stanza with multiple repetitions of "animal farm" and "animal home," which work as an incantation to focus his consciousness on a return to his Eden. In their rejection of the present, the singer of neither "Animal Farm" nor "Walter" is much different from those Davies characters who seek self-annihilation.

The version of "Walter" that appears on *To the Bone* (1996) is much different from the original on *Village Green*. The later version is much slower, more of a shuffle, more "Bavarian," as Ray says, and with acoustic guitars and a dominant accordion, it would seem appropriate in a German beer garden. The emotional content of the song, which is just as powerful as the original, is also very different; the singer is still defiant, but more reflective, more resigned, and less bitter.

"Village Green"

One of the highlights of the album is "Village Green," one of Davies's quiet masterpieces like "Young and Innocent Days" and "Art Lover," all of which use deceptively simple lyrics and a simple inescapable melody to reveal great emotional depth. Through a series of images, mostly visual, the singer, perhaps a stand-in for Davies himself, contemplates the village life he abandoned in search of fame in the city. He begins in the town center, the village green, and visualizes the oak tree, the church, the clock, the steeple, simple people, the homes, the grocery, his first love Daisy and her husband Tom, and recalls Sunday school, the morning dew, and fresh air—all sturdy images of warmth, stability, healthfulness, integrity, and certainty, with the exception of the clock, which reminds the singer and listener of life's transience and the inability to return to the past. By contrast, the city, for the singer, is full of soot, noise, and complicated or devious people—"I think people are scared to be innocent now," said Davies over four years after the album's release. "They feel they've got to have some dark side to them to make them mysterious."[48] Throughout his catalog, the suburban Davies expresses ambivalence toward city life, which can be alluring, entrapping, and destructive. Consider "Big Black Smoke" (1966), "Holloway Jail" (1971), "Killing Time" (1986), and "Don't" (1993), which succinctly summarizes the Davies city–town dilemma: "This city kills me, but it thrills me." In "Village Green," the singer questions the price of his presumable success.

The singer's melancholy develops from a personal sense of loss and deepens with the awareness that the loss is national as well. He laments the commoditization of old English values and "antiquities" through the grotesque, photograph-snapping American tourists who invade the village green and thus mark what John Osborne referred to in *Look Back in Anger* as the "American Age," with its crass commercialism, gadgetry, and cold architecture: "We are the Office Block Persecution Affinity" and "We are the Skyscraper Condemnation Affiliate." In "Village Green," the once vital, self-sufficient community and nation has been reduced to a tourist attraction, anticipating the bleak years of the 1970s.

In the final verse, the singer vows to return to the village green and reminisce over tea with Daisy, his first love. Yet such a reunion is unlikely as the singer lacks the self-deception that *might* operate in the singers of "Johnny Thunder" and "Walter." The song's abrupt ending, just about on the word *green*, in addition to the modestly crashing chords and bass line, the harpsichord, oboe, the piccolo, and hand-plucked violins, all underscore, as Ken Rayes notes, "the classical atmosphere of a distant place and time," one, for this singer, forever lost.[49] With its references to fame and its non-ironic sense of loss, "Village Green" might be the most personal song on the album, and might explain Davies's holding the song for over two years after its November 1966 recording.

The overall consciousness

Several songs on *Village Green* might be said to reveal the overall consciousness on the album. These songs, "The Village Green Preservation

Society," "Picture Book," and "Big Sky," are less about specific characters and more about statements and questions. "The Village Green Preservation Society" introduces the issue of preservation and the past's relation to the present while "Picture Book" considers the photograph as an instrument of preservation. "Picture Book" seems like an uncharacteristically cheerful song for Davies with images of relatives, vacations, and infants, and with its almost jubilant lead and backing vocals, its up-tempo rhythm and sprightly acoustic guitar runs. There is even an amusing appropriation of Frank Sinatra's *scooby-dooby-do* from "Strangers in the Night," a #1 UK hit in 1966. However, throughout the performance we are reminded several times that the depicted days of the photographs were "a long time ago." One line is particularly telling: "Picture book, when you were just a baby, those days when you were happy, a long time ago." Almost nonchalantly the singer suggests that happiness was only found in the past of childhood, a common theme throughout not only *Village Green* but also lost domain literature. "The Garden of Eden is the world of childhood," writes Alain-Fournier in *Le Grand Meaulnes*, "not the world of Adam before the fall."[50]

If there is ambiguity in "Picture Book," there is discomfort and pain in its companion song, the album's closer, "People Take Pictures of Each Other." The breathy vocals and the brisk pace established by the piano and the thumping bass reflect both the flight of time and the anxiety of the singer who is compelled to look at photographs of his past and happier times when, for instance, he sat under "the old oak tree" at age three. "Oh how I love things as they used to be," he sighs, and echoing the singer of "Walter," "when we were young and the world was free." The singer is overwhelmed by the disconnect between the burdens and loneliness of adulthood and the freedom and happiness of childhood. "Don't show me no more, please," he pleads, ending the album on a note of frustration.

However, Davies's most directly philosophical song on *Village Green* or anywhere else is "Big Sky." "That's one of my favorite songs," Davies said. "My publisher, Carlin, had asked me to go to the Cannes Music Festival, and I spent an evening with all these people doing deals. The next morning at the Carlton Hotel I watched the sun come up and I looked at them all down there, all going out to do their deals. That's where I got the 'Big Sky looking down at all the people' line. It started from there."[51] The inspiration points to the song's theme: the smallness of human action in the overall scheme of a vast universe and divine indifference.

More speculative and contemplative than definitive, "Big Sky" tries to sort out the nature of human existence and suffering and the human relation to God—an ambitious task for a less than three-minute pop song. Ambiguous and even contradictory, the singer states in one verse that Big Sky, a God substitute, "feels sad" about human suffering, and, in another, that "Big Sky is too big to sympathize." But the singer is certain of a few things: God does not respond to human pleas nor does it interfere with earthly existence, and yet the singer takes inspiration and consolation from Big Sky's indifference: "When I think that the world is too much for me / I think of the Big Sky and nothing matters much to me." These lines and others hint at a death wish, similar to the desired self-annihilation of Johnny Thunder, Phenomenal Cat, and the singer in "Sitting by the Riverside." In death, the singer will become disconnected, like Big Sky, from human activity and stress: "we'll be free, we won't care."

Despite Davies's stated dissatisfaction with the production of the song, which might at times be too busy or murky, the recording is powerful, bringing together Davies's vocals—alternately sung and spoken, strong and tender, consoling and resigned—with a muscular, hard-pushing guitar riff from Dave, forceful drumming from Avory, and well-placed falsetto *oohs* from Rasa, all building to a stunning crescendo at the song's close. An imposing achievement, "Big Sky" marks the high point of *Village Green* for Andy Miller, the author of a reliable and insightful study of the album: "['Big Sky'] is as good as anything written in the 1960's, by Lennon and McCartney, Bob Dylan or anyone else. . . . A fittingly divine inspiration seems to have visited them there, for the Kinks' version of 'Big Sky' contains some of the most beautiful, thunderous music they ever recorded, aligned to a vulnerability and warmth no other group—and I mean no other group—could ever hope to equal. It is a perfectly balanced production."[52] While Miller's praise might be lavish, certainly the depth of Davies's questioning in "Big Sky" compares very favorably to the very few similar songs in its category, like Lennon's "Imagine."

With all the distractions and disappointments of chart failure, poorly conceived tours, internal dissension, lawsuits, and the seemingly perpetual ban from America, not many thought that the Kinks would survive into 1968, let alone produce a masterful album. Yet it was this very anxiety and confusion that led to *Village Green*. Davies and the Kinks resigned themselves to their impending end and decided to make the album that they wanted to make, one with no concern for trends, movements, or topicality. "While everybody in the world was gravitating towards love, peace and San Francisco," remarked Davies, "the Kinks were in a London suburb making this strange little record about an imaginary village green . . . lost friends, draught beer, motorbike riders, wicked witches and flying cats."[53] The result was, as Davies said, "a farewell gesture," a very personal and "very intimate album," and a very Romantic album focused on contemplations of lost innocence, time, and personal and communal preservation.[54] The importance of the album to Davies and the integrity and independence that it came to represent were illustrated when, on October 3, 1981, at the peak of the Kinks' American success, Davies carried the album on stage before some 20,000 fans at Madison Square Garden.

125

7

ARTHUR

World wars and class culture

Within the first week of 1969, the Kinks received notice from Peter Quaife that he had decided to leave the band. However, unlike his accepted September 1966 resignation, the Kinks prevailed on their co-founder to remain, convincing him of the promising year ahead. They reminded Quaife that they had just completed *Village Green Preservation Society*, which, although not selling well, was their best album to date, one in which they could all justifiably take pride, and would be released within the next month in America. There were also a number of exciting projects confirmed for the Kinks: they had to record the first of six songs for *Where Was Spring*, the Ned Sherrin produced BBC-2 TV program; they had the spring single to work up; and, most importantly, they had to rehearse material for what would be *Arthur*, an album and television play commissioned by Granada TV.

Quaife agreed to stay on, but his dissatisfaction did not disappear. In fact, more than ever, he felt like a sideman: "I had nothing to say and I was simply a person playing bass."[1] The first release in January was "Hold My Hand," performed by the Kinks but released as a Dave Davies single, which although a very capable performance, failed to chart. Curiously, the B-side, "Creeping Jean," never issued on a Kinks album, has been a consistent feature of Dave's live sets beginning with the spring 1997. Most activity, of course, revolved around Ray rather than the band. In addition to the above projects, Davies was writing the title track for *The Virgin Soldiers*, a Sherrin produced feature film based on a best-selling novel by Leslie Thomas, and Ray was scheduled to fly to Los Angeles to produce the Turtles' next album, *Turtle Soup*, in April, an album that was marred by internal confusion within the Turtles and a dispute with the record label.[2] Quaife was becoming increasingly impatient with Ray's expanding ego and tyranny, too frequently excused, Quaife felt, by Ray's "genius" or his reputation as "Great Britain's God of musical composition—something he totally believed." More than ever, the bassist resented the trips to Ray's home in Borehamwood for rehearsals:

Borehamwood. It was possibly the most excruciatingly tiresome and frustrating time of my life! I had to walk to the tube station and take a tube to High Barnet where I would be met by Dave who would then drive me to the "mansion" where Rasa would open the door and let us into the totally empty house where we would all go into the large room to our right and WAIT! Sometimes for hours! We weren't even offered a cuppa! Then his majesty would walk in and go over to the piano where he would imperiously give us the key of the number and then proceed to play the number through. This was done with only the piano—no vocals or any idea of the tune or lyrics! When he had finished that one he would do the same with the next one—and the next one— and the next one . . . Then he would leave the room and not return, leaving us all wondering if we were finished or not. If we decided to leave Ray would come running down the stairs, yelling and screaming that we weren't interested in his new numbers and "who the hell do you think you are leaving like this?" etc. etc. Eventually we would all leave and that would be that. I could never get away from that place fast enough![3]

During one break Quaife recalls that the band decided to play Monopoly in the kitchen.[4] Faced with bankruptcy, Ray, instead of a graceful exit, made his bandmates recalculate the previous nine moves to be sure of his disqualification. Quaife steamed but cooperated, anxious to defeat the indulged star.

Quaife leaves—permanently

Clearly, Ray's star treatment rankled Quaife, a schoolboy friend and athletic rival, especially in track, and co-founder and integral part of the early Kinks. As Ray said, "I couldn't have done it without Pete. In the early days I was quiet and worried about the way I looked because of my teeth. Mick was a jerk. Dave was an angry wild kid, and Pete was an ambassador."[5] The last straw for Quaife came with what he called the "facile crap" of "Plastic Man," released in mid-March and the first Kinks single in nine months. "When I saw us performing 'Plastic Man' on the television I just wanted to cry with embarrassment and shame."[6] It is easy to understand Quaife's loathing of the trite satire of the robotic middle class. Even Ray's smirky delivery and occasional cockney clipped phrasing could not salvage the banal criticism, which lacked the wit of "Well Respected Man," the catchiness of "Dedicated Follower of Fashion," and the ironic melody of "Mr. Pleasant." The B-side "King Kong," however, is one of the many remarkable and unheralded Kinks songs, a forceful, hard-rocking stomp with a self-aggrandizing singer who revels in his oppressive force.

"Plastic Man" only appeared on the *Melody Maker* charts at #28 and sold only 26,000 copies, perhaps helped along by the BBC's objection to the use of *bum*, British slang for buttocks.

Shortly after the release of "Plastic Man," Quaife announced his permanent departure from the Kinks—for the third time. Despite efforts from those connected to the band, but not Ray according to Quaife, he could not be prevailed upon to stay. "I definitely needed a change," he declared.[7] Quaife said he might have reconsidered had "[Ray] offered me peace, friendship and a calm, fight free existence. . . . All I wanted was the music—nothing else."[8] His last official day as a Kink was April 3, 1969. Ray felt all the emotions of a divorce, a mixture of anger, pain, sadness, betrayal, and lingering resentment: "I definitely felt that [Quaife] had lost all his love for the band, and that hurt me. . . . I have this notion that perhaps I have never had a real friend in my entire life. . . . I always thought friends would be there forever. I had known Pete since school. We had grown up together and were always there to help each other."[9]

Ray's remarks are perplexing. It is questionable how close Ray was to anyone at school, including Quaife, as Ray was always a loner. Furthermore, neither school chum invited the other to his wedding, with each offending the other. Part of the problem with Quaife and the Kinks, and in fact, with almost everyone who deals with Ray is his lack of communication. Ray frequently withholds plans and details, which leads to confusion, resentment, and distrust. For his part, Quaife was less than direct with his fellow Kinks about his departure and new band. The other Kinks thought Quaife's band a side project and only read of his final decision to leave in the *NME*—perhaps the bassist's payback for the secretive and terse Davies.

It is also possible, as one close to the Kinks suggested to me, that Ray was secretly pleased with Pete's resignation. "Ray could control Dave and Mick," and Dalton, like most newcomers, would expect minimal input, but Pete was "too often the lone dissident voice."[10] Ray would thus have more unchallenged authority than ever.

However, Ray knew things would never be the same without Quaife: "When one of the founder members leaves the band is dead. Once you lose the thing—the four originals getting together, going through it together, forming the band together—once that goes, the group is a different group. That picture signs it off."[11] The Kinks have always been more to Davies than just a rock band or even a vehicle for self-expression. His self- and communal-identities, as they are for Dave, are closely linked to the Kinks—which explains, especially in later years, Ray's protectiveness of the name and the content and form of any musical releases (at least those he can control). While Quaife's departure may have hurt Ray's pride, more significantly, it wounded his sense of the band's artistic spirit and working-class solidarity, and thus it remains a major disappointment in Ray's life.

Quaife left the Kinks for Maple Oak, which he formed with some Canadian musicians. After about a year and a failed bubblegumish single, "Son of a Gun," the band broke up. "Those silly sods wanted to be just like The Band," Quaife recalls.[12] Not long afer the breakup, Quaife worked as a graphic artist and moved to Copenhagen, where he recorded "quite a lot of numbers with Michael Julin." After his second marriage in 1980, Quaife settled in Belleville, Canada, a few hours outside Toronto, where he continued work as a commercial and fine artist and took on other odd jobs, which included teaching classical guitar, airbrushing, and astronomy at the Loyalist College in Belleville, with occasional playing in amateur bands and recording some sessions at, of all places, Kink Studios—"the guy that owned it was Norwegian and his name was really Kink!"[13] He moved back to Denmark in 2003, where he resides as of this writing. His last concert performance as a Kink was most likely on March 15, 1969. He reunited with the Kinks during their encore of Chuck Berry's "Little Queenie" at the Maple Leaf Gardens in Toronto on September 25, 1981, and, again at the Rock and Roll Hall of Fame Induction Ceremony, where as John Entwhistle of the Who picked up a bass, the former Kink joked: "Why don't you give that to a real bass player?"[14] Someone handed Quaife a Telecaster and they both played. On May 23, 1998 at New York's Bottom Line, calls from the audience forced a reluctant Dave to invite Quaife to the stage to play bass on "You Really Got Me." The following night in Atlantic City he had a brief but cordial conversation with Ray before a performance of *20th Century Man*.

What should not be overlooked is Quaife's musicianship. One of the finest bassists of the British Invasion era, Quaife added little flourishes, from the *vroom* on "You Really Got Me" to the brief bass insert of a passage from Bach's "Jesu, Joy of Man's Desiring" in the middle of "Wicked Annabella," flourishes more readily appreciated with the clarity of CD reissues. Dave has called him "an advanced rock musician for his time,"[15] and early in 1966, in the initial stages of formulating a band which would ultimately become Cream, Eric Clapton asked Pete to join him, but Quaife was content with the Kinks. Asked if he ever regretted leaving the Kinks, Quaife responds firmly, "Never. I would have ended up in a madhouse had I stayed!"[16]

Beirut

Within days of Quaife's departure, Avory telephoned John Dalton who again assumed Quaife's place, appearing on television to lip-synch "Plastic Man" on April 5. This time, Dalton would remain a Kink for the next seven and a half years. A few weeks later, after Ray returned from his work with the Turtles, the Kinks began to record *Arthur*. Recording, however, was interrupted by a strange weekend visit in mid-May to Beirut, Lebanon, a country on the brink of civil war with soldiers and tanks patrolling the streets. In the then plush resort city, the Kinks lived out a dark comedy that included canceled gigs, a venue change from a concert hall to a make-shift outdoor stage near the hotel swimming pool ("awful . . . a terrible gig," recalls Dalton), a shady promoter who offered the Kinks final pay-ment in Mars candy bars, Dalton's cutting himself by walking through a plate-glass door, a roadie with extreme sunburn, requests for publicity photos of the Kinks' smoking hookah and eating goats' eyes and calves' brains, impounded equipment, threatened imprisonment, and confiscated passports returned three minutes before the departure flight. "We just couldn't wait to get out," says Dalton.[17] Within a day of their return, the Kinks happily resumed work on *Arthur*.

Arthur

At the end of 1968, Davies had accepted a proposal to write a televised musical play from Jo Durden-Smith, the producer of documentaries such as *The Doors Are Open* (on the Doors), *Johnny Cash in San Quentin*, and, that summer, *The Stones in Hyde Park*. A musical was a logical extension of Davies's work and interests. With agreements from Granada TV in place, Davies and Smith sought a co-author for the script. They considered

Figure 7.1 The Kinks around 1970: (L–R) Gosling, Dave, Avory, Dalton, and Ray

playwright Alan Bennett, poet laureate John Betjeman, novelist Colin MacInnes, and others who shared Davies's at least somewhat cynical sensibility, his ironic wit, and his darkish sense of humor. In rather short time, novelist Julian Mitchell was contracted for the script. Mitchell, nine years Davies's senior, had by 1969 published six novels, which were inventive, witty, and satirical, and typically featured smart, friendly, but inept heroes. In *The White Feather* (1964), one of his finest novels, Mitchell attacks Britain's consumerist culture, trendiness, and the exploitation of pop and "Swinging London." Mitchell welcomed collaboration with Davies, and the pair worked well together. They would discuss plot and characterization and Mitchell would draft scenes, often including phrases from Davies's lyrics. It is important to note that the script developed from the music, and not the other way around as is common with soundtracks or film scores. By August, Davies had much to be hopeful about. *Arthur*, album and script, were just about completed and filming was scheduled for the end of the year. It was an exciting time for the band. "After the setbacks of our last few records," said Dave, "I really sensed that we were back on course, that our music was more purposeful, more motivated than ever before."[18]

Arthur was at least partially inspired by Davies's brother-in-law Arthur Anning, who devastated Ray when he moved his sister Rosie ("Rosy Won't You Please Come Home") and cousin Terry to Australia in probably May 1964.[19] Davies had lived with the family during his troubled early teen years, growing close to Rosie and Terry who became more of a brother to him than Dave. On the day the Annings moved, the Kinks played a gig in Redcar, a sea resort in northern England. That night as Davies walked on the beach, he broke down. "I started screaming. A part of my family had left, possibly forever. . . . I collapsed in a heap on the sandy beach and wept like a pathetic child."[20] Dave confirms the story, "All of a sudden, the fact that they were really leaving finally hit Ray. He ran to the sea screaming and crying."[21]

Although there are parallels between the inspiration and the album, *Arthur* is far more imaginative and ambitious, and less personal than any parallels suggest. As related in Mitchell's liner notes to the 1969 album, the plot of *Arthur* is thin. Arthur Morgan, now retired from laying carpets, lives with his wife Rose in their London suburban home. They have two sons Derek and Eddie, named after Arthur's brother killed in World War I and himself a victim in the Korean conflict and survived by a son, Eddie, now a rebellious student. The drama takes place on the day in 1969 when Derek, his wife Marilyn, and their two children move to Australia, thrusting Arthur into profound introspection with personal and national implications.

Arthur does nothing less than present a cultural history of the first three-quarters of twentieth-century England and the psychological effects of that culture on its people, particularly the working class—all through some of the finest popular music ever made. Never far from the surface of *Arthur* is, as John Betjeman said, that "topic all-absorbing . . . CLASS."[22]

Arthur Anning corresponds more to Derek than Arthur, who, with Ronnie, might represent the Davies family response to the Annings' move. More importantly, Arthur represents an aging Englishman, born just before the turn of the century, and as such, reflects what Dennis Smith has identified as English ethnic characteristics: "a deep-ingrained resistance to assimilation with other ethnic cultures, a high degree of sensitivity to variations in the English class structure, and an unwillingness to be introspective."[23] He has lived according to cultural prescriptions with English pride cemented in his psyche from birth. Like many Englishmen born at his time, he was named for one of Queen Victoria's children with a moniker steeped in legend, grandeur, and pride. Arthur has lived through two world wars and a depression, but both England and he have emerged triumphant, proving for him in the words of a World War II pop hit, "They'll Always Be an England." However, his son's move jolts his comfortable retirement and his cultural assumptions. As Mitchell understates, "It's a sad day for Arthur."

"Victoria"

The album opens with "Victoria," an anthem whose irony is often missed in its jubilant rock-and-roll, precise lead guitar lines, sometimes low-in-the-mix vocals, and its rhythmic and infectious chant of the Queen's name. In "Victoria," Arthur escapes the present disappointment of his son's emigration and recalls the moral certainty and cultural stability of a powerful, well-governed Empire under Victoria's reign, 1837–1901, a time when, for instance, "sex was bad and obscene"—a reference that resonated with irony to *Arthur*'s original English audience who just witnessed a decade of sexual controversy and scandal. In 1959, to test the recently enacted Obscene Publications Act which was intended to protect serious works from charges of pornography, Penguin books published the first unexpurgated edition in England of D. H. Lawrence's *Lady Chatterley's Lover*, a novel banned since its publication in Italy in 1928. A dramatic obscenity trial followed with Penguin's acquittal and English publishing liberated.

Then, in 1963, England was obsessed with the Profumo Affair, which focused on Conservative War Secretary John Profumo's scandalous relationship with expensive call girl Christine Keeler, whom Davies mentions in "Where Are They Now?" on *Preservation Act 1*.[24] Clearly, England's traditional sense of decorum was being challenged and may have received a crippling blow with several legislative enactments in 1967, like the Abortion Act, the National Health Service (Family Planning) Act, and the

Sexual Offences Act, which de-criminalized homosexuality.[25] Such topics, buried in the Victorian era and for long afterwards, were addressed in Parliament, newspaper editorials, and on television with seemingly little reticence. Many in Arthur's generation who clung to Victorian values and affirmation were stunned, embarrassed, and disconcerted.

Arthur personifies what in 1963 John Mander called "a nostalgia for empire, powerful in Britain."[26] Empire and expansion had been part of the English consciousness since Elizabeth I in the late 1500s, and had given the country national purpose and unity. At the time of Arthur's birth, the Empire was at its peak, consisting of 20 percent of the Earth's land mass and 400 million of its inhabitants. The working-class English felt smug, superior, and privileged to those living in the territories. It is a feeling that stretched well into the twentieth century. Beginning in 1947, however, the Empire was dismantled with astounding speed, so that by 1969 only the remnants of Empire remained. Furthermore, there was no crisis like a world war or depression to focus and rally a nation. His son's departure for Australia emphasizes Arthur's national disorientation.

"Victoria" reveals Arthur's desire to return to simpler times, to his and England's lost domain. Arthur recalls the certainty and security he felt in his youth through solid symbols of "stately homes," "croquet lawns," and "village greens," and national pride and privilege in England's possessions from "Canada to India" and from "Australia to Cornwall," resting assured that "from the rich to the poor" Victoria, the ultimate symbol of Mother England, "loved them all." Even though the "rich were so mean," Arthur pledges his life to "the land of hope and gloria": "Let her sun never set." Davies at once mocks and sympathizes with Arthur, as he does with most of the working-class characters on the album. Such ambivalence adds tension and keeps the album's satire and sentimentality in balance. There is also a bit of Davies in Arthur, as there is in many of his characters, especially those who lament a passing England: see "Village Green Preservation Society" and "Village Green," for instance, and later "Did Ya" and "Yours Truly, Confused N10." For Arthur and others, personal reduction is interlocked with England's diminished status, so that in "Did Ya" (1991), England's "ill repair" becomes the singer's "despair."

If "Victoria" reveals working-class patriotism in the beginning of the twentieth century, "Yes Sir, No Sir" and "Some Mother's Son," the following tracks, document the exploitation of that patriotism and the expendability of the working-class soldier. In the opening stanzas to the sharply satirical "Yes Sir, No Sir," Davies stresses the subservience of the soldier as he awaits orders for everything, including breathing. As we heard in "Victoria," the soldier willingly submits—"for this land I shall die"—and as the repetition and monotone delivery of the title indicate he has been transformed into an automaton, one who is effectively brainwashed into knowing his place as a perpetual outsider in his own culture:

"You're outside and there ain't no admission to our play," an officer informs him.

The military setting of "Yes Sir, No Sir" serves as a metaphor for the class consciousness of the English and the class structure of England, which in its strict codes of behavior and expectations, Davies implies, keeps the working-class subservient. The song reflects the general triadic division of the English classes: the working-class soldier, his middle-class commanding officer, and the upper-class superior officer. The soldier is reduced to cannon fodder or "factory fodder" if he survives;[27] his immediate commanding officer mocks him and asserts his own superiority; and the top officer, who is introduced by a grand trumpet, strategizes in a posh accent: "Let them feel that they're important to the cause . . . Just be sure that they're contributing their all." And then, more brutally, "Give the scum a gun and make the bugger fight / If he dies we'll send a medal to his wife (*laughter*)." The song ends on the battlefield with the foot soldier counting bodies. Although distraught, he falls into his role as faithful servant of Empire, as Arthur's grandson will say later, completely "brainwashed": "What do I do, sir, what do I say / What do I say, how do I behave, what do I say."

"Yes Sir, No Sir" has been criticized for being tied too closely to the narrative,[28] but while it provides necessary exposition and support to the album's concept, the song creates sufficient drama to stand by itself if it had to. Avory's military drum rolls, Dave's stinging guitar under the lead vocals, the tempo shifts, and the poignant brass charts create an evocative performance. The song's unproduced visual accompaniment may be easy to imagine, but Davies, as he does so often, draws on his visual approach to songwriting, developed from his days at art college and from his interest in film.

With the next track, "Some Mother's Son," Davies's songwriting is at its most cinematic, with his verbal lens shifting or splitting the screen between the external battlefield to the internal landscape of a soldier's mind and then from a mother's living room to her despair, all while juxtaposing images of life and hope (games and school, for example) with images of death and despair ("head blown up" and the grave). This technique keeps the song from slipping into sentimentality, a tone too often and easily assumed in pop music. Furthermore, Davies's tender but understated vocals, along with the emotionally neutral but atmospheric intro of a parlor room piano and harpsichord with Dave's lead notes, balance the strings and *oohs* and *aahs* of the background vocals.

Especially noteworthy is the second verse. Fighting in a trench, a soldier is distracted by the sun, an image generally of life and healing throughout Davies's work, and "dreams" of his youthful days of innocent game playing. His fellow soldier calls too late to shake him from his dream state, and "a second later he is dead."

The song closes with a powerful image of a grieving mother alone with memories and her son's portrait with flowers decorating the frame. It is an especially profound image when we consider the superior officer's reference in "Yes Sir, No Sir" to the working-class soldier as "scum" and his condescending reference to sending medals home. The slain soldier is presumably Eddie, Arthur's brother. According to the liner notes, Eddie was killed in the Battle of the Somme, which saw 60,000 British soldiers killed on the first day of fighting on July 1, 1916, and over one million casualties by the battle's end that November. The image was inspired by Davies's recollection of the portrait of Arthur Anning's brother killed in World War II and the poppies decorating the frame.

These three opening songs provide both a general working-class perspective of English history in the early twentieth century and a specific history of Arthur's family and his psychological grounding. But with Arthur's painful recollection of his brother's death and his mother's sorrow, he begins to question his loyalty to the crown and the crown's to him. It is a painful ordeal for one unaccustomed to introspection, so in the next track, Arthur finds present escape in a memory of a past escape. "Drivin'," with its summery feel, was the first UK single from the album, but failed to chart.

"Drivin' " and "Brainwashed"

From Julian Mitchell's outline, we can conclude that Arthur bought a car in the late 1930s, which, most likely, would have made him one of the first working-class owners in his neighborhood. Arthur had planned on opening his own business, but it was the Depression and with savings too small and the risk too big, he opted for a car instead. "Drivin' " is rooted in Davies's childhood and pleasant memories of Sunday excursions with Arthur Anning behind the wheel of a Vauxhall 12, crammed with plenty of food and as many as nine family members and friends. In "Drivin'," Davies sings of sandwiches, tea, beer, gooseberry tarts, and "a picnic on the grass." Food, as both Elizabeth Field and Clare O'Donoghue demonstrate, is a recurring image in Davies's songs, one often associated with physical and emotional nourishment—consider "Autumn Almanac" and "Have a Cuppa Tea," for example.

The rhythm of the song coasts along like a leisurely car ride up and down hills and around curves, especially simulated in Dave's swirling lead guitar and, later, in his sputtering bass notes under his brother's vocals from the 1:28 to the 1:48 mark, and throughout, in Dalton's romping bass lines. Just as the recollection gives Arthur a little comfort during his troubling day, the car drive he recalls provided an escape from news of impending war ("Let all the Russians and the Chinese and the Spanish do the fighting"). In the memory, Arthur leads his family into a bucolic world of "thousands of trees," birds, cows, sheep, and a shining sun, under which they can "lie in a field"—a significant reversal from the previous song's image where "some mother's son lies in a field." The escape, then and in the present of the album, is short-lived, and just under the song's surface are restlessness and anxiety.

Arthur's daydream ends with the sinister bass-laden intro to "Brainwashed," a Marxist diatribe delivered by Arthur's grandson, Ronnie, in a scene to have taken place in a pub. The hardest rocking song on the album, "Brainwashed" is full of slashing power chords and a potent brass section. Ronnie, who is not emigrating, attacks the "aristocrats and bureaucrats" for shaping Arthur, but is more vehement in his attack on his grandfather and his class's complacency. Echoing "Yes Sir, No Sir," Ronnie sees Arthur as an automaton who only looks "like a real human being" and who has been brainwashed and bought off with an opiate of social programs ("social security . . . tax saving benefits") and comforts (house, car, etc.). He ridicules what he sees as Arthur's subservience and denigration by playing off his career as a carpet layer with the refrain, "Get down on your knees," and his lack of desire "to get up off the floor." Ronnie mirrors George Orwell who was preoccupied with class and who in *The Lion and the Unicorn*, divided England into "two nations": on one side "the moneyed classes . . . the ruling classes . . . [and] the reactionary classes," and on the other, "the poor . . . the common people," and "the mass of the people" who, Orwell and Ronnie hoped, would soon rise in rebellion.[29]

"Australia"

Not only does Arthur have to endure his grandson's tirade, but he also has to listen to his son's hyperbole on Australia. Derek seems to have rejected English propaganda for Australian propaganda. In "Australia," which closed side 1 of the vinyl album, Derek is indistinguishable from a commercial. "Opportunities available in all walks of life in Australia," he shouts. "So if you're young and . . . healthy why not get a boat and come to Australia?" Derek proclaims that in Australia there is no drug addiction and no class distinction, that the culture is comprised of straight talkers and adventurers, that everyone wears a "perpetual smile," and that on Christmas they can surf just as they do in America. Derek, it seems, has redirected his life based on an advertising campaign—perhaps indicating some of Ray's bitterness toward Anning and Australia for enticing their sister and nephew away from him.

An incisive parody of advertising promises, "Australia" is remarkably similar in content and tone to the promotional tracts John Smith wrote for America in the very early years of the seventeenth century. Davies's parody and Smith's promotions both present their lands as middle-class utopias, which reward hard work and make individual rejuvenation possible. Davies sings of Australia as "the chance of a lifetime [where] you get what you work for." Smith writes of America as a land where "nature and liberty affords us that freely, which in England we want, or it costs us dearly." He continues to say that "in contriving their own grounds to the pleasure of their own minds," that individuals can "recreate themselves before their own doors." Furthermore, Smith claims that "if a man work but three days in seven, he may get more than he can spend unless he will be exceedingly excessive." Like Australia, America, as defined by Smith, promises "profit, pleasure and content."[30] Smith, however, intends none of Davies's irony, which Davies suspects the Australians will miss: "They'll probably play our song 'Australia' in cabaret clubs with maracas and things."[31]

For its final four minutes, "Australia" breaks into a rare Kinks jam, featuring brass, Ray's piano, occasional vocal repetitions of key phrases ("chance of a lifetime," e.g.), and Dave's jazzy lead. The jam twists and turns with Derek's and Arthur's ruminations, but might be more effective as part of the film. As it stands, the jam is only adequate, more functional than inspired—especially when compared to the bootleg recordings of some hot onstage Kinks jams carried by Dave's guitar during the fall 1969 tour.

"Shangri-la"

"Shangri-la," which opened vinyl side 2, was released as the second single from the album, but like "Drivin' " it too failed to chart, greatly disappointing Ray as well as the band. Dave believed the song was misinterpreted as "purely a put-down," a mean-spirited attack on working-class complacency, which it is, at least partially.[32] Many critics, like Johnny Rogan, rank "Shangri-la" among Davies's best compositions,[33] and Mike Saunders says "it may stand forever as a masterpiece of rock songwriting."[34] Jon Savage considers it *Arthur*'s centerpiece,[35] and John Mendelssohn calls it "their most powerful" song, one "of positively astonishingly emotional complexity,"[36] which Rogan echoes by citing the "alternately affectionate and sardonic" tones.[37] There is what Dave calls an "underlying sympathy" in the song,[38] but it is overwhelmed at times by the satire, which can be incisive and cruel if less acerbic than "Brainwashed." Ray's clarification is itself ambiguous: "I'm not laughing at those people in the song at all . . . They're brainwashed into that, they brainwash themselves."[39] In fact, the sympathy comes largely from the song's context, which is to say, its relation to other songs like "Yes Sir, No Sir" and the closing and title track.

The singer of "Shangri-la" can be identified as the controlling consciousness of the album or an omniscient narrator, who peers into Arthur's psyche and turns Arthur's own thoughts of self-worth and achievement on him. The song opens with a gentle a cappella by Ray joined by an acoustic guitar and horn for verses two and three. However, his vocal tones prove more condescending than compassionate as he mocks Arthur's perceptions of "paradise," a "kingdom to command," his "reward for working so hard" (indoor plumbing—outhouses were common in working-class neighborhoods into the 1960s), and his material comforts of a car, fireplace, slippers, and rocking chair, images of affluent working-class comfort and complacency. "I'd wear hobnail boots by my fire rather than slippers," Davies said. "I can't stand slippers 'cause they symbolize giving up to me." Yet, ambivalently, "But at the same time, I love the people who are like that."[40] Through his images and his reference to Arthur as a "little man" who is "too scared to complain," Davies suggests that Arthur's life has been hollow, internally empty, and therefore inauthentic. Yet, in a note of empathy, the singer explains: " 'cos he's conditioned that way."

In the song's hard-rocking and explosive bridge with blaring horns and snarling vocals, the singer attacks the working-class suburban landscape, where every house looks the same, and the routinized and superficial lifestyle of tea and gossip reduces individuals to actors who "say their lines" and live out the cultural script too "insecure" to confront themselves and their false Eden. The bridge forms the center of the music as well as the center of the album's cultural landscape: "I did the sketch of chimney pots and endless suburbia," said Davies, "and the song just developed from there."[41] The bridge ends with the chanting of *Shangri-la*, more of a taunt which concludes with a stream of childlike *la-la-la-las* for some sixteen seconds. "They're happy, really," said Davies of the people in his landscape. "It becomes a religion to them. The glory of being boring. It's a glory. He shows you his stamp collection. It's a sense of greatness he's got around him that you can't penetrate because you feel you might upset him; he's that aura of *stuff*."[42] Again, Davies reminds us of England's transformation from the "land of hope and gloria" to "the land of the living dead," as he would term it in "Repetition" from *Think Visual* (1986).

The prime minister, royalty, and the working class

In the two tracks following "Shangri-la," Davies returns to the recent past of World War II and the post-war years. Both "Mr. Churchill Says" and "She Bought a Hat like Princess Marina" are *tour de force* performances that attack British leadership, working-class capitulation, and the development of a numbing consumerist culture. Since both songs can be said to spring from Arthur's memory and observations, they reveal the complexity of his national and self-examination. Arthur, over forty at the start of the war, did not serve in the armed forces—although conscription applied to men and women up to age fifty-five. If "Yes Sir, No Sir" and "Some Mother's Son" consider the soldier and the battlefield, albeit World War I,

138

"Mr. Churchill Says" considers the home front during what the English leadership called "the people's war."

"Mr. Churchill Says" is constructed around quotations from Churchill and other leaders and references war icons like General Bernard Montgomery, Lord Louis Mountbatten, and pop singer Vera Lynn, the "Forces' Sweetheart." Just after *Arthur*'s release, Davies commented on the song and Churchill: "Today TV exposes weaknesses in politicians. . . . But I don't know about Winston Churchill. He may have been a bit more ruthless than we've been led to believe. When the battle's over and you've won, you always look good. But what was achieved by it?"[43] Davies's question does not refer to the obviously positive effect of defeating Hitler, but to the unfulfilled promise of "the people's war" to end class distinction. During the war, the English believed that their unified and determined response to Nazi Germany was rendering the class structure obsolete. In 1940, a London correspondent of the *New York Herald Tribune* proclaimed that "Hitler is doing what centuries of English history have not accomplished—he is breaking down the class structure of England," and in December of that same year, Churchill said, "There is no change which is more marked in our country than the continual and rapid effacement of class differences."[44]

Early in the war, Churchill recognized the need for the support, perseverance, and sacrifice of the working class. But the working class was frustrated and angry, and, at times and in certain locations, seemed near revolt. Harold Nicolson, an advisor to Anthony Eden, Secretary of State for War, wrote in his diary: "Everybody is worried about the feeling in the East End. . . . There is much bitterness."[45] After a bombardment, residents booed the King and Queen who toured the area to demonstrate support. One evening, a Communist Member of Parliament led a group of East Enders to the Savoy Hotel, where they awaited the first siren of the evening and then demanded access to the hotel's luxurious shelter. When a bomb finally struck Buckingham Palace, the Queen admitted a sense of relief, using the catastrophe to make a democratic gesture to strengthen the bond between monarch and subject. Still, in some war factories, management and labor seemed to regard each other as a greater enemy than the Germans.

"Mr. Churchill Says" is about the powerful effects of the Prime Minister's words to rally the support of the working class, even if he were somewhat misleading in his claims of "the effacement of class differences." The song begins with one or perhaps two inspired working-class singers quoting first Churchill and then Lord Beaverbrook—the BBC reports that 70 percent of the population tuned to hear Churchill's radio addresses.[46] "We gotta fight this bloody battle to the very end," one quotes the Prime Minister, and "We gotta save our tin . . . garden gates and empty cans" to "make us win," from Beaverbrook. Davies establishes the sardonic tone for the first half of the song in Beaverbrook's promotion of what has been called the great aluminum fiasco. Beaverbrook, a highly successful newspaper publisher, brought his flair for the dramatic when he assumed the post of minister of Aircraft Production. At times, he passionately and foolhardily called for public support that he could not put to use. On July 10, 1940, he went before the nation:

> Women of Britain, give us your aluminium. We want it and we want it now. . . . We will turn your pots and pans into Spitfires and Hurricanes, Blenheims and Wellingtons. . . . Everyone who has pots and pans, kettles, vacuum cleaners, hat pegs, coat hangers, shoe trees, bathroom fittings and household ornaments, cigarette boxes, or any other articles made wholly or in part of aluminium, should hand them over at once to the local head-quarters of the Women's Voluntary Services. . . . The need is instant. The call is urgent. Our expectations are high.[47]

The response to Beaverbrook's call was overwhelming with "the people's war" in full throttle. Homeowners stripped kitchens and the secretary of the Fly Fishers' Club urged fishermen and golfers to surrender their gear. Yet it is difficult to surmise what Beaverbrook was thinking. More than likely, he wanted to keep the public motivated and committed to the war effort, but he had to be aware that "tin . . . garden gates and empty cans" could never yield enough high-grade aluminum to make such a drive meaningful. The public grew suspicious when they noticed aluminum goods still for sale in hardware stores and mounting aluminum scrap heaps. Similarly, while many necessary volunteer organizations proliferated during the war, others were knowingly needless, like the local Defence Volunteers (later the Home Guard), established by Anthony Eden to protect against the threat of Nazi parachutists. "What struck me," said Davies, "is that they accepted that, did what they were told."[48]

At the 1:36 mark of "Mr. Churchill Says," the Kinks suggest a Nazi air raid with a siren, a new and dreaded sound in 1939. Led by Dave's slashing guitar chords, the tempo quickens as the singers refer to a plane overhead, a destroyed house, and dead bodies—which reminds the listener of the devastation caused by Nazi bombs and English courage and perseverance.[49] Inspired by Churchill, the populace remains determined: "Do your worse and we'll do our best," one shouts at presumably a passing plane. They then proceed to clean the wreckage, prepare for another raid, and "show courage and discipline." Beginning at the 2:40 mark and continuing for over a minute, Dave's guitar solo seems scattered, suggesting the chaos and frenzy of an air raid and its aftermath as well as Arthur's complicated ruminations. If "Shangri-la" is more condemning than sympathetic, "Mr. Churchill Says" shifts the balance and is more sympathetic and even admiring of the wartime struggle of the working class, although somewhat critical of the leadership's false promises and false rallying cries. Timothy Crouse criticized the song as "vague," which is exactly its point. Arthur is left confused about Churchill, the war effort, and "the effacement of class differences," now a myth.

Despite the rhetoric of Churchill and others, the classes were as far apart as ever in the years following the war, which Davies illustrates in "She Bought a Hat like Princess Marina," a song that mocks the working-class imitation of the upper classes and prompted Dave to wonder, "I don't know whether you like these people or you hate them."[50] The track opens with Ray's singing or crooning in live performances to the accompaniment of the pleasant melody of a drawing-room piano and harpsichord, and, after the fourth vocal line, the contrasting sound of a brush scrubbing. Davies presents two characters who put aside all their problems and feel absolutely grand because of their hats. In a visually funny song, the woman buys a hat like that of Princess Marina, the most fashionable and beautiful of the royal women at the time, "to wear at all her social affairs," which include scrubbing floors and cleaning windows, and the male lead, who struggles to feed and clothe his family, buys a hat like that of Anthony Eden, the suave Prime Minister from 1955 to 1957 and described as "perhaps the best looking and the best dressed" of all prime ministers.[51] Emphasizing the class gulf, the song informs us that not only will this working-class woman not be seen at Royal Ascot, the four-day June tradition in English horse racing noted for its formality and fashion exhibitions, but also that she cannot afford the cost of transportation to the race where she would "rub shoulders with the titled, rich and famous whilst comparing the latest in millinery fashion."[52] In the first post-war years, life was austere for the British. Families juggled with points and coupons as just about everything was rationed, including food, clothing, even bread and chocolate, with rationing of meat continued until 1956.

To the woman and man in the song, the hats demonstrate pride in their Englishness, specifically pride in their nation's perseverance, triumph in the recent war, and faith in the supposedly emerging classless society. For Davies and the listener, however, the hats, like the slippers in "Shangri-la," suggest complacency, exploitation, and capitulation and emphasize the government's false promises of classlessness. As the song builds to its conclusion, the tempo speeds and yields to the music hall, aurally signaling the absurdity of the characters' imitation in an effectively chaotic mix which includes frenzied vocals, a kazoo, a honking bicycle horn, something that sounds like a washboard, background vocal laughs and calls, and perhaps a banjo or guitar strumming reminiscent of music-hall great George Formby. Only the farce of a music-hall skit, Davies seems to say, could reflect the absurdity of the war years' rhetoric of classlessness and the lower classes' faith in that rhetoric.

Curiously, in an effort to exhibit a common touch, especially in the wake of Princess Diana's recent death and to "demonstrate [her] close sympathy and relationship with the mass of people," Queen Elizabeth II staged fifteen-minute visits with average families throughout Great Britain during the summer of 1999. However, the Queen declined to remove her coat and hat during one call, which *Time* magazine referred to as a "painstakingly staged 15-minute visit," an assertion supported with a photograph of a stiff and apparently uncomfortable Queen.[53] As Davies sang on 1977's *Sleepwalker*, "Life goes on and on and on."

"Young and Innocent Days"

"Young and Innocent Days," the next track, is one of Davies's many seemingly effortless and moving ballads, marked by a graceful simplicity, that emerge on album after album unnoticed by the large rock audience. Peter Quaife spoke of how, during rehearsals, Ray would spellbind the group by seeming to pull such heartfelt songs out of the air. Dave said, "I remember that the day we did the vocal parts of 'Young and Innocent Days.' I had chills running up and down my spine and was brimming with emotion. It is such a gorgeous song."[54] The lead guitarist has performed the song frequently in his solo performances.

In "Young and Innocent Days," Arthur confides to his wife his longing to return to their Eden of "soft, white dreams with sugar coated outside," but he recognizes the impossibility from the recent events, his contemplations, and the lines on his wife's face. The Kinks perform the song without irony and sarcasm, and the melody, the wistful vocals, the harpsichord, and the acoustic guitar runs create one of the album's most sympathetic statements for Arthur and a class betrayed by the promises of the Welfare State.

Closing tracks

The penultimate track brings the plot to an unsatisfying conclusion. "Nothing to Say" is Derek's farewell statement to his father, but is loaded with ridicule and sarcasm, which, given the characters and circumstances, is not entirely convincing. It seems to be more about a generation gap than a married son's departure for a new country. It begins with Derek's nonspecific memory of walking as a child by his father's side, but he quickly informs his father that he has "no time for talking," "nothing to say," and "it's best we go our separate ways." Derek goes on to mock his father's petty health concerns, his life insurance policies, his trade union, his neighbors, and years of mundane conversation that "spit from [his father's] face" and Arthur's illusion that "everything's fine." As the song concludes, Derek leaves from boredom as both he and his father have "nothing to say." Only the bridge reveals some warmth as the son recalls happy days that neither thought would end. Musically, perhaps the least interesting song on the album, "Nothing to Say" rides on Ray's piano supported by clever horn charts, arranged here as throughout the album by Lew Warburton.

The title track, which probably would have played over the closing credits, is an upbeat rocker with a vigorous guitar workout from Dave and with lead vocals by both Dave and Ray before the brothers join together to deliver a rousing and climatic finish. The song summarizes Arthur's life ("plain simple man," "tried for a better life," "overtaken by the people who made the big decisions") and criticizes his complacency with references to previous songs ("Shangri-la," "Victoria"). But, most importantly, it resolves the ambivalent tone of the album, especially in the final three minutes—a sustained and unequivocal expression of understanding and compassion for Arthur in what Johnny Rogan termed a "gospel chorus."[55] "We know and we sympathize . . . Oh! we love you and want to help you," they sing repeatedly. Thus, despite the album's criticism of the working class, the Kinks ultimately reaffirm their class identity, solidarity, and "knowingness." "*Arthur* was a labour of love," says Davies. "I was angry with a society that had built me to be factory fodder; I wasn't angry about older people because I could see that they'd been victims of it."[56]

Response to *Arthur*

On October 10, 1969, *Arthur (or the Decline and Fall of the British Empire)* was released in both America and Great Britain. As with *Village Green*, many reviews praised the work as a monumental accomplishment. *Rolling Stone*, the most important counterculture organ of the time, published two reviews in its November 1 issue. Mike Daly called *Arthur* "a masterpiece on every level; Ray Davies' finest hour, the Kinks supreme achievement,"[57] and Greil Marcus said it was "by all odds the best British album of 1969." Then, after Marcus compares the album to *Tommy*, "It shows that Pete Townshend still has worlds to conquer, and that the Beatles have a lot of catching up to do."[58] Yet despite the reviews and an American tour, *Arthur* peaked at a disappointing #105 on the *Billboard* charts and failed to chart at all in England. However, once again like *Village Green*, *Arthur*'s statue has soared with the years. Writing in the mid-1980s, John Mendelssohn said that "*Arthur* isn't only The Kinks' finest hour, for my money, but recorded rock's,"[59] and in a special 1999 issue of *Guitar World*, *Arthur* is cited as one of the greatest albums in "the greatest year in rock."[60]

Unfortunately, Davies is unable to enjoy *Arthur*'s acclaim. Like much of the album's content, Davies has ambivalent memories and emotions towards the album. On one hand, it marks the end of the Kinks and, on the other, the close but unfulfilled vision of a groundbreaking multimedia production. "The record had some musical high spots," Davies wrote, "and was undoubtedly the first genuinely constructed musical play by a rock band, but as a whole I remember it for what it might have been, rather than what was eventually realized." He adds, "John Dalton played and sang well on *Arthur*, but I can't help feeling that the record would have been better if we had kept the original band."[61]

Davies's vision for *Arthur* came near completion. With most pre-production work completed and cast and crew in place, filming was scheduled to begin on December 1 and then rescheduled for January 1970. However, at a production meeting on December 9, Granada abandoned *Arthur* when producer Jo Durden-Smith failed to produce a formal budget and seemed too problematic for the network.

Ray and Julian Mitchell were especially outraged and Grenville Collins threatened a lawsuit—in reality, no one associated with the Kinks would have pursued litigation, not after the recently concluded lawsuit with Page over management and the still pending lawsuit over publishing rights with Kassner. Despite pressure from Collins, Granada held firm and the film has never been made. Furthermore, the script to *Arthur* has not been preserved by Granada, and Davies, who very likely has a copy, has never made it available. Rumors of a West End production of *Arthur* surfaced in 1971, but nothing materialized. What we do have, however, is an extraordinary album—musically inventive, emotionally complex, and an incisive study of England in the first three-quarters of the twentieth century.

8

A LONG WAY FROM HOME
Competing identities

"When we signed a letter apologizing, I didn't even read it," recalled Ray
Davies. "Just get this ridiculous situation over with."[1] With that letter as
the final part of applications and negotiations, the Kinks were able to take
the stage on Friday, October 17, 1969, at the Fillmore East in New York
for their first American appearance in over four years. Huge sold-out
crowds, however, did not exactly triumph their return. At the Fillmore
they supported Spirit, a respected but never very commercially successful
psychedelic rock band.

In many ways, the Kinks were starting over. They had not had a top-ten
hit in over four years ("Tired of Waiting for You," May 1965) nor a top-
twenty hit in three years ("Sunny Afternoon," October 1966), and their
last album to crack the top-100 was *The Kinks Greatest Hits!*, released in
August 1966. Their lack of commercial success in the States can only
partially be blamed on their absence. After his return from the disastrous
1965 American tour, Davies retreated into a distinctly English sensibility,
one with little appeal to America's increasingly radicalized youth. The
Kinks may have made some of their best music during these years, but it
went largely unheard in America.

Davies's songs were often ironic, wistful, and subtly introspective and
contemplative, while American rock was becoming louder and bolder,
both musically and lyrically, blasting its way through a very badly fractured
culture consumed by the Vietnam War, women's rights, racial tensions,
political assassinations, and drugs. American youths wanted aggression
and urgency in their music, preferring the extravagant and mythical *Tommy*
(#4 on the American charts) to the reflective and historical *Arthur* (#105).
"It was hard to imagine what the audiences really thought of us when
we played songs like 'Village Green,' 'Well Respected Man,' 'Victoria,'
'Mr. Churchill Says,' in the midst of 'heavy' American bands playing
stoned, with tedious over-indulgent solos that seemed to stretch long into
the night," writes Dave.[2]

As the Kinks toured in support of *Arthur*, the Jefferson Airplane released
Volunteers, their long-awaited album, which would be their fifth top-twenty

album in less than three years.[3] In sharp contrast with the Kinks, the Airplane, a band created and largely sustained by the events of those years, were, like the Who, stars on stage and in film at Monterey and Woodstock. On the opening track of *Volunteers*, the Airplane proclaims, "We are forces of chaos and anarchy.... Up against the wall, motherfucker." To open *Village Green*, released in America in early 1969, the Kinks utter, "We are the Village Green Preservation Society / God save Donald Duck, vaudeville, and variety." Boundary breaking was expected to be confrontational and reckless, not subtle.

Hoping to capitalize on favorable reviews of *Village Green*, such as the one in the June issue of *Rolling Stone*, Reprise authorized the legendary God Save the Kinks promotional campaign, which included an elaborate press kit complete with a tiny Union Jack, a plastic bagful of grass from the "Daviesland village green," a guide to Kinks recordings, a photo card with a matronly figure from the nineteenth century proclaiming through a speech bubble "God Save the Kinks," a God Save the Kinks button, and a promotional album *Then, Now and Inbetween*, featuring some fifteen Kinks songs, many abridged. The package reintroduced the Kinks to the American press in a novel and engaging way. While its effectiveness is difficult to gauge, from that point forward, "God Save the Kinks" has been a rally cry among Kinks fans.

On stage in America again

Understandably nervous, the Kinks took the stage at the Fillmore; not so understandable, however, was that, as Dave admits, they were "under-rehearsed."[4] Ray put it this way: "We went on and didn't know what we were doing."[5] They flubbed "Dedicated Follower of Fashion" and Dave forgot the words to "Death of a Clown." As his behavior on the tour indicates, Dave seemed to have forgotten that he had supposedly killed off the clown. "It was apparent that this tour was going to be hard work. It was like starting all over again. A long, hard slog back."[6] Remember, too, it was the hippie era, during which Ray never felt comfortable.

Doug Hinman, a drummer himself, was at the Kinks' gig at the Boston Tea Party, a week after their Fillmore debut:

> Sitting reasonably near to the stage, I could see the old metallic-sparkle drum kit still under their old logo. Up close I noticed what a beat-up little trooper of a kit it was by comparison with the huge kits used by the opening acts. The tom-tom shell was smashed and shoddily repaired. The amps were the only con-temporary equipment on stage—obviously leased for the tour. Out came the guitars: Ray's old Telecaster, beat to hell, and last but not least, Dave's legendary Flying V. After the announcement

146

out came the band, straight into their wall-of-sound rave up to "Till the End of the Day." Sloppy but energetic, electric and magic. The sound was not great—the singing was too low in the mix and probably slightly off—but the enthusiasm of the crowd virtually erased any fault. Dave was very visual, rocking out. Ray, emaciated in his red striped polo shirt, was frail and unsure, tentative. Mick looked basically the same. In retrospect, they seemed clearly split between an old-style pop act and a contemporary live band.[7]

The Kinks were feeling their way on this tour, which seemed more of an exploratory mission than an invasion and which, ultimately, galvanized Ray's competitive nature.

The tour had several low points, but none as low as Chicago. Somewhat humiliatingly, the Kinks opened for the Who, whose first hit, "I Can't Explain," was as Peter Townshend admitted, "straightforward Kink copying."[8] After the show, a demoralized Dave took to drinking in the Rush Street clubs, returning to trash his room and the hallway in the Holiday Inn. He injured his hand when he smashed a glass exit sign, resulting in stitches, a week of rest, and the cancellation of two shows—the tour called for mostly weekend dates as the Kinks were not a sufficient draw for the midweek. Dave, longing for his family and feeling no emotional support from Ray, decided to fly to Copenhagen for a few days where his wife and young son were visiting his in-laws. Ray flew back to London to see the premiere of *The Virgin Soldiers*, for which he wrote the theme song. The brothers thought about dissolving the Kinks at this time. "It was probably the nearest we had come to breaking up since Mick smashed [Dave] over the head with a cymbal [in Cardiff in 1965]," said Ray.[9]

The Kinks, of course, continued and by mid-November they found themselves in the small but prestigious Whiskey A Go Go in Hollywood for a four-night stand. As was becoming the norm, Dave yielded to rock-and-roll excesses of drugs, drink, and sex; Avory and Dalton took to the local bars, and Ray took care of interviews and other business. When in the proper frame of mind, Ray could always be among the most charming and seemingly forthcoming interviewees. He told a *Rolling Stone* reporter at this time, "I think the audiences are more knowledgeable now. When we came here before, we played arenas and coliseums, places like that. It was just the image then, but now the superficials are gone. . . . [Promoters have] already asked us to come back again, in February or March. . . . We're presently planning our next album and we hope to have it finished by the time we return. The way things look, we may record most of it here. Things are looking brighter now."[10] Other times, he could be painfully uncomfortable. One reporter in 1996 responded to Davies's awkward pauses and brief responses by simply ending the interview and enjoying dinner with the star.

The shows at the Whiskey were jammed and generated the kind of excitement that the Kinks had hoped. Rock luminaries attended, including members of Three Dog Night, rock-and-roll jack-of-all-trades Kim Fowley, and Mick Jagger, whose presence might have been bitter sweet as the Stones were in town for two shows at the Forum, home of the Los Angeles Lakers and performing before a total audience over thirty-five times larger than that of the Kinks. Although the shows were well received, Dave had to be prevailed upon to continue for the remaining two weeks of dates.

A week after the Whiskey, the Kinks headlined San Francisco's Fillmore West for two shows nightly on Thanksgiving weekend, with Taj Mahal and Sha Na Na, a rock-and-roll comedy troupe. In a bootleg from one of the Fillmore shows, the Kinks reveal themselves to be a much tighter band than sometimes reported. Dave's guitar work proves especially strong, demonstrating inventiveness and precision, as he leads the band through strong versions of "Mr. Churchill Says," "Big Sky," and "Victoria," and very competent extended jams on "Last of the Steam-Powered Trains" and "You're Looking Fine." Ray, not yet the showman he would shortly become, nevertheless sings proficiently, plays an assured harp on "Last of the Steam-Powered Trains," and is comfortable, if a little tentative, in his between-songs banter. It is a very capable set.

By any account, the tour was arduous and all were glad when it ended, but perhaps none more so than John Dalton. He may have solidified his standing in the Kinks, but he had become the brothers' scapegoat for the poorly performing leased amps, and he had to cope with Ray's and Dave's conflicting demands, rarely delivered in the other's presence. At one point, he volunteered to quit. "It was a very hard tour,"[11] said Dalton who relied on the friendship and advice of the good-natured Avory, now the group ambassador since Quaife's departure. "We were out there for so many weeks . . . So it was hard really, and they were small gigs."[12] It would not be until much later that Dave would acknowledge the "importance of [Dalton's] collaboration and involvement in the band."[13]

Back in England

Ray Davies returned to England more determined than ever to be a major player. "We wanted to reclaim what had been cruelly snatched from us," he said.[14] His competitive spirit was no doubt inflamed after opening for the Who and Joe Cocker and seeing the Stones sellout arenas. Davies knew he needed to assert himself on stage and develop his stage persona. He was always the front man, but as Dalton reported, "Ray used to include [Dave] a lot more in those days." Later, Dalton added, Dave "would get the one number,"[15] well, sometimes two, but Ray would never again schedule his brother to sing lead on approximately one-third of the program as he did on the 1969 tour. Dave came to feel used, creatively inhibited, and bitter: "As time went on, Ray became at times an almost vampire-like drain and pull on my creative and emotional energy . . . [Ray] always has to have an audience, and always has to have attention. . . . I am still totally frustrated and flabbergasted by Ray's detached and abusive attitude towards me. . . . I believe that Ray has never understood the true spirit or concept of collaboration."[16]

The Kinks scheduled two tours for early 1970. The first leg, from late January through February, focused on the East coast with a couple of dates in Texas and included a headlining weekend at the Fillmore East. The Kinks never got to the Fillmore, however, as the tour was canceled after two weeks when Mick Avory took ill with hepatitis. Still, in the two weeks, the Kinks had their share of disappointments with some unenthusiastic audiences, especially at gigs for which they were unsuited, like opening for Neil Diamond in Ontario. The West coast leg of the tour was scheduled for April, but was canceled as Avory still recuperated. The tour ultimately took place from the end of May until mid-July with stops throughout the country.

Between his premature arrival home in February and his departure in late May, Davies played the starring role in *The Long-Distance Piano Player*, a TV play about a young pianist out to set the world's record for non-stop playing. Televised in October, the play received poor reviews, but it served its purpose for Davies: "It cleared me of all music. I came back refreshed and energized."[17] More importantly, with the unexpected time, Davies worked and reworked the next Kinks single and began to write their next album. With *Arthur* having peaked in late December at #105, Davies knew the Kinks needed a hit to create demand and excitement. Great reviews were not enough.

"Lola"

As he has done so often through the years, first with "All Day and All of the Night" and later with *Sleepwalker*, the competitive Ray seized the challenge and wrote "Lola." He played the new song for Robert Wace, who often served as a sounding board or editor for Davies. The co-manager suggested it be recorded immediately. The first take, however, disappointed him: "It's terrible, really terrible," he told them. "They'd done it like a country and western song."[18]

At the same time as they worked on "Lola," the Kinks auditioned John Gosling as keyboardist. A classically trained musician who played music-hall numbers in pubs, Gosling was set to take his third-year final exams at the Royal Academy when he received a call from Grenville Collins. At first, Gosling thought the interested band was the *Kings*, with whom he said he was unfamiliar. A surprised Collins rattled off a series of Kinks hits.

Gosling realized his mistake before committing a *faux pas*: "The Kinks
... are they still going?"[19] Entering the studio with long hair, a beard,
and a cape, Gosling was rechristened "the Baptist."[20] "My audition was a
recording session for 'Lola,'" said Gosling. I was given chord sequences,
pieces of paper with chords written on them. I sat down and played them
and when 'Lola' was finished, I recognized it was one of the ones I'd played
on."[21]

Gosling's good-natured and fun-filled personality provided comic relief
on the road, especially for the besieged Dalton, and his superior keyboard
skills had a marked effect on Davies's production, songwriting, and performing: "Ray and I had 'in-jokes,'" he said. "We developed a sort of
empathy between us on stage, I think, and we could improvise between
the songs as well as within the songs. That's where the 'Mr. Wonderful'
thing came from and *Phantom of the Opera*, all that stuff. All those little
'link bits,' if you like, just came out of Ray knowing the styles I could
play in and taking advantage of them. I could usually suss his mood and
throw things in ad lib."[22]

Ray was very nervous about "Lola." He knew that if it weren't a hit or if
the next album did not place better than #105, the Kinks would be done.
Marion Rainford, their new publicist hired at this time, remembers her
first meeting with Ray: "He spent most of the afternoon gnawing his way
through the brim of his straw hat."[23]

Figure 8.1 Ray as Santa Claus for a mid-1970s Christmas card from the Kinks and
members of the staff of Konk

But not only was "Lola" a huge international hit, it had everything a great rock-and-roll record should have: an ear-catching opening riff, dramatic shifts in tones and tempos, memorable vocal and lead guitar hooks, a rebel hero, and a strange tale of love. The singer, now an older man, looks back at a youthful evening spent in a tawdry Soho club where, at the end of the evening, Lola invites him home. The singer falls into a panic caused not by the realization of Lola's gender but by the confrontation with his own sexuality. He seemed to realize early on that Lola was a man, noticing immediately her "dark brown voice," her tight squeeze, and her strength in sitting him on her knee. All the while, he *"almost* fell for *my* Lola" (italics mine), resisting a "fall" into what the culture would see as sexual deviance, which ultimately, as *my* signals, he may not have resisted. For when the singer tries to leave the club without his Lola, he *falls* to the floor and *falls* for Lola, unable to leave and unable to resist. On his knees, he and Lola stare into each other's eyes, obviously expressive of desire, and the song abruptly shifts to the present: "That's the way that I want *it* to be," (italics mine), he tells us—*it* being perhaps the moment of his commitment to Lola or the Lola fixed in his memory. He goes on to say that it's a "mixed up, muddled up, shook up world, except for Lola," who is comfortable with her identity and her alienation from the mainstream, as the singer hints in rock's most famously ambiguous line: "I'm glad I'm a man and so is Lola." As has been asked repeatedly, is Lola a man or is Lola glad the singer is a man? Both. For, more than likely, the singer not only went home with Lola that evening, but also has remained contentedly with her ever since, as the present tense *is* would seem to indicate. After all, in performance, Davies frequently introduces "Lola" as a love song.

Yet nothing, not even "Lola," ever seemed to go smoothly for the Kinks, who when Ray and Dave were not sabotaging the band, fate or the industry did. As the Kinks began their American tour in May, the BBC found "Lola's" reference to Coca-Cola in violation of its advertising policy. The UK release was postponed while Davies flew back to London after a Saturday, May 23 gig in Minnesota to overdub *Coca-Cola* with *cherry-cola*. After several efforts, Davies was unsatisfied. He met up with the band in Chicago for another round of dates before returning to London, where, this time, he nailed the overdub and met up with the band in New York. Released on June 12 in the UK, "Lola" raced up the charts, reaching #2 in *Melody Maker* and #1 in the *NME*.

Just after "Lola's" UK release, the Kinks taped a lip-synched performance of the single for the *David Frost Show*, to be aired on July 17 with the US release scheduled for July 14. It seemed a logical strategy, especially since the *Frost* show would mark their first American televised appearance in five years. However, the release was delayed for two weeks when the master tape was lost in transit from London to Los Angeles. They were spared the considerable chore of rerecording the song when the tapes turned up in New York. Still, the release was delayed until July 28, and, when it reached #9 near the end of October, "Lola" became the Kinks' first top-ten hit since "Tired of Waiting for You" in 1965 and their last until "Come Dancing" in 1983.

The campy showman

With "Lola" a massive hit and a new album set for release, the Kinks toured the States a hot act in mid-November, their fourth American tour in a little over a year. Driven by his competitive spirit, first honed during his days as a schoolboy athlete and now at least partially ignited by seeing the huge American success of Jagger and Roger Daltry, Ray was recreating himself into the flamboyant, campy showman that would mark his performing style from this point until the mid-1970s, a style that was influenced by "Lola," which afforded him an opportunity to be more actorly on stage; the burgeoning glitter-rock trend; and the music hall, where skits and numbers often involved gender-bending. Over the next few years, Ray would flit around the stage, speak with effeminate overtones, wiggle and dance, sing snippets of standards like "Mr. Wonderful," "Lily of Laguna" (a pretty love song first associated with black-face performers and then the music hall), "Banana Boat Song," "You Are My Sunshine" (which the Kinks had been performing for several previous years), "Have Nagila," "If I Were A Rich Man," "Baby Face," and imitations of Johnny Cash and Merle Haggard. In Davies the music hall met not just pop, but also camp.

"Lola" broadened the Kinks' audience among the mainstream and among gays and transvestites, who formed a fairly large subculture in cities like London and New York. Bette Midler, a star first within this subculture, and Candy Darling, transsexual actress and Andy Warhol protégé, went together to see the Kinks at New York's Felt Forum in November 1972, and the Cockettes, a group of outrageous transvestite dancers and singers, frequently turned up at Kinks press parties and concerts during these years. After "Lola," Davies's performances would no longer be perceived as nervous or tentative. Commenting on the Kinks' sold-out performance at the Santa Monica Civic Center on November 10, 1970, Judy Sims wrote that she had seen the Kinks on previous tours, "terrible each time"; however, she continued, "The Kinks, at Santa Monica, were wonderful; I don't know how they did it, but they changed the act."[24] Davies the great performer emerged over those three American tours of 1970, so that by 1982 no one familiar with him was surprised by the comment of journalist and playwright Barry Dickens: "To me, next to Jagger, he's one of the best performers in the world."[25]

It was on the 1970 tour that the Kinks, with a break in San Francisco, went to see Elvis Presley at the Cow Palace. John Dalton, who idolized

Elvis, commented: "Now that's what you call flash! He was fantastic. He did old numbers like 'Hound Dog' and new ones like 'Bridge over Troubled Water.' "[26] The bassist imitated his idol on "Willesden Green," his lone lead vocal as a Kink. Grenville Collins, however, reports that neither he nor the Davies brothers were as impressed. According to Collins, the audience had a long wait for Elvis to take the stage and perform for only 22 minutes. "The Kinks were pretty put-out that the set had been so short and the printed price of the tickets so high. I immediately jumped in and said, 'Now you know how people feel when you play short time.' "[27] It is difficult to know, as Collins admits, whether Elvis's performance or his comment influenced Davies. Gosling found the Elvis show significant for another reason: "Once Ray had seen Elvis in a white suit that was the start of a huge rift between him and the rest of the band. That was it; it was Ray's dressing room, his bottle of champagne, his limo. He'd obviously got it in his mind that he was going to be like Elvis and the rest of us were his band."[28]

Davies, the over-the-top performer of the early 1970s, gave rise to two frequently asked questions: is he gay and did he perform drunk? The answer to both is no. Davies is arguably rock-and-roll's master actor. During this era, he delivered his songs with drunk and gay posturings—with generally positive results, although many longed for the contemplative, sensitive songwriter. John Dalton comments, "Ray was an actor on stage; he was acting. 'Alcohol,' 'Mr. Wonderful,' he was always acting. . . . That was music hall, old-fashioned music hall is all it is."[29] Asked how much of his effeminacy was an act, Dalton responded, "All of it."[30] Ray might feign drunkenness, spray beer on the audience, and balance a beer on his head, but all close to him are adamant that he was never drunk on stage. "I know that it came across that Ray was a total boozer," says Dalton, "but he'd probably only had one light ale that day!"[31] Although as Gosling notes, the Kinks were sometimes called the Juicers, that sobriquet resulted from offstage drinking by others and by their routine of carting any beer and alcohol from the dressing room to the hotel. Collins, sounding managerial, said, "The Kinks were never really a druggie or boozy band. They had enough difficulties on their own."[32] About his onstage posturing and gesturing, Collins says succinctly, "It's all show-biz."[33]

Philharmonic Hall, New York City

On March 30, 1971, Ray's "show-biz" may have reached new heights at a legendary and revealing performance at New York's Philharmonic Hall. There are several different eyewitness accounts of Ray's onstage tumble. We can say with certainty, however, that Davies kept the audience waiting before he took the stage, that as he swayed sideways during "Apeman" he stumbled backwards at which point Dave stepped aside rather than break his fall, and that Ray crashed into a stack of amps and hit the floor. From there, the story gets murky. Avory believes the fall was real, caused by a spiked drink that Ray unknowingly took before going on. "Someone gave him a funny drug. . . . This loony who used to hang around used to administer drugs to groups and knock their heads up for the show. He'd spike your drink with something. [Ray] was under the influence of something. I don't think that he would have done that on purpose. . . . He just lost control. He wasn't right before that. He wasn't performing right. . . . Yeah, that was the only time I've ever seen him out of control."[34] Collins remembers that Ray's delay in taking the stage left many in the audience angry. "It was an important performance," he said. "The Kinks started without Ray. I had to convince him to go on. The audience was hostile. Ray, the performing genius, had to do something to win them over. He intentionally stumbled back into the amplifiers and fell. Amazingly, the audience gave a collective 'Oh, no!' People thought he was dead as he lay there. I ran to him, and Ray said, 'Get away, Grenville. I'm all right.' From that moment on, he had them in the palm of his hand. It was all an act. Ray played it up."[35] Like Avory, Dave said that he could see something was wrong with his brother. In *Kink*, Dave blames the sudden effects of the tequila Ray had drunk, but, later, in the liner notes to the CD release of *Everybody's in Show-Biz*, remembers that the frontman's drink was spiked.

Although years later Ray spoke about the fall with his usual clandestine evasiveness, he adds credibility to Collins's story: "that's when I really started to go for the audience. And I, mmm . . . let's say had an accident and fell into an amplifier and got knocked out. The audience took over for me. They came up and sang the songs because I couldn't sing. That's when I realized that the audience really likes to get involved; they became a part of the show as much as us. It's worked from then on."[36] What Ray and Dave in *Kink* confuse is the fall with the encore when, according to the *New York Times*, "several dozen people" climbed onto the stage, singing and playing with available instruments in a chaotic scene that, for Ray and Dave, strengthened the bond between the Kinks and their fans. The staid and condescending coverage in the *Times* illustrates just how little the mainstream media understood rock music in 1971: "The Kinks are an above average band given to polite and pleasant songs about love or . . . the bankruptcy of middle class British life. Occasionally, they produce a song of note. . . . In all, it was a pleasant affair musically, but the audience made it a bit sordid."[37] Of Davies the performer, Collins says, "Ray is at the genius level at working audiences. I would tell performers to watch and learn from him."[38]

Lola versus Powerman

Davies had the Kinks working at a feverish pace. In a one-year period from November 27, 1970 until November 24, 1971, the Kinks released three albums of new material and toured steadily. The workload, especially touring, was taking its toll on Dave, who sought relief through sex, alcohol, and drugs, specifically hallucinogens. "I was extremely paranoid and depressed on the road," he said.[39] Less than two weeks after the Philharmonic gig, Dave was hospitalized for depression, necessitating the cancellation of some half dozen dates of the tour in support of *Lola versus Powerman and Moneygoround, Part One.*

Lola versus Powerman introduces a new and preoccupying theme for Davies: the music industry. Davies attacks the industry's exploitation of artistic integrity, its manipulation of artistic identity, its destruction of artistic innocence, and its undermining of the artistic process. Davies would never tire of these themes, exploring them further on *Everybody's in Show-Biz* (1972), *(The Kinks Present) A Soap Opera* (1975), *Think Visual* (1986), and several individual songs, including "A Rock 'n' Roll Fantasy" (1978) and "The Road" (1987). The protagonist of *Lola versus Powerman* is not Lola, but rather "the Contender," an innocent, who leaves home for a career in music. (Surely, *Lola* in the title was a ploy to capitalize on the success of the single.)

The Contender soon learns that no one in the industry cares about music. In "Denmark Street," Davies introduces us to the shady world of publishing, a perspective certainly influenced by his dealings with Edward Kassner and Larry Page. The carnival-style piano of the intro, the cockney-barker overtones of the singer, and the resonator guitar, strummed like a banjo, all suggest the flimflam nature of a publishing circus. Of course, the Contender is signed by the publisher, who hates his music but hates more to be wrong. The hero then must contend with unions ("the man who decides if I live or die, if I starve or I eat"—"Get Back in Line"), the media, television appearances, and screaming fans ("Top of the Pops"), non-stop touring, or, in short, "perpetual motion" ("This Time Tomorrow"). The revenue he produces spins around on the moneygoround before he ends up with whatever is left. Full of bitterness, emphasized rather than masked by its music-hall piano and performance, "The Moneygoround" attacks the cruel absurdity and accepted thievery of the system. Robert Wace and Collins felt betrayed by, to them, the insensitive and unjustifiable opening lines: "Robert owes half to Grenville / who in turn gave half to Larry [former manager Page] . . . so he gave half to a foreign publisher . . ." And on and on the revenue splitting goes, until the composer ends up with "half of goodness knows what."

What the Contender comes to realize is that he is under the control of the impervious Powerman with "money on his side," and his Rats with their "pinstripe mind," or as he terms it in *X-Ray*, the Corporation. Typical in Davies, the Contender, driven "insane" by Powerman, longs for an Edenic return to innocence, "to sail away to a distant shore and make like an ape man" where he can be Tarzan to his girl's Jane ("Apeman"). While

Powerman has his money and publishing rights, he has love: "I've got my girl and I'm alright." In the final track, the Contender pledges to fight Powerman: "got to be free to say what I want / make what I want and play what I want." It is a triumphant end in both its individual assertion and its faith in love, something which Davies does not seem capable of holding out in *Think Visual*, not after two divorces and a painful breakup with live-in lover Chrissie Hynde. Additionally, the *Part One* of the album's title promises a conclusion, one never completed, perhaps prophetically, as the Kinks' problems with the industry would continue, not in small part because of Ray's difficult personality. As Wace once said, "Everything was just too much of a struggle."[40]

Underlying *Lola versus Powerman* is the Contender's and Davies's fear of losing personal identity and authenticity in the quest for stardom. It is a fear at the heart of Davies's artistic restlessness and his refusal to conform to his past art and to fan and industry expectations. Thus, Davies has led the Kinks through various styles, musical formats, and stage personas through the years. In *X-Ray*, his fear of conformity is dramatized on the very first page, as the fictional septuagenarian Davies admits to losing the battle: "The only individualism in me lurks somewhere so deep inside my desolate soul that it may never emerge to my human exterior, which was bred with the sole purpose to conform." This artistic restlessness, his failure to conform to expectations, explains to some extent why the Kinks have never had the commercial success of the Rolling Stones or the Who. As Mick Avory says, "Ray has always had this sort of integrity. . . . It might have held things up . . . so it's never gone to the full commercial height that it could have done. In a way, I don't think he wanted that."[41] As Joseph Marotta has noted, "For Davies, curiously, public acceptance is viewed as something to be shunned (though obviously sought), a trap which the true artist must avoid, for to accept the public's adulation, material or otherwise, might only get in the way of the search for something more artistically or personally valuable, authentic." Davies prefers to remain, as Marotta says, "the perennial outsider, free of the hypocrisies that might attend the artist who has sold out, and free to continue the search for something not yet discovered."[42]

Throughout the years, Davies's songs have addressed this fear of losing one's authentic self: "Brainwashed" (1969), "Full Moon" (1977), "Destroyer" (1981), "How Do I Get Close" (1989), "Surviving" (1993), and "Over My Head" (2006), to list a few. In "A Long Way from Home" on *Lola*, Davies handles the theme through what can be interpreted as an interior monologue in which he assumes the voice of a close friend or a parent—in Ray's case, presumably his mother to whom he was closer. The underappreciated song, as well as much of Davies's work over the next several years, illustrates William Butler Yeats's concept that "Of the quarrel with others, we make rhetoric; with ourselves, poetry."[43] Through the Contender, Davies studies his own position as an apparently "self-assured" rock star with wealth, handmade clothes, and other trappings of success. And while he has come a long way from a "runny-nosed and scruffy kid," he is still "a long way from home," which is to say, a long way from authentic self-fulfillment and true contentment. Later, on *Preservation*, Davies would imagine himself as a tramp, and, much later, on *Phobia*, sing, "Still looking, all alone, till I find myself a home." His art thrives on this quest for self-identity often through the persona of a fractured man searching for wholeness, fulfillment, and self-acceptance, best exemplified perhaps by the three voices he uses to tell his story in *X-Ray*, his "unauthorized autobiography." "Ray Davies is a sad individual," one close to him said. "We wouldn't have the lyrics, the whole damn thing if not for the nightmare that is Ray Davies. He is not a balanced individual."[44]

Percy

Shortly after *Lola versus the Powerman* and its #35 peak US chart position, the Kinks released *Percy*, a soundtrack to, by all accounts, a terrible film, starring Elke Sommer and Britt Ekland, about a man who undergoes a penis implant—*Percy* is British slang for penis. With the exception of Ray, the Kinks were not interested in the project. Dave was especially resentful and saw it as Ray's use of the band for another side project, coming when they could have used the time for either rest or the recording of a proper album. Ray accepted the assignment largely to learn more about film-making, one of his passions. "In a way *Percy* was really good training, having to write with a stopwatch, the same as *Arthur* was good training because I had to work with a script [and] *Piano Player* was good because I worked with theatre."[45] Just as *Piano Player* helped prepare Ray for *Starmaker*, *Percy* helped prepare Ray for *Return to Waterloo*.

Percy made for an unusual album, but not as John Dalton says, "one of the worst albums we made. It was a case of 'Let's do it, let's get it over with.' "[46] As with most soundtracks, especially of that era, *Percy* includes several background instrumentals, including a hackneyed version of "Lola." However, there are several first-rate Davies songs that have been lost in the obscurity of the UK only release, or as Dave says, "wasted on that awful project"[47]—although the failed single "God's Children" and the humorous "Willesden Green" received attention from their inclusion on *Kink Kronikles*. John Gosling, who plays a spirited and for the Kinks rare Hammond B-3 blues solo on "Completely," sees the album differently. "I've always cited that as my favorite Kinks album besides *Muswell Hillbillies*," he says.[48] When asked in an early 1990s radio interview to cite his favorite Kinks songs, Gosling listed three from *Percy*: "God's Children," "The Way Love Used to Be," and "Moments."

One song rarely if ever mentioned is the eerie "Just Friends," sung by Ray to only a baby grand piano and strings. The singer tries to seduce a woman, but there is something ominous and threatening in the suspiciously delicate piano, the quivering strings, and his crooning and quaking voice: "I won't molest you / I shan't break your brain." Given the nature of *Percy*, we can interpret the song as a dark comedy sung by a madcap buffoon rather than a monster. Still, something unsettling persists, which instills a challenging tension in the song. An early 1970s stage performance by Davies would have been welcomed—perhaps as music-hall slapstick, not unlike his treatment of "Alcohol."

Australia

In late May 1971, with "Lola" a huge international hit, the Kinks made their first tour of Australia in six years. Curiously, "Lola" had been banned from the Australian airwaves for its controversial content and, according to a newspaper clipping, for one especially objectionable but unspecified line—perhaps "I want to make you a man."[49] Of course, the ban renewed interest in the Kinks and contributed to a sellout tour. Beginning with the departing flight, on which Gosling accidentally struck a stewardess with an empty beer can, the Kinks were at their naughtiest. "Pop Star Attacks Air Hostess" proclaimed a headline in Melbourne's *Truth*, which described the Kinks' in-flight behavior as "loud, raw, rude and offensive."[50] Their behavior did not improve on the ground, where Gosling hopped a luggage trolley across the tarmac, or during the tour itself. Grenville Collins, who was no doubt frazzled from regularly traveling with the Kinks since 1969, turned over on-hands managerial duties to his partner Robert Wace, who may be responsible for the anonymous statement from "a person connected with them": "On stage they were great and the audience loved them but once the applause stopped they became difficult and almost impossible to deal with." Indeed, the Kinks left with the threat of a lawsuit when they bailed out on a scheduled television performance. "They just said they didn't want to do it," said "a stunned tour official," as the Kinks caught an earlier flight home.[51] While in Australia, Ray and Dave reunited with sister Rosie and saw Arthur for the last time before his death from cancer in October 1973.

RCA

In July, with the contract with Pye and Reprise set to expire, Davies and Collins traveled to New York for a round of meetings with record label executives. Serious negotiations ensued with Clive Davis, anxious to bring the Kinks to Columbia, and RCA, with whom the Kinks signed a demanding but lucrative contract with stipulations including a strict release schedule (five albums of new material in five years) and a moral clause concerning controversial material. In exchange, RCA gave in to Davies's demand for a large advance, the decisive factor in choosing RCA over Columbia. From experience, Davies had grown wary of label accounting practices which, among things, could siphon off questionable expenses from royalties. He therefore pushed Collins to garner the advance.

For the tight-fisted and relatively modest-living Davies, his desire for money stems more from his insecurities and less from his avarice— although stories of his frugality are legendary, from dividing a restaurant check among his daughters to taking extraordinary measures to avoid a round at the pub. Money represents security and artistic freedom to Davies, who saw his mother struggle through difficult times with an unemployed father and who realized that much of his own income depended on the fickle record-buying public. However, his poor salaries to his fellow Kinks, especially those who joined after Quaife, are not easily justified. "The basic wage was about the same as I'd get as a motor mechanic," says Dalton's replacement Andy Pyle, "which is what I used to be. . . . I got twice as much from Savoy Brown five or six years earlier!" The tour-end bonus, Pyle continued, depended "on what side of the bed [Ray] got out of. The bonuses varied so much from tour to tour that it was a joke."[52] Dalton asked, "How come nobody [else] ended up with any money? Very strange. People left the band broke."[53] Only on rare occasions has Ray let the possibility of commercial success and financial gain influence his music. Collins says briefly, "Ray does separate money from his art. If he couldn't, he would be a monster."[54]

With the advance from RCA, Davies invested a large portion in what became Konk Studios, the main headquarters for the Kinks and Davies ever since, located in Hornsey, about two miles from Davies's childhood home. The negotiations marked Grenville Collins's last important duty with the Kinks. He departed shortly after on friendly terms. Robert Wace, however, remained until the very end of the year at which time he left bitterly over a dispute with his management fee. "They owed me a lot of money and I got fed up waiting for it," he said.[55] By 1972, the Kinks or rather Ray controlled nearly all the band's activities, or as Avory says, "he steered the ship."[56]

Muswell Hillbillies

In late November 1971, The Kinks released their first RCA album. In its social consciousness and Romantic sensibility, *Muswell Hillbillies* is classic Kinks and one of their best albums. From its gatefold cover featuring the Kinks at the bar of the Archway Tavern, a north London hangout of the Davies family, to the inside photograph of the band in front of a corrugated iron fence surrounding a World War II bomb site of a row of two-story

Figure 8.2 The early 1970s Kinks: (L–R) Dalton, Dave, Ray, Avory, and Gosling

shops and flats apparently slated for urban renewal, *Muswell Hillbillies* is rooted in family, working-class struggle, and tradition, especially the music hall, and features some of Davies's deepest character-songs. Oddly enough, although the album is as English in subject as *Village Green Preservation Society* and *Arthur*, it is very American in its musical underpinnings of blues, Dixieland jazz, country, and slide guitar, and its references to American locations, films (*Oklahoma!*), stars (Errol Flynn, Doris Day), and the album's title, a take-off of *The Beverly Hillbillies*, a popular sitcom. To reflect urban blight and despair, Davies and engineer Mike Bodak recorded the album so it would suggest an antiquated, almost Depression-era sound, which included microphones not used for some ten years—an eternity given the developments of recording technology in the 1960s. Everything about the album—music, lyrics, sound, artwork—was intended to imply the economic, psychological, and overall cultural quagmire of the English working class since the advent of the Welfare State, a term coined in the 1930s referring to the totality of services by which the central government would raise the standard of living for the poor.

The opening track, "20th Century Man," serves as both a manifesto and an overture or a prologue, setting a context for the characters that follow. It begins with a soft intro of Davies's slow strumming of an acoustic guitar for some three four-beat bars, followed by the staccato slashing of the same guitar for another five bars, before the entrance of the drums and bass, and then the vocals. At about the 1:36 mark, Dave's slide acoustic

160

guitar comes in, followed about a minute later by his electric guitar and, still later, Gosling's Hammond organ, which is especially dramatic in the second half of the song, filling out the sound and drama and, with the vocals, emphasizing the escalating angst and despair of the singer in the "age of machinery." It is a powerful arrangement, still forcefully performed by Davies as late as 2006.

Without irony or ambiguity, "20th Century Man" states succinctly Davies's world view, which has remained consistent and which is most fully expressed in *X-Ray*. The singer rails against, what Davies calls in *X-Ray*, the Corporation, a global economic, technological, and military ruling complex, which in "20th Century Man" has given us a "wonderful world of technology," "napalm, hydrogen bombs, and biological warfare," sophisticated surveillance systems ("got no privacy"), a polluted and decimated landscape, faceless bureaucracies of "people dressed in grey," "trigger-happy" policemen, and uninspiring art. The singer defines himself as "a paranoid schizoid product of the twentieth century," which is to say "disillusioned" and riddled with "aggravation and insanity." Like many Davies characters before and since, he longs for a return to innocence and an Edenic landscape of "the green pleasant fields of Jerusalem" and the certainty implicit in the art of Rembrandt, Titian, Gainsborough, Leonardo da Vinci, and Shakespeare, whose very forms and subjects (like religious art, royalty, landscapes of English parks and cathedrals, sonnets) reflect a more confident world view.

In the remaining eleven songs on the initial release, Davies introduces us to a range of working-class characters and their responses to the "mechanical nightmare" of the twentieth century and, more specifically, the English Welfare State. But while "20th Century Man" is sobering and bleak, Davies modifies the tone throughout the album with wit and humor, a dark humor more sustained on *Muswell Hillbillies* than on any other Kinks or Davies work. In "Acute Schizophrenia Paranoia Blues," a shrewd, funny, and rousing song with dizzying brass charts and Dave's ringing slide, a paranoid is too terrified to leave home as the grocer follows him, the woman next door works for the KGB, and the milkman is a spy. In "Holiday," a disappointed singer is sent away only to find himself lonely on a beach under cloudy skies and polluted air gazing at the "open sewer" of a sea; still, as the bridge indicates—often a revealing section in Davies's songs—he has at least escaped the pressures of the city and relaxes without sleeping pills and sedatives.

In "Skin and Bones," an up-tempo rocker with Dixieland horns, Fat Flabby Annie finds her solution in a crash course diet that leads to anorexia and the singer's jeer to "rattle them bones"; in performance, Davies often includes "Dry Bones" ("the foot bone's connected to the leg bone . . ."). Perhaps not so incidentally, Davies's mom Annie was a large woman. In "Alcohol," the singer issues a cautionary tale about the "old demon" and its effects on a man who lost all. These tracks, all audience favorites, lend themselves to the campy, music-hall Davies who through these songs would playfully interact and tease audiences. With their critique of the Welfare State, the class system, self-deprecating but sympathetic working-class portraits, humor, and arrangements, these songs could have been performed on the music-hall stage. As Peter Townshend said of Davies, "He is unique because he linked Britain's Music Hall tradition with pop."[57]

Several other characters on *Muswell Hillbillies* also evade the pressures of life: the singer of "Complicated Life" who finds life "overrated"; the woman in "Oklahoma U.S.A." who escapes through daydreams; and the protagonist of "Uncle Son," who, based on Davies's actual Uncle Son, resigns himself to the dictates of state ("generals"), religion ("preachers"), and occupation ("unionists"). "Most of the people I know in life are just ordinary people like Uncle Son," said Davies. "They're not extremely talented. . . . He had TB from working on the railway, and he died because of his job. . . . like Rosie Rook [on 'Muswell Hillbilly'], he symbolized something to me."[58] Other characters defy the culture, like the singer of "Here Come the People in Grey," who pledges to fight governmental "compulsory purchase" with "a one-man revolution someway," or the young apparently coerced prostitute of "Holloway Jail," who is defeated in her quest for a better life in London, similar to other Davies heroines in "Big Black Smoke," "Polly," and "Starstruck."

A notable exception to the above and providing some comic relief following "Here Come the People in Grey" is Granny in "Have a Cuppa Tea," who always finds comfort and wisdom in tea. Inspired by Davies's grandmother who lived to be ninety-eight, Granny demonstrates a certainty that has been largely lost in post-World War II England, a loss which jolted Arthur. In the 1980s, Davies once said of his grandmother, "I just wish she and her *knowledge* could be around now."[59]

In its social concerns, its working-class dreams and defiance, its dark humor, and its American and music-hall references, the closing track, "Muswell Hillbilly," brings together the album's various musical and thematic motifs. The singer is being displaced from his East End London home and relocated to the suburb of Muswell Hill as part of a slum clearance drive. Davies envisioned the song opening a film version of the album, which RCA refused to finance, with Ray and Dave on the back of an overloaded flatbed truck like the one featured in *The Beverly Hillbillies*. The defiant singer says his goodbyes to friends like Rosie Rook, who despite her "bloodshot alcoholic eyes," found her "finest hat" for the farewell, and he pledges never to lose his cockney swagger and accent, despite the relocation to "a computerized community" with the enforced study of elocution. He may live in one of the "identical little boxes," but "they'll never make a zombie out of me," he avows. "It's just a lack of consideration

162

for people," says Davies. "The government people think they are taking them into a wonderful new world but it's just destroying people."[60]

For inspiration the Muswell hillbilly turns to America. Not only does the song feature a country-rock arrangement with Dave's twangy guitar refrains, Dalton's popping bass rhythm, and Avory's pounding drums, but also several references to the American landscape of West Virginia, New Orleans, Oklahoma, Tennessee, and, in one of Davies's masterful ironies, the Blacks Hills of South Dakota: "Take me back to the Black Hills that I ain't never seen." While referencing some of the musical roots of *Muswell Hillbillies*, all these places, especially in 1971, are somewhat removed from the American mainstream and not yet consumed by America's homogenization and suburban sprawl. Furthermore, the Black Hills calls to mind the relocation resistance of the Indians, which led to Custer's Last Stand and to the massacre at Wounded Knee. The identification of England's working class with America's marginalized is further suggested by "Mountain Man" and "Kentucky Moon," recordings omitted from the original release, but included as CD bonus tracks.

Coalescing the major Romantic and social preoccupations of Davies, *Muswell Hillbillies* marks Davies's continued but most sustained concern for those marginalized and exploited by post-war power structures. "I think what I try to do," says Davies, "is to try to write about freedom of people. Whether it's *Muswell Hillbillies* or *Everybody's in Show-Biz* or *Misfits*, I'm trying to work out what freedom is."[61] In 1997, dissatisfied with Tony Blair's candidacy for prime minister, Davies quipped, "I might declare my own candidacy, standing for The Extremely Tormented People Party."[62] Although the Kinks toured steadily in its support and although it marks the artistic high point of the Kinks' RCA years, *Muswell Hillbillies* did not have the commercial success either the band or the label had hoped, reaching only #100 in the US and failing to chart in the UK. In an all too familiar pattern, the album collected excellent reviews but low sales.

Kink Kronikles

In between the Kinks' first and second RCA albums, Reprise released *The Kink Kronikles* in March 1972, a double-album retrospective of the years 1966 to 1970 with selections and liner notes by John Mendelssohn, who was also involved with the God Save the Kinks campaign. The superb compilation includes two US hits ("Lola," "Sunny Afternoon"), several UK hits (among them, "Waterloo Sunset," "Autumn Almanac"), several misses ("Wonderboy," "Victoria"), album tracks ("Fancy," "Village Green Preservation Society"), and rarities ("King Kong," "Did You See His Name?"). Reprise did not include any of the early US hits, like "You Really Got Me" or "A Well Respected Man," which may have increased

163

sales. But *The Kinks Greatest Hits!* was still in print, just repressed the previous year, although it had been off the charts for some four-and-one-half years. In its breadth and astute choices, *Kronikles* conveniently filled in a sizeable gap for an American audience who lost the Kinks between "Sunny Afternoon" and "Lola." Although it only reached #94, the album or subsequent CD has remained in print and earned a #231 slot on *Rolling Stone*'s "500 Greatest Albums of All Time." From another perspective, however, *Kronikles* represents what would become a continual problem for the Kinks, who have found their new material and new stage shows in competition with repackagings of hits and resulting audience expectations. In England, the problem has been especially acute as the Pye catalog has been sold and resold for many, many reissues through the years, making it difficult sometimes for the unfamiliar Kinks to get a listen.

Everybody's in Show-Biz

As with *Muswell Hillbillies*, Davies had hoped their second RCA album, *Everybody's in Show-Biz*, would be the cornerstone of a multimedia production, but, again, RCA refused funding. Released in the late summer 1972 as a double album with one studio and one live disc, *Show-Biz* summarizes the Kinks, circa 1970 to summer 1973, and pits Davies the sensitive, introspective composer against Davies the buffoonish, high-camp performer. The album does not reconcile the contrast, nor can Davies the individual—as became apparent at White City in July 1973. Despite some very humorous moments and brightly colored cover art with cartoonish portraits of comedians and actors, nothing can mask the album's underlying melancholy and self-doubt.

Davies's increasingly fractured identity is suggested by not just the live-studio, clown-artist contrast, but perhaps more so by the closing track on each of the four original sides—none of which ends with the affirmation and defiance of "Got to Be Free" from *Lola versus Powerman* or *Muswell Hillbillies*. Side 1 concludes with a strained contemplation of self in "Sitting in My Hotel"; side 2 with a desire for self-annihilation in "Celluloid Heroes"; side 3 with the humorous but desperate escape of "Holiday"; and side 4 with an oddly abridged version of "Lola," which for 1:40 minutes consists almost exclusively of the audience clapping and singing the single word *Lola*—thus ending the album with a concrete image of the fragmentation and isolation into which Ray was slipping. "I was seeing less and less of Ray, as he was away a lot," said Rasa, his wife at the time. "When he was at home, he was very into himself and working, writing a lot. . . . It's as if he's got this thirst; he's got to be busy. He's unable to relax. His mind is working all the time. . . . He's a loner."[63] He was growing increasingly distant from the other Kinks as well, excluding them from Kinks' decision-making and spending very little time with them offstage.

"Sitting in My Hotel" addresses directly this theme of alienation from self, others, and community. Supported primarily by Gosling's piano, the song recalls "A Long Way from Home," but penetrates more deeply. In both songs, the singer examines himself by projecting questions from friends to himself. "'If my friends could see me now'—that was the key line to that song," says Davies. Such a perspective suggests Davies's awareness of his detachment from his working-class roots and his core identity. The singer questions his glitzy stage outfits ("satin strides and two-tone daisy roots . . . bow tie"), his over-the-top performance style ("like some outrageous poove"), his exploitation by the industry ("just being used"), his escape from personal responsibilities ("hiding from the dramas of this great big world"), the meaningfulness of his art, both cultural ("writing songs for old time vaudeville reviews") and personal—"what it's all leading to?" The song ends on this question, punctuating side 1 and its complaints of touring, specifically, the pace of travel ("Here Comes Yet Another Day"), the exploitive and dehumanizing conditions ("Maximum Consumption"), and the inauthentic people along the way ("Unreal Reality"). Of "Sitting in My Hotel," Davies said, "We had all the trappings of that success around us, but there I was, in the middle of it all, asking the question: 'Who am I?' I was really concerned about who I was. So the hotel was just a symbol for my isolation. The song ought to be subtitled, 'Who Am I Trying To Kid?' "[64]

"Celluloid Heroes" closes the studio sides with one of Davies's most powerful vocal performances, with tonal shifts conveying reflection, vulnerability, irony, compassion, and, ultimately, desperation. "When Ray put down the vocals to that, I stood in awe of the man!" said Gosling.[65] More subtle and more penetrating than "Sitting in My Hotel," "Celluloid Heroes" reveals Davies's Keatsean attraction to death, as his singer longs for the oblivion of celluloid, similar to other singers who long for Lavender Hill, misty water, and sleep in "I Go to Sleep." Here, the singer yearns for "a fantasy world" where he will "never feel any pain" and "never really die," since, of course, there is no life to lose on celluloid. Gosling's baby grand adds an aura of grandeur and tragedy to the track, or what the keyboardist called a "classical feel."[66] "Celluloid Heroes," the second single from the album, overwhelms in performance and content the album's modestly successful single, #16 in the UK, "Supersonic Rocket Ship," a song in quest of a regained innocence and an Edenic Return with a nursery-rhymish melody, childlike vocals, and lilting acoustic guitar lines.

For the live sides, Davies made some unusual selections. "I don't know if Ray was trying to make a statement," says Gosling, "but he put the worst tracks on the live side; they were rubbish. Old music hall songs, all the camp stuff at the expense of the decent hits. At the time you wonder what the hell he's doing."[67] Davies's choices are surprising. Of the eleven tracks, five were released on *Muswell Hillbillies*; an album track each from

Lola versus Powerman and *Arthur*; music-hall takes of "Baby Face," the fragmented "Mr. Wonderful," and "Banana Boat Song," complete with *Wey-o* call-and-response; and finally the "Lola" sing-along. A few hits, the usual fare of live albums, might have led to a better chart showing for *Everybody's in Show-Biz* than its #70 *Billboard* ranking.

Johnny Rogan calls the live sides "unrepresentative of a Kinks concert,"[68] but even minus hits it captures the high-camp Kinks very well. Between songs, Davies croons, "I really love you and you," and when an audience member calls out, "I need you," most likely a request for a lesser known Kinks song, Davies responds in a giggly effeminate tone, "Thank you. It's lovely to be wanted." At the time of the CD reissue in 1998, perhaps embarrassed by the recorded response, Davies unconvincingly explains that he was playing to a group of transvestites in the front row—the only part of the audience he could see: "So bear that in mind when you're listening to the album, and to me talking to the audience." Davies can be subtly funny as well, as in his introduction to "Acute Schizophrenia Paranoia Blues": "I want to warn you. This is a really heavy number. If you can't take it, leave the building. Maestro." He can also be subtly condescending as when he introduces his brother as Dave "Death of the Clown" Davies, a backhanded compliment which offended Dave, implying that his contributions to the band are minimal, revolve around a single hit, and that his best work lies in the past. Left off the album but at the same Carnegie Hall performance, Ray announced, "[Dave's] going to sing a song now. Give him a big round of applause so he'll have confidence."[69] Hardly shy, Dave mocked Ray and his "best arse in show-biz" by wiggling his own posterior to the audience. Worse still, at other performances, Ray has referred to Dave as "the little twerp" who "will *try* to sing one for you now"—remarks characterized by adolescent cruelty rather than good-natured brotherly teasing. Davies's introduction of himself on *Show-Biz* is, in retrospect, more revealing than might have been supposed. "My name's Johnny Cash," he says, a humorous maneuver to avoid the awkward self-introduction but, still, reflective of ever-increasing questions of self-identity.

Included on the live album is fan favorite "Alcohol," performed regularly by the Kinks but never more effectively than during these high-camp years. "Alcohol" brought together the music hall and the Saturday night parties in the Davies childhood home, which usually featured his father's boozy rendition of "Minnie the Moocher." But not only is "Alcohol" a friendly parody or burlesque of the music-hall and the front-room traditions of the Davies family, it also serves as a spoof of the nineteenth-century melodrama and the popular temperance plays of the mid-nineteenth century— although it is extremely unlikely that Davies had the nineteenth century in mind when conceiving "Alcohol." Nevertheless, as common in the nineteenth-century melodrama, the music hall, or, for that matter, silent films, "Alcohol" presents stock characters: a demanding wife, a "floosie," and the fallen husband, who loses wife, career, and home to "demon alcohol." Davies, however, signals his parodic and comedic intentions through use of almost archaic slang ("floosie," "Skid Row," "lag") and the melodramatic music with its haunting *Phantom of the Opera* organ strain and soaring trumpet from Mike Cotton.

During the song, particularly the chorus (the drunkard's lines—"Oh demon alcohol, sad memories I . . ."), Davies would spray beer on the front rows—something he did for the first time in Montreal on February 5, 1970, to shake an unresponsive, stoned audience, who responded with surprising enthusiasm to what was supposed to be an affront. It was not long before audiences came with rain gear, ready for the beer shower. Band members, particularly Dave, imitated a drunken swagger, and the audience joined the chorus, which sounded more celebratory, more Dionysian than moralistic. The performance often ended with Ray as the lost drunkard desperately trying to save his depraved audience, only to break down and cry for mercy from demon alcohol. This favorite stage piece struck just the right factious tone in its blend of comedy, parody, satire, absurdity, and showmanship.

The vaudevillian Ray, however, did not always satisfy audiences. Many came looking for the Davies of *Village Green Preservation Society*, *Arthur*, and *Kink Kronikles* or the rarely performed "Sitting in My Hotel." It seemed as if Ray could not be serious in performance for an extended period, which led to his and the band's "criminally misrepresenting themselves on stage," as John Mendelssohn said of the Kinks in the liner notes to *Kronikles*. The Kinks could be sloppy, under-rehearsed, and in shambles on stage, which contradicted the studio perfectionism of Davies and his carefully crafted songs and their sometimes overworked productions. During the Carnegie Hall performances, but left off *Show-Biz*, one audience member shouted, "Stop being such a clown." Many concertgoers were confused by the contradiction of Ray the performer and Ray the composer, or as Dave said in another context, the "puzzling dichotomy" of Ray Davies.[70] Part of the confusion lies with the audience's inextricable linking of the performer with the song and the composer with the voice, and more so, in 1972, linking authenticity with autobiography. Many, unfairly, thought the onstage Davies insincere and a sellout, largely uninformed about his connection to music hall, which was rarely discussed, as Davies said, since it was "in rock and roll terms, quite an uncool thing to be associated with."[71]

On January 14, 1973, as part of the prestigious Fanfare for Europe concert series, the Kinks staged what was intended as a concept concert based on *Village Green*. The five-piece Kinks were, as then usual, supplemented by the three-piece brass of the Mike Cotton Sound, and for this performance only, an additional six-piece brass section and a six-person chorus. The multimedia production, which Ray had long hoped for, included a set that suggested London's Vauxhall Gardens, the legendary public entertainment grounds for the English from about 1660 until its closing in 1859, and a backdrop for movie footage and photos, which during the premiere of "Where Are They Now?," featured the Rolling Stones in a lightly sarcastic gesture. The Kinks rehearsed intensely and, although the performance was more of a typical Kinks show than a concept concert, reviews were glowing. It looked as though Ray would lead the ever-resurgent Kinks to a new peak.

White City

After the Drury Lane gig, the Kinks continued a steady pace of touring, recording, and promos. The continual work, industry pressures, and self-imposed pressures were taking its toll on Davies, who has never been able to relax or even sleep regularly. "He's one of those people who allows things to get on top of him," said Robert Wace.[72] On June 20, a day before his twenty-ninth birthday, he received a surprising and crippling blow when Rasa and the children abruptly left him. "I really felt that I was getting nowhere with my own life," explained Rasa who had been worn by an inattentive husband consumed by work and subject to volatile moods. "I think he needs somebody there in the background. But who's going to be in the background and cope with the way he is? . . . The marriage just crumbled."[73] Davies wrote about her departure in "To the Bone," the title track on the 1996 Kinks album and a song which he introduced during his *20th Century Man* shows. Apparently, Rasa left behind a vinyl record, a reminder of "our first summer together" and "guaranteed to drive me mad." Of course, the singer tortures himself as "every single groove" cuts him to the bone.

On a damp July 15 at the end of a particularly sloppy set at White City Stadium in London, Davies stunned the rock world and the other Kinks by announcing his retirement, after, by one account,[74] gently kissing Dave on the cheek: "I'm fucking sick of the whole thing," he said. "I'm sick up to here with it."[75] With typical Kinks irony, pre-recorded music partially shrouded the statement, but while the 30,000 in the audience may not have heard clearly, the press and band did. "I thought he was joking," laughed Dave.[76] "We didn't have any clues," said Dalton. "He just quit."[77] "Our jaws just drooped," recalled Gosling. "It was a very depressing experience."[78]

Davies's announcement received widespread coverage. Within a week Ray's photograph appeared on the front cover of *Melody Maker* with a damage control statement by Kinks press secretary Marion Rainford, who called Davies's announcement an "emotional outburst," caused by overwork, fatigue and the recent breakup of his marriage. "He will carry on," she said, "for the fans' sake."[79] What was omitted was that Ray had been hospitalized some two weeks earlier after an overdose of valium and Dom Perignon and that he had been taking amphetamines throughout the White City show. After leaving the stage, Davies was treated at Whittington Hospital, Highgate, where his stomach was pumped. Against a doctor's foreboding recommendation, Davies soon checked himself out of Whittington and recuperated for the next few weeks at Dave's home before traveling with his younger brother's family for a vacation in the countryside of Denmark. By the end of August, however, Ray and the Kinks were in the studio completing *Preservation Act 1*.

9

HERE COMES FLASH

The rock musicals

After his recuperation from the debacle at White City, Ray Davies took the Kinks in a new direction, one that would last for three years and result in four albums (one double) and three elaborate and exhausting stage productions. For years, Davies had wanted to mix media, whether through a pantomime to complement *Village Green*, the television musical of *Arthur*, films to accompany *Muswell Hillbillies* and *Everybody's in Show-Biz*, or the recent Fanfare for Europe concert. For one reason or another, however, none had quite materialized as he had envisioned.

Finally, in the fall 1974 with the landmark *Preservation* tour, Davies saw through his long determined vision and transformed the Kinks into a traveling troupe. The five-piece core band was supplemented by a brass section and back-up singers for a total of fifteen performers, along with a choreographer, lighting director, stage director, and producer. The musicians and singers would dress in costume and assume minor roles as assigned by Ray, who played the starring roles. "I had to join Equity," says Avory, referring to the actors' stage union.[1] The Kinks would open the evening as themselves and perform an approximately 45-minute set of hits and favorites, and then, after an intermission, return for the approximately 90-minute *Preservation*. It was a long, demanding evening for the band.

At first, the other Kinks supported Ray's grand concept. "The dressing up was good fun," Gosling said.[2] "It was in The Kinks' character. We dressed up as clowns, gangsters, and schoolboys. . . . I could really spread out on the keyboards trying different sounds, but again it went on too long; it got far too complicated."[3] Dave, who preferred the studio to the stage at this time, bought into the concept during the recording of the first *Preservation* album. Eager to learn the new equipment at Konk, Dave engineered the album with Roger Beale and was especially enthusiastic when Ray adopted his idea for the guitar sound and tuning on "Daylight," one of the first tracks recorded. But his enthusiasm, like Gosling's and the others', waned and turned into resentment by the *Soap Opera* sessions in the late summer of 1974, before the first *Preservation* tour. "I was beginning to

170

get frustrated and bored with Ray's concept ideas. I really wanted to get back to playing straight ahead rock 'n' roll again. I thought that surely Ray had had enough of this self-indulgence by now. Our albums weren't selling that well, although we had a tremendously loyal following in the States. Frankly, I was concerned about our direction."[4]

If Dave was concerned about the band's direction and album sales, so too was RCA, who had signed the Kinks after "Lola." None of the musicals produced a hit single, none charted in the US top-forty, and none charted at all in England: *Preservation Act 1* (released November 1973, #177), *Preservation Act 2* (released May 1974, #114), *Soap Opera* (April 1975, #55), and *Schoolboys in Disgrace* (Nov. 1975, #45). RCA got the prestige band it wanted in the Kinks, but it did not get the expected sales.

The albums generally received lukewarm reviews while the stage productions generally earned very favorable and enthusiastic reviews. The acclaim of the New York and London productions of *Preservation* are representative. Dave Hickey found it "visually and verbally as funny as anything in rock & roll: sophisticated rather than cynical, bemused rather than outraged. The production—rear-screen projection and a few costume changes—does the most with the least. . . . I left the Felt Forum in a state of euphoria."[5] *Melody Maker* called the London Christmas production "extremely impressive . . . [deserving of] a long run in a large theatre," and *Sounds* said it "combines the best elements of Christmas pantomime,"[6] which must have particularly gratified Davies who contemplated such a production some six years earlier.

Despite the large cast and multimedia presentation, none of the musicals was as elaborately staged as Davies might have hoped—in part because RCA refused funding. "They weren't spectacular!" recalls Avory. "Although they were well organised they were not big productions in great big stadiums. They were 'Low Budget' affairs really," not "like Pink Floyd might have."[7] Davies too explains, "But when it's limited funds . . . it makes you think creatively." For Flash's televisions set, he had a cardboard cutout of a television set constructed for $2.00. It worked, he explained, as did the whole production because "the ideas were big [and] that's the thing that hits you more."[8]

By the *Schoolboys* tour, which required the band to dress in public school uniforms similar to those later worn by guitarist Angus Young of AC/DC, the other Kinks were weary. "We had too many people on the road," remarks Gosling. "We'd lost that 'intimate' band thing that we had. A rock n' roll band that had just suddenly become a touring road show with back projections, dancing girls and a man dressed as Max Miller. We then became like a West End Show and I can't abide West End shows! Ray seemed to be on a different planet from the rest of us."[9] As John Dalton says, "We were all getting a little bit fed up, well, obviously, not Ray."[10]

Figure 9.1 Ray in the early 1970s

No, obviously not Ray, who years later said, "That was a great band, a great period. It deserves a book of its own."[11]

Preservation

Of the Kinks' three rock musicals, *Preservation* is the most fully developed, most ambitious, and most artistically successful. Spanning three discs of approximately 105 minutes, the albums can be sprawling and uneven. Several songs serve more of a narrative than musical function, "Demolition" and "Flash's Dream" most obviously, and several stage announcements could be considered intrusive. However, the musical quality is consistently high on the albums with Davies's drawing from his favorite sources: traditional rock-and-roll, English folk, the music hall, blues, and Dixieland jazz.

Initially, Davies had planned *Preservation* as one double album. Sessions began in the spring of 1973, but dissatisfied with the results, Ray decided to rerecord the music in the late summer, shifting from Morgan Studios to the band's new home at Konk. "There is a danger when you get your own studio," said Gosling, "that you get unlimited time." The result, Gosling continued, was that the music was often "over-produced" and "over-cooked." "Ray re-mixed the stuff so much, it ironed out a lot of the original emotion, the dynamics, and so possibly that makes it sound a bit flat."[12] *Preservation* was not ready in time for the Christmas rush, so Ray opted to release *Act 1* in the late fall with *Act 2*, a double album, to follow in the spring.

One complaint with *Preservation* is that the sonic difference between *Act 1* and *Act 2* is extreme. *Act 1* is more acoustic and more folkish, more the Kinks of the *Village Green* without the demo quality, while *Act 2* is heavier, more rocking, underscored by Dalton's booming bass. But as Davies explains, *Act 1*, although ominous, depicts "ordinary, mundane things, the everyday world of everyday people" while *Act 2* concerns the destruction of that world. The music necessarily conforms: "The second half is blacker and more violent and more athletic. Musically athletic."[13] In *Act 2* the war and action escalate.

Plot and themes

Preservation tells the story of Flash, a repressed working-class youth who rises through violence and corruption to be the decadent dictator of an unnamed country, but presumably England, where citizens are subject to "his every whim." Flash destroys the old England of village greens and thatched cottages to gain wealth which, he believes, will secure his own power and preservation. *Act 1*, a prologue, depicts life under Flash, where dreams may still exist, however barely.

The vinyl album opens with "Morning Song," a wordless choral ode which evokes the sunrise through vibrations, hums, and quivering flutes, and which anticipates Davies the composer of *The Flatlands*, a choral work commissioned by the Norfolk and Norwich Festival in 1998. Not unlike the opening of *Under Milk Wood*, where the first voice chronicles the movement from darkest night to dawn, "Morning Song" and the next track "Daylight" sound the hopeful note of a new day which, in hindsight, will suggest that life under Flash, although grim, was preferable to that under Black. Before long, rumblings of revolt surface in "There's a Change in the Weather" and "Money & Corruption / I Am Your Man," yet the oblivious Flash carries on with his abuse and schemes. In "Here Comes Flash," Davies creates suspense for Flash's entrance as the chorus and "scared housewives" warn us to hide our daughters and stay inside. More importantly, in its mildly shrieking chorus girls, in Ray's operatic vocals in the bridge ("Once we loved . . ."), and in its speedy tempo and guitar riff echoing Aram Khachaturian's "Sabre Dance," a composition adapted for madcap cartoon chases and slapstick comedy routines, "Here Comes Flash" establishes *Preservation*'s darkly humorous tone, which links the play to Bertolt Brecht and absurdists like Samuel Beckett and Harold Pinter. *Act 1* closes with Flash and his cronies' plotting further destruction through compulsory purchase.

In *Act 2*, with its emphasis on narrative rather than tone and exposition, Mr. Black unites the nation through his Puritanical reformist campaign. In "Shepherds of the Nation," a parody of self-righteous political speeches and ministers' sermons, Black unites people against pot, debauchery, vulgarity, and "breasts that are bare and pubic hair," pledging that he and his new centurians will protect them against Satan and sodomites. Black goes on to lead the People's Army in a successful coup d'état overthrowing Flash, who seemed more concerned with amassing personal wealth and satisfying his lust than in establishing a defense force. As the musical ends, Black constructs a "brave new world" or as Davies terms it on *Muswell Hillbillies*, "a computerized community," inhabited by a "master race" of "artificial people" with Black to "monitor the human brain" and keep everyone under "constant observation even when [their] dreaming"—like Davies, Black understands the power of dreams. Unlike *Arthur*, which ends with a jubilant expression of love and sympathy, and *Muswell Hillbillies*, which ends in defiance, *Preservation* concludes with the creation of a dystopian world and only muted hope in the disappearance or escaped Tramp.

Preservation explores and expands some of Davies's favorite themes: governmental and corporate exploitation of the individual, the "control of the masses by the dictatorship of the media,"[14] political hypocrisy ("Fidel Castro, Winston Churchill. Complete opposites—capitalism, socialism—and both smoked Havana cigars. There's always a common denominator somewhere, the same hypocrisy"[15]), individual and cultural preservation (cricket, thatched cottages, village greens—"I like these traditional British things to be there. I never go to watch cricket any more, but I like to know it's there. . . . I'd rather have the actual things here not just pictures of things we used to have"[16]), the over sanitization and resulting sterility of contemporary life, and the importance of rock-and-roll, which, Davies has said, "is just as important as painting."[17] On "One of the Survivors," Davies reintroduces Johnny Thunder from *Village Green*, who escapes Flash and political rhetoric and maintains his individualism by riding off on his motorcycle with "twelve bars flowing through his brain" and the strong Chuck Berry riff of the song.

Preservation, however, is largely consumed with not the self-preservation of the characters or the culture but rather with the self-preservation of Ray Davies, who, more than politics, is the dominant subject of the musical. "There were two points in my life," said Davies, "when I should not have been allowed to put records out: [in 1968 at the time of *Village Green*] and in 1973–1975. I was searching and a bit lost."[18] *Preservation Acts 1* and *2*, along with the previous album, *Show-Biz*, and the following album *Soap Opera*, reveal a fractured artist increasingly concerned with the loss of his own identity, authenticity, and autonomy. Lost though he may have been and a little more than a year after his marriage to Rasa collapsed, Davies married school teacher Yvonne Gunner in early November 1974. The marriage was kept amazingly quiet. Most fans only heard about it when the childless couple divorced in 1981 as a result of Ray's very public affair with Chrissie Hynde of the Pretenders.

Ray as Tramp

Preservation features three main characters: Flash, Mr. Black, and the Tramp. Of the 27 songs on the original albums, the Tramp sings six, Flash sings nine, and Black four. Ray played the Tramp and Flash onstage and Mr. Black, the least developed of the three, on film projected behind the stage. It is through the Tramp and Flash, his alter egos, that Davies reveals his dreams and fears, his inner tension and imbalance.

The Tramp, who serves as narrator and commentator, represents an ideal for Davies of one who, through movement, avoids both cultural conformity and self-examination. In actuality, Davies may avoid conformity but he can only wander restlessly inside himself with endless self-questioning and self-searching. "I'd really like to wander from country to country, as a sort of tramp, but with the security of money," he said in 1964. "I'd have a bank account I could draw on in different countries when I needed it, but I would like to do what I wanted and be free to watch people and life!"[19] Davies's artistic ambition and his frugality could never bring him such a peaceful existence.

175

The Tramp has returned to his home village at least in part to repair his love relationship with Genevieve. In "Sweet Lady Genevieve," he claims that he is no longer the rogue who seduced her one drunken night and asks to be forgiven and taken back. However, the bright melody and folk-rocking rhythm with Ray on harmonica suggest that his apology is only halfhearted and somewhat playful, especially when we detect a smirk in the shaky delivery of "put your trust in me." Somewhat equivocally, too, he pledges to make only promises that he "*can* keep" and to provide only "*some* security." The song has long been interpreted as Davies's plea to his estranged wife, but both Rasa and Genevieve reject the offer. As the equivocal tone of the song suggests and as the musical will reveal, the Tramp has the sharpest instincts of self-preservation of anyone in the play, a feature he shares with his creator: "Ray has the best sense of self-preservation of anyone I have ever seen," said a former colleague. "It's uncanny and highly developed."[20]

After members of the working, middle, and upper classes sing of impending political chaos in "There's a Change in the Weather," the Tramp sings of lost individuality in "Where Are They Now?" which is more of a lament than a wistful longing for the 1950s and 1960s. The Tramp catalogs individuals, controversial and innovative, actual and fictional, like John Osborne and his creation Jimmy Porter, Alan Sillitoe and Arthur Seaton, fashion icon Mary Quant, Teddy Boys and Beatniks, the Rockers and the Mods, call girl Christine Keeler and Carnaby Street icon John Stephen, and all the angry young men and protest songs. Under Flash, individuals capitulate from fear while Black rallies support with his vision of a single-minded, "antiseptic world." Both the Tramp and Davies, however, find hope and individual expression alive in music, "Oh, but rock and roll still lives on," the song concludes and the following song about Johnny Thunder, "One of the Survivors," dramatizes.

The Romantic Davies emerges in full voice for the Tramp's final appearance in *Act 1*, "Sitting in the Midday Sun." With Flash terrorizing the community, Black organizing the resistance, and a "holocaust rising over the horizon," the Tramp disengages himself, losing himself in nature and, for Davies, the ever restorative sun, which is as satisfying here as a "currant bun." As in other sun songs, like "Waterloo Sunset" and "Lazy Old Sun," the singer does not brood but finds oblivion and escape from the surrounding chaos and tension of not just the current political situation of the drama but also from modern life, as he gleefully and proudly boasts of not holding a job or a mortgage and of being an "out of work bum." In its softly joyful arrangement featuring bright, uplifting piano and guitar fills, a warm flute, and Ray's convincingly relaxed vocals, "Sitting in the Midday Sun" is one of many graceful ballads that have come to mark the albums of the Kinks.

However, in "Introduction to a Solution," the opening song of *Act 2*, the Tramp assumes the role of narrator and updates the audience about the impending revolution. But the Tramp, although he may try, cannot remain emotionally detached. Gone are the cheerful equivocator of "Sweet Lady Genevieve" and the smug escapist of "Midday Sun." "It's painfully clear that the battle is near," he sings, with Dalton's thumping bass and Dave's slashed chords and frenetic solo mirroring his anxiety. "I wish I could just disappear," he concludes more desperate than self-absorbed.

In his last two songs, the Tramp assumes the role of an informed but innocent and pragmatic observer, who is frustrated by the folly of war and the absence of love, in which he still places faith. In "Nobody Gives," he places the current war in historical context, and notes that wars "throughout all history" result from a lack of trust, communication, and compromise. His frustration and anger expressed in Dave's sometimes twisting and sometimes scorching riffs and Dalton's pounding bass, used throughout the album to establish much of its dark tone. In the bridge, above Gosling's electric piano and under a string section, he pleads for a truce, "Why can't we work it out? . . . Why not negotiate and try to be civilised?" But just as quickly as he asks, Dalton's bass enters and his anger escalates as he realizes that history will not be defied: "I'll tell you why because nobody gives a damn. . . . no one will listen, no one will understand," and each will blame the other. A minor triumph in the context of *Preservation*, "Nobody Gives" provides some historical and philosophical underpinnings to what is essentially a dark comedy or tragicomedy. It sustains its 6:33 length, however, not through reflection, but through the Romantic longing of the Tramp, who wavers between frustration, hopefulness, cynicism, and world weariness, reflected in the twists and turns of the arrangement and Dave's guitar.

The Tramp makes his final statement on "Oh Where Oh Where Is Love?" a lament and a duet with one of the woman "do-gooders," probably Marianne Price. The up-tempo rhythm and lilting melody conjures the lost domain for which the Tramp yearns, a world of storybooks and fairytales, joy and simplicity, and love and romance. One of *Preservation*'s strongest tracks, the song could have found a home on *Village Green* or even *Muswell Hillbillies*. Realizing that "sincerity don't stand a chance," the Tramp leaves the country which is about to fall under Black's control and escapes transformation into an artificial man. Similar but less bitter than the septuagenarian Davies of *X-Ray*, the Tramp preserves his individual integrity through withdrawal, thereby bringing at least some hope to the musical's conclusion and joining Johnny Thunder "as one of the survivors."

Flash

Flash, Davies's other alter ego, is the most developed character in the musical. In the prequel *Schoolboys in Disgrace*, Davies tells how the young

Flash was expelled from school for a romantic tryst, but not before suffering humiliation from the perverted Headmaster. The experience left Flash "a hard and bitter character," who vowed that "he would always get what he wanted."[21] As *Preservation* opens, Flash is at the pinnacle of his power, controlling an empire built on brutality, lust, and greed. Yet although Flash destroys what Davies seeks to preserve (thatched cottages, village greens, fairy-tales), Flash remains a sympathetic villain, one to whom Davies can easily relate. Like Davies, Flash and his Cronies understand themselves as "mass produced factory fodder," born into a Welfare State, which, the Second-hand Car Spiv says, "owned my mind and my body and my soul." Flash and Davies are both "slum kids" who "never stood a chance" and who recreate themselves by materializing their dreams: Davies as an artist, Flash as a "capitalist gone mad," as Davies describes him.[22] "I'm in a business," Davies said, "where I think up something in my dream world, I think up something fabulous. And in my little dream world I put it down on paper, or tape, and I play it for people who are outside that world, and they judge it by the world that they live in."[23] If Davies's dreams motivate creation, Flash's motivate destruction. In "Demolition," Flash destroys a part of old England to manufacture "identical boxes" and "to treble the profits."

Davies manipulates the reader's sympathies for Flash through contrast, humor, and confession, presenting Flash as a lovable villain, victimized by his own dreams. Compared to the other characters in the musical, Flash is an enthralling and dynamic character, brash and fun to watch. He appears onstage and on the cover of *Preservation Act 2* on a neon sign with a goofy, fishlike grin, under a huge hat (courtesy of music-hall comedian Roy Hudd), and dressed with maroon bow tie, polka-dot shirt, and a multi-colored blazer of thick and thin bars and smaller circles in larger ones. The costume, which takes to an extreme the "satin strides and two-tone daisy roots" of "Sitting in My Hotel," was adapted from music-hall legend Max Miller, "one of my idols from music-hall days," said Davies, "a rebellious comedian" who "kept his audience in touch with reality."[24] Flash thus appears more comic than threatening, a tone Davies sustains with his protagonist's introduction in "Here Comes Flash" and reinforced by the Tramp's immediate response in "Sitting in the Midday Sun."

Although decadent and corrupt, Flash is full of life, unlike the leader of the opposition, the self-righteous Mr. Black. The contrast is sharply drawn in the sequencing of songs early in *Act 2*. Flash reveals his obsession with wealth in the pulsating and passionate "Money Talks," an orgiastic tribute to Mammon and its power, which reveals at least some self-awareness: "money talks you out of your self respect." Black counters inadequately, especially for the rock-and-roll fan, with the dogmatic but stiff "Shepherds of the Nation," in which, among other things, he pledges in a Salvation Army-like melody to "put all the pervs in jail"—Davies's humor salvages the over four-minute track. The song establishes Black as a cliché of western culture, the insincere leader who resurfaces periodically avowing to restore traditional values, very similar to the moralistic Spiro Agnew, who resigned the American vice presidency in disgrace a month before the release of *Act 1*. Flash reclaims center stage with "Scum of the Earth," in part a dirge in which he hilariously pleas for pity and attempts to justify his wickedness by alluding to Shylock's soliloquy in Shakespeare's *Merchant of Venice* ("Hath not a Jew eyes?"), concluding with an appeal to his victims' common humanness and understanding, for "deep down we're still the same as one another." Whatever his flaws, Flash and his strong life impulse and boldness win the audience's sympathy.

Furthermore, while Black leads an army and obviously has close advisors, he is depicted in isolation, in his attic for instance, while Flash is generally surrounded by his cronies and floosies, especially Belle, his lover. Unlike Black, Flash, Davies suggests, is capable of friendship and love. In "Mirror of Love," the twice-released and twice-failed single from *Act 2*, Belle expresses her love for Flash, "even though you treat me bad." Right out of the music hall, "Mirror of Love" lumbers along to Gosling's jangling electric keyboards, Dave's trembling mandolin, and John Beecham's plodding tuba, and on the alternate version, the second single, Alan Holmes's soaring clarinet. Importantly, despite her complaints and as the mirror image indicates, Belle feels Flash's love for her, which he later proclaims in "Nothing Lasts Forever."

Of course, to remain lovable, the villain must confess. After, for Flash, a terrifying and, for the audience, funny dream, Flash apologizes for "my cruelty, my ego, and conceit" and for becoming "everything that I once despised." Moreover, his nightmare reveals his darkest fear, which explains his hunger for control and flamboyance: "I had no identity or individuality / No thoughts of my own, no mind or personality. / I was just a no one, a total nonentity." As Black assumes power, Flash's nightmare comes true as, *en masse*, Black and his mad scientist transform individuals into "artificial people," who all join hands and proclaim their supposed happiness in the finale, "Salvation Road."

Flash's fear is, of course, Ray's. Davies is obsessed with his own authenticity and individuality, and fears losing himself and his imagination in a business that thrives on recycling. He has subverted his own success by refusing to follow pop trends and refusing to conform to his audience's or record companies' expectations, even when not inconsistent with his and the Kinks' creativity. "If something good happens," Dave said, "Ray will construct a situation to make it go wrong. Maybe he feels safer when things are uncomfortable than when they are comfortable."[25] Dave is right. Ray feels most alive, most challenged, when uncomfortable and restless, a condition, as Dave indicates, he frequently imposes on himself. As Ray suggests in *Arthur*, the comfort of slippers, rocking chairs, and fireplaces render the imagination mordant and thus destroy the artist. On the very fist page of *X-Ray*, his septuagenarian self, like Flash, has fallen to his greatest fear: "The only individualism in me lurks somewhere so deep inside my desolate soul that it may never emerge to my human exterior, which was bred with the sole purpose to conform." Above all, *Preservation* is about Davies's self-preservation and autonomy, the fear of losing he expresses through Flash but the confidence of retaining through the Tramp, the quintessential outsider for Davies.

Konk Records

"I thought it would be a great idea to have a little label so we could put out 5,000 records of a new band," said Ray. "In the seventies you had to be a megastar to get a record deal. I thought we could get these little bands, almost like having a football team. That's what I really intended it to be."[26] As well intentioned as he may have been, however, Davies was too consumed by his musicals to nurture and develop the artists as he had hoped.

Conceived as early as 1968, Konk released only a handful of albums, none of which charted. Davies produced Konk's first release, Claire Hamill's *Stage Door Johnnies* in September 1974, but it soon became apparent that he could not follow through on the production of other albums. He turned Andy Desmond's *Living on a Shoestring* over to Dave and Gosling, who had developed a solid working relationship. The pair recorded a number of tracks at the time for what could have evolved into a Dave Davies solo album. "It was far superior to stuff we were doing with the Kinks on *Preservation*," claims Gosling.[27] The tracks, however, went unreleased.

Ray's inaccessibility led to a bitter dispute with Tom Robinson of Café Society. Robinson, who would have some success as a solo artist with "2-4-6-8 Motorway" and "Sing If You're Glad to Be Gay," grew weary of Davies's continual delays. In two and a half years with Konk, Café Society released just one album. In a scenario all too familiar to anyone who has dealt with Davies, Robinson explained, "You could never get anything defined. It was always, 'Oh well, we'll go into the studios soon. We'll do it one day next week.' And come Thursday you'd call up and say, 'Wasn't it going to be this week?' 'Oh no, the Kinks are in America this week.' It was really frustrating."[28] In time, Robinson began performing "Tired of Waiting for You" with a dedication to his would-be mentor. One evening while on stage in London's Nashville Rooms in December 1976, shortly after he had left Café Society, Robinson exchanged verbal jibes with Davies, who apparently was taunting his former protégé from the audience.

A year later, the Kinks released Davies's blistering rock-and-roll assault on Robinson in "Prince of the Punks," the B-side of "Father Christmas."

Unnamed in the lyrics, Robinson was the obvious target as Davies alludes to his "playing folk in a country bar" and his shift to punk to "make a little more bread," while exposing him as a middle-class "phony" in working-class guise. The two sides of the uncharted Christmas greeting combine to blast both the authenticity of the holiday season and, whether Robinson or not, meretricious pop artists.

For his part, Robinson expressed at least some gratitude toward Davies: "What Ray did do was to let us support the Kinks a couple of times. I learned everything I know about how to deal with the audience just from watching Ray Davies from the side of the stage."[29]

Starmaker

Sometime in 1972, Granada Television, who was to produce *Arthur*, asked Davies to create a musical play. While the project was never far from his mind, Davies did not conceive of, for him, a satisfying concept until April 1974, when he lay sick with the flu in a Chicago hotel room and watched the glamorous denizens of American soap operas. Davies decided to deepen the theme of "Unreal Reality" from *Everybody's in Show-Biz* and focus on Starmaker, who "can turn the most ordinary man in the world into a star," and who, more importantly, is the alter ego of Norman.

Conceived, written, and starring Ray Davies, *Starmaker* premiered on British television on September 4, 1974 to overwhelmingly negative reviews—the *NME* used descriptives like "glib, shallow and . . . superficial."[30] "I knew it was going to be bad," said Ray, who left the film set discouraged. "We always get resentment from [theatrical and film] people because we're a rock band . . . infringing on their territory."[31] If reviewers and Ray were dissatisfied, so too were the other Kinks, who played the music from the side of the stage and were seldom visible except at the very end. Dave was especially irate: "We were treated worse than a house band. The sound was atrocious, there was not one camera line-up for the band during the whole broadcast, and I had to sit and play stuck in the corner with the others while Ray pranced around the studio like a ponce, as if lost in a megalomaniacal trance . . . I felt really hurt."[32]

Dave told his brother not to make further plans for the band beyond the upcoming *Preservation* tour. Ray, however, not only smoothed over differences but also convinced Dave to develop *Starmaker* into the next Kinks album and stage musical.

Soap Opera

After the *Preservation* tour, Davies entered the studio in January 1975 to mix the late summer/early fall tapes of *(The Kinks Present) A Soap Opera*. Released in the spring, *Soap Opera*, Davies said, is "about mental illness,"[33] although it seems to be more about escape and the willful use of fantasy. *Soap Opera* tells the story of Norman, a frustrated office worker, who relieves the tedium of his job and life by assuming more glamorous identities, previously a painter, astronaut, athlete, and now a rock star. In *Soap Opera*, his wife Andrea reaches the breaking point and forces him to confront himself, which, as "(A) Face in the Crowd" suggests, will be as painful for Norman as it has been and continues to be for Davies.

As with *Preservation*, the plot serves several interrelated, by now familiar themes of Davies, principally the dehumanizing effects of technological culture. Life and individuality have been lost in "computerized trivia" and the inspiration of nature negated by neon signs, "slabs of concrete," "artificial moonlight," and "simulated sunshine," which is especially devastating to Davies who frequently finds inspiration in the sun. "Underneath the Neon Sign" voices his Romantic nightmare. Throughout *Soap Opera*, significantly, individuals are referred to in a collective: "ordinary people," "commuters," "mechanical minds," "robots," "bores," and "the crowd." The result is a world where the imaginative, like Norman who is made to "feel like a mole in the ground" and "part of the machinery," find escape in fantasy while others turn to alcohol in two drinking songs, "When Work Is Over" and "Have Another Drink."

The obliteration of the individual and individual authenticity is suggested by the album's artwork, the cover of which parodies God's creation of man from Michelangelo's vault of the Sistine Chapel. On *Soap Opera*'s cover, the Starmaker's index finger, featuring a large, space-age ring, extends from a wrist with gold bracelets and a glimmering, bright sleeve to touch the finger of Norman, reaching from a cufflinked, lavender shirt, and a pin-striped suit. Instead of an omnipotent, fiercely determined God inspiring his innocent and naked subject, the new creation myth features a glitzy image maker infusing a well-dressed bureaucrat with illusion, the absurdity of which is signaled by three ducks flying under the hands, hardly Michelangelo's angels surrounding God. The parody suggests the decadent, unsatisfying life Emerson saw in his "Divinity School Address": "Life is comic or pitiful, as soon as the high ends of being fade out of sight, and man becomes nearsighted, and can only attend to what addresses the senses."[34] *Soap Opera*, like much of Davies's work, is about the appropriation of raw power and integrity by those who profit from technology. "My ongoing theme," Davies said in 1993, "is about control of the masses by the dictatorship of the media."[35]

In addition to a less colorful and smaller reproduction of the front cover in the left corner of the gatefold, Joe Petagno provides nine other illustrations, none more than three inches each, set in between the lyrics of the songs. The thirteen portraits or human figures in the illustrations are all faceless. In another illustration, a hand emerges from what appears a pint of stout and, in another, shepherd's pie steams from a woman's trunkless

182

waist, which serves as a container. The implication is clear. The culture has reduced the individual to a function: a commuter, consumer, cook, bureaucrat, and performer. Petagno's artwork brilliantly reflects *Soap Opera*'s dual concerns of overpowering technologies and individual fragmentation.

As with the Tramp and Flash, Davies identifies with Norman, made especially obvious with the stage production. "It was me onstage, pretending to be a man called Norman, who was pretending to be me," Davies said.[36] On stage, near the end, Norman insists that he is indeed Ray Davies of the Kinks. The backup singers strip him and in psychedelic tights he and the band perform a few Kinks hits like "Sunny Afternoon," "Dedicated Follower of Fashion," and "Well Respected Man." However, the ending is not quite so happy. But Norman does take the necessary first step to an authentic life with the self-questioning of the penultimate song, "(A) Face in the Crowd," which, like "Sitting in My Hotel," is meditative, self-doubting, and psychologically autobiographical. "I've got to stop acting like a clown," Davies sings to Gosling's moving piano. "I don't want to lie to myself anymore . . . can you tell me who I really am?" Davies has, of course, struggled for a long time with these issues: "It's very difficult if you've been brought up to be factory fodder to then find that people are interested in what you have to say. Always, what am I? Who am I?"[37]

Davies, as he did in "Where Are They Now?" and "One of the Survivors," suggests that authenticity can be found in rock music. In "You Can't Stop the Music," which, interestingly, combines in tempo and theme those two *Preservation* songs, Davies drinks a toast to the rock stars of the past for their inspiration. The star imagery may have weakened with the years, he sings, but not the power of the music, which the song separates from its promotion and image makers. *Soap Opera* may not end with happiness, but it does end with hope.

Schoolboys in Disgrace

With *Schoolboys in Disgrace*, the Kinks produced their last rock musical and their last album of new material with RCA. While very much a musical onstage, the album, their best selling with RCA, marked a shift in direction. There was no heavily plotted narrative, no stage directions or announcements, and the role of the brass section was minimized. Dave's enthusiasm for the Kinks returned with what he called the "fabulous little album,"[38] a "rock-oriented record, a bit gutsier, going back to where I thought the Kinks should be musically—guitar-based tracks, strong riffing and intelligent but funny lyrics."[39] While the liner notes inform us that the album is about the early days of Flash, the hero's name does not appear in any of the songs. Although the onstage production formed a narrative, the album is organized around a concept, closer to *Muswell*

Hillbillies than either of the *Preservation* albums or *Soap Opera*. Only the first three songs on the original side B ("I'm in Disgrace," "Headmaster," "The Hard Way") advance a plot, one based on Dave's teenage love affair and resulting humiliation and expulsion. Along with Dave, the other Kinks were just as pleased. "It was a lot more rock and roll," said Dalton, "but it was a bit silly dressing up in those bloody clothes all the time"— referring to the performances.[40] Of the ten Kinks albums on which he worked, Gosling ranks *Schoolboys* only behind *Muswell Hillbillies* and *Percy*.[41] Rumors have persisted that the Kinks had recorded some thirty tracks for a possible double *Schoolboys*, but nothing has been confirmed and no bonus tracks were released on the 1998 CD reissue.

For *Schoolboys'* musical inspiration, Davies turned to the sounds of his youth. "Jack the Idiot Dunce" is a straight-ahead rock-and-roll novelty song with driving bass and Jerry Lee Lewis piano while "The First Time We Fall in Love" draws from doo-wop and "The Last Assembly" from 1950s sentimental balladry and school choirs. Dave even refers back to "You Really Got Me" with the power chords of "I'm in Disgrace" and, especially, "The Hard Way," which also includes Dave's prototype soaring solos.

The masterpiece of the album, however, is the coolly reflective "No More Looking Back," a song of great emotional depth in which the singer tries to convince himself to press on and forget an old love. Most likely, the song was inspired by the parental breakup of Dave's relationship with Sue Sheehan. Dave said the "unresolved feelings I had for her, and my inability to express them to her, would haunt me for many years to come."[42] For the singer of "No More Looking Back," a simple walk down the street triggers emotional trauma as images and sounds evoke her memory and visions of her beside him. But just as the image fades he sees a book that she read or hears a song she sang—Dave recalls Sue's singing at a dance— and the torment begins again, with Ray's vocals conveying the shifting moods of pain, anxiety, desperation, and perseverance. "No more looking back," he sings. "Got to be hard."

The Kinks set the somber mood and underlying ache of the song in the lengthy intro. Gosling plays a slight, murky melody on the electric keyboards to Avory's steadily ticking beat and Dalton's occasionally bubbling bass. At the half-minute mark, Dave plays a tenacious and piercing riff, high in the mix, followed by a quick but stinging guitar solo. At 0:54, Ray's controlled but anxious vocals enter, first escalating in anxiety at 1:24 ("is it something . . ."), then more so at 1:47 ("but lately . . ."), and even more so at 2:02 ("and just when . . .") before subsiding at 2:25 when the song repeats the pattern and closes at 4:27. The arrangement with its nearly two-and-a-half minutes of rising tension conveys the dread of resurfacing memories, brought on in part by the desperate need, unachieved, of the singer to come to peace with his past. A towering song,

"No More Looking Back" adds weight to the more glib moments of the album like "Jack the Idiot Dunce" and the somewhat trite and obvious insights of "Education." In an interesting observation, Uli Twelker notes the similarities of "No More Looking Back" to a Pete Townshend composition and imagines Roger Daltry's vocals and Townshend's slashing windmill chords.[43] While the influence is almost certainly indirect, Davies did reclaim "I Can't Explain" (borrowed from "You Really Got Me") with "Starmaker," the opening track of *Soap Opera*.

With the last performance of *Schoolboys* in Hamburg, West Germany, on March 31, 1976, the Kinks performed their final musical. While the musicals did not sell as many albums as RCA and Ray may have hoped, they reveal an energetic and resourceful artist, challenging himself, his band, and his audience. The Kinks Kult, particularly in America, remained unwavering during the RCA years, but the larger rock audience generally ignored the musicals, unfairly associating them with conventional theater while, paradoxically, finding Davies too idiosyncratic. (The Who's *Tommy* had the advantage of being, arguably, the first rock opera and of being loud, brash, and extravagant.) From time to time Davies's musicals are restaged in small productions. The Boston Rock Opera presented first a modest production of *Preservation Act 2* in 1993 and then a full-scale production of *Preservation* in 1998, with some advisement from Davies himself and to very positive reviews in the *Boston Globe* and the *Boston Herald*.

The Hamburg performance is significant too in that it marks the last stage appearance of John Dalton as a Kink. Tired of the exhausting pace, the travel, the low pay, and anxious to spend more time with his wife and three young children, Dalton decided to stay on only through the completion of the new album. He then bought a café with a friend and returned to construction, rebuilding the bar at Konk and remodeling part of Ray's house. Two years removed from the Kinks, he returned part time to music to form a local band and has played consistently since, in recent years performing Kinks songs with the Kast-Off Kinks with Gosling, Avory, and Dave Clarke (not of the Five), sometimes performing to raise money for the cure of leukemia, which claimed one of his sons.

Arista

Davies fulfilled the contract with RCA when he delivered the masters for a compilation, *The Kinks Greatest—Celluloid Heroes*. Citing the Trades Descriptions Act, Davies said he could not include *Hits* in the title since the Kinks had no hits with RCA—only "Supersonic Rocketship" charted in the UK at #16 and that was left off the album as were any selections from *Schoolboys*, their highest charting and best-selling RCA album. *The Kinks Greatest* sold poorly, reaching only #144 in the US and holding the charts for a mere five weeks. RCA may have been disappointed with the sales of the Kinks, but it would recover shortly with the death of Elvis in 1977 and ever-increasing sales from his back catalog.

In April 1976, Davies began negotiations with Clive Davis, who had founded Arista Records in the fall of 1974. Davis, a longtime Kinks fan, had tried to sign the Kinks to Columbia in 1966 when the band was renegotiating with Warner/Reprise and then again in 1971 when he lost out to RCA. This time, with little competition, Davis signed the Kinks to a ten-year deal. "I liked the idea of going with someone who had been thrown out of a major corporation," said Ray, referring to Davis's recent ouster from CBS Records.[44] Davis did not, however, grant Ray the artistic freedom that RCA had. He insisted on the right to suggest the band's artistic direction, to monitor recordings, and, if necessary, to reject submitted recordings. In one of his first actions after the signing, Davis gave Ray three songs to consider covering, which Davies ignored. Clearly, Arista was not expecting musicals or concept albums. The relationship with Davis would lead to the Kinks' greatest commercial success in America.

At about the same time, Ray rented an apartment on Manhattan's upper West Side, just down the street from John and Yoko's residence in the Dakota—once again, Davies was more diminutive than his chief English competitors. With more time spent in New York away from his still primarily home in north London, the Kinks sound became more aggressive, louder, and more urban and less idiosyncratic.

10

JUKE BOX MUSIC
Alienation and love

While Ray Davies spent most of 1976 writing and recording the Kinks' Arista debut, the British punk scene was gaining momentum and fast becoming rock's new movement. In July, the Kinks recorded backing tracks for "Brother" and "Juke Box Music" as the Ramones staged their legendary July 4 concert at London's Roundhouse with members of the Sex Pistols, Clash, and the Damned in attendance. In September, the Kinks recorded "Full Moon" and "Life Goes On" just as the 100 Club Punk Festival featured the Buzzcocks, Siouxsie and the Banshees, and the Sex Pistols, with then fan Sid Vicious in the middle of a brawl which led to a ban of punk from the club. In early December as Davies made a last minute decision to include "Mr. Big Man" on *Sleepwalker*, the drunken Sex Pistols gave their infamously provocative and profane interview on Bill Grundy's *Today* show, which led to outraged headlines throughout England, cancellations of Sex Pistols performances, and Grundy's two-week suspension.

While the punks attacked disco, the progressive rock of Yes and Genesis, and the dinosaur rock of the Beatles and Stones, they respected the Kinks, who might have seemed a likely target. The Kinks, still visible, had not had chart-topping success in the UK for a while and were considered something of an oldies band with frequent repackagings of 1960s hits for sale. Perhaps it was the Kinks' insistence on performing and releasing new material that safeguarded them from the punks; perhaps it was their working-class origins and what Glen Matlock of the Sex Pistols referred to as the "hammer and tongs" sound of early hits like "You Really Got Me" and "All Day and All of the Night," which influenced, the bassist said, "the Pistols' construction of songs";[1] or perhaps it was the band's off- and onstage battles—although the Kinks didn't spit at audiences they did spit at each other, and worse. Certainly, there was some kinship between the Kinks and the punks, which led to the cover of Davies's songs by hybrid punk acts. In 1976, the Buzzcocks intended to cover a Kinks song in their debut performance, but the management apparently pulled the plug on them before they got to it.[2] More successfully, in August 1978, the Jam

scored a #25 hit with "David Watts," and, in February 1979, Chrissie
Hynde and the Pretenders landed the first of their dozen UK top-forty
hits with "Stop Your Sobbing" and then, in November 1981, a #7 with
"I Go to Sleep." In 1978, metal rockers Van Halen scored a top-forty
American hit with "You Really Got Me," which jump-started their career.

However, major success would elude the Kinks in the UK, but not in
America, where the Kinks would stage a major comeback under the guid-
ance of Elliot Abbott, a Chicagoan, who Dave described as "positive,
businesslike, with a pleasant laid-back manner,"[3] and, especially, Clive
Davis, who has a reputation for trusting his artists and his own instinct,
which he calls "the key to the music business." Davis has been described
as "the kind of executive who listens to demos with his eyes closed and
knows a hit when he hears one"[4]—maybe not always. He disagreed with
Ray's choice of "Come Dancing" as the single from *State of Confusion*, which
he thought "a ditty" and too slight to be the 1983 smash hit it became
(#6 in the US, #12 in the UK).[5] However, unlike the executives Davies
had written about in "Moneygoround," the Arista president could not
be accused of profiting off a song that he never heard—at least a Kinks
song.

Figure 10.1 The Kinks began the Arista years with a lineup of: (L–R) Ray,
Dalton, Dave, Gosling, and Avory

Sleepwalker

As Davies rethought and reworked the Kinks' very important Arista debut, its planned release for the 1976 Christmas rush and simultaneous tour were postponed until after the new year. Reports hold that Davies wrote some thirty songs for *Sleepwalker* with the Kinks recording twenty of them before settling on the nine for the album. From time to time, Clive Davis would listen to the results and make suggestions. He recommended, for instance, that strings be added to "Brother" to give it a grand, sweeping effect like "Bridge over Troubled Water," which Davis had worked on. The song was sure to be a major crossover hit, he told Ray. Davies complied with the executive's urging and went through great care to get the sound right, only to be disappointed that Arista never released "Brother" as a single. Davis, however, was savvy enough not to impose too much on the sensitive and temperamental head Kink.

The sessions for *Sleepwalker* were not completed until just before Christmas with Davies's completing the final mixing not until late January, with the album rushed out for a February 12 release. It was not a fortuitous time, as the Kinks were two weeks into a three-week tour of the US. Audiences therefore heard the new songs for the first time in concert with no record available for immediate purchase. Avory said it was a typical situation resulting from Ray's perfectionism: "We usually had a new album that maybe only came out the day that we toured and it usually took six weeks to come out and we'd have a six-week tour promoting something they couldn't get. . . . Timing was never very good with the Kinks."[6]

Sleepwalker, however, accomplished everything Arista and the Kinks wanted. It re-established them as a five-piece unit, although they would continue to tour with brass and backing vocalists, and it re-established the Kinks as a vital and more mainstream rock act again, not as an idiosyncratic rock-theatre troupe and not withstanding the punk movement or the New Wave movement, the friendlier term preferred by labels and industry marketers. *Sleepwalker* was greeted by mixed reviews in the UK, but generally outstanding reviews in the US. Billy Altman's review in *Rolling Stone* was typical: "the first Kinks album since *Lola* that's unencumbered by either a horn section or female vocal chorus . . . is a clear-cut triumph both for Davies and the band . . . The Kinks' playing on *Sleepwalker* is easily their most powerful since *Lola*. Dave Davies' aggressive guitar work is pushed into the forefront, and the intensity of his lead work seems to rouse the entire group."[7] With massive promotion by Arista, the album reached #21 on the US charts, the highest showing for a Kinks album since *Greatest Hits* peaked over ten years earlier in 1966.

The Kinks were back and a remarkable run with Arista was underway. Over the next eight years, Ray followed Davis's advice to de-emphasize the

189

Figure 10.2 Ray on stage at the Veteran's Memorial Auditorium, Columbus, Ohio, September 1981. Courtesy of Marianne Spellman

concept album—although each album would feature tracks with inter-locking themes—and return to focusing on the individual song as a complete entity unto itself. The result was that of the Kinks' seven Arista albums, between 1976 and 1985, six charted in the top-forty with four of those in the top-fifteen: *Sleepwalker* (1977, #21), *Misfits* (1978, #40), *Low Budget* (1979, #11), *One for the Road* (1980, #14), *Give the People What They Want* (1981, #15), *State of Confusion* (1983, #12), and *Word of Mouth* (1984, #57). In 1986, Arista released *Come Dancing with The Kinks*, a compilation, which peaked at #159 and, in 1985, Ray's soundtrack to his film *Return to Waterloo*, which did not chart.

The Kinks became a highly successful touring band, headlining America's huge arenas. Especially gratifying were two headlining dates at Madison Square Garden in October 1981 and December 1984. The Kinks had played the Felt Forum, located directly underneath the main arena and now called the Theater at Madison Square Garden, where Elton John had once performed simultaneously above them. A promoter had told Davies that the Kinks would never be popular enough to headline the main arena. On the West Coast, the Kinks headlined the Los Angeles Forum on three occasions, October 1980, August 1981, and May 1983. By contrast, in 1969, the Kinks played the Whiskey A Go Go in Hollywood with Mick Jagger's dropping by while the Stones were in town for two shows at the Forum.

Departures and additions

With John Dalton's tenure completed at what was thought the conclusion of the *Sleepwalker* sessions, the Kinks recruited Andy Pyle, one of apparently two bass players whose audition consisted of session work for the band. Pyle may have had an advantage in that he knew John Gosling from earlier days, which would have influenced Ray who preferred at least somewhat familiar musicians to those completely unknown. Pyle, the first veteran musician added to the Kinks lineup, had played in Blodwyn Pig, Savoy Brown, and Alvin Lee & Company. His Kink debut was on "Mr. Big Man," the final track recorded on *Sleepwalker*.

Pyle joined the Kinks with great enthusiasm, but his tenure would be short, a mere thirteen months. He found intolerable the mood swings of Davies, the conflicting demands of the brothers ("never really saw eye to eye on anything"), the onstage fights ("almost expected of us"), and the low pay: "I got twice as much from Savoy Brown five or six years before!"[8] In the studio he was confused by Avory and Gosling, both glum and silent, but afterwards in the pub, fun and lively. In time, they told the bassist, he would understand.

The time came on tour when he experienced a classic Ray Davies assault: "I can remember this real tirade in the dressing-room in Chicago and at first I thought the bloke was joking. I'd seen him do this before with other people, airline pilots and people like that. For no reason at all he'd pick on me and lay into me in not a very nice way. I didn't think he could be serious because I hadn't done anything. . . . And we didn't speak to each other for another fortnight."[9] Pyle also recalled an incident backstage at the

Santa Monica Civic Center, where after Dave spat upon everyone in the band Gosling refused to perform an encore. Ray threatened the keyboardist to take the stage, but Gosling held firm. Davies, the former schoolboy boxer, flattened the Baptist and returned to the stage all smiles to play the keyboards himself.

Pyle did enjoy some of his time on stage with the Kinks, but it would not seem to last long: "There is a certain wonderful feeling when you're onstage and 20,000 people are singing along with you. . . . until you get another kick in the shins!"[10] Pyle's most enjoyable moments with the Kinks came after the shows or sessions when he, Avory, and Gosling would jam with local bands. Rarely would Dave join and only once Ray. During a break from some disappointing *Misfits* sessions, Ray ordered the equipment into a van for a trip to John Dalton's bar, where the Kinks jammed through some standard rock-and-roll numbers. "He never liked us playing with other people," recalls Gosling. "He made that quite clear, but we still did it, particularly in America. . . . We had some fun, but it was never when the two brothers were together."[11] Pyle gave Ray notice during the *Misfit* sessions and played his final concerts as a Kink with the Christmas shows at the Rainbow Theatre in north London. The bassist continued with session work, recorded a solo album, and toured with former Thin Lizzy guitarist Gary Moore and then with Wishbone Ash.

More significant to the band, however, was Gosling's decision to leave during the *Misfits* sessions. By that point, he says, "My involvement had reached an all time low and my motivation had been exhausted so I was desperate to try something new, preferably using some of my own material."[12] The studio was especially draining: "We did so many performances of each song in the studio that we rarely had any energy left to put anything new in."[13] When Ray called for take 64 of "Get Up," the Baptist had had enough. "I left the studio and never went back! It was an unpleasant end to such a long standing relationship but I don't have any regrets."[14] The next day, after his departure, both he and Pyle received notices that their services were no longer needed.

No band member's departure, with the possible exception of Quaife, affected the Kinks' sound and Davies's songwriting more than Gosling's. Ray came to rely on the keyboardist's skilled versatility—calling for music hall in "Mirror of Love," boogie-woogie in "Skin & Bones," a classical overtone in "Celluloid Heroes," and much more. With Gosling, Davies's resourcefulness gained added breadth. Furthermore, Gosling's even temperament and fun-loving personality helped balance the tension as much as possible, especially on the road, where he would console Dalton and Avory.

In their final days with the Kinks, Gosling and Pyle had begun writing together, forming United with Ron Berg, formerly of Blodwyn Pig, and guitarist Dennis Stratton, who later joined Iron Maiden. United would be

192

ill-fated, however. They recorded an album for Phonogram, who insisted the band change its name to Network, but with punk or New Wave in full swing and the label sold to Polydor, the album went unreleased. Opting for a quieter life like Dalton before him, Gosling decided to manage a music store in Berkhamsted. In 1989, he and his son formed Rough Diamond, a local band, which featured an occasional guest appearance by Pyle. As of this writing, Gosling plays in the Kast-Off Kinks and teaches music in several Berkhamsted schools.

While session players completed the bass parts on *Misfits*, there was talk of inviting Quaife back into the fold, but an invitation was never extended. Instead, Pyle's permanent replacement was Jim Rodford, another veteran who met the Kinks first in late 1964 as a member of the Mike Cotton Sound who toured briefly with the Kinks, and then again in 1972 and 1973, when his band Argent opened occasional dates for the Kinks. Rodford remained officially a Kink until 1999, when his retainer was not renewed. He tours today with his cousin Rod Argent and Colin Blunstone in the Zombies.

Gosling's first replacement was Gordon Edwards, who had played with the Pretty Things in the 1970s and then the disbanded Sunshine. Edwards played only a year with the Kinks, mostly on tour, and was dismissed when he failed to show for the *Low Budget* sessions. Ian Gibbons took over as keyboardist from 1979 until 1989 and then again from 1993 to 1995. The years in between saw Mark Haley on keyboards, who toured and did limited studio work, but contributed the synthesizer riff on "Down All the Days (Till 1992)"—on *Phobia*, Davies played all keyboards. Gibbons, however, did leave his mark on the 1980s Kinks. While he tended to be more bluesy and hard rocking than Gosling, he added a more contemporary sound to the Kinks through synthesizers. Of course, with everyone under Davies's firm hand, it is difficult to measure the contributions of any of the other Kinks, excepting Dave, since Ray directs all music and constantly experiments with sounds and styles, reinventing the Kinks sometimes album to album. As Gibbons says, "There were so many different styles of music that encompassed their career before I joined them: some of which I knew about, the earlier stuff; some of which I really just learned as I went along . . . on-stage, sometimes. I mean, there'd be stuff coming out that I'd just join in on, I had no idea. . . . There'd be a basic running list of songs, but Ray would change it around. If he wasn't getting the right response from the audience, he'd just sort of scrap it and go in some other direction to get them in the palm of his hand."[15]

Through all his explorations with form and music, Davies has remained consistent with his Romantic spirit and Romantic themes, sometimes emphasizing one theme over another, deepening an inquiry here or there, or working the theme through a different perspective. Through the Arista years and beyond, Davies continued to concern himself with the fractured self, exploited and disenfranchised individuals, the corruption of institutions, and the sanitization and lifelessness of contemporary culture. More than ever, though, he seemed concerned with human alienation and problematized love, obviously in response to his broken relationships. While not rigidly focusing albums on a concept, like *Lola* or *Muswell Hillbillies*, or on a story, like the rock operas, albums would be threaded with themes and images, like somnambulism and mental breakdown in *Sleepwalker*, nonconformity and eccentricity in *Misfits*, or broken relationships in *State of Confusion* and *Other People's Lives*. But these themes and images are never overwhelming. To the casual record buyer, these are simply rock albums, collections of songs, or as Davies signals on *Sleepwalker*, "Juke Box Music."

Alienation

The concept of alienation, a dominant theme of twentieth-century art and philosophy, frames the discussion for existentialism, a protean context but one to which all twentieth-century thought responds. Through his restless wanderers and dreamers, Davies expresses a similarly existentialist vision to that of Albert Camus, who in *Le Mythe de Sisyphe* described the mid-twentieth-century individual as a "stranger" and "an irremediable exile ... deprived of memories of a lost homeland [and who] lacks the hope of a promised land to come."[16]

This condition results for many Davies's characters because of the failure of institutions. His characters no longer find logic and support in centuries-old traditions. Eugène Ionesco put it this way in "Dans les armes de la ville," "Cut off from his religious, metaphysical, and transcendental roots, man is lost; all his actions become senseless, absurd, useless."[17] Many of Davies's characters crave the certainty of earlier generations, even an implausible certainty like that of the granny in "Have a Cuppa Tea" or the illusionary certainty of the young Arthur of "Victoria."

Davies has called *Muswell Hillbillies*, with its gallery of marginalized individuals, "my own existentialist type record."[18] He also said, "There's one section of the population that doesn't seem to have a voice, that doesn't have songs speaking its mind, I'm talking about ordinary people, the ones who're not part of any movement or fashion. That's who I write for because that's me."[19] More often than not, Davies's "ordinary people" are in crisis and struggle with the symptoms of alienation—restlessness, identity crises, and paranoia. Sometimes they are defiant, but mostly they just capitulate to the contemporary world.

Frustration, restlessness, and lost identity

Sleepwalker is filled with characters who cannot sleep through the night. The singer of "Life on the Road" talks about his bloodshot eyes and holes

194

Figure 10.3 Ray at the Summit, Houston, Texas, May 1983. Courtesy of
Marianne Spellman

in his shoes from "walkin' the streets all night"; the couple in "Stormy Sky" waits for the coming dawn and morning light; and the singer of "Sleepless Night" lies awake jealously as his ex-girlfriend makes raucous love upstairs with her new boyfriend. In the title track, the singer plays the role of a vampire to avoid confronting his problems, which, he says, arise at midnight. As in "David Watts" and "Superman" (*Low Budget*), his assertion is more a power fantasy than a threat. Of course, the irony of the song is that it could be very much about its insomniac composer, who was a sleepwalker as a child. "It's about a vampire," Ray said, "but not the bloodsucking kind. It's more somebody who feeds off of people's lives rather than people's blood—somebody who feeds off of their stories. It's like a writer going around getting people to talk in their sleep and then coming out with all of the things they say in their subconscious."[20] Then, in possibly a revealing or playful statement, "I feel close to [the song]." Dave, perhaps not so coincidentally, has talked of Ray's "almost vampire-like drain and pull on my creative and emotional energy."[21]

The uncluttered production, in contrast to the lavish production of "Brother," the following track, displays Dave's dynamic electric guitar work which adds tension to the irony and humor, established through Ray's lighthearted vocal delivery, his jangling acoustic guitar, and the upbeat rhythm. Dave's performance on "Sleepwalker" is indicative of his fine ensemble playing and reveals the unbalanced mind of the protagonist through slashing chords, jabbing runs underneath and around the vocals, a flurried solo, and a soaring ending. In some ways, "Sleepwalker" is a more sophisticated arrangement of "You Really Got Me" or "All Day and All of the Night"—not necessarily better.

Throughout Davies, but especially on *Sleepwalker*, the inactivity of the night causes characters to dwell upon themselves, with little resolution, except to yearn for the distractions of day time. At first, the singer of "Full Moon," which Davies says he wrote entirely at night, tries to convince us that his despair and identity crisis are under control. After Gosling's dark piano intro, he tells us not to be alarmed by the madness in his eyes, his mumbling "like a loon," or his crawling across the floor—the actions have been brought on simply by the full moon. However, Dalton's wrenching bass line and the ethereal background vocals, a motif on *Sleepwalker*, indicate that claims of self-acceptance are thin, another disguise.

In fact, what we see in "Full Moon" is a singer in the process of mental collapse, whose voice, after the false calmness of verses one and two, escalates in intensity with verses three through five and with the progression of the night. In verse three, he blames the curse of the moon for his condition ("full moon's a-callin"); in four he longs for the day to break the curse ("I wish the day would come soon"), and even after a brief respite between verses four and five with Gosling's light piano tones and Avory's drums paused, he admits in five to not recognizing himself in the mirror. Despite

Figure 10.4 Ray in Milwaukee, June 1978. Courtesy of Marianne Spellman

the playful werewolf imagery, "Full Moon" has none of the lightness of "Sleepwalker." It is an eerie song, which in its final lines addresses the audience ("If your hands start shakin' . . ."), indicating not just the singer's deeper self-separation and disintegration, but also suggesting that his "State of Confusion" and anxiety might be common and shared by his audience.

In *L'Aveu (The Confession)*, an autobiographical account of spiritual and psychological crisis, Adam Adamov anticipates what several Davies's characters and the R.D. in *X-Ray* could have said: "I am separated. What I am separated from—I cannot name it. But I am separated."[22] Like the singer in "Full Moon" who blames "the curse" of the moon, Davies's characters cannot often explain the reasons for their alienation nor can doctors and therapists help them through the confusion. Davies treats the theme comically in "Acute Schizophrenia Paranoia Blues," "Permanent Waves" (from *Misfits*), and "Destroyer" (*Give the People What They Want*). "Permanent Waves" is a heavy thumping rocker with a singer who believes himself "finally breakin'." His doctor tells him he needs a change and recommends a new hairstyling: "put in some permanent waves . . . you'll be made, you'll get laid." Johnny Rogan has suggested that the song is Davies's riposte to punk, suggesting that punk or New Wave is no more than a different haircut.[23] But in "Permanent Waves" as maybe in punk, the new hairstyle works if only for a time, or until the rain washes out his waves and his neurosis returns. But just wait, the singer proclaims,

197

"Till I get back my permanent waves. . . . I'll be cool, I'll be smooth, I'll be laughing." For Davies, there is no permanent solution to the sense of separation and alienation from self and from community and from those traditions Ionesco cites as once sustaining. As Pyle's sturdy, thumping bass suggests in "Permanent Waves," the neurosis persists and can only be repressed temporarily, or as a singer on *Muswell Hillbillies* shouted, "There ain't no cure for acute schizophrenia paranoia disease."

"Destroyer" is a witty stadium rocker with drum roll intro, loud crashing chords and anthemic chorus ("Paranoia the destroyer") with references to "All Day and All of the Night" in its chords and lyrics ("Girl, I want you here with me") and to Lola, who spends the night with the singer who awakes feeling "kind of queer." The singer visits his doctor who seems as crazed as his patient as he animatedly confirms his "acute schizophrenia paranoia disease": "There's a man in ya, gnawin' ya, tearin' ya into two." The booming drums and crashing symbols, proof of Avory's ability to adapt to the arena circuit, and Dave's searing lead lines, along with Ray's humorous cynicism and homage to the Kinks' past create an engaging performance, one Davies said, "was simply made up on the spot while we were recording. . . . I just shouted out some chords and when I got to 'All Day' . . . I just said, 'Stop!' And because of that, there's a lot of excitement there."[24]

Of course, many of Davies's characters do know the source of their alienation. Frequently, as illustrated on *Muswell Hillbillies*, it is the Welfare State with its unfulfilled promises, nightmarish technology, and, during the Arista years, corporate privilege, so that all individuals, even executives, are subject to layoffs for the "sake of the company," as Davies sings in "Massive Reductions" (*Word of Mouth*), a synthesized rocker with Avory's fiercely pounding drums and a half-minute intro of session preparations, including Dave's repetition of "sorry," seeming to simulate a factory floor. On the same album is "Sold Me Out," a punk rant about dreams and ambitions destroyed by a pocket calculator. In *Return in Waterloo*, the song is delivered by threatening and angry punks aboard a commuter train, signaling the disenfranchisement of the young. In "Definite Maybe," powered by Dave's thunderous chords and rumbling riffs underneath the vocals, a computer glitch informs the singer that he does not exist. To resolve the error, the singer is redirected from office to office, from line to line, and "'round and 'round" with no resolution, only a "definite maybe," finding only compassion in the humorous background vocals of the chorus: "Somebody help this poor man."

In the title track of *Low Budget*, Davies gives us a self-deprecating, playful self-portrait as he works out, for him, a nightmarish predicament. One of Davies's fears is to be penniless, without the security and time for creativity that money provides him. In "Low Budget," self-referents make it clear that Davies is not only talking about himself but also mocking his preoccupation with money. The destitute singer identifies himself as once a "toff," a swanky dresser, and cigar-smoking executive like Flash (see album covers to *Acts 1* and *2*), but now he sucks polo mints and shops at Woolworth's, wearing discount clothes, even if the shoes are too small and the trousers too tight. But he is still somewhat vain about his appearance, as Ray, with the once self-proclaimed "best arse in show-biz," sings that his hair and teeth are still his own, claims Davies has made apart from the song. In a line to cause some to wince, Ray sings of his need to economize, "So don't think I'm tight if I don't buy a round ... I'm on a low budget"—many would claim he has always set himself a tight budget. Ray's explanation as he sings here, "Art takes time, time is money." Since its release, "Low Budget," powered by Dave's loudly resonating three-chord riff, has been a crowd favorite, still performed as of this writing by Ray, who seems to enjoy its self-mockery.

Resignation and defiance

In songs like "Lavender Hill" and "Oklahoma U.S.A.," Davies's characters create dream worlds into which they escape and lose themselves. During the Arista years and beyond, many of his protagonists feel the same need to dream, but often their visions fail to create a self-convincing alternative world, thus resembling more the singer of "Celluloid Heroes." Consider the protagonist of "Clichés of the World" (*State of Confusion*) and the singers of "Drift Away" (*Phobia*) and "(Wish I Could Fly Like) Superman" (*Low Budget*), in which a 9-stone or 126-pound weakling with "knobby knees" and a "pigeon chest" tries to energize his fantasy in the closing mantra: "Superman Superman wish I could fly like Superman." As a result, many characters resign themselves to sterile, conformist existences, depicted compassionately in "Little Bit of Emotion" (*Low Budget*) and scathingly in "Young Conservatives" (*State of Confusion*).

In "Predictable," the Everyman singer is entangled in a web of monotony, stuck in a non-communicative marriage and dull job with frowning co-workers, whom he attempts to escape in typical Davies fashion by dreaming of "far away places," and, typical again, longing for a past, actual or not, when life was lived with "dignity and grace." Yet through his cynicism and perhaps looking forward to the album's close with "Better Things," he hopes "things will get better" or even temporarily worse with "something better" eventually emerging. The slow, reggae-influenced rocker, with calypso-styled keyboards from Ian Gibbons, was released as a single with Julien Temple's amusing video featuring Ray in various guises from a bored housewife, to dope-smoking hippie, and a fashionable early 1980s dude—all bored, isolated, discontent, and barely functioning, repeatedly thwarted by supposedly modern improvements and technologies.

Few of Davies's characters find contentment in their resignation, but one notable exception is the complacent dreamer of "Quiet Life," a kind of video insert in *Absolute Beginners*, a feature film directed by Temple in 1986. Intended to illustrate the "weirdo" family of Colin, the film's protagonist, "Quite Life" focuses on Colin's father, played by Davies, and "the sweetest bloke you'd ever want to meet." While his shrew of a wife cavorts with the lodgers in the family's boarding house, the father performs a multitude of chores and turns a "blind eye" to the goings-on in his home, taking comfort in his superiority ("can't communicate with minds that are small"), his belief in his control through knowledge ("confidentially between these walls, I'm on top of it all"), an occasional act of passive-aggressive rebellion (accidentally siphoning off his wife's lavish dress with the vacuum), and, most importantly, moments of quiet solitude with his pipe before the television or at his desk.

The singer's mantra, "anything for a quiet life," inverts the tone but works to the same self-empowering end as the angst-ridden, working-class mantra of Arthur Seaton, who finds escape through clothes and the pub in *Saturday Night and Sunday Morning*: "Don't let the bastards grind you down," says Seaton. However, with its soft shuffle beat, cheerful melody, easeful strings, choreography, color film, and cinematic styling, "Quiet Life" is hardly kitchen sink, and while to the viewer, the father's escapism is more illusory than actual, it is self-sustaining and the father survives, which to Davies is always something to be celebrated, no matter the means—whether through a motorcycle like Johnny Thunder, a dance like Jack the Idiot Dunce (*Schoolboys*), or "an emotional plan," like the singer of "Surviving" (*Phobia*).

As in the kitchen-sink films, defiance is admirable in Davies, but it often leads to increased isolation for protagonists, who are further cut off from their communities. In "Around the Dial," the protagonist is a radio DJ who was removed for reasons unknown, but most likely because he "never followed any trends" and "was honest to the end," never yielding to "the record bums [who] tried to hack [him] up." His good ratings, "the best in town," could not protect him from corporate greed and corruption. The executive spin is that he has suffered a "minor nervous breakdown," which the singer disbelieves as he searches madly around the dial for his favorite DJ. The inspiration, Ray said, "was a guy in Buffalo who got fired for playing the records he wanted to play, because they weren't in rotation."[25]

Much maligned as a noisy generic rocker and a ploy for US air time, "Around the Dial" is, rather, a zestful and riveting rock-and-roll pastiche, powered by vibrating chords, screeching guitar licks, and emblazoned Chuck Berry riffs around Ray's anxiety-ridden vocals supported at times by Beach Boys-like harmonies. The song was a dramatic concert opener for the Kinks, and, as the opening track on *Give the People*, introduces both the "anti-media" theme, developed in songs about bloodthirsty spectators (title track), the prying news media ("Killer's Eyes"), bad television ("Pre-dictable"), and the theme of violence—social, emotional, and physical. Ray's dark humor, however, keeps *Give the People* from being whiny, didactic, or self-inflated. He explains the title of the album, "'Hey Show Biz! The Kinks giving the people what they want.' It's anti-that if any-thing. I really want to get the point across that it's not the Kinks giving the people what they want . . . that is not the intention behind the album. It's anti-media, in a sense: the lengths people will go to—see riots, see murder, snuff movies on television—to get higher ratings. That's really what it's all about."[26]

In his championing of outsiders and rebels, Davies has long been sym-pathetic of criminals, which is relatively easy given the protagonists and their situations in songs like "Did you See His Name?," "Holloway Jail," and "Once a Thief" (recorded 1982–3, released bonus track *State of Confu-sion* CD, 1999). But on *Give the People*, Davies struggles for understanding and sympathy for a murderer. He explains the origins of "Killer's Eyes," inspired by both young Turkish terrorist Mehmet Ali Agca, who shot Pope John Paul II in May 1981, and the Yorkshire Ripper, Peter Sutcliffe, who in a five-year reign of terror killed thirteen women and seriously wounded seven others, until his capture on January 2, 1981:

> The guy that shot the Pope is the one who initially inspired the song "Killer's Eyes." . . . I saw that guy's face in the paper, and it just wrote the song for me. His face. There was a quote in the story from his mother, and halfway through the song, I sort of take the role of the parent. I saw Peter Sutcliffe's parents doing an interview on TV, and they were as confused and baffled as anybody else. They just didn't know that they had this monster living with them. . . . I'd like to have known what made Peter Sutcliffe what he was.[27]

Davies adapts the perspective of an intimate—a family member or friend—who seeks to understand the rational explanation for the mur-derer, a fictional composite of Sutcliffe and Ali Agca. With conflicting feelings of sympathy, rage, and confusion, the singer considers poverty, childhood abuse, a corrupted youthful "vision" or fanatical "mission,"[28] smoldering childhood hate, even the broad "bullshit of the world," but is ultimately left, as Davies said above, "confused and baffled," a point that the sturdy but contemplative ballad dramatizes in its lilting but grinding power chords that punctuate several lines. Implicitly, the song suggests that the truth will not be found in the media, which demonstrates "so little compassion" and is "so icy cool." While writing, Davies also recalled an interview with Sonia Sutcliffe, the killer's wife: "There's this madness, this attention people want in the Sunday papers. 'Sonia's Terrible Torment'. But they didn't give a shit about Sonia Sutcliffe, she's just good copy."[29]

Problematized love

Like any pop music composer, Ray Davies has written conventional love songs focused around the usual topics: yearning for love ("You Still Want Me," the Kinks' first self-penned single), physical attraction ("You're Looking Fine"), first love ("The First Time You Fall in Love"), boy meets girl ("Something Better Beginning"), blossoming love ("I've Got That Feeling"), love's ecstasy ("Till the End of the Day"), contentedness ("Don't Ever Change"), frustration ("Tired of Waiting for You"), breakups ("Stop Your Sobbing," "It's Too Late," "Days"), and love sickness ("Just Can't Go to Sleep," "End of the Season," "No Return"). For *Kinks Kontroversy*, Davies even organized a sequence of love songs, but very few of Davies's conventional love songs are in his first rank—with "Days," if conventional, a notable exception.

By 1967, by which time Davies was husband and father, he had written the majority of his conventional love songs. But even before then Davies was interested in the underside of love with love's obsessive and neurotic claims: "You Really Got Me," "All Day and All of the Night," and "I Need You." As time went on, Davies wrote fewer and fewer traditional love songs and perhaps, more than any other pop songwriter, he wrote about unusual love relationships ("Monica," "Lola," "Out of the Wardrobe") and then, love gone wrong, a major theme for Davies during the Arista years and beyond, when he writes about bitter breakups ("All She Wrote"), divorce ("Property"), and materialistic former lovers ("Bernadette," "Add It Up" with "Gucci Gucci, Cartier Cartier" background vocals by Chrissie Hynde). Most of these songs have their inspiration in Ray's three divorces and breakup with Hynde. For sure, even in his earliest days, Davies has written much more effectively about problematized love and lovers than conventional love.

However, while details in his songs may not correspond to actual details in his relationships and breakups, the emotional qualities in the songs provide insights into Davies's struggles. Thus, his songs of problematized love are more emotionally than factually autobiographical, and even then we cannot underestimate the imagination of the artist, especially one who favors ambiguity and personal concealment like Davies, who enjoys teasing his audience with contradictions. In the liner notes to *Other People's Lives*, for instance, he writes, "If on this CD I've found myself accidentally drawing from my own personal life, I hope I am accomplished enough by now to conceal some things so that I can still have some privacy." And, shortly after, with pure Davies ambiguity, he concludes the notes: "I certainly feel that I have lived every line along side my various protagonists but before any one jumps to any conclusions here, I would like to state categorically that even though I am the singer songwriter, the *rest* is about other people" (italics mine). It is difficult to determine what he says here about the autobiographical nature of the songs and what specifically he means by the *rest*. To what exactly does the *rest* refer?

Divorce and estrangement #1

Davies's marriage of eight-and-a-half years to Rasa Didzpetris ended in June 1973 when Rasa left with their two daughters. The period immediately following was agonizing for Davies, leading to his collapse after the infamous White City performance in July and a failed appeal to Rasa for reconsideration through his brother Dave and sister Joyce. Ray made a less than desperate appeal in the thinly veiled "Sweet Lady Genevieve," and only wrote directly about the emotional impact of the breakup over twenty years later in "To the Bone."

"Art Lover," one of Davies's most moving songs of the 1980s, draws its emotional depth from his experience as an estranged father. Without being able to tour America in the late 1960s, Ray spent much time at home with his two daughters Louisa and Victoria. After the divorce, he did not see them for several years, absent for most of their adolescence and young teen years—although two years after "Art Lover's" release on *Give the People* eighteen-year-old Louisa sang backing vocals on several tracks on *Word of Mouth* and *Return to Waterloo*. In "Art Lover," an estranged father jogs in the park on Sundays to "look at all the little girls"—*jogging* one of the self-referents Davies inserts from time to time, as in "Autumn Almanac," to tease his audience into thinking that the song may, in part, be about him. The song, as the second verse makes clear, is not about "a flasher in a raincoat," but an estranged father who finds Sunday afternoons in the park to be therapeutic, "something special . . . like another world," a green world of vegetation, beauty, hope, and art, which is how he views the young girls: "Pretty little legs, I want to draw them, / Like a Degas ballerina . . . I'm an art lover," he sings.

"Art Lover" may be "a rough song for parents," as manager Elliot Abbott said,[30] and there is an underlying melancholy in Ray's soft, breathy vocals and a sad edge in the electric guitar lines, but it is not sentimental or overly bleak. The riff from what sounds like a xylophone, probably off a keyboard, establishes a warm tone while the *oohs* of the background vocals express sympathy, and the singer leaves song and park refreshed to cope with another week. Despite Davies's suggestion that "there's a double edge" since the art lover, like himself, is "a little bit of a pervert because I do love looking at beautiful bodies," there is no ambiguity in the song as the listener detects the singer's situation by the opening of verse two.[31] However, "It's a sad song," as Davies said, and one that resonates with him: "And I'd love it to be a single. I wouldn't care if it bombed and died a death because I believe in that song so much."[32]

Figure 10.5 Ray during the Arista years.

Davies illustrated the importance of "Art Lover" to him at the US Festival in San Bernardino, California, on September 4, 1982, before a crowd of over 200,000. The Kinks, scheduled to perform at 6:20 p.m., delayed until the sun sat low enough in the sky for a dramatic rendition of "Waterloo Sunset." Promoter Bill Graham, who prided himself on efficient concerts, ranted backstage, noting the discomfort of the fans who had endured heat of 100° and threatening to turn over Abbott's Mercedes if the Kinks did not take the stage. Finally, forty minutes late, Ray led the Kinks to the stage. All expected a big bang of an opener, "Around the Dial" most likely. "But not us," says Avory. "*Ding, Ding, Ding*—'Art Lover!' No one else could get away with that, only the Kinks. Because a lot of people like to start off with something dynamic, that 'here-we-are' sort of thing, but not us, no. . . . But what a funny song to pick. . . . Brilliant!"[33]

Divorce #2

Davies's marriage to Yvonne Gunner, a school teacher, ended after seven years in 1981 with Ray's adulterous relationship with Chrissie Hynde cited in the divorce decree, finalized that fall. Neither Ray nor Yvonne has spoken publicly about their marriage, but some insight might be gleamed from a few songs on *Give the People* and *State of Confusion*, specifically "Yo-Yo," "Labour of Love," and "Property." To be clear, however, not "A Little Bit of Abuse," a darkly humorous track about a battered wife—there have been no reports, rumors, or divorce papers to suggest that Davies has been an abusive husband. Rather, "A Little Bit of Abuse" seems to have its roots in *Chorus Girls*, a play Ray collaborated on with Barrie Keeffe and which ran for five weeks in the spring of 1981 at the Theatre Royal in northeast London. Inspired by Aristophanes's *Lysistrata*, *Chorus Girls* features topical songs by Davies from a feminist perspective. Unfortunately, none of the music has been released, but Ian Gibbons has said that "some of the music in that is brilliant" and "really cleverly written . . . so funny."[34]

Less humorous or cleverly written is "Labour of Love," a bitter, cynical statement about how marriage, "a two-headed transplant," transforms partners into "Mr. and Mrs. Horrible." Recalling "Plastic Man" in its bland directness, the song is only partially redeemed by Dave's heavy-metal guitar and the Hendrix-style intro of "Here Comes the Bride." "Labour of Love" especially pales when we consider the immediately preceding tracks, "State of Confusion" and "Definite Maybe," and the following track "Come Dancing."

Similarly direct but more emotionally complex is "Property," which follows "Come Dancing" and closes side A of the vinyl *State of Confusion*. In "Property," Davies captures the final moments of a failed marriage as the singer leaves the marital home. As he looks around, the photographs, "the ones of you and me," and the "souvenirs bought on holiday" all trigger emotions of sorrow, loss, and confusion—the album's emotional motifs and an emotional experience similar to that of the singer in "No More Looking Back." The melancholy and unrest in the lyrics are reflected in Ray's synthesizer, at times mournful and brittle; the rhythm guitar parts, never dominant but quietly scratching away at chords; and a bass line which under the melody of the first two verses appropriates the riff of the Temptations' "My Girl" to emphasize the loss of a once blissful relationship now reduced to mere objects or property. The slight melody, sometimes more talked than sung, draws on the recitative technique of Hank Williams, one of Ray's early idols. In the coming years, Davies would use the recitative more and more—most notably on "How Are You" (*Think Visual*), "How Do I Get Close" (*UK Jive*, 1989), and "The Informer" (*Phobia*).

But "Yo-Yo" is the most interesting of these songs and perhaps the most personally revealing. In "Yo-Yo" Davies uses a tripartite narrative structure, which he would later use with more complexity in *X-Ray*. Here, three voices—a narrator, a husband, and a wife—depict a collapsing marriage. In portentous voice, to first slowly strummed and picked electric guitar chords, then dark acoustic chords with Avory's booming drum, Davies as narrator begins a two-verse introduction in which he sings of people's leading "double lives," one at home and one at work, and then sets up the specific situation of the song with the husband barely cognizant in front of the television and his wife's fighting back tears in the kitchen. As power chords intensify the drama, the wife and husband exchange verses for the remainder of the song. It is not always clear, however, which characters sing which verse, especially since Ray is the lone lead vocalist. "I think ambiguity is a good tool, a good weapon," said Davies at the time, who might not have wanted to be too revealing in a song with obvious autobiographical implications.[35]

In verse three, seemingly the wife sings, "You needed me when you were crying." Ray met Yvonne shortly after his breakup with Rasa and during the rock musical years when record sales were disappointing. Later, the wife warns her husband that "you might be popular [now], but it won't last for long," an almost direct reference to the Kinks' commercial resuscitation. For his part, the husband responds that he was her "little boy" and she thought herself "at the controls," immediately followed by a sarcastic, "yeah, yeah, yeah, yeah." The implication throughout the song is that the wife needed to be needed and the husband took up with her at a time when he needed some nurturing. Now that he is "popular" and "laughing" again, he no longer needs her. While it is tempting, it cannot be said with certainty that this reflects Yvonne and Ray's relationship. Surely, however, Yvonne was a stronger personality than Rasa. During

206

his first meeting with the couple, Dave recalls that he stormed out of a restaurant after he and Yvonne disagreed on basically everything with neither yielding any ground. In time, Dave says, they came to tolerate one another.[36]

The central image of the song, the yo-yo, describes the husband, the wife, their relationship, and his career, but additionally, it describes the feelings of Davies and anyone ever connected to him. Ray has long kept those in his personal and professional life "dangling like a yo-yo on a string," subject to his moods, his whims, his indecisiveness, and his strong, even volcanic personality. But perhaps no one more than himself has been kept "dangling" as he mulls over which of his always many ideas and projects to pursue. As a former associate said, "It's incredibly difficult being Ray Davies. Where does he get his peace and joy?"[37]

Chrissie Hynde

If Ray's marriage to Yvonne was quiet and unpublicized, his relationship with Chrissie Hynde, lead singer of the Pretenders, was public and eventful. The relationship may have begun as early as the summer 1980 and lasted into the spring 1984, providing plenty of material for gossip columnists.[38] In late August 1981, the couple not so coyly expressed their love when Davies joined Hynde on stage with the Pretenders at the Santa Monica Civic Auditorium to sing a duet of Jackie Wilson's "Higher and Higher": "your love keeps on liftin' me higher and higher." It was an unusual display for the before and since reticent Davies. Hynde, seven years younger than Davies, seemed to delight in the openness of their love and spoke of their relationship to the national press in the fall 1981: "Obviously, I'm besotted with him," she said. "It's a major part of my life."[39]

Constantly together, the couple began to irritate fellow band members. In June 1982, a few days after the death of Pretenders' guitarist James Honeyman-Scott, who once reportedly punched Davies backstage at a Pretenders' concert, Ray invited Hynde to perform with the Kinks at Philadelphia's JFK Stadium, where Joan Jett and the Blackhearts had played earlier in the day. After Ray asked the audience to "welcome the greatest female rock-and-roller in the world," Dave admitted to taking a "swipe" at Hynde before storming off the stage only to return a moment later. Although he came to like Hynde after the breakup with his brother, Dave said that he immediately "sensed something of the vampire in her . . . she was very rude. Maybe she and Ray were well suited, the pair of them."[40] Hynde added another level of tension in the Kinks, who after twenty years still had their onstage battles with verbal abuses, shoves, and even flying guitars.

The tumultuousness of the Davies–Hynde relationship with reports of tossed televisions and broken fireplace mantels has formed the stuff of Kinks–Pretenders' apocrypha and rock-and-roll legend. But their unfulfilled marriage plans have resulted in several spirited stories. In one version, the couple fought so vehemently just before their civil ceremony that they decided to call off the wedding and return home, where they reconsidered. However, by the time they returned to the registry, depending upon the story, the registrar refused to marry them because either they missed their appointed time or because he objected to their earlier fighting.[41]

Someone close to Davies told me another version. Ray, who insisted on the civil ceremony despite Chrissie's desire for a more lavish celebration, met his bride-to-be at the Croydon Registry Office, to which Davies arrived by train as if to punctuate the simplicity. Just before standing in front of the registrar, Davies excused himself from Hynde, saying that he had to use the men's room. He then exited the building, returned home, and left Hynde at the proverbial altar. Since Davies has told conflicting stories about the non-event, it is difficult to say which is accurate. What is certain is that the couple came very close to marrying, but never did; that they had a daughter, Natalie, born January 22, 1983; and that the relationship came to a devastating end for Davies when he heard the shocking news that Hynde had married Jim Kerr of Simple Minds in New York on May 5, 1984. Until then, Davies was not certain that their relationship was over. "It was a relationship doomed for disaster from the outset," said Dave, "since they both had selfish and manipulative tendencies, even though they truly loved one another."[42]

In time, Davies resolved the relationship with himself as he indicates in "Animal," which he introduced as "a favorite" at the Jane Street Theatre in New York in August 2000 and recorded as one of two studio tracks for *To the Bone* (1996). The singer, in control and "on reflection," looks beyond the pain and violence of the relationship with its "cuts and bruises" and "broken bottles and abuse" to remember the "sunsets on the sands" and the "absolute compassion in the air." It was a relationship of extremes, "truly natural" and "really animal," which, in Davies, is something to be celebrated when we consider the number of his songs lamenting the absence of the natural and emotional from contemporary existence, songs like "Artificial People," "Little Bit of Emotion," and "How Do I Get Close." Hynde and Davies may have been an explosive couple, each with, as Davies sings, "vampire fangs," but together they were alive and in the tight grip of Ying and Yang.

Divorce #3

Davies met Irish dancer Pat Crosbie while both were in physical therapy. Besides chronic back pain, Davies reportedly broke his kneecap and tore several ligaments in a fall during a performance in Hampton, Virginia, in

early 1984. On January 25, 1986, Ray and Pat married in a small ceremony and reception in Ray's home with music by his daughter Victoria
and her band, which included drummer Simon Davies, Dave's son. "It was
really special," wrote Dave, who described Pat as "really nice, quiet and
sensitive."[43] In the coming years, Pat would tour with the Kinks and
choreograph dances to among other songs, "It (I Want It)," "Welcome to
Sleazy Town," and "Aggravation." She and Ray had a daughter, Eva, born
sometime in the middle of 1997. The couple divorced while Ray was
working on *Other People's Lives.* The divorce, the "really big fall" alluded to
on the CD, gives focus to several songs—not Ray's gunshot wound in the
leg suffered after he tried to chase down a New Orleans mugger who
swiped his girlfriend's handbag in early January 2004. By then, the album
had been largely written.

On *Other People's Lives,* breakup songs resonate with experience and self-
assurance unlike earlier songs like "Property" and "Good Day." While the
singers may be in anguish, they are more rational, confident of their survival, their ultimate renewal, and their ability to love again. They have
been there before. After the album opens with a siren, ominous feedback,
and a human groan, Davies kicks off with a sturdy rocker that proclaims
the opening song's title and the CD's keynote, "Things are gonna
change." The singer accepts his calamity and vows to "dig inside," promising that before long he'll be "resurrecting the clown"—significantly, an
image of self-deprecation not self-pity. Although confident that "love will
return," he realizes that he will struggle, reminded sonically by the song's
pumping bass line and the wrinkly e-bow guitar of Mark Johns.

In "After the Fall," the following track, the singer like his counterpart
some forty years earlier in "Big Sky," looks for answers in the heavens, but
finds none. "I started writing 'After the Fall' after my marriage broke up
and I was in Ireland visiting my daughter; it was about retribution and
guilt and life changes and how you've got to be responsible for your own
actions."[44] Even with crashing power chords reigning on him, the singer
"in [his] bleak mid winter" realizes that "the sun will shine again"—as
ever, the restorative sun shines in Davies forming a powerful connective
with his earliest work. "After the Fall" also introduces the importance of
patience in the healing process, a recurring idea on the album, as the
singer first needs refuge before he tackles the "wrecks . . . in this war
zone," confronts himself, and atones, with the song warning against fabri-
cated public smiles and masks, for ultimately "the way we come in is the
way we're gonna go," which is to say naked and exposed to the truth.

"All She Wrote," which Davies said draws on all his breakups, treats
the one in the song humorously and with resignation, whereas, by contrast, the singer of "To the Bone" feels as if a vein has been torn open. In
"All She Wrote," the singer stoically reads his lover's goodbye note and,
later, an old love letter. "Almost everything in that song is true," said

Davies. "She met a new guy. In a disco. And she wrote that the guy reminded her of me when I was young. That's the worst thing a woman can tell a guy."[45] The note of the song, written on the back of an old brown envelope, is intended to irritate, frustrate, and disturb the singer, full of references to, as he sings, "get my goat." She writes, for instance, that her new love "laughs a lot not like you," and she tells her old lover that he is now free to hunt young girls in "titty bars and low life clubs" and, in a humorous refrain, seek "that big Australian barmaid," a reference, Ray said, to a woman who once mistook him for Dave. Ray sings the opening verse accompanied only by his acoustic guitar before drums introduce verse two and the tempo quickens. The voice, however, reflects the cool acceptance of the speaker as does the abrupt ending to the song.

In 2001, with just about the entire album written, Davies traveled for an extended stay in New Orleans to write new songs and experience the place which holds the roots of so much of his music. "It was as though," he writes in the liner notes, "all of my American musical influences had been floated down the Mississippi from all over America and picked up other styles along the way until it ended in New Orleans," a location he cites in "Muswell Hillbilly." While Davies said he wrote several songs during the stay, only two songs found their way onto *Other People's Lives*, "The Tourist" and "The Getaway." However, the album's strongest track, "Over My Head," reveals a NOLA (New Orleans, LouisianA) influence in its funk rhythm, especially in its bass line and electric guitar, and its brief jazz-fusion solo from 3:14 until 3:34, probably performed by Steve Bolton, who in the early 1970s played with the progressive band Atomic Rooster.

In "Over My Head," the singer feels betrayed: "Thought that you were my friend / In a world that is full of hatin'." This is a powerful statement in Davies, where so often the couple provides individuals refuge from a ruthless world—as in "Powerman," "Apeman," and "How Do I Get Close," for example. However, unlike the singers in "To the Bone" or "Summer's Gone" (*Word of Mouth*), this singer does not torment himself but recognizes the need to withdraw, to let her words fly "over his head," to put himself emotionally "a million miles away" and "get to my bed." There is no irony or humor, just a singer who recognizes the need for first quiet and then self-examination, to "see my life in perspective"—a hopeful attitude, especially when he avows that "tomorrow I'll be back in the race." This could be Davies's most compelling and insightful breakup song, capturing the stunned anguish of the singer who can nonetheless foresee his renewal.

Perhaps only coincidental, there seems to be a connection between the singer's self-examination and Ray's rediscovery and use of his NOLA musical roots in the song, suggesting that renewal, musical and personal, might require a look at roots. Although Davies's quest in New Orleans resulted in only two songs on this album, he recorded all the released tracks after his first stay and then mixed two songs ("Things Are Gonna Change" and "All She Wrote") in New Orleans during his 2003–4 stay. Certainly, his Crescent City exploration contributed to the incisiveness and freshness of *Other People's Lives* and, in some way, enabled him to look beyond his own intimidating back catalog and deeper into his musical influences to create new sounds.

Songs of encouragement

While he can be cynical and distrustful, particularly of institutions, Davies is generally a hopeful writer, whose Romantic nature trusts in the enduring capacity of the individual for renewal. His darkest works offer at least some hope, even if in *Everybody's in Show-Biz* it comes from the exuberance of his live performance. In overtly cynical works like *Preservation*, hope is found in the survival of the Tramp, and in *X-Ray*, the young narrator feels "born again" as he escapes the Corporation, determined that it will not destroy his dreams again and that he will live "without having to answer to anyone." In the closing image of the book, he blows a kiss to a departing black cloud, creating a clearing for the sun and personal renewal.

Albums of the Kinks have ended on hopeful notes, *Village Green* ("All My Friends"), *Arthur* (title track), *Soap Opera* ("Can't Stop the Music"), and on. During the Arista years, some songs of encouragement were a bit heavy-handed, lacking subtlety in melody, production, or lyrics—"Get Up" and "Live Life" wound the otherwise excellent *Misfits*, and "Life Goes On" seems a forced closer to *Sleepwalker*. However, many of Davies's songs of encouragement comprise his best songs from the Arista years and beyond: "Brother," "Misfits," "Better Things," "Come Dancing" and "Don't Forget to Dance" (*State of Confusion*), "Good Day," "Don't" and "Scattered" (*Phobia*), and "Is There Life after Breakfast?" (*Other People's Lives*), which, as Davies said in the liner notes, "is basically me looking in the mirror and singing to a more down and depressed self."

The sparkling "Better Things" opens with cheerfully anxious piano chords, followed by a crackling electric riff from Dave and the booming drums of Avory, and then Ray's soothing, avuncular vocals: "Here's wishing you the bluest skies . . ." In its hard-rocking edge, its sparse production, and its closing position on *Give the People*, an album about victims of abuse, routine, bad marriages, separation from children, paranoia, and more, "Better Things" is optimistic without being saccharine. "Don't Forget to Dance," a slow ballad and perhaps too busy a production in its use of synthesizer, is more specific in that the singer addresses a middle-aged woman with a "broken heart." The tender singer tries to inspire her out of her depressed state with her fear of aging and loneliness, and warns against withdrawal into self-pity, noting how the "young punks whistle at you" and, how "if this were a party," he would ask her to dance. In 1983, the single peaked at #29 on the US charts and, with "Come Dancing," gave the Kinks two US top-forty singles in the same year for the first time since 1966.

One of Davies's most accomplished songs of encouragement is the first song he wrote after his relationship with Hynde ended. "Good Day" opens with echoes of "Better Things" and the many sun songs of Davies: "The sky is blue but there are clouds in my head. . . . the sun is out . . . but the room is so grey." In the chorus, the singer tries to rally himself: "Today has got to be a good day." But despite the calm tones of the verse and chorus, the singer reveals his desperation in the bridge, or what Ray called "an apocalyptic moment," when, with some humor, the singer looks forward to the end of the world, realizing at least then he will be out of his misery.[46] While the song may capture the singer's despair, self-pity, loneliness, and even false hope that his love will return, "Good Day" reveals a determination to survive, "my only aim," and to fight off the melancholy—reflected in the lilt of the electric keyboards and the gleeful church bells at the end, both of which stand in opposition to the bluesy harmonica. Furthermore, the singer finds inspiration in British sex symbol and film star Diana Dors, who died at fifty-two from cancer just one day before the Hynde–Kerr marriage, but never withdrew from the public despite her illness and three failed marriages. "Hey Diana, I've really got to learn to take a tip from you," sings Davies, intent on a good day. In its combination of despair, hope, and humor, "Good Day" looks forward to the songs on *Other People's Lives*.

11

THINK VISUAL

TV, CD, and stage

Beginning in 1980, the Kinks reverted to touring as a five-piece unit, something they had not done since early 1971.[1] With their signing to Arista and with their movement away from the rock musicals, the touring Kinks gradually diminished in number, eliminating the back-up singers for the *Misfits* tours of 1978 and reducing the horn section to just one on the *Low Budget* tour of 1979—Nick Newall, who played not only saxophone, but also second keyboard and congas. One result of the decrease was that the ongoing tension between band members escalated, especially that between Avory and Dave. The rock musical years had, as Avory said, "diluted any sort of rifts that we might be having . . . because we had so many different people . . . [the supporting troupe] screened the band off."[2] However, in January 1984, during a brief American tour, the friction between Avory and Dave reached the point that after one gig the drummer attempted to attack the guitarist. Nothing much happened as others intervened to prevent a full-scale battle, but Dave made a decision: Avory would have to go.[3]

Avory remained until that summer when during the *Word of Mouth* sessions, the tension became so pronounced that, rather than use Avory, Ray programmed a drum machine for "Good Day." "By that point," Mick said, "I wasn't really enjoying it at all. I had to go. It was mainly Dave, really. Dave and myself."[4] Finally, in July 1984, Ray and Avory had a quiet discussion and both agreed that the drummer should end his twenty-year tenure with the Kinks. Avory realized that the Kinks were, at least in a way, "a family business,"[5] and neither brother would surrender his position—despite earlier rumors of Dave's departure. Nonetheless, it was a heartbreaking moment for Ray, who regarded Avory as a confidant and "touchstone."[6] To Dave, however, Avory was a sycophant or a yes-man who rarely if ever challenged his brother.

Shortly after Avory's resignation, Ray offered Mick a job as manager of Konk, a position he still holds as of this writing. Avory has never stopped drumming, performing today in local pubs, sometimes a short walk from his south London home, and as a member of both the Kast-Off Kinks and the Class of 64, which in addition to Avory, features former members of the Hollies and Tremeloes. On occasion, he has taken a few drum lessons as a way to keep sharp and to stay on top of new developments. His Kinks replacement, Bob Henrit, drummed on Dave's second and third solo albums, *Glamour* and *Chosen People*, and had played with Jim Rodford in Argent. A very different drummer from Avory, Henrit builds a bigger, louder sound, more suited to arenas than the generally quieter style of Avory, who focuses more on flourishes and fills. "I always envisaged getting a drummer like Bob Henrit," Dave said. "When we first worked with Bobby Graham [booming session drummer on 'You Really Got Me'] I thought 'that's it,' that is the drummer who should be in [the Kinks, but] things like 'Princess Marina' and all those vaudeville family type things might not have worked with someone like Bob."[7] Henrit, who would be the Kinks' final drummer, says that he and Rodford restored "solidity" and "some anger into [the Kinks], musical anger."[8]

Return to Waterloo

Just before Avory's departure, Davies finished *Return to Waterloo*, an experimental film which he had conceived in late 1981 as a Kinks project. Early on, however, Dave opted out. Perhaps he was wary of the plans after first the *Percy* soundtrack and then the rock musicals, reluctant to encourage Ray in what was sure to be a distraction in the midst of a commercial

Figure 11.1 Jim Rodford who joined the Kinks in 1978 stands between Ray and Dave on stage in Texas in 1983. Courtesy of Marianne Spellman

peak. Whatever the reason, he later said, "I didn't feel that it was some-thing I could really get my teeth into."[9] The other Kinks, however, cooperated with Ray and recorded the soundtrack in July 1983 with Ray playing all guitar parts. Davies was basically in charge of all aspects of the film, including the script, the music, and direction. He began filming in October 1983 with editing completed by the following March.

Return to Waterloo relies on song and image with rare snippets of dia-logue from only secondary characters. While the camera follows The Traveller, a suspected rapist played by Ken Colley, on his commute from home to office, the film's deeper focus is on Margaret Thatcher's England. About two-thirds into the approximately 57-minute film, two old soldiers voice its central question: "What has this great nation become?" Davies offers a disturbing response, depicting England as riddled with moral corruption, violence, conformity, and frustrated and non-communicative individuals who live with dashed dreams and the broken promises of the Welfare State. In "Not Far Away," Davies sings of "total chaos, total destruction, [and] social collapse," and an England whose "ending is near" as no emergent rescuing vision seems apparent. In fact, England seems locked in a "state of confusion"—to borrow the title of the album released while Davies worked on the film.

In *Return to Waterloo*, Davies expresses this pervasive confusion and uncertainty through ambiguity, distortion, and indirectness. Characters often see objects and people at least once removed—through windows and camera lenses, in reflections, in mirrors, in photographs, in sketches, in memories, in manikins, and in imaginations. This doubling technique indicates that the characters and audience are only viewing representa-tions, which are a distortion, however minor, of reality. Therefore, the characters and viewer are certain of very little in the film: is The Traveller a rapist? Did he have an incestuous relationship with his daughter? Is he having an affair? And, above all, what has become of England?

In addition to the sight imaging, another central image, as Stephen Paul Miller notes, is movement and non-movement, or "self-contained move-ment, a movement that paradoxically stays where it is." The film begins and ends in Waterloo Station, whose lofty name might suggest Empire, but here only reminds the viewer of the diminishment of Great Britain, which, like The Traveller, is stuck in a "perpetual loop."[10] The central image of entrapment is the train, which shuttles characters from home to work and back and where all characters control one another through a strong culture of surveillance, making unnecessary the need to address under-lying dissatisfactions and pent-up rage. Throughout the film, characters spy on and stalk one another, reminding each other, for instance, of smok-ing restrictions and the need "for conforming to our plan" ("Ladder of Success"). Similarly, images of frustration and individual powerlessness proliferate—The Traveller bangs a malfunctioning coffee machine, phone

Figure 11.2 Ray in the 1980s.

calls exasperate communication, young punks sing "got no dreams, got no ambitions" ("Sold Me Out"), and an advice columnist tells perhaps The Traveller's wife that "if he's going to leave there's no way that you'll win him back."

There are few images of hope in the film, but the most poignant one comes near the end when The Traveller sees a young boy, an image of himself in the past, rushing down the stairs of a dilapidated housing project identified as "Coronation Buildings," a reference to the failure of the post-World War II Welfare State. As his train pulls into a station decorated with a series of Union Jacks and just after Davies sings "another dawn is breaking" ("Expectations"), The Traveller through the train's window hands the boy a set of keys marked "Abbey Road," clearly visible several times in the film. With this reference to the Beatles, Davies suggests that free expression, necessary for hopefulness, lies in the integrity of rock music, where, at its best, honesty prevails and contrasts with England whose "lies are beginning to show . . . no one breaks promises the way that you do" ("Expectations"). Davies conveys a similar sense of hopefulness and individual and cultural authenticity at the end of *Soap Opera* with "You Can't Stop the Music" and, in *Preservation*, with "Where Are They Now?" and "One of the Survivors," and subsequently, the importance of music to the individual life impulse in "Juke Box Music" and "A Rock 'n' Roll Fantasy."

On November 4, 1984, *Return to Waterloo* premiered in the UK on Channel 4 TV to mostly mixed reviews. Davies's experimental techniques caused one reviewer to compare it to "a long and very good poem" while another said it "made me yearn for something really old-fashioned."[11] Indeed, the lack of dialogue and ambiguity does not make the film immediately accessible, especially for the 9:00 p.m. Sunday night television audience for whom it premiered. Although created for the small screen, the film played in the US in art houses and independent theaters beginning in May 1985, with the soundtrack released in the US only that July. *Return to Waterloo* is a major triumph for Davies, one that inventively captures in song and image what for him is his beloved but dying nation.

MCA: a new label

With *Return to Waterloo* completed by May 1984 and his relationship with Chrissie Hynde abruptly over, Davies shifted his attention to the Kinks, who began writing and recording *Word of Mouth*, and Konk, where major renovations called for updated recording equipment and a second studio. In a surprise move that July, Davies rehired Larry Page as the band's UK manager. Page was part of the band's management team from December 1963 until September 1965, but was terminated for what Ray considered his abandoning the Kinks on their first American tour. Page with Edward Kassner then locked the Kinks, their remaining managers, and their music publisher, in protracted and complex litigations that took several years to resolve. This time Page would remain with the Kinks until April 1989.

Word of Mouth would be the Kinks' final album of new material for Arista. Certainly, the Kinks' relationship with Arista had been beneficial to both, and the Kinks and Clive Davis were very pleased with one another. Lead guitarist Dave Davies called the executive a "class act,"[12] and drummer Mick Avory recalled that "Clive Davis actually liked the band" and found Arista "more of a personal label and it paid off with a big revival."[13] In 2002, Ray Davies was asked about a favorite Kinks period: "I loved the period around '78 or '79 when we'd found a way of moving forward and making records. We had an active record company, good head of the company, good A&R. . . . We focused and found our audience. That was a wonderful time."[14] Unlike any other Kinks' recording contract before and since, *both* label and band believed they had benefited. Thus, when the contract expired with *Word of Mouth* it seemed that both Arista and the Kinks would recommit to one another. But something went wrong.

In January 1985, Larry Page announced that the Kinks would be open to negotiations with other labels. Perhaps to determine the Kinks' value and to strengthen the band's bargaining position with Arista, Davies and still US manager Elliot Abbott began to explore the marketplace. In October, Davies and Abbott met with MCA Records in New York, and, then, on November 8, 1985, MTV prematurely announced that the Kinks had signed with MCA. Arista broke off negotiations and, in early January 1986, the Kinks did indeed sign with MCA for all their American releases—shortly thereafter the band signed with London Records for all European releases. It was a shortsighted decision, however, as Davies simply accepted the offer with the most money—much as he had done some fifteen years earlier with RCA.

The Kinks and MCA were not well suited for one another. Dave Davies had a bad feeling the moment he walked into MCA headquarters to meet the head of promotion, who would not or could not make eye contact with him. Dave's fears were confirmed when during the meeting he heard ABBA in the backroom. He said that MCA "didn't understand how to promote a British rock 'n' roll act," especially one as idiosyncratic as the Kinks. Dave considered the Kinks' tenure with the label "an unfortunate episode for everybody"[15]—meaning the Kinks, MCA, and Arista. Only the first of three of their MCA albums charted in *Billboard*'s top-100— *Think Visual* at a weak #81. *The Road*, a mediocre live album of 1988, reached only #110, and *UK Jive* in 1989, only #122; none charted in the UK.

Think Visual: concept, art, and videos

Relationships with MCA were strained after *Think Visual* failed to meet sales expectations. To be clear, the Kinks did not make it easy for MCA, who, in fairness, did work hard to promote *Think Visual*, released in

218

November 1986. While *Think Visual* is a strong album, musically and thematically, it is a dark record, a subtle concept album about one of Ray Davies's favorite themes, the music industry and its effect on the performer, or as Davies phrased it in broader terms, "the fears caused by big monopolies."[16] In a Reagan America sympathetic to big business, starry-eyed about individual triumph, and even tolerant of individual excess, *Think Visual* and what some saw as a pop star's whining did not appeal to the record-buying public. Furthermore, in a pop landscape dominated by individual performers like Madonna and Michael Jackson, and, to a lesser extent, Whitney Houston, all of whom used elaborate videos to develop cults of personality, and narcissistic hair bands like Bon Jovi, Poison, and Whitesnake, and even next to resurging 1960s icons like Steve Winwood and Paul Simon, both of whom employed brighter rhythms, *Think Visual* seemed out of place. Thus, in an industry which thrives on imitation, the album had little chance of commercial success.

What is surprising, especially given the album's title and Ray's interest in film and art, is the lack of effective visuals to promote it, especially the cover art. The cover, designed by Richard Evans in consultation with Ray, may reflect the dark quality of the album but did not appeal to the average record buyer, especially a teen-impulse shopper who is more often than not a male, sexually insecure and perhaps slightly homophobic. The cover, with deep black background, features four words separated by ellipses (*The Kinks ... Think Visual*) and a photograph of an androgynous model, set between the *s* and *u* in *Visual*, posing in an imitation of Rodin's *Thinker*.[17] Each of the four words appears in different font size and print style with *The* and the ellipses colored red, *Kinks* and *Think* white, and *Visual* gray. As a result, the words seem in motion and the presentation looks chaotic. The androgyne may reflect the album's content but gets lost in the movement of the letters and gender considerations. Unlike *The Thinker*, the seemingly bronzed, stylishly short-haired blonde figure in leotard, sits in profile on a stool with one hand serving as a rest for the Billy-Idol-like head bent in thought, and with the other hand, a clenched fist, set a few inches above the waist, emphasizing an athletic frame with muscular arms and small breasts. Like the parody of Michelangelo's God touching Adam on the cover of *Soap Opera*, this parody reflects a similar diminishment in human concerns. While Rodin's *Thinker* contemplates human nature, right and wrong, and good and evil, *Think Visual*'s androgyne seems to ponder bodily fitness, appearance, and striking a pose— which is to say style over substance and which reflects the music industry's concern with sales and profit rather than creativity and art. Perhaps ironically or perhaps fittingly (given the album's content and Ray's criticism), the cover might be stimulating art, even in its unattractiveness, but it did not help record sales.

Three videos, directed by Davies, were released in support of *Think Visual*, but none found their way into MTV's or VH1's rotation. The reason may be found in Davies's statement: "I want to make music for an audience . . . not a demographic."[18] All three videos have their merits as videos or short films, but they may not be appealing to a younger demographic. The first video—for Dave's "Rock 'n' Roll Cities"—seemed to have the best chance of success. It features a youngish-looking and flustered Dave apparently working in a chaotic daycare center. He is anxious to get back on the road, but brother Ray has disappeared. It is a fun-loving, brightly colored, and spirited video, featuring a brief shot of an audition for Ray look-alikes, which instead turns up impersonators of Boy George, David Bowie, Mick Jagger, Freddie Mercury, and even Tina Turner. However, the central plot of a missing forty-something rock star may not have been of sufficient interest to the teen audience, and the song itself might have seemed to MTV programmers as a too heavy-handed ploy for airplay.

Neither of the other two videos seemed to stand much chance of rotation. For "Lost and Found," the Kinks perform with an orchestra before a screen running a black-and-white, silent film of Ray as an eighteenth-century fop, first pining for and then recovering his true love—remember, at this time Ted Turner claimed that his colorization of classic movies made the films more accessible to youthful viewers who typically shunned black-and-white programs. Through the "Lost and Found" video, Ray may have been trying to prove Turner wrong or he may have been waging a subtle protest against Turner's process, but such protest and subtlety would be lost on the MTV audience—and perhaps its programmers. For "How Are You," the third video, Ray walks suburban English streets and contemplates memory and loss. The song and video seem too introspective and melancholy for an audience used to the excesses and fantasies of videos from Madonna, Guns N' Roses, and rap stars. Without a hit video, the Kinks would not be able to return to the top-twenty album charts.

Thematically, *Think Visual* picks up where three other Kinks albums leave off. *Lola versus Powerman and Moneygoround*, *Everybody's in Show-Biz*, and *Soap Opera* are all, for the most part, about the music industry. Yet each album either voices a strong note of affirmation and triumph—from the assertiveness and certainty of "Got to Be Free" from *Lola*, the spirited and freewheeling live performances of sides 3 and 4 of *Show-Biz*, to the determination of self-discovery ("[A] Face in the Crowd") and the joyful tribute "to the rock stars of the past" ("You Can't Stop the Music") of *Soap Opera*. But *Think Visual* ends only searching for hope, one not yet realized. Furthermore, "When You Were a Child," the final track, is a Dave Davies composition intended to rally his brother from the despair of "Killing Time," the previous track, and to rescue the album from what could have been an overwhelmingly gloomy close.

Out of the darkness and into the darkness

Think Visual was recorded after an emotionally dark period for the Kinks, lasting from 1983 through 1985: sales, although respectable, started to decline with *Word of Mouth*; Ray struggled to complete *Return to Waterloo*; Chrissie Hynde's marriage to Jim Kerr devastated him; he was saddened by Avory's departure; and Dave battled depression, some say severe, after the commercial failure of *Chosen People*. Several times during this period the Kinks seemed on the verge of collapse. But, by January 1986, with the signing to MCA and Ray's marriage to Pat Crosbie, optimism seemed restored—although it would be short-lived. That same month the Kinks went into the studio to rehearse and record "How Are You" and "The Video Shop," new material which would eventually end up on *Think Visual*. However, after a promising start, rehearsals and recordings ended and did not resume until the last day of March by which time the band had lost its way again.

After a bout with writer's block and a few lackluster rehearsals, Ray began to question the band's relevance and continuation. According to Dave, Ray was questioning everything at this time, "even the shirt he was wearing."[19] In an effort to see if the band could find itself, Ray scheduled a quick ten-day tour of Spain and Portugal. The Kinks played well on the May tour and any doubts about new drummer Bob Henrit's suitability were removed. Davies returned home and found his voice again in one of his favorite themes: the record industry and corporate insensitivity, greed, and individual exploitation. Once again Davies would defend and identify with underdogs and outcasts, just as he had done with Johnny Thunder, Lola, the Tramp, and the cast of characters from *Misfits*. *Think Visual* with its defense of the individual and its attack on corporate conglomerates both connects Davies with his past work and looks forward to *X-Ray*, in which he would wage his most sustained attack on corporate global culture.

Once the Kinks resumed sessions for *Think Visual* in June and July, all went remarkably smoothly, especially for Kinks sessions. "It was a very planned-out album," Ray said. "It's the first album The Kinks have ever made where we knew the songs and made demos for them before we started to record."[20] The result is a solidly cohesive album, thematically interesting, if bleak, and musically strong, with few low points ("Repetition," "Natural Gift") and several high ones ("Working in the Factory," "The Video Shop," "How Are You," "Killing Time," "When You Were a Child"). In fact, *Think Visual* includes one of Ray Davies's best songs of the 1980s ("Lost and Found"). Despite this, the album and its videos received little radio and, as noted, television airplay, and it remains largely underrated.

"Working in the Factory"

The emotional tenor of *Think Visual* is sounded in the intro to "Working in the Factory," the album's first track, when Ray Davies strums a solitary acoustic guitar for eight beats. The melancholy strumming, which seems tentative, suggests resignation, helplessness, and isolation, and has nothing of the bright cheerful chords of the unaccompanied guitar which opens "The Contender," *Lola's* first track, or the fiery blast of distorted power chords that introduce the angst and bravado of "You Really Got Me," which opened the Kinks' career. *Think Visual* gets fully underway when Dave's electric guitar leads a crash of sound which drowns the acoustic guitar and carries all the force of a screeching work whistle or a foreman's shout—the workday and album have begun. The consciousness of "Working in the Factory" might be identified as *Lola's* Contender in maturity with all innocence destroyed or simply Davies himself, who like the Contender saw music as his escape from manual labor and the factory. However, as "Working in the Factory" expresses, Davies felt betrayed by a business which gave him "new life" and "hope back in 1963," only to realize later that he had been "sold . . . a dream, that in reality was just another factory." As the music business evolved into a large industry in the 1960s, "the corporations and the big combines," the song continues, "turned musicians into factory workers on assembly lines" with no ownership over their creations. "I made the music, thought that it was mine," sings Davies in an allusion to the difficulties and protracted lawsuits over the control of his compositions and recordings. The vocals of "Working in the Factory" may be controlled, yet they give full voice to his disillusionment, resignation, and his underlying rage which he explains rather than emotes. It is a reflective voice but not without bitterness.

Davies's overriding complaint with the industry is that it commodifies everything associated with the artist: dreams, quests for freedom, individuality, and, of course, art. As "Working in the Factory" suggests, the music is irrelevant to record companies as long as there is a hit to carry the album and some consistency to keep old fans coming back. "Take the money," yes, but "make the music pay." But while the artists may take the huge advances, they often give them back. "It's the way the business has evolved and developed," Davies says. "Artists get better deals now, although I have to say the rip-off factor is still there. What they give on paper—contracts are now about 80 pages long—is taken back on some back page somewhere."[21] Courtney Love compares the recording artist to a sharecropper, and says that "the system's set up so almost nobody gets paid"[22]—except, of course, label executives and managers, and Bart Bull, the manager and husband of Michelle Shocked, says succinctly, "There's no contract you can sign in modern life that resembles a recording contract; they're absolutely unconscionable."[23] Davies vacillates over advising young bands recording at Konk about their record deals: "I feel a bit like one of those natural history photographers making a documentary. Do you stop the baby antelope being eaten by the lion, or do you film it?"[24]

"Lost and Found"

"Lost and Found," as the title suggests, is about recovery, which is what album and artist need after the bitter opening track. With typical craftsmanship and depth, the song is one of those majestic Davies statements, like "Celluloid Heroes." On the surface the song tells of a ship barely surviving a hurricane to pull into port, now ready to face a "new frontier." Of course, ship and storm serve as a trope, but for what? The video suggests it is about love, and focuses on the Ray Davies character struggling through separation before he and his lover renew their bond. Olga Ruocco has written, appropriately enough, that the imagery represents something unpleasant that the characters need to confront before they "emerge cleansed and almost reborn."[25] Given the context of the album and the then recent history of the band, we can be more specific. The song is about the seemingly unsinkable construction of the Kinks, particularly the relationship of the Davies brothers, the only original members left in the group. Several times in recent years and just weeks before recording "Lost and Found" Ray thought of disbanding the Kinks, deciding to continue only after the inspiring tour of Spain and Portugal.

That "Lost and Found" can be said to be about the recovery and revitalization of the Kinks is reinforced by the bridge, when Ray seems to address brother Dave: "This thing is bigger than the both of us / It's gonna put us in our place / We were lost and found, just in time / Now we got no time to waste." While *This thing* could refer to the band as well as the storm, the lyrics indicate Davies's renewed sense of vigor and urgency as he rallies his brother to the cause. Confronted with adversity throughout their career, the Kinks always seem to "say what really matters," which is the music and which Davies seems ready to work on after acknowledging his factory-like situation and surviving recent personal traumas and professional disappointments. With all storms passed, the Kinks find themselves revitalized and the song ends triumphantly: "Now it all seems clear / We were lost and found, standing here / Looking at the new frontier"— perhaps referencing the new album and label, a hopeful recovery of the mass audience of the recent Arista years, and Kinks 85 Ltd., a company formed by Ray and Dave through which all Kinks-related monies will flow. Reflective and intensely emotional, "Lost and Found" represents Ray's most optimistic moment on *Think Visual*, as it demonstrates that despite industry demands and inequities, artistic renewal is possible.

Furthermore, the slow ballad represents one of Davies's finest moments as producer of *Think Visual*. Bob Henrit's pounding beat and Jim Rodford's sturdy bass line, both high in the mix, propel the song or ship forward, while steel drums (probably via synthesizer) and Ray's acoustic guitar runs convey drama and struggle. More than halfway through the song, Dave Davies launches his first guitar break, a trademark Dave solo in its upward sweep, which supports the notion that "Lost and Found" is really about the Kinks fighting their way to triumph through "the dead of winter." Although a real sax would have been preferable to the synthesized one, "Lost and Found" is a wonderfully arranged and assembled track.

"Repetition," "Welcome to Sleazy Town," and "The Video Shop"

The three songs ("Repetition," "Welcome to Sleazy Town," and "The Video Shop") which close side 1 of the LP (*Think Visual* was released simultaneously in LP and CD formats) are about corporate control through self-surveillance and reflect Davies's conspiracy theory, which he would fully develop in *X-Ray*, where the Corporation seeks to control all human activity for its own power and profit. The world view on these three songs and in *X-Ray* is not unlike the worlds depicted in Orwell's *1984*,

RAY DAVIES   DAVE DAVIES

Figure 11.3 In the 1980s

Thomas Pynchon's *Gravity's Rainbow* (ruled by They), or the non-fiction study of Hardt and Negri's *Empire*. All songs and books present images of solitariness and human isolation. "Repetition," a mediocre rocker saved by its bridge, is about dehumanization through routine, which leaves individuals "incommunicado in the land of living dead" and which Samuel Beckett once referred to as "the cancer of time."[26] For the Corporation, and in the context of this album, routine serves as a very effective and low-cost form of surveillance or self-surveillance, a concept Davies suggests in *Return to Waterloo* as well.

In "Welcome to Sleazy Town," Davies sings of corporate control through the manipulation of public space. It is a theme that Davies has long been sensitive too, given his parents' history and references to the "office block persecution affinity" in "Village Green Preservation Society" and to slum clearance drives on *Muswell Hillbillies*. "Sleazy Town," inspired by the urban renewal of downtown Cleveland,[27] is a traditional electric blues—a fitting form for a song about the corporate makeover and sanitization of a Midwestern city. Davies gives his singer a unique perspective, one infused with what Barbara Carroll called Davies's obsession with "the *ideal* of place" (italics hers).[28] Tragically nostalgic, the singer tries to entice his listener to Sleazy Town, fully aware that Sleazy Town no longer exists, any more than the blues does as a mainstream form of mid-1980s pop music. The singer can only talk about Sleazy Town in the past tense: it *was* "bouncing . . . hot . . . dark . . . dirty . . . cruel . . . mean," but "dull it was not." However, the "corporations came long" and built "office blocks and parking lots . . . motorways and shopping malls" and "closed this city down." The singer laments that Sleazy Town is "just a dream," one now alive only in memory and imagination—not unlike Davies's earlier worlds of "Village Green" and "Victoria." Through his protest and song, however, the singer demonstrates a not yet repressed life impulse—unlike his unresponsive listener, identified in the opening verses as one driven into the isolation of the video world and very much in danger of evolving into the freeze frame he studies.

"The Video Shop," which through its keyboard and bouncy melody bears some resemblance to "Come Dancing," is set in a small community hit with skyrocketing unemployment after "an overseas corporation" closes the factory. On the one hand, it seems as if the singer and shop owner, one of Davies's spiv characters, wages a small, if somewhat self-gaining battle against corporate power by renting out bootleg videos. However, he unwittingly serves as a corporate instrument as his videos encourage isolation and escapism. He promises that his videos will "fly, fly you away" and "relieve your situation," thus driving the unemployed factory workers from individual or public confrontation and further into inauthentic and unexamined lives, so that when "another factory's been knocked down . . . nobody ever complains." Davies has long explored the reduction of individuals in the contemporary world—see, for instance, "Mister Pleasant,"

"Plastic Man," "Artificial Man," "A Little Bit of Real Emotion," and "Predictable." However, with *Think Visual*, we see the theme deepening and moving in the direction of *X-Ray*, as the three closing tracks of side 1 focus on corporate strategies to automate and incapacitate individuals.

"Rock 'n' Roll Cities"

Side 2 opens with "Rock 'n' Roll Cities," the first of Dave's contributions and the first of three failed singles. The much maligned, muscular rocker was dismissed by David Wild in *Rolling Stone* as "the worst sort of hucksterism . . . the sort of desperate, airplay-seeking number that only a radio programmer could like." The criticism is not without reason. After all, Dave shouts radio stations' call letters, even overdubbed for particular markets, and the song does seem imitative—which might explain its release as *Think Visual*'s first single. It might strive a little too hard to be the next "We're an American Band," Grand Funk's #1 smash and puffy tour song from 1973, or the more recent "We Built This City" [on rock-and-roll], the Starship's bombastic #1 from 1985, and it is not unlike Bob Seger's mammoth hit "Old Time Rock & Roll," released in 1979, featured in 1983's *Risky Business*, and a DJ staple at weddings ever since. However, now some twenty years removed, "Rock 'n' Roll Cities" deserves reconsideration.

Ray Davies's comment on the song is telling: "When I first heard that song it made me sick. But then the next day I saw the humour in it."[29] "Rock 'n' Roll Cities" refuses to take itself seriously, unlike the three hits just mentioned. Drawing from the perspective of Rob Reiner's mocumentary *Spinal Tap* (1984), Dave mocks himself and the Kinks as aging rockers exhausted from their air flight even before the tour begins. Armed with their promo MTV video and ready for a bacchanalia, the band receives no airplay, no attention from the "pretty girls getting younger every year," suffers from headaches, and seeks travel directions while settling for "pizza to go" and a hotel with cable TV. As Dave's cry of the call letters WSOS suggests, touring is now more hazardous to the band than to any city they might be invading, unlike Grand Funk's pledges or threats of "comin' to your town . . . to help you party it down" and "tear that hotel down." "Rock 'n' Roll Cities" is a delightful spoof not only of touring but of touring songs as well. Inexplicably, the song seems little appreciated even by its composer, who has not included it in his solo shows.

"How Are You"

One of the album's highlights, and perhaps the vocal highlight, is the moving "How Are You." Davies, a harsh self-critic and relentless with multiple takes, was so pleased with his performance on the demo that he transferred it to the twenty-four track machine and created an instrumental performance around the vocal.[30] Tinged with regret, sadness, and a sense of what could have been, and delivered in an emotional and at times quivering conversational voice, "How Are You" *seems*, like "Lost and Found" *seems*, to be about two lovers, except here the reunion is left uncompleted. However, the song was not prompted by one of Davies's broken relationships, but rather a chance encounter between Ray and former Kinks manager Grenville Collins. Thus, "How Are You," like "Lost and Found," not only reflects Davies's emotional investment in the band, but also his especial affection for the original band members and managers, an affection he expressed in his *20th Century Man* and *Storyteller* performances. Both Collins and Robert Wace were offended by the lyrics from "Moneygoround" in which Ray suggested that the pair may have taken an unfair revenue cut. In "How Are You," Davies may be apologizing: "No harm was ever felt or ever meant," he sings.

As the song indicates, Ray and Collins were once close. Therefore, although they may not have seen each other for "at least a year or more," Davies does not need to specify his recent but longstanding problems of work and marriage. "Are you still struggling the way that I am?" the singer asks. Without needing to be specific, the song attempts but not necessarily succeeds in concealing as much as it reveals. For what it reveals is a singer in constant state of despair and anguish, who proclaims unconvincingly that "Somehow I got through, I always manage to." Then, he deflects self-examination and turns outward to his friend: "And by the way how are you?" The conversation is strained and uneasy, as the singer remains only on the verge of revelation. His anxiety and agitation is reinforced by Dave's thin guitar lines that lilt after the chorus, rather than fade to wholeness; by the electric keyboards which skip and halt, almost like plucked guitar runs, and the use of echo and Ray's haunting falsetto. The track is an emotional performance that reveals the torment of Ray Davies.

The label executive

The following two songs, "Think Visual" and "Natural Gift," move away from a conversation with a former manager and friend and from implicit memories of more innocent days to more recent discussions with label executives. Both songs depict label executives infiltrating artistic consciousness so that the artist surrenders artistic impulse and autonomy to corporate authority and commercial success. As Bob Henrit's pounding drums and Dave's scratchy opening chords suggest, corporate strategies are pummeled and etched into the artist's consciousness. The concern is not with art but, as the song says, with "productivity . . . profitability . . . competition . . . advertiz[ing] . . . merchandiz[ing] . . . econom[izing]

... marketability ... [always a] goal to chase." The day's buzz words figure prominently in the song ("think digital, synthesize, computerize"), and, above all, in the MTV age, "think visual." Such inculcation, the label hopes, will result in an artist who will not only produce hit records, but also become self-monitoring and therefore quite cost effective. The song suggests that record companies are only about profit, not art. As Chuck D of Public Enemy once said, "If [record labels] could sell Brillo pads with a slice of cheese on them, they'd do that, because the music is irrelevant to them."[31] Similarly, Ray once complained of MCA, "the people at the record company just wanted us to sell T-shirts."[32]

While "Think Visual" remains Davies's bleakest song-commentary on the music industry, it has its humorously self-referent moments. For instance, the executive tells the artist to maintain "the clean cut image," "to show your personality," and "to flash those teeth." The Kinks! The band, frequently scruffy, has long had a rowdy reputation of both in- and out-fighting, and Ray, charming at times but genuinely shy and moody, can be a difficult interview. And "flash those teeth" recalls the episode from the early days when Ray visited and escaped a dentist hired by management to close the gap on his teeth.

"Natural Gift," with "Repetition," marks a musical low point of the album. It portrays a manipulative and callous label executive who tries to encourage, berate, and finally frighten the artist into creation. He tells the artist to "use your natural gifts" and "rise above your stupidity ... you're dumb but don't give in," and "with some luck and dedication and some careful manipulation," you might sell some records. At the 1:30 mark, a plucked synthesizer is introduced and then returns later, with still clipped but alternatively rising and falling chords. The sound recalls the haunting choral voices from the *Omen* soundtrack (1976) and creates an especially eerie moment, especially while the executive demands his artist "stop this depression you're in" and warns of "bad people, mad people, bitter people, scared people" all waiting to attack the star—a rhythm and repetition recalling the doctor of "Destroyer." No doubt Davies has had to endure such "motivational" talks several times through the course of his career.

Closing tracks

In Davies's final composition on the album, the penultimate track "Killing Time," the consciousness of the album, which is to say Davies, falls to his nadir. Angst and frustration have been replaced with resignation born out of despair and hopelessness. Images of emptiness proliferate in the song: the music industry is an "empty mine" and the singer has a corresponding "idle mind" and is only "killing time"; we hear of "empty streets," counter-productive human activity ("complaining," "watching me ... watching them," "petty crime") and trivial concerns ("soap operas full of vanity" and "commercials full of luxuries"). The singer is helpless and can barely register a rhetorical protest as he worries that "these lunatics will take my mind." *Lunatics* seems a reference to the executives of "Think Visual" and "Natural Gifts," who indeed try to program the consciousness of the artist. In the closing couplet, the singer expresses his frustration at the dehumanization of human activity and the diminishment of human concerns, reflected in the album cover: "Why can't life be more sublime? / Than all of this waste and killing time."

"Killing Time," one of the most stubbornly melancholic songs in the Davies catalog, sounds a deep note of despair from which Davies cannot, at least on this album, find a way out, the way he could on previous LPs about the industry—the fragmentation suggested by the abridged "Lola" at the end of *Show-Biz* at least demonstrates zest and external support. But on *Think Visual*, an album on which the Kinks censure the assembly-line treatment of music making, the brutal rock-and-roll cycle of recording and promotion, executive manipulation, lost friendships, and corporate domination over individuals, landscapes, and art, Davies concludes only that there is "nowhere to go" and that he must "bite the bullet" and he asks for someone, perhaps his bandmates, to "help me through it." However, *Think Visual* does not end with the despondency of "Killing Time," but it is not Ray Davies who provides the hope. Instead, it is brother Dave, who earlier provided comic relief with "Rock 'n' Roll Cities." On "When You Were a Child," Dave points the way to renewal for his brother. Dave, who had helped Ray through earlier mental breakdowns, found himself helpless after Chrissie Hynde split with his brother: "this time I couldn't get close . . . I knew he was deeply hurt and upset . . . I felt bad for him but there was nothing I could do."[33]

"When You Were a Child" voices a Romantic sentiment which directs Ray to find inspiration in childhood. As Dave said, the song is "about how people grow old and lose touch with the inner child, becoming bitter and resentful of the way life has treated them."[34] The response to "Killing Time" is remarkably direct as Dave sympathizes with Ray as a victim of the industry: "Can't believe what they've done to you . . . Taught [you] to hide all that's true inside . . . They've got you just where they wanted you . . . Don't it make you weep?" He calls on Ray to revisit his childhood, and to rediscover the purity of place, external and internal, from which the music came, "for in your heart there's innocence waiting to be free." Throughout the song, Dave tries to ignite Ray's memory and imagination with the refrain, "What was it like when you were a child?"

Dave's efforts are hardly naïve. As Picasso said, "Every child is an artist. The problem is how to remain an artist once we grow up."[35] Not only Dave, but also Ray seems to be aware of the need to draw from and return to "young and innocent days," to quote an earlier song title. In the early 1980s, Ray talked about the composing process of "You Really Got Me":

"How could I possibly write those lyrics? So simple. I wish I could do it now," thus referring to the innocent and unreflexive artlessness that has since left his composing process.[36] With "When You Were a Child" Dave not only tries to inspire Ray, but he also recommits himself to his brother and the Kinks, much as Ray did in "Lost and Found," both putting aside, however briefly, years of bickering, pettiness, and brawls—although a fistfight did break out during the *UK Jive* sessions when Dave was enraged at his brother's editing of his guitar solos. "I believe that we were meant for each other," Dave sings. "We'll get along somehow / If they leave us alone"—the operative word might be "somehow." The song is inspirational and affirms the possibility of healing and individual regeneration after great despair.

Think Visual would be a much different album without "When You Were a Child." Not only does the track offer hope and a way out of despair, but, to the careful listener, it also radiates back to the preceding tracks, coloring them with a little bit of optimism, suggesting that despair need be only temporary. Thus, *Think Visual* ends with at least a tentative hopefulness and possible reclamation of a lost vision, maybe not as optimistic an ending as other Kinks LPs, but not as bleak as "Killing Time" would have left the album.

Think Visual may not be in the first rank of Kinks albums, but it has nonetheless been neglected and underappreciated. It provides a more comprehensive view of the music industry than any other rock album, including others by the Kinks, and not only tells but also demonstrates the toll the industry exacts on its artists. When *Think Visual* did not meet sales expectations of MCA, the Kinks fell victim to an incredibly bitter irony. In June 1987, Ray and perhaps Dave were summoned to a meeting with MCA executives, including president Irving Azoff. The meeting was not pleasant as MCA told Davies that in the future the label expected a more marketable product from the Kinks, or, as "Working in the Factory" put it, "make the music pay." Ray mentioned his idea of a double-live album with accompanying video, which MCA immediately rejected. That night during their New York performance, Ray cursed MCA from the stage, a gesture which he would repeat elsewhere. Still, MCA threw an after-show party for the Kinks, for in the music industry all is irrelevant except sales. MCA executives, it would seem, lived out depictions on *Think Visual*.

80 Days

In the late summer 1985, Ray received an inquiry from Broadway producer and director Des McAnuff asking if he would be interested in working on a musical based on *Around the World in 80 Days*, the novel by Jules Verne. Davies was recommended by Barrie Keeffe, who had been developing the concept with McAnuff and who worked with Ray on *Chorus Girls.* After some discussion, Davies agreed to the project and with the completion of *Think Visual* a year later, he turned his attention to the musical. Davies, who wrote the music and lyrics for *80 Days,* also conceived two substantial features of the script: "I wanted it to be about Verne rather than the sort of travelogue like the Mike Todd movie. And I also wanted it to be about the Empire, about imperialism. I've always had a passion for that."[37] With his suggestions, Verne became a major character and Empire a major theme.

Through Verne, Davies explores the creative process: "What was he thinking when he sat down to write his novel, and what were the problems along the way?"[38] In the opening song, "Let It Be Written," Verne experiences "chills . . . anger [and] rage" as he stares at a blank page and confronts an eighty-day deadline, immediately linking his journey of creation with Phileas Fogg's journey around the globe: "In 80 days I am condemned to write this book . . . In 80 days to circumnavigate this plan" ("80 Days"). While both face self-doubt, distractions, and loss of control, their main struggle is with time. "The story has a neurotic involvement with progress and timetables," said Snoo Wilson, who wrote the script.[39] Thomas Bartoldus and Ralf Junkerjürgen note that all characters, not just Verne and Fogg, are "bound to the dictate of time and thus accelerated modernization, a condition visualized by the set, which is moving at almost any time . . . [Everyone in the play] has the task not to conquer the world but time"[40]—a familiar theme for the always over-extended Davies.

The opening songs contextualize Fogg's adventure in terms of creative struggle, time demands, and Empire, so that despite the drama and humor of the subsequent action these underlying themes are never far from the surface. After "Let It Be Written," in which Verne calls the Englishman "the most icy inscrutable creature known to science," Davies mocks notions of Empire and class elitism in "Well-Bred Englishman," the third song, and "The Empire Song," the second one: "It was God that made this nation great / It was our fate to dominate the world / This is our world," which is sung by Prime Minister Gladstone, the Archbishop of Canterbury, and a preacher, who, like the minister of "Cricket" in *Preservation,* serves Empire more than God.

For one especially interested in Davies, "The Empire Song" references past and future Davies songs: "Victoria" with its reference to the sun's never setting; "There's a Change in the Weather" (*Preservation Act 1*) with its lifting of the phrase "holocaust risin' over the horizon"; and "Yours Truly, Confused N10" with its borrowing from Shakespeare's *Richard II* and its allusion to England with its "throne of kings . . . set in a silver sea." Similarly, in its cataloging of great Englishmen from Sir Francis Drake to Lord Byron and Charles Dickens, "Well-Bred Englishman" anticipates a similar list in Davies's "London Song." While many songs draw from familiar Davies sources, music hall, for instance, perhaps the most mysteriously beautiful song in the production is the raga rock of "Just Passing Through" with its echoes of "See My Friends" and "Fancy." Unfortunately, no cast album or official collection of the music of *80 Days* has been released, although a bootleg has surfaced of Ray's demo sessions recorded in New York City in 1987.

80 Days: A New Musical opened on August 23, 1988, at the La Jolla Playhouse, San Diego, and closed on October 9 of the same year. It was a lavish production with "40 set changes, 40 costumes changes, 24 actors playing 200 parts, and a stage built atop another stage that contains two mechanical treadmills and a raised slip-stage with a revolving platform. . . . [It costs] $700,000 for the entire production, making it the most expensive show ever done at the La Jolla Playhouse."[41] The play did not live up to expectations, however, as both McAnuff and Davies looked forward to a Broadway hit, which was not unreasonable. *Big River*, a musical adaptation of Mark Twain's *The Adventures of Huckleberry Finn* and previously staged at La Jolla, won McAnuff a Tony Award as Best Director, as well as seven other Tonys and ran for over a thousand performances from April 1985 until September 1987. In a cruel irony for Davies, McAnuff went on to achieve a Broadway hit with another English rock artist and Davies rival Peter Townshend. *The Who's Tommy*, which opened at La Jolla in July 1992 and ran on Broadway from April 1993 to June 1995, collected five Tony Awards, including Best Direction of a Musical for McAnuff and Best Original Score for Townshend.

12

20TH CENTURY MAN
The 1990s and beyond

Davies spent a busy November 1987 in New York. He saw through the completion of the master tapes for *The Road*; he negotiated unsuccessfully with MCA for a full-length video to accompany the live album; and he further developed *80 Days* with Des McAnuff and Snoo Wilson. All work halted on November 23, however, when he received news of his mother's death, coming twelve years after the passing of his father, who died after convincing his oldest son to place a bet on the Wimbledon victory of Arthur Ashe, an underdog who, Fred Davies said, "will slap the bastards in the face for us."[1] Ray flew back to London for his mother's funeral and delivered the eulogy, which Dave described as "extremely moving" and "insightful."[2] In a letter to his mother in the weeks before her death from cancer, Ray told her that she was the main source of his inspiration and that without her he would never have written anything.

Still, Dave and other family members were upset with Ray for not leaving New York to be with his mother during her final days.[3] Upon his arrival for the funeral, Ray did not receive a warm welcome, which he dramatizes—if not in all the specifics, certainly in the overarching emotional discomfort of his protagonist—in a short story first entitled "Scattered: Home" and then simply "Home," in both editions of *Waterloo Sunset*. At one point, the character feels as if his family were "watching him do penance." However, character, like creator, also found the inspiration to complete "that unfinished song that had been going around his head for so long."[4]

"Scattered"

"Scattered," which Davies said took ten years to write,[5] is one of his most complex lyrics and one of his best songs of the 1990s and appears on *Phobia* with a dedication to his mother and to Carol Bryans, a friend who also died of cancer. First inspired by a broken relationship, probably with Chrissie Hynde, the ambitious "Scattered" contemplates nothing less than human existence. More certain and less speculative in its meditation than

233

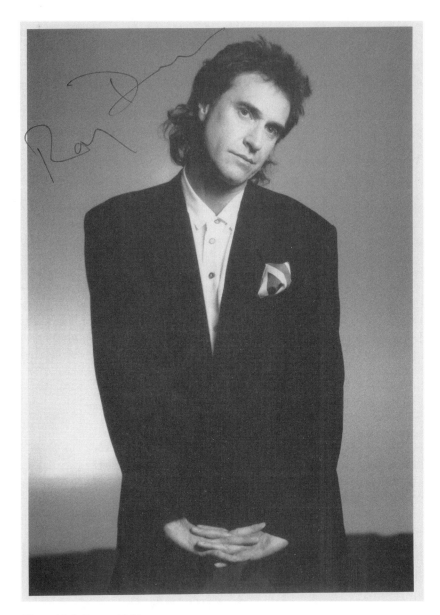

Figure 12.1 Ray c. 1990

"Big Sky," "Scattered" concludes that the defining principles of life are dynamism, fragmentation, impermanence, and randomness, with individuals "torn" and "shattered" and "barmy and battered," or simply "scattered." Through alliteration ("like a *seed* that is *sewn*" or "a *breeze* that is *blown*") and rhymes and near rhymes interlocking stanzas, the song suggests that conception, growth, decay, and death are ruled by an entropic principle, where even in the afterlife one is "scattered . . . in time and space . . . like the universe." More folkish and less hard-rocking than most of the tracks on *Phobia*, "Scattered" would not have been out of place on *Village Green*.

Despite the dark overtones of song and video, "Scattered" is not bleak. There may be references to struggle, bruising, and lack of autonomy in the lyrics and images of overcast skies, stark fields, and funerals in the video, but there are also references to human endurance and survival "with emotional glue" and images of singing and dancing. Furthermore, the tempo is upbeat and song and video conclude with an image of home and a loving reunion in the afterlife. In "Scattered," the singer moves toward acceptance, an ability to live with Keats's negative capability, which has largely eluded Davies and his singers. Here, the singer accepts what he cannot "know" or "prove," which is "why this life on earth is scattered like the universe." Ultimately, he sings, "You're going *home* so what does it matter" (italics mine). It may not be a cheerful acceptance, but it is acceptance nonetheless, embedded in the comforting and stable image of *home*.

Autobiography and *Weird Nightmare*

In January 1988, Davies entered a Dublin hospital to be treated for excessive fluid in his lungs and for the removal of a blood clot. He was not, as some media reports had it, hospitalized for bronchitis, exhaustion, or a heart attack. While recovering at his in-laws in Cork, Davies began writing his autobiography, which publishers had been after him to write since the mid-1970s. According to Doug Hinman, Davies wrote about a hundred pages during his recuperation, but abandoned the book by the middle of March to tour with the Kinks in support of *The Road* and then to finish preparations for *80 Days*.[6]

Work on the autobiography would further be delayed by additional Kinks and non-Kinks projects, including the film, *Weird Nightmare: A Tribute to Charles Mingus*, which Davies directed and co-produced with Elizabeth Silver and which premiered on UK television in June 1993. The over-hour length film documents the life and career of the jazz composer, bassist, and bandleader, and films sessions from the Mingus tribute album also called *Weird Nightmare*, produced by Hal Willner and featuring Henry Threadgill, Keith Richards, Charlie Watts, Vernon Reid, Elvis Costello, and many others.[7] Davies intertwines Mingus's words, photographs, and archival footage, including previous interviews of long-time Mingus drummer Dannie Richmond, with footage from the tribute recording sessions and new interviews of former wives, children, friends, Mingus's psychologist, jazz critic Nat Hentoff, and musicians like Richards, Reid, Watts, Costello, and trumpeter Jack Walrath, a former band member.

Weird Nightmare is a dynamic and tight presentation, not only paying homage to the artist but also revealing in its characterization of Mingus as a person, composer, musician, businessman, and bandleader. However, in the context of this book, it is interesting to note the many similarities between the subject and the director. Both Mingus and Davies have been called perfectionists and geniuses, difficult taskmasters who can torment musicians for the song—although musicians rarely turned down offers to work with either. Both are extraordinarily complex, prone to outbursts of temper, occasionally violent, and yet capable of extraordinary sensitivity in their work and sometimes in life. Both are insomniacs who have been treated for depression. Both have been married or in close relationships with several women, and both were acutely aware of their marginal status—for Mingus, as a black American, and for Davies, as a member of the working class.

Work on the documentary seemed to have a direct influence on Davies's autobiography. At the beginning of *Weird Nightmare*, Mingus proclaims, "I am Charles Mingus. . . . To me, I am nothing." Later, he tells his psychologist that as a child, "I was never a person." This is not unlike the beginning of *X-Ray*: "My name is of no importance. . . . I am one of the faceless thousands manufactured by this corporate society. . . . my individuality has not been allowed to surface yet."

X-Ray

X-Ray, subtitled *The Unauthorized Autobiography*, was published in September 1994 in the UK by Penguin/Viking and in September 1995 in the US by Overlook Press. Davies did not write the comprehensive and fact-filled story that the genre usually demands, nor did he include photographs, except on the jacket. Instead, as the subtitle suggests, he took a more imaginative approach, one that fuses fiction and non-fiction. He creates, for instance, Julie Finkle, a composite character drawn from groupies and girlfriends; he sets the present of the book in approximately 2025; and, most significantly, he develops a tripartite narrative perspective in which we hear from a young journalist; an embittered and cantankerous septuagenarian usually referred to as R. D., and the author Davies, approximately fifty years of age controlling all information and whose actual voice is never far from the surface. The result is an autobiography in which the author distances himself from his subject or himself, thereby concealing as he reveals, blending fact and fiction, and frustrating readers and critics longing for directness.

While reviews were generally at least somewhat favorable, Lauren Thierry in the *New York Times* wrote that "it remains unclear what he has to say," but "Mr. Davies seems to be saying that he is the most misunderstood artist in rock and roll. His book seems to be intended to keep it this way." In the *Sunday Times of London*, Robert Sandall found the book somewhat tedious, stating that "*X-Ray* would be twice as entertaining at half the length," but his counterpart in the weekday *Times*, Alan Jackson, enjoyed the experimental work: "Pop biographies rarely come more inventive than this, an enjoyable mix of true confessions and quasi-fictional scene-setting."[8]

X-Ray begins with a young journalist just hired by the Corporation to document and debunk Davies's life and work, particularly his ideas. However, as the journalist's work progresses, he comes to understand the truth of R. D.'s Orwellian and Pynchonian vision, which claims that since World War II the individual has lost autonomy to the increasingly powerful Corporation, a global, industrial, military, and governmental conglomerate that controls all and exploits and marginalizes individuals for its own end. "People never realize this," Davies said, "but the young journalist is the character that's closest to me right now, not the 75-year-old R. D. I suspect R. D. is what I'll be like when I'm 75, if I'm still around."[9] Like R. D., who dies near the end, the young narrator withdraws into isolation at the conclusion of the book.

In many ways *X-Ray* is about the very nature of the autobiographical and biographical forms and, more to the point, their limitations. The text seems to ask whether or not we can ever fully know an individual. Davies explains his intention succinctly in the song "X-Ray," which he wrote for the stage version of the book. In the song, he hints at the inadequacy of "the photograph, video and the printed word" to reveal truth and then, echoing *Hamlet*, he sings, "But there is more in this heaven and earth than what is revealed on the x-ray"—medical photograph or book?[10] Probably both. Ostensibly, the song concerns Davies's youthful football injury, but given the context of the song—a performance to promote the book— Davies ironically throws into question the content of *X-Ray* and the credibility of biographies and autobiographies, including his own. As he sings in "X-Ray," "the world only *sees* what it *believes*"—the reversal of *sees* and *believes* from its usual positioning implies that rather than seek truth people only desire confirmation of what they are comfortable with or what they think they know.

The young journalist addresses similar concerns near the end of his assignment: "I felt that while the physical world can see two people—the outer and inner person—there is also the third person, a spiritual driving force that constantly intermingles with the first and second person. Intangible and totally separable."[11] With "intangible," which echoes both "Scattered" and the allusion to *Hamlet* in "X-Ray," Davies suggests that the quest to capture an image of the spiritual dimension or the deepest life force of an individual is ultimately futile. In an odd way, the statement is

Davies's ironic admission of failure as he informs the reader that he has not been able or willing to penetrate his own depths.

Waterloo Sunset

While *X-Ray* marks Davies's highest achievement in literature, *Waterloo Sunset* is a solid if less inventive collection of short stories, first published in 1997 in a 17-story edition and then in 2000 in a 24-story edition. Conceived by Davies as "a concept album on paper,"[12] *Waterloo Sunset* presents recurring characters like Les Mulligan, the protagonist of the collection and an aging rock star existing on the margins; Richard Tenement, his upper-class manager who enjoys the thrill of the deal; and Donna, the former girlfriend of Les with their "love nest" having turned into "a war zone"—the same image used in "After the Fall." The stories find their inspiration in Davies's songs, building on song characters, themes, and sometimes details—almost all stories take their titles from songs.

Davies's strategy of developing stories from songs is not always successful, however. In "Rock-and-Roll Fantasy," Davies may effectively develop Danny, "the wacko rock-and-roll fan," who evolves from the character on *Misfits*, but with Lavinia from "Holiday Romance" on *Soap Opera*, Davies seems redundant, adding no surprising detail to a character fully suggested in the song. Perhaps the worse instance of this redundancy is in "Return to Waterloo," written from the first-person perspective of The Traveller, which is noteworthy in its exploration of the creator–creation relationship but detrimental to the film in that it demystifies the central character, clarifying, for instance, his crime of rape. Similarly, the space of the story sometimes stretches Davies's sharp detailed descriptions. "The day was blurred," begins "Waterloo Sunset." "Like one of those old French impressionist paintings where the viewer is never sure whether the artist was drunk or needed spectacles." Certainly, a lively and effective description, but not as concise as we find in songs like "Art Lover": "Pretty little legs, I want to draw them / Like a Degas ballerina / Pure white skin, like porcelain." Consider too the openings of "Autumn Almanac" or "Waterloo Sunset."

As Davies does in songs, he teases readers with the obvious parallels between his characters and himself. Mulligan is "English through and through" ("The Shirt"), "born to write" about London "like a latter-day William Blake" ("Misfits"), who in 1977 takes up residence on New York's upper West Side in a building similar to Davies's. Mulligan is, however, a substantial character, interesting enough to sustain the collection. Overall, though, *Waterloo Sunset*, unlike *X-Ray*, seems to suffer from restraint as the stories seem tied too tightly to the songs which inspire them. Davies seemingly took more leaps with his own life in *X-Ray* than with his own fictional characters.

20th Century Man

"I was doing readings in these quaint, little-old-lady shops in Canterbury and Oxford," said Davies. "And I thought, 'This is a nice, relaxed atmosphere. I'd love to play a few tunes here as well.' " *20th Century Man* grew out of these promotional appearances for *X-Ray* and into a form that accessed his abilities as singer-songwriter, actor, performer, and author in a way that few formats could. The show—which is part play, part reading, part concert, part performance art—is not "a factoid-night-out-with-tunes," as Davies says. "It's a story, it's song, it's anecdotes. It's just all the stuff you can't condense in a two-and-a-half minute pop song."[13] Davies performed the show first in March 1995 and then toured regularly with the show from that fall through the fall 2001, suggesting the creative fulfillment he experienced from the work, the importance of it to him, and its flexibility. *20th Century Man* is the title Davies used most frequently for the two-act version of the show, while *Storyteller*, generally but not always, referred to the one-act later version of the play, which has been captured on a CD (1998) of the same title. In 1996, he performed a version of the show to inaugurate *Storytellers*, the VH1 series. Closing credits of subsequent episodes cited Davies as the series inspiration. Every so often Davies has spoken of staging *20th Century Man* / *Storyteller* with additional cast members but nothing has developed. To date, he has performed the show only with guitarist Pete Mathison.

The following discussion focuses on the two-act production, as it reflects Davies's most complete vision of what he wanted the performance to embody, while also representing the high point of Davies's theatrical achievement as creator, performer, and innovator, once again moving him a step or more ahead of his contemporaries. Much of the discussion is, of course, applicable to the one-act production and *Storyteller* CD. I will refer to the two-act production by its original title *20th Century Man*, so as to avoid confusion with the one-act production and the CD. *20th Century Man* can require some three hours to perform, and covers Davies's life from its beginning to the breakup of the original Kinks lineup, with reference to the Drury Lane *Village Green* concert in 1973—*X-Ray* goes a few months later ending with the bleak White City incident. The initial *Storyteller* requires under two hours' performance time and concludes with the Kinks' recording "You Really Got Me." In perhaps an effort to mitigate weariness, Davies, it seems, shifted to the one-act version because of the demands of touring small United States markets where one performance per location seemed the rule.

There are five primary reasons for the success of *20th Century Man*: the songs, the text, the performer, the humor, and the statement.

239

Figure 12.2 Ray performs *Storyteller* in the late 1990s. Courtesy of Kevin Reynolds

The songs

Davies performs some twenty-five songs in the show, including Kinks classics such as "You Really Got Me," "Lola," "Waterloo Sunset," and "Days"; infrequently performed Kinks songs like "Two Sisters," "The Moneygoround," and "Village Green"; new songs, some written for the show, like "X-Ray," "London," "Art School Babe," perhaps "To the Bone," and the still unreleased "Americana"; and covers like "That Old Black

Magic." Certainly, the songs give *20th Century Man* a head start, but this is too simple an explanation for the show's success.

What happens during *20th Century Man* is that the songs, text, and performer operate in a reciprocally illuminating system. "Two Sisters," for instance, is literally about Priscilla, who, restricted by her duties as wife and mother, feels jealous of her sister Sybilla, who lives in a swinging London flat, "free and single." On stage, Davies explains that although he did not realize it at the time of composition, the song represented his relationship with his brother Dave, who was leading the stereotypical life of a rock star. The song and its introduction pierce to an emotional root in the brothers' rivalry, rendering unnecessary and anticlimactic any gossipy chat that the audience may have thought it wanted to hear. The song also illustrates something about Davies's songwriting process and how he draws from his subconscious without excessive or censoring analysis. Thus "Two Sisters" serves several functions in the show: it reveals something about Davies as jealous brother and "suburban husband";[14] it provides insight into his songwriting process; and it advances the narrative.

Furthermore, "Two Sisters," performed near the beginning of *Act 2*, reintroduces themes established in *Act 1*; helps to establish the theme of the brothers' relationship; and, like "See My Friends," strikes more deeply than narrative could. Introducing "See My Friends," Davies speaks of the melodic inspiration—he heard the early morning chanting of fishermen in India, which also inspired the sitar-like drone on the recording. However, the controversy that surrounds the song—many hear homosexual implications—is subtly discredited. Davies uses the song to illustrate not sexuality, but spirituality. "My most religious experience," says Davies introducing the song, "was not at St. James School, but when playing with Dave in the early days in the front room." The song creates an emotional moment, deeply expressive of love and loss, an expression that perhaps the original recording does not quite achieve. In *20th Century Man*, the singing is plaintive as it grieves the lost innocence of youth, while on record, the singing seems more anxious and restless. In the context of the show, the performance adds specificity and intensity to the often broadly defined and casually dismissed love–hate relationship of the brothers. Not all songs, however, assume deeper tones; some are lightened. "Tired of Waiting for You," for instance, becomes a wry, but humorous, commentary on the romantic frustrations of the various boyfriends of Ray's sisters.

The text

And there is a text, and a narrative. *20th Century Man* is the story of a young Englishman, who at the beginning of the performance repeats the opening sentence from *X-Ray*: "My name is of no importance." We see his childhood, his home life, his familial joys and pains, his education through art college, his first job as draftsman for an architect, his early bands, the founding of the Kinks, artistic and commercial success, union bans, commercial failure, and ultimately triumph. This 20th Century Man with no name is every working-class English youth who has struggled through an oppressive culture to escape his fate as "factory fodder" and find identity as an artist. "My name is Raymond Douglas Davies," he proclaims victoriously near the show's end.

The text, however, is more flexible than the above scene summary might suggest. It allows for song additions and substitutions, audience interaction and participation, and ad libs and improvisation. The ad libs, or seeming ad libs, form a connection, as "Alcohol" did in Kinks shows, with both the music-hall performer and the nineteenth-century actor. During music-hall performances and nineteenth-century plays, even those of Shakespeare, the star might step out of character to make a humorous or topical aside to the audience. By creating a dialogue with the audience, the performer incurred its favor and established intimacy in even the largest of theaters.

The technique, not necessarily insincere or only self-serving, works for Davies as it did for those earlier performers. When the audience sings along to "Tired of Waiting for You," Davies jokes, "You sound like a Welsh rugby team," or "You sound like a washroom at the YMCA." In several shows he addressed his deceased father: "Dad, you were such a ham. I'm glad I didn't turn out like you." Or for another bit of tongue-in-cheek denial: " 'You Really Got Me' had to be a hit or we would be dropped from the label—I hear that's humiliating." Such lines, deprecating of audience or self, give those in attendance the sense that this performance is unique, and that they are part of a special audience, one the performer trusts to take into his confidence and one he is familiar enough with to joke. As a result, the audience feels the need to respond enthusiastically as a way to reciprocate the performer's trust. It's an old technique, but when employed by someone with the wit and perception of Davies, it seems fresh and enhances the evening's adventure and inspires both performer and audience.

Some improvisations have been startling. At one performance, Davies introduced "To the Bone," inspired, he said, by the failure of his first marriage and by a record album his wife left behind to torment him. He paused. An audience member shouted "Ducks," alluding to "Ducks on the Wall," a comic gem from *Soap Opera* (1975) about a wife's poor decorative taste. The somber mood broke and the unpredictable Davies laughed. Then before continuing his tale about the old stereo and album loaded with memories that "cut to the bone," he broke into a verse or two and a chorus of "Ducks on the Wall," which he seemed to enjoy as much as the audience. Perhaps inspired by that moment, later in the same show, Davies spoke about the Drury Lane concert in which the Kinks performed *The Village Green Preservation Society*. He led a sing-along of what might have been a complete rendition of that album's title track. Amazingly, the audience never faltered, despite the non-repetitive and complex cataloging of the lyrics, and despite Davies's lack of cues. The attempt itself indicates a bold and confident performer, well in touch with his audience.

In a sense, at every performance Davies constructed a new text as he responds to script, song, memory, himself, audience, and location.

The performer

A script, however, is only as good as its performers and *20th Century Man* is a fitting text for Davies, one with which he was obviously comfortable and a vehicle that allowed him to unfold his various talents and accomplishments and to perform as a fifty-year-old-plus rock composer and singer. Ironically, he did this while re-enacting events and performing songs from over thirty years ago. But the difference between him and other rockers, who perform or try to perform in much the same way as they did decades ago, is that Davies and his audience acknowledge the passage of time. There was no attempt in *20th Century Man* to feign youth or deny age. There was never a doubt that the point of view in the script is that of a mature, experienced narrator looking back at his past. This perspective gives the show its quality of "human truth."

20th Century Man allows Davies to say "I am"—not only as an individual and artist, but as an actor in the Stanislavskian sense, i.e., one submerged in the emotional currents of the script. Stanislavski defined the state of "I am" as follows:

> In our theatre parlance this means that I have put myself into the very centre of imaginary circumstances . . . that I exist at the heart of the imaginary life, in a world of imaginary things. . . . The smallest action or sensation, the slightest technical means, can acquire a deep significance . . . only if it is pushed to its limit of possibility, to the boundary of human *truth*, faith and the sense of "I am." When this point is reached, your whole spiritual and physical makeup will function normally.[15]

> (italics his)

Fairly consistently, Davies achieved this sense of "I am," this total immersion in the scene, which compelled him to act from impulse, not calculation. It happened regularly, it seemed, with certain scenes more than with others: when, for instance, he sang "See My Friends" and considered his days playing guitar with Dave in the front room; when he re-enacted the recording of "You Really Got Me"; when he talked of meeting John Lennon as the Kinks prepared to perform just ahead of the Beatles; when he related the moment his father expressed pride in his sons' achievement; when he talked of his marriage to Rasa and sang "I Go to Sleep"—at one February 1997 show he quickly wiped a fallen tear, perhaps a ploy, but maybe not; and when he discussed the imminent breakup of the original Kinks during the recording of "Days."

These moments were dramatic and emotional without being sentimental (Davies's humor prevented that), and provided Davies the opportunity to reach "I am." On those nights when he gets to "I am," he never failed to take the audience with him. "One of the most exciting parts in the show for me," says Davies, "is reliving when Dave first did his guitar solo in 'You Really Got Me.' It's a moment I still remember in slow motion. When that works on-stage, when I feel like the audience really *gets* it . . . there's simply nothing like it"[16] (italics his).

However, "I am" can be both an exhilarating and terrifying place for an actor, as instinctive, emotional responses imply, somewhat falsely, loss of control: "When it gets too emotional," says Davies, "I pretend I'm talking about somebody else, and that's the whole joy. . . . And the interesting thing about the show is that people forget who I am sometimes and then they say, 'Hang on, that's the real person up there.' "[17] As in *X-Ray*, Davies often reveals more about himself when he tries to hide or conceal himself from his audience.

The humor

20th Century Man was a very funny show. There were, as expected, amusing anecdotes, ad libs, self-deprecating comments, and pretended arrogance: "Never mock a man at prayer," Davies might say in an effete, upper-class voice as he sashayed towards a beer. But he also mimicked voices, played with double entendre, and delivered recurrent jokes.

Almost no one in Davies's life escaped being mimicked and mocked, and not always affectionately. Whether it be the deep and very masculine south London accent of drummer Mick Avory; the effeminate, posh affectations of managers Grenville Collins and Robert Wace; the deep, slow Liverpudlian drawl of John Lennon; the high-pitched voice of a youthful Ray Davies and the higher-pitched shrill of brother Dave; the redneck, gum-chewing customs agent at John F. Kennedy Airport; or the gruff New York accent of a dubious Allen Klein, whom Davies did not identify by name: "The Kinks. I always wanted to meet The Kinks. 'You Really

Got Me' is a great record. Me and my wife dance to it all the time. What can I do you for?" After hearing the Kinks are broke: "That's disgraceful. Sometimes I'm ashamed of the industry I'm in." During one spring 1997 performance in Peekskill, New York, Davies improvised cartoon voices of characters such as Tweety Bird and Sylvester the Cat.

But what made the mimicries so effective was that they grew out of the character or caricature that Davies created. Each voice was funny because each voice suited the character so well—whether that character or voice matched the actual person or not. In addition, contrasts were cleverly emphasized: between, for instance, a young Davies's high-pitched squeak and Klein's deep rasp, or between manager Larry Page's slow, East End ruggedness and Wace's and Collins's frenetic effeminacy.

Davies also enjoyed playing off the double entendre. Sometimes at the very beginning of the show, Davies might announce that he would "prime" the audience with a few songs: "You don't mind being primed. Now do you, Madam?" Or we could have heard of a sister who was not "going down too well" with a boyfriend, "which is to say that the relationship wasn't flourishing as it should. Or, in other words, my sister was not going down too well." One night in New York he followed that with an ad lib addressed to no one in particular: "Are you offended, madam? *Tommy*'s up the road. Go see that." Or when he talked of the redneck chauffeur driving him through the wild, wild West: "I'm glad he was only waving his revolver at me."

Davies seemed to have two favorite recurrent jokes: Mick Avory's homophobia and the "I-know-a-man-who-knows-a-man" routine. After his audition, Mick tells the band that he enjoyed playing with them, the music, that is, but he quickly informs them that he is straight: "We'll soon change that, darling" is the suspicious reply. Throughout the narrative, whenever the Kinks get into trouble, which is frequent, they seek advice from "a man who knows a man who knows another man." So when they need funding to re-record "You Really Got Me," their wealthy manager Robert Wace comes through because "Robert knows a man, who knows another man, who knows Robert's father." This refrain reflects the complex and convoluted circumstances behind most of the Kinks' dealings, from bad record deals, to four-year bans from America, and multiple and protracted lawsuits.

The statement

20th Century Man worked so well because it said something significant about several themes, including lost innocence and the magic of innocence. In episode after episode, young Ray Davies and his fellow Kinks get taken in or abused—whether it be at their first gig at a local dance hall, in a car with Big Fat Cowboy, or at the hands of Allen Klein. Yet somehow their innocent faith in their music sustained them. At least until Peter Quaife left. There was sadness when Davies spoke of Quaife's departure and sadness in Davies's performance of "Days," which in the show commemorates the end of an era for the Kinks. With innocence and Quaife both lost, the music inevitably changed. But the sadness of the scene lifted when Davies broke into "Waterloo Sunset," which affirms faith in innocence, although one of a different kind: the innocence of two lovers and the speaker's comfort in the natural image of the sunset.

20th Century Man also concerns itself with family, one of Davies's dominant themes, particularly the family in post–World War II England. Discussing *X-Ray*, Davies said, "My thing was family. And the book is dedicated to my family. That's what the kid journalist in the story has lost, and that's what R. D. has turned his back on."[18] As he does in the stage show and elsewhere, particularly *Arthur*, Davies considers his own family representative of the English working class— especially since they "experienced things that millions of other families did."[19]

But Ray's familial relationships are, of course, at least somewhat unique. While Ray addresses his relationship with his brother, perhaps the most ambiguous and ever-evolving relationship depicted (in terms of the performance, i.e.) is between Ray and his father. How to present the relationship seems to have posed problems for Davies. In Stamford, Connecticut, in October 1996, he said of his father, "An interesting character. [Pause.] Well, not really, but for the sake of the show, let's say that." Less than a month later in New York, he said as a beer was handed to him, "My father allowed me to call him 'Dad' after three or four pints of that stuff." There is certainly love in the relationship, but there is also distance. At times, Ray seemed to have been trying to please his father, a father who was closer to Dave, the more comprehensible son, and a father who perhaps lived more for weekends at the pub and his late-Saturday-night parties than for his children. The relationship becomes closer when Ray plays the scene in which he apologizes to his father for being a rock star and not a football player as he thinks his father would have preferred. His father, however, expresses pride in his son and confides that Ray is doing just what he would have liked to have done himself. Then to undercut sentimentality, the father says, "Now, let's get pissed." By show's end, Davies reaches an understanding toward his father, but it seems tentative and unassured.

To a lesser extent, *20th Century Man* is about the artistic process and the way songs are composed, recorded, and performed. Throughout the evening, Davies takes us into his creative process, revealing inspiration, method, and strategy. Consider the comments above on "Two Sisters" and "See My Friends." Somewhat predictably, the show attacks the music industry and its disregard for the artist and artistic integrity.

Less predictably and unplanned, the performances frequently revealed artistic frustration with the audience. One night, after the audience applauded Davies's reference to "All Day and All of the Night," Ray responded, "We're not playing that tonight." The audience sighed. Davies relented, and followed with "Apeman." Then he commented on the enthusiastic response, "Oh, so that's it. You only came for the hits." He was not completely kidding. One night, while leaving the theater in Philadelphia, I overheard someone say, "I like the songs, but I wish he didn't talk so much." After the same show I watched as another fan expressed his disappointment to Davies, who was signing an autograph for him: "How come you didn't sing 'Celluloid Heroes'?" Davies explained politely that it did not fit into the show's context. Unsatisfied, the fan asked if Davies could sing it for him now. These responses to Davies during and especially after the show might explain why Mick Jagger continues to present himself as Jumping Jack Flash: "Give the People What They Want."

Ultimately, however, *20th Century Man* is about individual triumph. Despite the English class system and its Welfare State, a corrupt music industry, union chest thumping, managerial ineptitude and desertion, and more, the individual succeeds because he believes in what he is doing. He has a sense of passion and commitment, and as Joseph Campbell might have said, he follows his "bliss." It's a very hopeful story and, through Davies, a very plausible and insightful one of a young boy growing up, struggling into maturity, and finding and celebrating himself as an individual and as an artist.

Ever restless

Although *20th Century Man / Storyteller* consumed much of his time in the mid- to late 1990s, Davies continued to develop other projects. In October 1998, he premiered *The Flatlands*, a choral piece with orchestration commissioned by the Norfolk & Norwich Festival in East Anglia. Inspired by Davies's sense of a lost England as well as the East Anglian landscape, "a mystical place, full of history,"[20] *Flatlands* places St. George, England's patron saint, in the contemporary world where he slays another dragon and rescues another damsel. Marcus Davey, artistic director, was very pleased with not only the sellout audiences for *Flatlands*, but also Davies's eagerness to bring his own style and approach to the choral tradition. Female lead vocalist Jane Haughton characterized the piece as having "a very nice element of popular folk feel about it."[21] Unfortunately, *Flatlands* has not been officially recorded for release and it has not been performed since a week after its premiere.

Throughout the late 1990s and into the new century, Davies continued the songwriting course that he first offered in 1993. The workshop approach brings together between fifteen and twenty students for an intense week of discussion, writing, and tutoring. Davies meets collectively and individually with his students and assigns various exercises—writing a song from the perspective of a specific character, for instance. By the end of the week, students will have written several new songs with at least one for a group musical based on a theme or a film, like *Thelma and Louise* or *On the Waterfront*. According to reports, Davies can be a challenging and demanding instructor, but also a sensitive and enthusiastic one intent on opening students to new possibilities and approaches.

In the late 1990s, Davies began writing songs for his first solo album—he does not consider the soundtrack to *Return to Waterloo* or the CD version of his stage show *Storyteller* to be solo albums. In late August 2000, he premiered several new songs during a three-night stay at the Jane Street Theatre in New York. Backed by Pete Mathison and Yo La Tengo, an Indie band and great admirers of the Kinks, Ray played several songs that found their way onto *Other People's Lives*, like "Things Are Gonna Change," "Creatures of Little Faith," "Next Door Neighbour," "Stand Up Comic" and "Thanksgiving Day," and others that have yet to be released, like "The Deal," "Empty Room," "Vietnam Cowboys," and the exceptional "Otis Riffs." It was a generous set mixed with Kinks hits, like "All Day and All of the Night," "Celluloid Heroes," and "Low Budget," as well as obscure Kinks songs and album tracks that Davies said Yo La Tengo "persuaded me to do . . . songs that I would never ever play,"[22] like "No Return," "Animal Farm," "This Is Where I Belong," and "Strange Effect," the last of which would not be released officially by the Kinks until 2001 on *The Kinks: BBC Sessions, 1964–1977*. The Jane Street shows were extremely well received and the new album eagerly awaited—although it would not be released for almost six years.

While Davies worked and reworked the songs for *Other People's Lives*, he lived partly in New Orleans. His marriage to Pat Crosbie had fallen apart and Ray thought he would "discover America." "I was in a relationship with someone who was moving there, and the music that inspired me came from there—apart from Noel Coward and the English stuff."[23] Davies settled in Faubourg Marigny, a residential neighborhood just outside the French Quarter. "It was just great," he said. ""I felt comfortable there because . . . New Orleans felt like a village to me," he said. "The music community didn't have any snobbery to it. It's the most laid back place in America and it's genuine."[24] It did not take long for Ray to become part of the NOLA community. He rode his bicycle around town, exercised occasionally at the New Orleans Athletic Club, and listened to music at local clubs like the Circle Bar and the Mermaid Lounge. Quint Davis, the producer and director of the New Orleans Jazz and Heritage Festival, came to know Davies, stating that he was "becoming a guy on the scene. . . . Which is a cool thing. . . . He's an important artist, not just some English cat hanging out."[25]

Life in New Orleans, however, took an abrupt change for Davies in the early evening of January 5, 2004. Having just resolved to finish what would be *Other People's Lives*, he walked with his girlfriend after dinner on Burgundy Street near Esplanade Avenue, not far from their residence. Suddenly, a car pulled up and a passenger exited, snatching his companion's handbag. Ray pursued the thief who escaped in the car, but not before he shot Davies in the thigh. Taken to Charity Hospital, Davies was assured by doctors that he was in good hands. After all, they explained that "they had . . . plenty of practice."[26] The shooter was arrested later that evening as Ray's girlfriend was able to record the license plate number of the car.

Ray's wounds were not as clean as first thought, and he had to be hospitalized again on March 31. What most surprised Davies, however, was that he was affected emotionally as well as physically. As a result, his relationship with his girlfriend ended and *Other People's Lives* was delayed. Ray had an especially difficult time finishing "The Tourist" and "The Getaway," both written and recorded before the shooting. "I had to abandon mixing the album because I couldn't listen to those songs," he said. Still, Davies has no ill feelings towards New Orleans. "I really loved the place and the people—it's impossible to go very far there without encountering music."[27] Indeed, he was serenaded in Charity Hospital by a nurse "who whispered slow, mournful gospel songs in the style of Mahalia Jackson."[28] Davies, it seems, has put the shooting in perspective: "Despite what happened to me, I have such happy memories."[29]

In March 2004, with the aid of a walking stick, Davies accepted a CBE (Commander of the Order of the British Empire) from Queen Elizabeth II. Davies had very little apprehension about accepting the award. "My family had a big issue with the idea of Empire," he commented. "But I think I was just so relieved to be alive and for the opportunity to go there with my daughter, who lives in Ireland. I was getting presented with it on St. Patrick's Day and I thought it was too poetic to turn down. I deserve a medal for staying [in the country] and paying tax when it was 95 percent."[30] Afterwards Davies created a minor controversy when he reported what supposedly the Queen had whispered to him: "I hope they catch the bastards who shot you!" The Palace insisted that Her Majesty would never have used "that sort of language."[31] Previously, in June 2002, Davies had sung "Lola" before the Queen, the Royal Family, and 12,000 ticket winners on the grounds of Buckingham Palace as he and many other pop music luminaries performed at the Party at the Palace in celebration of Elizabeth's Golden Jubilee. For Davies, who had watched the young Queen's Coronation on his sister's small television screen, both events had to be thrilling.

Since the release of *Other People's Lives* in 2006, Davies has worked on an accompanying documentary, still unreleased to date—although in the spring 2006 he premiered footage at South by Southwest (SXSW), an annual music festival and conference in Austin, Texas. Davies has also toured steadily in support of the CD, performing some fifty concerts throughout America and Europe in 2006. Appearing fit and in good voice, Ray seems to enjoy his time on stage with his four-piece band as they weave through Kinks hits, classics, relatively obscure album selections—including sometimes a cluster of songs from *Village Green*—and most of the selections on the new album.[32] Like *Other People's Lives*, his performances have received largely positive if not enthusiastic reviews from fans and critics. Reviewing a bootleg CD of a July 2006 performance, *Rolling Stone* said, "Overall, the show is so good that it's almost enough to make you stop praying for a Kinks reunion."[33]

Davies and the Kinks

The Kinks last performed together on June 15, 1996 in Oslo at the Norwegian Wood Music Festival, hardly a climactic site for the final performance of one of rock music's most important bands, and, last released an album as a working unit on October 15, 1996 with *To the Bone*.[34] At neither time did any of the Kinks realize that either would mark finality. *To the Bone*, a double CD, especially sends ambiguous signals. It collects live concert performances from 1993 and 1994, several tracks from in-studio performances at Konk before a select audience in April 1994, and studio recordings of new songs, "To the Bone" and "Animal." Old songs are given reworkings, like "Do You Remember Walter," and some rarely performed tracks are energetically delivered, like "Set Me Free" and "Picture Book." On the one hand, the band seems to be securing its legacy while, on the other, it looks forward to future possibilities.

Since the Kinks' last performance at Oslo, rumors, not unfounded, have persisted of a Kinks reunion. In the fall 1997, for instance, Ray approached the original lineup about re-forming and recording. Some time later, Ray and Dave met to discuss details of a reunion—which quickly collapsed as the brothers faced off in a swirl of demands and counterdemands. According to my source, among other far less significant conditions, the brothers could not agree on the drummer with Ray's preferring Avory over Bob Henrit, Dave's choice. Ray, however, did agree not to produce a new Kinks album—of course, how much autonomy an outside producer would have is questionable.

Neither brother has definitively stated that the Kinks are finished. In 2006, Ray reported that he was "going to get together with [Dave] to see if the music is still there." No meeting, however, has been reported. One detail has always been certain about a reunion: "There's got to be new music. We can't just play old hits."[35] Neither Ray nor Dave is content to cash in on nostalgic impulses of potential audiences and have long shunned high-paying dates at any type of British Invasion or 1960s reunion shows. Furthermore, the brothers have not been self-serving in their equivocal responses to reunion questions. The truth is that neither knows for sure whether the Kinks will reunite or whether they should reunite.

The only thing certain

Since Davies tends to begin more projects than he can possibly complete, it becomes impossible to predict the time or form of any new work—official release dates not withstanding. He has, for instance, been working on a film complement to *Other People's Lives*; he has written music and recorded demos for *Come Dancing*, a Broadway or West End type musical; he has several film scripts in various stages of completion; he has discussed a possible CD-ROM or DVD for *Village Green Preservation Society*; and he has enough songs from New Orleans for a second solo album. The question is which of these or others will receive his priority.

Mick Avory, who at Ray's direction contacted Peter Quaife with tentative Kinks reunion plans, provides insight into Ray's work habits. "He says something as if he wants to do it next week. Then you don't hear about it for another year. [*Imitating Ray*] 'So, by the way, did you talk to Pete?' I said, 'Yeah, a long time ago. But I thought you had already forgotten about it.' "[36] At that particular time, Ray probably got distracted by other projects, perhaps *Flatlands* or *Storyteller*.

The only thing certain is that new work in one form or another will be forthcoming from Ray Davies.

CONCLUSION

"Stockhausen, an adventurous composer, saw his life's work as a continuum," said Ray Davies in 1996. "That's a correct attitude to adopt. Even though each project may view separately [sic], the survey will be that it's a single body of work."[1]

Since 1964, with and apart from the Kinks, Ray Davies has produced a substantial and diverse body of work—masterful three-minute pop songs, concept albums, rock musicals, more traditional musicals, experimental films and documentaries, an inventive autobiography, a collection of short stories, a choral piece with orchestration, and a one-man stage show. Yet behind all his work is not only the same force but also the same subject: himself. His vast output and artistic resourcefulness results from his yet unfulfilled quest for self-definition, self-understanding, and self-acceptance.

But what enlarges his art, besides a fervent and curious imagination, is his insistence on his own representativeness as a post-World War II individual, indeed, a *20th Century Man*, one with a great capacity to sympathize with others who may be less aware of their marginalization. His art speaks for them as well as for himself. Through his creations, Davies wrestles with his and the contemporary individual's relationship with family, place, the past, national identity, technology, the state, and internal forces. More often than not the villain is the state, or as termed in *X-Ray*, the Corporation, which has increasingly empowered itself at the expense of individual certainty and liberty, leaving the individual in various states of confusion and incompleteness.

Davies has never remained close to any large institution, record companies included. Since the Kinks' relationship with Pye and Reprise ended in 1971, he has changed labels at the termination of every contract, no matter how supportive the label. His suspicion has only grown through the years. In the late 1990s, he reached terms with Capitol Records for the release of the album that would eventually be *Other People's Lives*. But not only did he fail to deliver the album, he also refused to play demos for executives, instead inviting them to his concerts at the Jane Street

Theatre. In 2002, the exasperated label dropped Davies after waiting over three years for the album. Capitol executive Dave Ayers, who was eager to work with Davies, was disappointed: "[He has] an intense mistrust of the system," commented Ayers. "There's a line in [X-Ray] that says, 'When in doubt, trust your paranoia,' which says a lot."[2] The result was that *Other People's Lives* was released by the smaller V2 Records, which has since let go of all its artists to focus on its back catalog and digital distribution.

Ray could well have been the model for the Master in the short story "The Lesson of the Master" by Henry James. Asked by a young author if the artist is ultimately "a man all the same," the Master, Henry St. George, replied, "I mostly think not. You know as well as I what he has to do: the concentration, the finish, the independence he must strive for from the moment he begins to wish his work really decent. Ah, my young friend, his relation to women, and especially to the one he's most intimately concerned with, is at the mercy of the damned fact that whereas he can in the nature of things have but one standard, they have about fifty."[3] Furthermore, the Master says, the artist works "on the supposition that a certain perfection's possible and even desirable . . . one's children interfere with perfection. One's wife interferes. Marriage interferes. . . . [An artist marries] at his peril—he does so at his cost."[4]

Davies has not been an easy husband or partner for his three former wives and love mates. Relentless in his artistic pursuits, he undertakes more projects than he could ever hope to complete and he never takes an extended hiatus. "I used to get very lonely," says first wife Rasa. "He makes himself busy all the time. . . . He's unable to relax. His mind is working all the time, I'm sure, even when he's sleeping. I think Ray's just got to be on his own a lot of the time. He's a loner."[5]

Davies has tried to explain. "Whilst pop music is simple and should be understood by everybody," he said, "the reality is that for some people there is something deeper that drives them to do what they do—and I think I'm one of those people."[6] That "something deeper" is not easily defined, but in "Self-Reliance" Emerson called it "genius" and "whim," although he admitted that *whim* was not quite the right word. "I shun father and mother," said the Transcendentalist, "and wife and brother, when my genius calls me. . . . I cannot sell my liberty and my power, to save their sensibility."[7] Davies has neither been slowed by age nor by his shooting in New Orleans: "It put me back on the trajectory of being focused," he said. "It's just put me back into fight mode . . . I'm just a driven chap."[8]

It seems as if Davies's restlessness, personal and artistic, results from a need to avoid consistency and acceptance, which, for him, are forms of confinement through definition. "I always shun the idea that I might be accepted," Davies once said, "because maybe if I was, I'd stop searching. I want the right to change."[9] He has resisted any kind of career summing

Figure C.1 At the time of *Phobia*, the Kinks were: (L–R) Dave, Ray, Haley, Henrit, and Rodford

up, whether it be *To the Bone* or a yet to be compiled Kinks box set—certainly, any issues with the various labels are resolvable. Ray seems troubled by such retrospectives, which would reduce the Kinks' over thirty-year career to perhaps four hours of supposedly defining moments. Too neat, too final.

In "Still Searching" from *Phobia*, Davies comes as close to defining himself as he does anywhere else: "a restless spirit who can't reach his goal / Can't find a home until I've found my soul." It is his failure to reach his goal—artistic perfection and personal fulfillment, unachievable to Henry James—that has kept him on the quest, kept him tormented and struggling through sleepless nights, but also kept him creating. The result is a rich artistic legacy, spanning some five decades and still growing.

APPENDIX A

My twenty-five *favorite* Ray Davies songs

1. "Waterloo Sunset"
2. "Days"
3. "Victoria"
4. "All Day and All of the Night"
5. "Lola"
6. "Sunny Afternoon"
7. "Autumn Almanac"
8. "You Really Got Me"
9. "Sitting in My Hotel"
10. "Art Lover"
11. "A Well Respected Man"
12. "Muswell Hillbillies"
13. "Better Things"
14. "Oh Where Oh Where is Love?"
15. "Village Green Preservation Society"
16. "King Kong"
17. "Sweet Lady Genevieve"
18. "Lost and Found"
19. "Around the Dial"
20. "Permanent Waves"
21. "Over My Head"
22. "Good Day"
23. "In a Foreign Land"
24. "Dedicated Follower of Fashion"
25. "Lavender Hill"

APPENDIX B

My ten *favorite* Kinks/Ray Davies albums
(including compilations and live albums)

1. *Arthur (or the Decline and Fall of the British Empire)*
2. *The Kinks Are the Village Green Preservation Society*
3. *Muswell Hillbillies*
4. *Preservation Act 2*
5. *The Kink Kronikles*
6. *Something Else by the Kinks*
7. *Everybody's in Show-Biz*
8. *To the Bone* (double CD)
9. *Give the People What They Want*
10. *Word of Mouth*

2 *SOMETHING BETTER BEGINNING*

1. Said during performance of *20th Century Man*, the John Harms Center for the Arts, Englewood, NJ, Oct. 24, 1997.
2. Qtd. in Michael J. Kraus, "A Conversation with Bob Henrit," in *Living on a Thin Line: Crossing Aesthetic Borders with The Kinks*, Thomas M. Kitts and Michael J. Kraus, eds. (Rumford, RI: Rock 'n' Roll Research Press, 2002), 236.
3. Qtd. in Alan di Perna, "A Kink's Kronikle," *Guitar World* (Jan. 1997): 58.
4. Qtd. in Johnny Rogan, *The Kinks: A Mental Institution* (London: Proteus, 1984), 3.
5. Qtd. in Kraus, "Conversation with Bob Henrit," 235.
6. Qtd. in Danny Kirby, "Peter Quaife: Interview Part One," *Now & Then*, 7 (1994): 5.
7. Qtd. in Nick Hasted, "Ready Steady Kinks!!!" *Uncut* (Sept. 2004): 49.
8. Qtd. in Kirby, "Part One," 4.
9. Qtd. in Johnny Black, "The Hellfire Club," *Mojo* (Sept. 2000): 64.
10. Qtd. in Jon Savage, *The Kinks: The Official Biography* (London: Faber and Faber, 1984), 8.
11. Ray Davies, "Guitars and Greasy Spoons," *Electronic Telegraph*, Feb. 22, 2001, http://www.telegraph.co.uk (accessed Feb. 24, 2001).
12. Dave Davies, *Kink* (London: Boxtree, 1996), 3.
13. Quaife lasted only about three weeks at art college, although he went on to work in post-Kinks years as a commercial artist and illustrator.
14. Mark Paytress, "Tales of Ordinary Madness," *Mojo* (Mar. 2006): 72.
15. Qtd. in Rogan, *Mental Institution*, 7.
16. Ray Davies, *X-Ray: The Unauthorized Autobiography* (Woodstock: Overlook, 1994), 69.
17. *X-Ray*, 70.
18. *X-Ray*, 69.
19. *X-Ray*, 68.
20. Qtd. in Chris George, "The Kitchen Sink Kink," *Independent*, Aug. 27, 1994. Rpt on *Dave Emlen's Unofficial Kinks Web Site*, http://kinks.it.rit.edu (accessed Mar. 13, 2006).
21. Rob Patterson, "Ray Davies: 'God Save the Kinks!' " *Fi* (Dec. 1998): 22. Rpt. in the newsletter of the Official Kinks Fan Club, Jan. 2000: 6.
22. Qtd. in Robin Denselow, "London Calling," *Guardian*, Oct. 3, 2005, http://www.guardian.co.uk (accessed Oct. 13, 2005).
23. Qtd. in Walter Tunis, "Kinks Leader Has His Own Story to Tell," *Lexington Herald-Leader on the Internet*, May 10, 1998. Excerpt rpt. in newsletter of the Official Kinks Fan Club, July 8, 1998: n. pag.
24. Interview by author, Aug. 15, 2005.
25. See Rogan, *Mental Institution*, 164.
26. Interview by author, Aug. 15, 2005.
27. Qtd. in Russell Smith, *The Songs I Sang for Auntie* (Warwickshire, UK: Official Kinks Fan Club, 1996), 1.
28. Qtd. in Rogan, *Mental Institution*, 191, said to rock journalist Keith Altham, c. Sept. 1964.
29. Qtd. in *The Kinks: Virgin Modern Icons* (London: Virgin, 1997), 46. Rpt. from *Melody Maker*, 1964.
30. Qtd. in Hasted, 50.
31. Qtd. in Doug Hinman, *The Kinks: All Day and All of the Night* (San Francisco: Backbeat, 2004), 11.
32. *Kink*, 25.

33. Qtd. in John Mendelssohn, *The Kinks Kronikles* (New York: Quill, 1985), 20.
34. See Hinman, *All Day*, 12.
35. Qtd. in Mendelssohn, 28.
36. Interview by author, Aug. 15, 2005.
37. Qtd. in Black, "The Hellfire Club," 64.
38. Qtd. in Mendelssohn, 28.
39. Telephone interview by author, May 18, 2000.
40. *Kink*, 147.
41. Qtd. by Collins, telephone interview by author, May 18, 2000.
42. For a detailed account of Mickey Willet's firing, see Rogan, *Mental Institution*, 10–13.
43. Qtd. in Black, "The Hellfire Club," 65.
44. Qtd. in Rogan, *Mental Institution*, 14.
45. See the following for accounts of the naming of the Kinks: *X-Ray*, 102–4; *Kink*, 32; Hinman, *All Day*, 17; Rogan, *Mental Institution*, 17–18; Savage, 17; Mendelssohn, 25–6. In *My Generation: The Kinks*, Dir. John Pigee, Granada Television, 1995, Page says firmly, "I gave them that name, the Kinks."
46. *X-Ray*, 103.
47. Interview by author, Aug. 15, 2005.

3 YOU REALLY GOT ME

1. Probably Regent Sound Studios in central London to record three Davies originals: "You Still Want Me," "You Do Something to Me," and "I Don't Need You Anymore."
2. For the six-hour session the Kinks with session drummer Bobby Graham recorded at least five songs.
3. Qtd. in Ray Davies, *X-Ray: The Unauthorized Autobiography* (Woodstock: Overlook, 1994), 104.
4. Telephone interview by author, May 18, 2000.
5. Liverpool's *Mersey Beat* asks, "How can anyone make such an exciting song so boring?" while the *New Musical Express* says that "my preference is for 'I Took My Baby Home' with its hypnotic twist beat and pleasing melody"—qtd. in Doug Hinman, *The Kinks: All Day and All of the Night* (San Francisco: Backbeat, 2004), 21.
6. Qtd. in Robin Mackie, "The Kinks: A Band to Preserve," *Record Mirror*, Jan. 13, 1973: n. pag. Rpt. in the newsletter of the Official Kinks Fan Club Jan. 2000: n. pag.
7. *X-Ray*, 120, 121.
8. Olga Ruocco, e-mail message to author, May 12, 2006.
9. *X-Ray*, 207.
10. See *X-Ray*, 156–60. The story was pivotal in *20th Century Man* and *Storyteller*.
11. Telephone interview by author, May 17, 2000. See also Hinman, *All Day*, 31.
12. Hinman, *All Day*, 53.
13. Davies has said this repeatedly while introducing the song in concert—at Irving Plaza, NY, for instance, Mar. 24, 2006.
14. Both Ray and Dave agree that the little green amp was not very powerful and that Dave slashed the speakers, but they differ on the details. Ray reports that the amplifier was 8 watts and Dave 10 watts; Ray claims that Dave slashed the speakers with their mother's knitting needles and Dave claims he used a razor blade, which offers a tougher and more rock-and-roll image—see *X-Ray*, 32–3; *Kink* (London: Boxtree, 1996), 1, 2.

15. *Kink*, 3.
16. Qtd. by Avory, interview by author, Aug. 15, 2005. Dave and Ray also report Nash's defense of the Kinks and quote him directly. The sense of the quotations is the same, but the exact words are different—see *Kink*, 41; *X-Ray*, 119; Jon Savage, *The Kinks: The Official Biography* (London: Faber and Faber, 1984), 24.
17. Davies refers to the Dave Clark Five as "product" (*X-Ray*, 116). The DC5 relied on talented singer, keyboardist, and composer Mike Smith, who was uncomfortable fronting a band.
18. Qtd. in Neville Marten and Jeffrey Hudson, *The Kinks: Well Respected Men* (Surrey: Castle, 1996), 35.
19. See Dave Marsh, *Louie Louie* (New York: Hyperion, 1993), 143–4.
20. Qtd. in Johnny Black, " 'Who, Me?' " *Mojo* (Sept. 2000): 70.
21. Qtd. in Hinman, *All Day*, 31; Berry scored a major hit in Belgium and Holland with Ray's "This Strange Effect."
22. *X-Ray*, 151.
23. Avory did not play on the original recording, not because of his ability, but because he had not yet signed a contract with Pye and because Talmy knew that the studio-experienced Graham would more quickly find the proper sound for recording—drums were the most difficult instrument to record in the days of mono. Avory sneaked in to play tambourine, and Arthur Greenslade played piano. Despite persistent rumors, Jimmy Page did not play the guitar solo on "You Really Got Me."
24. Qtd. in Savage, 34.
25. Qtd. in Hinman, *All Day*, 29.
26. Gavin Martin, "Ray's Back with a Bullet," *Mirror* Feb. 10, 2006, http://www.mirror.co.uk (accessed Feb. 14, 2006).
27. Qtd. in Savage, 40.
28. Peter Townshend, "Meaty, Beaty, Big and Bouncy," *Rolling Stone* (Dec. 9, 1971): 37.
29. Qtd. in *The Kinks: Virgin Modern Icons* (London: Virgin, 1997), 71. Rpt. from *Q*, 1995.
30. John Osborne, *Look Back in Anger* (1957, reprint, New York: Penguin, 1982), 15.
31. Savage, 38.
32. Qtd. in John Mendelssohn, *The Kinks Kronikles* (New York: Quill, 1985), 44.
33. Qtd. in Gary Eskow, "Ray Davies: The Storyteller," *Mix* (Aug. 1998): 57.
34. *Kink*, 57.
35. Qtd. in Mendelssohn, 77.
36. Telephone interview by author, May 18, 2000.
37. E-mail message to author, May 16, 2006.
38. Telephone interview by author, May 18, 2000.
39. Qtd. in Savage, 38.
40. *Kink*, 49.
41. Qtd. in Savage, 40, italics his.
42. *X-Ray*, 175.
43. *Kink*, 64.
44. Costello's "Tired of Waiting for You" appears on *One of the Attractions*, a bootleg; Green Day's version appears on *Basket Case* (UK release) and the soundtrack for *Private Parts*, and Yoakam's on *Under the Covers*. Ramone performed "Tired" and "Set Me Free" at the Loser's Lounge Tribute to the Kinks, Westbeth Theatre, NY, Oct. 6, 2000. Ramone died from lymphatic cancer on Apr. 15, 2001.

45. Qtd. in Michael Heatley, "Classic Career: Dave Davies," *Classic Rock*, n.d. Rpt. in the newsletter of the Official Kinks Fan Club, Jan. 2002: n. pag.
46. *X-Ray*, 223–4.
47. *X-Ray*, 224.
48. *X-Ray*, 225.
49. Qtd. in Alan Freeman, "Iron Man of the Kinks," *Rave* (Dec. 1964). Rpt. on *Dave Emlen's Unofficial Kinks Web Site*, http://kinks.it.rit.edu (accessed Apr. 30, 1997).
50. Interview by author, Aug. 15, 2005.
51. *X-Ray*, 233.
52. Qtd. in Hinman, *All Day*, 65.
53. *Kink*, 68.
54. Interview by author, Aug. 15, 2005.
55. *X-Ray*, 34, 369.
56. This Eleven Plus examination was administered to all students just after their eleventh birthday. How the students scored determined whether they would enter a secondary modern school or a college preparatory program. Few went from secondary modern schools to college.
57. Qtd. in Savage, 139.

4 A WELL RESPECTED MAN

1. Telephone interview by author, May 17, 2000.
2. Interview by author, Aug. 15, 2005.
3. Qtd. by Collins, telephone interview by author, May 17, 2000.
4. Qtd. in Hinman, *The Kinks: All Day and All of the Night* (San Francisco: Backbeat, 2004), 56.
5. *Kink* (London: Boxtree, 1996), 80.
6. Collins, telephone interview by author, May 18, 2000.
7. Interview by author, Aug. 15, 2005.
8. Interview by author, Aug. 15, 2005. Curtis was the father of two sons, Adrian and Paul Gurvitz, who with Ginger Baker formed the Baker Gurvitz Army in 1974. They disbanded in 1977 after recording three albums, of which their self-titled debut had minor chart success in the UK and US.
9. See Johnny Rogan, *The Kinks: A Mental Institution* (London: Proteus, 1984), 48, and Jon Savage, *The Kinks: The Official Biography* (London: Faber and Faber, 1984), 51.
10. Qtd. in Savage, 52.
11. Qtd. in Savage, 52.
12. Qtd. by Avory, interview by author, Aug. 15, 2005.
13. Qtd. in Savage, 88.
14. Both Avory and Quaife have expressed appreciation to me about the post-tour hospitality of Zacharlini, who showed both around the southern California area in a pink Cadillac—Avory, interview by author, Aug. 15, 2005; Quaife, interview by author, May 25, 1998.
15. Avory, interview by author, Aug. 15, 2005.
16. Qtd. in Rogan, *Mental Institution*, 53.
17. *X-Ray*, 180.
18. *X-Ray*, 386.
19. Qtd. by Collins, telephone interview by author, June 1, 2000.
20. Telephone interview by author, May 18, 2000.
21. Qtd. in Jeff Tamarkin, "The Kinks: Seventeen Year Itch," *Hit Parade* (Mar. 1982): 27.

22. Qtd. in Tamarkin, 27.
23. See Rogan, *Mental Institution*, 75. Hinman reports that Avory "had fun" with a "hapless journalist" who he also told that the Kinks were "holding rehearsals in a scout hut near the Avory family house" to put together "an entirely new stage show" (*All Day*, 93).
24. *X-Ray*, 350.
25. Qtd. in Alan di Perna, "A Kink's Kronikle," *Guitar World* (Jan. 1997): 200.
26. Roy Hudd, Introduction, *Music Hall* (London: Eyre Methuen, 1976), n. pag.
27. V. C. Clinton-Baddeley, *The Burlesque Tradition in the English Theatre after 1660* (London: Methuen, 1973), 81.
28. *X-Ray*, 261.
29. Qtd. in Savage, 64.
30. Qtd. in *X-Ray*, 279.
31. Qtd. in Savage, 65.
32. Tamarkin, 27, and *X-Ray*, 311.
33. *Kink*, 89.
34. *X-Ray*, 279.
35. Qtd. in Savage, 67.
36. *X-Ray*, 278.
37. Qtd. in Hinman, *All Day*, 79.
38. *X-Ray*, 279–80.
39. Qtd. in *X-Ray*, 281.
40. Hinman notes that "the title of this LP has been alternately cited as *The Kink Kontroversy* or *The Kinks Kontroversy* depending whether or not one relies on the title as stated on the original UK record label or record cover. One UK catalog incorrectly listed the title as *The Kinks of Kontroversy*"—*The Kinks Part One: You Really Got Me: An Illustrated World Discography of the Kinks* (Rumford, RI: Hinman, 1994), 55.
41. Interview by author, Aug. 15, 2005.
42. *X-Ray*, 286.
43. See Arthur Marwick, *British Society Since 1945* (London: Penguin, 1982), 158, 121.
44. Qtd. in Savage, 75.
45. *X-Ray*, 286.
46. Davies commented immediately after the recording: "[Razorlight] wanted me to do 'Sunny Afternoon' and they wanted me to sing a lot on it and in the end I sang a lot of it and helped produce it. . . . We'll see how it works out. If we think it's tacky we won't put it out. Actually, if we think it's tacky we will put it out"—"Razorlight team up with the Kinks," *NME* [*New Musical Express*] *News*, June 8, 2006, http://www.nme.com/news/kinks/.23272 (accessed Sept. 15, 2006).
47. Marwick, 121. By the end of the decade, Marwick also notes that almost 70 percent of the homes had refrigerators and about 60 percent had washing machines.
48. Savage, 81.
49. *Kink*, 100.
50. Qtd. in Rogan, *Mental Institution*, 74.
51. *X-Ray*, 324.
52. See Rogan, *Mental Institution*, 81.
53. *Kink*, 56.
54. Qtd. in John Mendelssohn, *The Kinks Kronikles* (New York: Quill, 1985), 46.
55. *Melody Maker*, April 10, 1966, qtd. in Rogan, *Mental Institution*, 73.

5 WATERLOO SUNSET

1. E-mail message to author, Nov. 12, 2006.
2. *My Generation: The Kinks*, Dir. John Pigee. Granada Television, 1995.
3. Dave Davies, *Kink* (London: Boxtree, 1996), 101. Dave implies that Ray was more of an arranger and producer than co-writer, developing the middle and creating the remarkable intro for the track by opening the lid of a piano and plucking the strings with a guitar pick.
4. In addition to overdubs on *Live Kinks*, it is possible that, as Andy Miller notes, the "audience hysteria is an extended, repeating tape loop"—Andy Miller, *The Kinks Are the Village Green Preservation Society* (New York: Continuum, 2003), 24.
5. Michael J. Kraus, "The Greatest Rock Star of the 19th Century: Ray Davies, Romanticism, and the Art of Being English," *Popular Music and Society*, 29.2 (2006): 202.
6. Ross Wetzsteon, "Theater: Dedicated Follower," review of *20th Century Man*, *Village Voice*, Feb. 27, 1996, 75.
7. Qtd. in Stephenson [no first name given], "Ray is Still a Dedicated Follower of Fashion," British Press Association, c. spring 1997, http://www.pa.press.net/spotlight/music_davies.html (accessed Nov. 7, 1999).
8. David Perkins, *The Quest for Permanence: The Symbolism of Wordsworth, Shelley and Keats* (Cambridge, MA: Harvard University Press, 1959), 3, 2.
9. Meisel not only states that he reads rock-and-roll through the lens of Romanticism, but that he also reads "Romanticism through the lens of rock and roll"—Perry Meisel, *The Cowboy and the Dandy: Crossing over from Romanticism to Rock and Roll* (New York: Oxford University Press, 1999), 7.
10. *Ray Davies: The World from My Window*, Dir. Matthew Longfellow, Isis Productions, 2003. Geldof was the force behind several fundraising activities to benefit Africa, including the hit single "Do They Know It's Christmas?" (1984) and the mammoth concerts Live Aid (1985) and Live 8 (2005). He was awarded an honorary knighthood and was nominated for the Nobel Peace Prize in 1986.
11. *I'm Not Like Everybody Else: The World of Ray Davies and The Kinks*, Pro. and Dir. Vanessa Engle, BBC, 1995.
12. Jon Savage, *The Kinks: The Official Biography* (London: Faber and Faber, 1984), 84. At one point, Davies claimed the "Liverpool Sunset" story was a deliberate fabrication—see Johnny Rogan, *The Kinks: A Mental Institution* (London: Proteus, 1984), 194, note 49. But he has since repeated that the inspiration was Liverpool and Merseybeat—see *X-Ray: The Unauthorized Autobiography* (Woodstock: Overlook, 1994), 338.
13. *Kink*, 101.
14. *X-Ray*, 338.
15. E-mail message to author, Nov. 13, 2006.
16. *X-Ray*, 338.
17. E-mail message to author, Nov. 13, 2006.
18. *The Kinks: All Day and All of the Night* (San Francisco: Backbeat, 2004), 96.
19. Qtd. in Savage, 84.
20. E-mail message to author, Nov. 13, 2006.
21. *X-Ray*, 335.
22. Olga Ruocco, "Sunny Afternoons and Full Moons: Sunlight, Moonlight, and Stormy Skies in the Songs of The Kinks," in *Living on a Thin Line: Crossing Aesthetic Borders with The Kinks*, Thomas M. Kitts and Michael J. Kraus, eds. (Rumford, RI: Rock 'n' Roll Research Press, 2002), see 55–6.

23. William Wordsworth, Preface to *Lyrical Ballads* (1800), *Bartleb.com: Great Books Online*, http://www.bartleby.com/39/36.html (accessed Jan. 23, 2007).
24. Qtd. in Savage, 84.
25. In "My Heart Leaps Up," Wordsworth wrote that "The Child is father of the Man."
26. Davies had originally given the characters the unmusical names of George and Mabel, but apparently changed them after seeing Terence Stamp and Julie Christie in *Far from the Madding Crowd*—see Rogan, *Mental Institution*, 80, and Neville Marten and Jeffrey Hudson, *The Kinks: Well Respected Men* (Surrey: Castle, 1996), 78. But Terence could also refer to Rosie's son to whom Davies felt especially close as a youth, and Julie could be an early incarnation of Julie Finkle, the mythical woman of Davies's dreams, whom he evokes in *20th Century Man*.
27. Joseph G. Marotta, "The Loss of Identity and the Myth of Edenic Return in Ray Davies," in *Living on a Thin Line*, 69.
28. From Wordsworth's "Lines Composed a Few Miles above Tintern Abbey," ll. 25–30.
29. Bowie released "Waterloo Sunset" on the DVD edition of *Reality* and the Japanese CD (2003). Davies and Bowie performed the song together at New York's Carnegie Hall on February 26, 2003, at the benefit for the Tibet House. Davies also performed the song with Blur's Damon Albarn on UK television's *The White Room* in 1995.
30. *X-Ray*, 353–4.
31. "Andy Partridge of XTC 'Autumn,' " excerpted from Mac Randall, *Musician Magazine*, May 1997. Rpt. on *Dave Emlen's Unofficial Kinks Web Site*, http://kinks.it.rit.edu (accessed Nov. 10, 2006).
32. "Afternoon Tea," in Ray Davies, *Waterloo Sunset* (London: Viking, 1997), 190.
33. Davies said, "There is one line, 'Oh my poor rheumatic back', because I suffer from a spine problem. So I thought I would throw that in for the people who knew me"—qtd. in Savage, 96.
34. Letter to George and Thomas Keats, Dec. 21, 1817.
35. Anonymous, interview by author.
36. Camille Paglia, *Sex, Art, and American Culture* (New York: Vintage, 1992), 20.
37. Harold E. Toliver, *Pastoral Forms and Attitudes* (Berkeley: University of California Press, 1971), 17.
38. Frank Kermode, Introduction, *English Pastoral Poetry: From the Beginnings to Marvel* (London: Harrap, 1952), 10.
39. See Savage, 96.
40. Bernard Gendron, "Theodore Adorno Meets the Cadillacs," in *Studies in Entertainment: Critical Approaches to Mass Culture*, Tania Modleski, ed. (Bloomington: Indiana University Press, 1986), 35.
41. Lisa Robinson, "Raymond Douglas Davies: 'Some People Like to Live with Dreams,'" *New York Daily News*, c. late November 1974. Rpt. in the newsletter of the Official Kinks Fan Club, Apr. 1999: n. pag.
42. Davies adapts this line from Shakespeare's *Richard II*, Act II, sc. i, ll. 40, 46, which reads, "This royal throne of kings, this sceptred isle . . . This precious stone set in a silver sea."
43. *All Day*, 142.
44. See Savage, 115.
45. *My Generation: The Kinks*.
46. Qtd. in Nick Hasted, "Ready Steady Kinks!!!" *Uncut* (Sept. 2004): 64.
47. See Vic Garbarini, "Ray Davies: The Kinks' Innocent Abroad," *Musician* (Aug. 1983): 63.

48. See Natalie Zemon Davis, *Society and Culture in Early Modern France* (Stanford: Stanford University Press, 1975), 129–51.
49. *I'm Not Like Everybody Else.*
50. *I'm Not Like Everybody Else.*

6 THE VILLAGE GREEN PRESERVATION SOCIETY

1. Qtd. in Vince Bockris, *Keith Richards: The Biography* (London: Penguin, 1992), 88.
2. Qtd. in Timothy White, *The Nearest Faraway Place* (New York: Holt, 1994), 252.
3. Qtd. in White, 270.
4. Qtd. in Mike Hammer, "The Kinks Kronikled," *RockBill* (May 1988). Rpt. *Dave Emlen's Unofficial Kinks Web Site*, http://kinks.it.rit.edu (accessed Nov. 28, 2006).
5. Jagger reports the conversation in Jonathan Cott and Sue Cox, "Rolling Stone Interview with Mick Jagger," *Rolling Stone* (Oct. 12, 1968): 16.
6. Qtd. in Hammer.
7. "Ray Davies Reviews the Beatles LP," *Disc and Music Echo Magazine* (Aug. 1967). Rpt. on *Dave Emlen's Unofficial Kinks Web Site* (accessed Nov. 28, 2006).
8. Qtd. in James Miller, *Flowers in the Dustbin: The Rise of Rock and Roll, 1947–1977* (New York: Simon and Schuster, 1999), 261.
9. Bill Williamson, *The Temper of the Times: British Society since World War II* (Oxford: Basil Blackwell, 1990), 167.
10. Grace Slick, *Somebody to Love? A Rock-and-Roll Memoir* (New York: Warner, 1998), 140.
11. Qtd. in Andy Miller, *The Kinks Are the Village Green Preservation Society* (New York: Continuum, 2003), 28–9.
12. Qtd. in Jon Savage, *The Kinks: The Official Biography* (London: Faber and Faber, 1984), 97.
13. Qtd. in Doug Hinman, *The Kinks: All Day and All of the Night* (San Francisco: Backbeat, 2004), 112.
14. Qtd. in Johnny Rogan, *The Kinks: A Mental Institution* (London: Proteus, 1984), 89.
15. Qtd. in Savage, 97.
16. Qtd. in Andy Miller, 27.
17. Qtd. in Andy Miller, 29.
18. Peter Quaife, e-mail message to author, Nov. 26, 2006.
19. Qtd. in Russell Smith and Bill Orton, *The Official Kinks Fan Club Present Dogs, Squirrels and Black Crowes* (Warwickshire, UK: Official Kinks Fan Club, 1999), n. pag.
20. Ray Davies, *X-Ray: The Unauthorized Autobiography* (Woodstock: Overlook, 1994), 360.
21. Qtd. in Smith and Orton, n. pag.
22. Qtd. in Savage, 104.
23. Telephone interview by author, June 1, 2000.
24. Dave Davies, *Kink* (London: Boxtree, 1996), 108.
25. *X-Ray*, 362.
26. *Kink*, 108.
27. Qtd. in Rogan, *Mental Institution*, 93, which provides the most detailed and yet succinct summary of the complicated lawsuit. See pages 58–9, 76–9, and 90–4.

28. Qtd. in Hinman, *All Day*, 116.
29. Interview by author, Aug. 15, 2005.
30. From *New Musical Express*, Aug. 3, 1968, qtd. in Andy Miller, 37.
31. Interview by author, May 25, 1998.
32. *X-Ray*, 362.
33. E-mail message to author, Jan. 12, 2007.
34. Qtd. in liner notes, *The Village Green Preservation Society*, Castle, 1998.
35. Jonathon (*sic*) Cott, "Afternoon Tea with Ray Davies," *Rolling Stone* (Nov. 26, 1970): 31.
36. Qtd. in Danny Kirby, "Peter Quaife: Interview Part Two," *Now & Then*, 8 (1994): 10.
37. Qtd. in Savage, 101.
38. Gerald DeWitt Sanders, John Herbert Nelson, and M. L. Rosenthal, eds., *Chief Modern Poets of Britain and America* (New York: Macmillan, 1970), I–8.
39. Qtd. in Jonathon Cott, 31.
40. Qtd. in Andrew Bailey, "Can Anybody Depend on the Kinks? Yeah," *Rolling Stone* (June 20, 1974): 18.
41. Letter to George and Thomas Keats, Dec. 21, 1817.
42. Qtd. in Savage, 101.
43. Ken Rayes, "The *Village Green* and *The Great Gatsby*: Two Views of Preservation," in *Living on a Thin Line: Crossing Aesthetic Borders with The Kinks*, Thomas M. Kitts and Michael J. Kraus, eds. (Rumford, RI: Rock 'n' Roll Research Press, 2002), 154.
44. Jack J. Boies, *The Lost Domain: Avatars of the Earthly Paradise in Western Literature* (New York: University Press of America, 1983), 1–2.
45. *X-Ray*, 17.
46. Johnny Rogan, *The Complete Guide to the Music of The Kinks* (London: Omnibus, 1998), 63.
47. See especially "The American Scholar," 1837. Rpt. in *The Portable Emerson*, Carl Bode, ed. (New York: Penguin, 1981), 54–8.
48. Robert Palmer, "Kink in Manhattan: Ray Davies Loses His Innocence," *Rolling Stone* (Jan. 4, 1973): 14.
49. Rayes, 160.
50. See Boies, 219.
51. Qtd. in Savage, 101–2.
52. Andy Miller, 70, 71–2.
53. *X-Ray*, 361.
54. "farewell gesture" in *X-Ray*, 360 and "intimate album" qtd. in Savage, 101.

7 ARTHUR

1. Qtd. in Danny Kirby, "Peter Quaife: Interview Part Two," *Now & Then*, 8 (1994): 11.
2. Davies spent several weeks in the spring and then again in early summer producing *Turtle Soup* for the California pop band known for singles like "Happy Together" and "Elenore." However, after Davies returned to England, the Turtles remixed *Turtle Soup*. Davies's mix would not be available until a Rhino reissue in 1986.
3. E-mail message to author, Jan. 12, 2007; punctuation, ellipses, quotations marks, etc., all Quaife's.
4. Interview by author, May 25, 1998.
5. Qtd. in Jon Savage, *The Kinks: The Official Biography* (London: Faber and Faber, 1984), 104.

6. E-mail message to author, Jan. 12, 2007.
7. Qtd. in Doug Hinman, *The Kinks: All Day and All of the Night* (San Francisco: Backbeat, 2004), 128.
8. E-mail message to author, Jan. 12, 2007.
9. Ray Davies, *X-Ray: The Unauthorized Autobiography* (Woodstock: Overlook, 1994), 314, 315.
10. Anonymous, interview by author.
11. Qtd. in Savage, 106.
12. E-mail message to author, Jan. 12, 2007.
13. E-mail message to author, May 6, 2007.
14. Danny Kirby, "Peter Quaife: Interview Part One," *Now & Then*, 7 (1994): 6.
15. Qtd. in Ken Sharp, "Working Out the Kinks: Dave Davies Comes into His Own," *Goldmine* (Nov. 21, 1997): 50.
16. Interview by author, May 24, 1998.
17. "Interview with John Dalton: Early Days," *John Dalton: Bass Lines* (Atherstone, UK: Official Kinks Fan Club, 1996): 12.
18. Dave Davies, *Kink* (London: Boxtree, 1996), 117.
19. Dave gives the date as November 1963 in *Kink* (99), but he probably misremembers since the Kinks did not play a seaside resort at that time. His version of Ray's reaction, with the confirmed date of the Redcar gig, suggests that Ray's placing of the date as May 1964 is accurate.
20. *X-Ray*, 137.
21. Qtd. in Tom Beaujour, "The Kinks: *Arthur (Or the Decline and Fall of the British Empire)*," *Guitar World—1969: The Greatest Year in Rock* (June 1999): 93.
22. "Beside the Seaside," 1948, upper case Betjeman's.
23. Dennis Smith, "Knowing Your Place: Class Politics and Ethnicity in Chicago and Birmingham in 1890–1983," in *Class and Space: The Making of Urban Society*, Nigel Thrift and Paul Williams, eds. (London: Routledge and Kegan Paul, 1987), 304.
24. The Profumo Affair linked Christine Keeler to Captain Eugene Ivanov, a former member of the Russian Embassy, and Dr. Stephen Ward, a society osteopath. The extensive press coverage and embarrassment drove Ward to suicide during his trial.
25. The Abortion Act legalized abortion and the National Health Service (Family Planning) Act permitted local authorities to dispense contraceptives and contraceptive advice.
26. John Mander, *Great Britain or Little England?* (Cambridge: Houghton Mifflin, 1964), 57.
27. *X-Ray*, 34, 369.
28. Johnny Rogan, *The Complete Guide to the Music of The Kinks* (London: Omnibus, 1998), 70.
29. For a discussion of Orwell's obsession with class, see David Cannadine, *The Rise and Fall of Class in Britain* (New York: Columbia University Press, 1999), 149.
30. John Smith, *The General History of Virginia, New England, and the Summer Isles* (1624), in *The American Tradition in Literature*, vol. 1, George Perkins and Barbara Perkins, eds. (New York: McGraw-Hill, 2007), 46–7.
31. Qtd. in Jonathon (*sic*) Cott, "Afternoon Tea with Ray Davies," *Rolling Stone* (Nov. 26, 1970): 31.
32. *Kink*, 119.
33. Johnny Rogan, *The Kinks: A Mental Institution* (London: Proteus, 1984), 106.
34. Mike Saunders, review of *The Kink Kronikles*, *Rolling Stone* (May 25, 1972): 64.
35. Savage, 110.

36. John Mendelssohn, *The Kinks Kronikles* (New York: Quill, 1985), 105.
37. Rogan, *Complete Guide*, 71.
38. *Kink*, 119.
39. Qtd. in Cott, 31.
40. Qtd. in Cott, 31.
41. *I'm Not Like Everybody Else: The World of Ray Davies and The Kinks*, Pro. and Dir. Vanessa Engle, BBC, 1995.
42. Qtd. in Cott, 31, italics his.
43. Qtd. in Timothy Crouse, "The British Scourge," *Show Guide Magazine* (1969). Rpt. on *Dave Emlen's Unofficial Kinks Web Site*, http://kinks.it.rit.edu (accessed Jan. 21, 2007).
44. Qtd. in Cannadine, 150. Churchill from his Address at Harrow School.
45. Qtd. in E. R. Chamberlain, *Life in Wartime Britain* (London: Batsford, 1972), 53.
46. Anthony Aldgate and Jeffrey Richards, *Britain Can Take It: The British Cinema in the Second World War* (Oxford: Blackwell, 1986), 49.
47. Qtd. in Susan Briggs, *The Home Front: War Years in Britain, 1939–1945* (London: McGraw-Hill, 1975), 185 and Angus Calder, *The People's War: Britain—1939–1945* (New York: Pantheon, 1969), 149.
48. Qtd. in Crouse.
49. After five years—from August 24, 1940 to March 29, 1945—of 70,995 tons of Nazi high explosives and thousands of incendiaries, England suffered the deaths of 60,595 civilians, injuries to another 86,182, and destruction of 222,000 homes with damage to nearly five million others—see Chamberlain, 74.
50. Qtd. by Ray Davies in Cott, 31.
51. Robert Blake, "Anthony Eden," in *British Prime Ministers in the Twentieth Century*, vol. II, John P. Mackintosh, ed. (New York: St. Martin's, 1978), 75.
52. Brendan John Worrell, *Racing at Royal Ascot 2000*, http://www.upnaway.com/~worrelle/rat.htm (accessed Jan. 22, 2007).
53. "If It's Thursday, It Must Be Tea with the Queen," *Time*, July 19, 1999, 93.
54. *Kink*, 118.
55. Rogan, *Complete Guide*, 73.
56. Qtd. in Savage, 114.
57. Mike Daly, review of *Arthur*, *Rolling Stone* (Nov. 1, 1969): 39.
58. Greil Marcus, review of *Arthur*, *Rolling Stone* (Nov. 1, 1969): 39
59. Mendelssohn, 102.
60. Brad Tolinski, "Woodshed: Sixty-Nine, Dude!" *Guitar World—1969: The Greatest Year in Rock* (June 1999): 22.
61. *X-Ray*, 361, 368.

8 A LONG WAY FROM HOME

1. Qtd. in Nick Hasted, "Ready Steady Kinks!!!" *Uncut* (Sept. 2004): 60.
2. Dave Davies, *Kink* (London: Boxtree, 1996), 121.
3. *Surrealistic Pillow* #3, 1967; *After Bathing at Baxter's* #7, 1967; *Crown of Creation* #6, 1968; *Bless Its Pointed Little Head* #17, 1969; *Volunteers* #13, 1969.
4. *Kink*, 120.
5. Qtd. in John Mendelssohn, *The Kinks Kronikles* (New York: Quill, 1985), 108.
6. *Kink*, 120.
7. Qtd. in Jon Savage, *The Kinks: The Official Biography* (London: Faber and Faber, 1984), 111.

8. Peter Townshend, "Meaty, Beaty, Big and Bouncy," *Rolling Stone* (Dec. 9, 1971): 37.

9. Qtd. in Savage, 111.

10. Qtd. in "Kinks 'Enormously Gratified' in US," *Rolling Stone* (Dec. 27, 1969): 12.

11. Qtd. in Savage, 111.

12. "Interview with John Dalton: Early Days," *John Dalton: Bass Lines* (Atherstone, UK: Official Kinks Fan Club, 1996), 14–16.

13. *Kink*, 118.

14. Hasted, 60.

15. "Interview with John Dalton," 16.

16. *Kink*, 159–60, 268.

17. Qtd. in Savage, 115.

18. Qtd. in Savage, 115.

19. Qtd. in Johnny Rogan, *The Kinks: A Mental Institution* (London: Proteus, 1984), 109.

20. It cannot be said with certainty who gave Gosling his nickname. Gosling thinks it was Collins ("The John Gosling Interview: Part One." Rpt. in Rebecca Bailey, ed., *The Kinks: Reflections on Thirty Years of Music* [Morehead, KY: Trillium, 1994], 118), Dave says Dalton (*Kink*, 134), and roadie Ken Jones takes credit himself (qtd. in Savage, 115).

21. Qtd. in Savage, 114.

22. Qtd. in Michael J. Kraus, "A Conversation with John Gosling," in *Living on a Thin Line: Crossing Aesthetic Borders with The Kinks*, Thomas M. Kitts and Michael J. Kraus, eds. (Rumford, RI: Rock 'n' Roll Research Press, 2002), 215.

23. Qtd. in Savage, 115.

24. Judy Sims, "Kinks at their best, and worst," c. Nov.–Dec. 1970. Rpt. in *The Kinks: A Live Experience* (Atherstone, UK: Official Kinks Fan Club, n.d), n. pag.

25. Qtd. in Savage, 153.

26. Qtd. in Rosalind Russell, "Why You Just Can't Classify the Kinks," clipping, c. early 1971. Rpt. in *The Kinks: A Live Experience*.

27. E-mail message to author, Jan. 30, 2007.

28. Qtd. in Neville Marten and Jeffrey Hudson, *The Kinks: Well Respected Men* (Surrey: Castle, 1996), 145.

29. Qtd. in Kraus, "A Conversation with John Dalton," in *Living on a Thin Line*, 209.

30. Qtd. in Mendelssohn, 134.

31. "Interview with John Dalton," 19.

32. Telephone interview by author, May 17, 2000.

33. Telephone interview by author, June 1, 2000.

34. Interview by author, Aug. 15, 2005.

35. Telephone interview by author, May 17, 2000.

36. Qtd. in Doug Hinman, *The Kinks: All Day and All of the Night* (San Francisco: Backbeat, 2004), 152.

37. Mike Jahn, "The Kinks Draw an Unruly Crowd," *New York Times*, Apr. 1, 1971, 50.

38. Telephone interview by author, May 17, 2000.

39. *Kink*, 145.

40. Qtd. in Mendelssohn, 34.

41. *Not Like Everybody Else: The World of Ray Davies and The Kinks*, Pro. and Dir. Vanessa Engle, BBC, 1995.

42. Joseph G. Marotta, "The Loss of Identity and the Myth of Edenic Return in Ray Davies," in *Living on a Thin Line*, 69.

43. William Butler Yeats, "Anima Hominis" (1924), section v, in *Per Amica Silentia Lunae*, http://www.horrormasters.com/Text/a1989.pdf (accessed Feb. 22, 2007).
44. Anonymous, interview by author.
45. Qtd. in Hinman, *All Day*, 146.
46. "Interview with John Dalton," 18.
47. *Kink*, 143.
48. Qtd. in Kraus, "A Conversation with John Gosling," 216.
49. "Lola Completely Banned." Rpt. in *The Kinks on Tour* (Atherstone, UK: Official Kinks Fan Club, c. 2002): n. pag.
50. Alec Martin, "Pop Star Attacks Air Hostess," *Truth* [Melbourne], June 5, 1971. Rpt. in *The Kinks on Tour*.
51. "Kinks Walk Out on ABC," clipping, c. June 1971. Rpt. in *The Kinks on Tour*.
52. Qtd in Rogan, *Mental Institution*, 164.
53. Qtd. in Kraus, "Conversation with John Dalton," 210.
54. Telephone interview by author, May 18, 2000.
55. Qtd. in Mendelssohn, 34.
56. Qtd. in Michael J. Kraus, "A Conversation with Mick Avory," in *Living on a Thin Line*, 188.
57. Qtd. in Ken Sharp, "A Conversation with Pete Townshend," *Goldmine* (Feb. 2, 2007): 18.
58. Qtd. in Jane Schact, "Ray Davies Unravels the Muswell Puzzle," *Circus* (Feb. 1972). Rpt. on *Dave Emlen's Unofficial Kinks Web Site*, http:/kinks.it.rit.edu (accessed Feb. 8, 2007).
59. Qtd. in Savage, 124, italics mine.
60. Qtd. in Schact.
61. Qtd. in Fred Schruers, "The Once and Future Kinks," *Rolling Stone* (Nov. 7, 1978): 11.
62. Qtd. in Margaret Rooke and Ruby Wellington, "First Person," *Telegraph Magazine*, c. early 1997. Rpt. on *Dave Emlen's Unofficial Kinks Web Site* (accessed Apr. 30, 1997).
63. Qtd. in Savage, 129.
64. Qtd. in liner notes, *Everybody's in Show-Biz*, CD reissue, 1998.
65. "The John Gosling Interview: Part Two," *Now & Then*, 6 (1993): 27.
66. Qtd. in Kraus, "Conversation with John Dalton," 215.
67. Qtd. in Marten and Hudson, 106.
68. Rogan, *Mental Institution*, 131.
69. Qtd. in Lisa Mehlman, "Kinks at Carnegie Hall: What a Performance," clipping, c. March 1972. Rpt. in *The Kinks: A Live Experience*.
70. *Kink*, 85.
71. Qtd. in Alan di Perna, "A Kink's Kronikle," *Guitar World* (Jan. 1997): 200.
72. Qtd. in Mendelssohn, 34.
73. Qtd. in Savage, 129.
74. Jerry Gilbert, "Ray Quits Kinks," loose clipping, summer 1972.
75. See Roy Hollingworth, "Thank You for the Days, Ray," *Melody Maker*, July 21, 1973; see also *Kink*, 163.
76. *Kink*, 163.
77. Qtd. in Kraus, "Conversation with John Dalton," 206.
78. "The John Gosling Interview: Part Two," 30.
79. Qtd. in "Kinks: Now a Ray of Hope," *Melody Maker*, July 21, 1973: cover inset.

9 HERE COMES FLASH

1. "An Interview with Mick Avory: Part Two," *Now & Then*, 2 (1991): 10.
2. Qtd in Dave Thompson, "The Kinks: Thirty Years Gone," *Goldmine* (Aug. 19, 2005): 18.
3. "The John Gosling Interview: Part Two," *Now & Then*, 6 (1993): 28–9.
4. Dave Davies, *Kink* (London: Boxtree, 1996), 165.
5. Dave Hickey, review The Kinks: Felt Forum, *Rolling Stone* (Feb. 2, 1975): 78.
6. Qtd. in Doug Hinman, *The Kinks: All Day and All of the Night* (San Francisco: Backbeat, 2004), 190.
7. "An Interview with Mick Avory," 10.
8. Qtd. in Richard Skanse, "20th Century Man, Ray Davies Online Kinks Anthology Interview," *Rollingstone.com* (Dec. 11, 1998), http://www.rollingstone.com/news/story (accessed Mar. 7, 2007).
9. "John Gosling Interview: Part Two," 29.
10. Interview with John Dalton: Early Days," *John Dalton: Bass Lines* (Atherstone, UK: Official Kinks Fan Club, 1996), 20.
11. Qtd. in Alan di Perna, "A Kink's Kronikle," *Guitar World* (Jan. 1997): 202.
12. "John Gosling Interview: Part Two," 28.
13. Qtd. in Scott Cohen, "*Preservation Act II*: Interview," *Circus*; 1974. Rpt. on *Dave Emlen's Unofficial Kinks Web Site*, http://kinks.it.rit.edu (accessed Feb. 8, 2007).
14. Liner notes, *Preservation Act 2*, Velvel CD.
15. Qtd. in Mark Paytress, "Tales of Ordinary Madness," *Mojo* (Mar. 2006): 80.
16. From *Record Mirror*, May 10, 1969, qtd. in Johnny Rogan, *The Kinks: A Mental Institution* (London: Proteus, 1984), 96.
17. Qtd. in Bill Holdship, "Ray Davies Unravels the Kinks," *Creem* (Dec. 1981): 40.
18. Qtd. in Jon Savage, *The Kinks: The Official Biography* (London: Faber and Faber, 1984), 101.
19. Qtd. in Savage, 133.
20. Collins, telephone interview by author, May 18, 2000.
21. Liner notes, *Schoolboys in Disgrace*, Velvel CD.
22. Qtd. in Skanse.
23. Qtd. in Lisa Robinson, "Raymond Douglas Davies: 'Some People Like to Live with Dreams,'" *New York Daily News*, c. late Nov. 1974. Rpt. in the newsletter of the Official Kinks Fan Club, Apr. 1999: n. pag.
24. Qtd. in Savage, 134.
25. *I'm Not Like Everybody Else: The World of Ray Davies and The Kinks*, Pro. and Dir. Vanessa Engle, BBC, 1995.
26. Qtd. in Savage, 134.
27. Qtd. in Savage, 133.
28. Qtd. in Savage, 139.
29. Qtd. in Savage, 139.
30. Qtd. in Hinman, *All Day*, 186.
31. Qtd. in Thompson, 14.
32. *Kink*, 166.
33. Qtd. in Paytress, 79.
34. "Divinity School Address," 1838, rpt. in *The Portable Emerson*, Carl Bode, ed. (New York: Penguin, 1981), 77.
35. Liner notes, *Preservation Act 2*, Velvel CD.
36. Paul Nelson, "Ray Davies Gets His Kinks Out," *Rolling Stone* (Mar. 24, 1977): 14.

37. Qtd. in Paytress, 79.
38. *Kink*, 173.
39. Liner notes, *Schoolboys*, Velvel CD.
40. "Interview with John Dalton," 20.
41. Qtd. in Michael J. Kraus, "A Conversation with John Gosling," in *Living on a Thin Line: Crossing Aesthetic Borders with The Kinks*, Thomas M. Kitts and Michael J. Kraus, eds. (Rumford, RI: Rock 'n' Roll Research Press, 2002), 216.
42. *Kink*, 24.
43. Uli Twelker, "The Kinks: Brit-Broadway Schoolboys in Commercial Disgrace," in *Living on a Thin Line*, 116.
44. *Kinks: Come Dancing*, electronic press kit. Dir. Ray Davies, Weird Films, 2000.

10 *JUKE BOX MUSIC*

1. "Hearing the Kinks, Small Faces and Yardbirds going hammer and tongs . . . that's where the Pistols' construction of songs came from." Qtd. in Clinton Heylin, *Babylon's Burning: from Punk to Grunge* (Edinburgh: Canongate, 2007), 80.
2. See Heylin, 99.
3. Dave Davies, *Kink* (London: Boxtree, 1996), 177.
4. Robert Levine, "Clive Davis: Greatest Hitmaker," *New York Magazine*, Dec. 20–7, 1999, 81.
5. *Kinks: Come Dancing*, electronic press kit. Dir. Ray Davies, Weird Films, 2000.
6. Interview by author, Aug. 15, 2005.
7. Billy Altman, review of *Sleepwalker*, *Rolling Stone* (Apr. 21, 1977): 95.
8. Qtd. in Johnny Rogan, *The Kinks: A Mental Institution* (London: Proteus, 1984), 155, 164.
9. Rogan, *Mental Institution*, 155
10. Qtd. in Rogan, *Mental Institution*, 157.
11. Qtd. in Neville Marten and Jeffrey Hudson, *The Kinks: Well Respected Men* (Surrey: Castle, 1996), 141.
12. "The John Gosling Interview: Part Three," *Now & Then*, 7 (1994): 16.
13. Qtd. in Michael J. Kraus, "A Conversation with John Gosling," in *Living on a Thin Line: Crossing Aesthetic Borders with The Kinks*, Thomas M. Kitts and Michael J. Kraus, eds. (Rumford, RI: Rock 'n' Roll Research Press, 2002), 218.
14. "The John Gosling Interview: Part Three," 16.
15. Qtd. in Kraus, "A Conversation with Ian Gibbons," in *Living on a Thin Line*, 219–20.
16. Albert Camus, *Le Mythe de Sisyphe*, qtd. in Martin Esslin, *The Theatre of the Absurd* (New York: Penguin, 1983), 23.
17. Eugène Ionesco, "Dans les armes de la ville," qtd. in Esslin, 23.
18. Qtd. in liner notes, *Muswell Hillbillies*, CD reissue, 1998.
19. Qtd. in Rogan, *Mental Institution*, 165.
20. Qtd. in Paul Nelson, "Ray Davies Gets His Kinks Out," *Rolling Stone* (Mar. 24, 1977): 14.
21. *Kink*, 159.
22. Adam Adamov, *L'Aveu (The Confession)*, qtd. in Esslin, 93.
23. Johnny Rogan, *The Complete Guide to the Music of The Kinks* (London: Omnibus, 1998), 122.
24. Qtd. in Jeff Tamarkin, "The Kinks: Seventeen Year Itch," *Hit Parade* (Mar. 1982): 26.

25. Qtd. in Vic Garbarini, "Ray Davies: The Kinks' Innocent Abroad," *Musician* (Aug. 1983): 64.
26. Qtd. in Bill Holdship, "Ray Davies Unravels the Kinks," *Creem* (Dec. 1981): 42.
27. Qtd. in Holdship, 42.
28. Sutcliff claimed that a voice from God directed him to kill prostitutes—his insanity plea at his trial failed and he was sentenced to life imprisonment. Ali Agca claimed membership in the Popular Front for the Liberation of Palestine, which the organization denied, and then later that he was assisted by Bulgaria and pressured by the KGB to assassinate the Pope because of his support of Poland's Solidarity Movement.
29. Qtd. in Rogan, *Complete Guide*, 132.
30. Qtd. in Holdship, 58.
31. Qtd. in Jon Savage, *The Kinks: The Official Biography* (London: Faber and Faber, 1984), 159.
32. Qtd. in Holdship, 58.
33. Interview by author, Aug. 15, 2005.
34. Qtd. in Kraus, "A Conversation with Ian Gibbons," in *Living on a Thin Line*, 221.
35. Qtd. in Holdship, 58.
36. See *Kink*, 187–8.
37. Anonymous, interview by author.
38. In *Kink* (201), Dave reports that Ray took Hynde with the Kinks to France and Belgium from July 4–6, 1980.
39. Qtd. in Rogan, *Mental Institution*, 179.
40. *Kink*, 203.
41. See Rogan, *Mental Institution*, 184, and John Mendelssohn, *The Kinks Kronikles* (New York: Quill, 1985), 190.
42. *Kink*, 204.
43. *Kink*, 244.
44. Qtd. in Chris Willman, "Return of the Kink," *EW.com*, Feb. 17, 2006, http://www.ew.com (accessed Mar. 26, 2007).
45. Qtd. in "Ray Article in German Mag. [*Der Spiegel*]," May 2006, trans. RumbleDoll, *Ray Davies Website*, http://raydavies.3.forumer.com (accessed May 17, 2006).
46. Qtd. in Rogan, *Complete Guide*, 142.

11 *THINK VISUAL*

1. In March 1972, the Mike Cotton horn section began supporting the Kinks, missing only two dates that month because of prior commitments.
2. Interview by author, Aug. 15, 2005.
3. Dave Davies, *Kink* (London: Boxtree, 1996), 234.
4. Interview by author, Aug. 15, 2005.
5. Qtd. in Michael J. Kraus, "A Conversation with Mick Avory," in *Living on a Thin Line: Crossing Aesthetic Borders with The Kinks*, Thomas M. Kitts and Michael J. Kraus, eds (Rumford, RI: Rock 'n' Roll Research Press, 2002), 198. Dave also referred to the Kinks as a "family business": "Dave Davies in Conversation with Bill Orton & Russell Smith," *Dave Davies, Unfinished Business: The Magazine* (Warwickshire, UK: Official Kinks Fan Club, 1998): n. pag.
6. Qtd. in Anthony DeCurtis, "Rocking My Life Away," *Rolling Stone.com* (Mar. 29, 2002), http://rollingstone.com/news/newarticle (accessed Apr. 10, 2002).

7. "Dave Davies in Conversation," n. pag.
8. Qtd. in Kraus, "A Conversation with Bob Henrit," in *Living on a Thin Line*, 231.
9. *Kink*, 231.
10. Stephen Paul Miller, "Elevated Tracks: The Films of Ray Davies," in *Living on a Thin Line*, 143, 145.
11. Qtd. in Doug Hinman, *The Kinks: All Day and All of the Night* (San Francisco: Backbeat, 2004), 272.
12. *Kink*, 199.
13. "An Interview with Mick Avory: Part Two," *Now & Then*, 2 (1991): 10.
14. Qtd. in Keith Phipps, "Ray Davies," *The Onion A.V. Club*, Jan. 23, 2002, http://www.theonionavclub.com (accessed Jan. 24, 2004).
15. *Kink*, 236.
16. Qtd. in Hinman, *All Day*, 282.
17. Rodin designed *The Thinker* to be placed in the center of the tympanum of *The Gates of Hell*, his monumental work in which the Thinker contemplates the tortured figures below him in hell—see William Harlan Hale, *The World of Rodin, 1840–1917* (New York: Time-Life Books, 1973), 87, 96–9.
18. Qtd. in Gina Vivinetto, "Business Puts a Kink in Music," *St. Petersburg Times* (Florida), Mar. 18, 2001, 9F.
19. *Kink*, 240.
20. Qtd. in Hinman, *All Day*, 252.
21. Rob Patterson, "Ray Davies: 'God Save the Kinks!' " *Fi* (Dec. 1998): 21. Rpt. in the newsletter of the Official Kinks Fan Club, Jan. 2000: 5.
22. Courtney Love, "Courtney Love Does the Math," *Salon.com* (June 14, 2000), http://archive.salon.com (acessed Nov. 8, 2005).
23. Qtd. in Neil Strauss, "A Chance to Break the Pop Stranglehold," *New York Times*, May 9, 1999, sec. 2: 1f.
24. Qtd. in Dan Cairns, "Yes, He's a Dedicated Saboteur of Fashion," *Sunday Times* [London], March 18, 2001. Rpt. on *Dave Emlen's Unofficial Kinks Web Site*, http://kinks.it.rit.edu (accessed Aug. 31, 2005).
25. Olga Ruocco, "Sunny Afternoons and Full Moons: Sunlight, Moonlight, and Stormy Skies in the Songs of The Kinks," in *Living on a Thin Line*, 58.
26. Qtd. in Martin Esslin, *The Theatre of the Absurd* (New York: Penguin, 1983), 33.
27. Johnny Rogan, *The Complete Guide to the Music of The Kinks* (London: Omnibus, 1998), 148.
28. Barbara Carroll, "Two Views of Paradise: The Inner Geography of Ray Davies and Brian Wilson," in *Living on a Thin Line*, 165.
29. Qtd. in Rogan, *Complete Guide*, 149.
30. See Hinman, *All Day*, 280.
31. Qtd. in Strauss, "A Chance to Break," 51.
32. Qtd. in Nick Hasted, "Ready Steady Kinks!!!" *Uncut* (Sept. 2004): 66.
33. *Kink*, 240.
34. *Kink*, 244.
35. Qtd. in *All Great Quotes*, http://www.allgreatnotes.com/pablo_picasso_quotes.shtml (accessed Aug. 29, 2005).
36. Qtd. in Jon Savage, *The Kinks: The Official Biography* (London: Faber and Faber, 1984), 32.
37. Qtd. in Sandra Kreiswirth, "Ray Davies Working Out the Kinks," *The Daily Breeze* [Torrance, CA], Aug. 26, 1988, E16.
38. Qtd. in Kreiswirth, E16.

39. Richard Stayton, "80 Days Is a Work of Years for McAnuff," *Herald Examiner* [Los Angeles], Aug. 21, 1988, E2.

40. Thomas Bartoldus and Ralf Junkerjürgen, "The most icy inscrutable creature known to science: an Englishman—*Le Tour du monde en quatre-vingts jours dans une adaptation musicale de 1988*," *Iris*, 28 (2005): 214, trans. Oliver Bűrenkemper. Unpublished.

41. Greg Joseph, "*80 Days*: If play seems lavish, there's good reason," *Tribune* [San Diego], Sept. 6, 1988, D1.

12 20TH CENTURY MAN

1. Qtd. in Ray Davies, *X-Ray: The Unauthorized Autobiography* (Woodstock: Overlook, 1994), 374. On July 5, 1975, Ashe became the first black male to win the Wimbledon singles' championship.

2. Dave Davies, *Kink* (London: Boxtree, 1996), 246.

3. See *Kink*, 245–6.

4. "Scattered: Home," in Ray Davies, *Waterloo Sunset* (London: Viking, 1997), 244, 248.

5. See Doug Hinman, *The Kinks: All Day and All of the Night* (San Francisco: Backbeat, 2004), *All Day*, 306.

6. Hinman, *All Day*, 292.

7. Also in the film and on the album are Michael Blair, Don Alias, Geri Allen, Greg Cohen, Art Baron, Bill Frisell, Bernard Fowler, the Uptown Horns, and Bobby Keyes.

8. Lauren Thierry, review of *X-Ray*, *New York Times Book Review*, Sept. 24, 1995, 24; Sandall, qtd. in Hinman, *All Day*, 326; and Alan Jackson, qtd. in Neville Marten and Jeffrey Hudson, *The Kinks: Well Respected Men* (Surrey: Castle, 1996), 189.

9. Qtd. in Neil Strauss, "The Pop Life," *New York Times*, Oct. 5, 1995, C22.

10. "There are more things in heaven and earth, Horatio, / Than are dreamt of in your philosophy"—*Hamlet*, Act I, sc. 5, ll. 166–7.

11. *X-Ray*, 418–19.

12. Qtd. by Hyperion editor Leigh Haber in "Between the Lines," *EW.com*, Nov. 6, 1996, http://www.ew.com (accessed Apr. 21, 2007).

13. Qtd. in Chris Norris, "One Kink's Story." Rpt. of clipping in *The Year in Review—1996* (Warwickshire, UK: Official Kinks Fan Club, 1997): n. pag.

14. *X-Ray*, 227.

15. Constantin Stanislavski, *An Actor's Handbook*, Elizabeth Reynolds Hapgood, ed. and trans. (New York: Theatre Arts Books, 1963), 73.

16. Qtd. in Norris.

17. Qtd. in Jim Sullivan, " 'I'm a 20th Century Man . . . But I Don't Wanna Be Here,' " *Boston Globe*, Sept. 29, 1996, N1.

18. Qtd. in Strauss, "Pop Life."

19. Qtd. in Ken Sharp, "He's Not Like Everybody Else: God Save Ray Davies," *Goldmine* (Mar. 1, 1996): 4.

20. *Ray Davies: Visions of England*, Pro. and Dir. Ray Davies and Ron Trickett, Anglia Programme, 1998.

21. *Ray Davies: Visions of England*.

22. On stage at the Jane Street Theatre, Aug. 25, 2000.

23. Qtd. in Robin Denselow, "London Calling," *Guardian*, Oct. 3, 2005, http://www.guardian.co.uk (accessed Oct. 13, 2005).

24. Qtd. in Mark Guarino, "20th Century Man," *Daily Herald* [Arlington Heights, IL], Mar. 30, 2006, sec. 4: p. 4.

25. Qtd. in Keith Spera, "Singer for the Kinks Wounded in N.O.," *Times-Picayune*, Jan. 6, 2004: clipping.
26. Ray Davies, "New Orleans: The Ideal Place to Get Shot," *Times Online* [London], 7 Sept. 2005, http://www.timesonline.co.uk (accessed Sept. 8, 2005).
27. Qtd. in Gavin Martin, "Ray's Back with a Bullet," *Mirror*, Feb. 10, 2006, http://www.mirror.co.uk (accessed Feb. 14, 2006).
28. Davies, "New Orleans."
29. Qtd. in Gavin Martin.
30. Qtd. in Gavin Martin.
31. Qtd. in Stuart Mitchner, "Put the Kettle On, Mate, and Have a Cuppa Ray Davies," review of *Other People's Lives*, *Town Topics* (Mar. 1, 2006), http://www.towntopics.com (accessed Apr. 26, 2007).
32. In 2006, members included Mark Johns on guitar, Dick Nolan on bass, Gunnar Frick on keyboards, and Toby Baron on drums.
33. Andy Greene, review of *Ray Davies*, bootleg, recorded at the Wiltern Theater, Los Angeles, *Rolling Stone* (Sept. 7, 2006): 108.
34. *To the Bone* was released in the UK on Mar. 3, 1997.
35. "Ray Davies Confirms Kinks Return," *Contactmusic.com*, May 30, 2006, http://www.contactmusic.com (accessed June 2, 2006).
36. Interview by author, Aug. 15, 2005.

CONCLUSION

1. Paul Freeman, "Ray Davies, Always a Kink," *The Year in Review—1996* (Warwickshire, UK: Official Kinks Fan Club, 1997): n. pag.
2. Qtd. in Chris Willman, "Return of the Kink," *EW.com*, Feb. 17, 2006, http://www.ew.com (accessed Mar. 26, 2007).
3. Henry James, "The Lesson of the Master," 1888, in *Henry James: Representative Selections*, Lyon N. Richardson, ed. (Urbana: University of Illinois Press, 1966), 342–3.
4. James, 338.
5. Qtd. in Jon Savage, *The Kinks: The Official Biography* (London: Faber and Faber, 1984), 129.
6. *I'm Not Like Everybody Else: The World of Ray Davies and The Kinks*, Pro. and Dir. Vanessa Engle, BBC, 1995.
7. "Self-Reliance," 1841, rpt. in *The Portable Emerson*, Carl Bode, ed. (New York: Penguin, 1981), 138, 142, 155.
8. Qtd. in Willman.
9. Qtd. in Tony Schwartz, "The Rock of Ages," *Newsweek*, June 26, 1978, 79.

REFERENCES

Aldgate, Anthony, and Jeffrey Richards. *Britain Can Take It: The British Cinema in the Second World War*. Oxford: Blackwell, 1986.

All Great Quotes. 29 Aug. 2005 <http://www.allgreatnotes.com/pablo_picasso_quotes.shtml>.

Altman, Billy. "Rev. of *Sleepwalker*." *Rolling Stone*, Apr. 21, 1977: 95.

Avory, Mick. Personal Interview. Aug. 15, 2005.

Bailey, Andrew. "Can Anybody Depend on the Kinks? Yeah." *Rolling Stone*, June 20, 1974: 18.

Bailey, Peter. *Popular Culture and Performance in the Victorian City*. Cambridge: Cambridge University Press, 1998.

Bailey, Rebecca, ed. *The Kinks: Reflections on Thirty Years of Music*. Morehead, KY: Trillium, 1994.

Bartoldus, Thomas, and Ralf Junkerjürgen. "The most icy inscrutable creature known to science: an Englishman—*Le Tour du monde en quatre-vingts jours* dans une adaptation musicale de 1988." *Iris*, 28 (2005): 205–18. Trans. Oliver Bűrenkemper. Unpublished.

Beaujour, Tom. "The Kinks: *Arthur (Or the Decline and Fall of the British Empire)*." *Guitar World—1969: The Greatest Year in Rock*, June 1999: 93.

"Between the Lines." *EW.com*. Nov. 6, 1996. Apr. 21, 2007. <http://www.ew.com>.

Black, Johnny. "The Hellfire Club." *Mojo*, Sept. 2000: 60–9.

——. " 'Who, Me?' " *Mojo*, Sept. 2000: 70.

Blake, Robert. "Anthony Eden." *British Prime Ministers in the Twentieth Century*. Vol. II, ed. John P. Mackintosh. New York: St. Martin's, 1978: 73–115.

Bockris, Vince. *Keith Richards: The Biography*. London: Penguin, 1992.

Boies, Jack J. *The Lost Domain: Avatars of the Earthly Paradise in Western Literature*. New York: University Press of America, 1983.

Briggs, Asa. *Victorian Cities*. New York: Harper & Row, 1963.

Briggs, Susan. *The Home Front: War Years in Britain, 1939–1945*. London: McGraw-Hill, 1975.

Cairns, Dan. "Yes, He's a Dedicated Saboteur of Fashion." *Sunday Times* [London], Mar. 18, 2001. Rpt. on *Dave Emlen's Unofficial Kinks Web Site*, Aug. 31, 2005.

Calder, Angus. *The People's War: Britain—1939–1945*. New York: Pantheon, 1969.

Cannadine, David. *The Rise and Fall of Class in Britain*. New York: Columbia University Press, 1999.

Carroll, Barbara. "Two Views of Paradise: The Inner Geography of Ray Davies and Brian Wilson." Kitts and Kraus 165–70.

Chamberlain, E. R. *Life in Wartime Britain*. London: Batsford, 1972.

Clinton-Baddeley, V. C. *The Burlesque Tradition in the English Theatre after 1660*. London: Methuen, 1973.

Cohen, Scott. "*Preservation Act II*: Interview." *Circus*, 1974. Rpt. on *Dave Emlen's Unofficial Kinks Web Site*, Feb. 8, 2007.

Collins, Grenville. Telephone Interviews. May 17, May 18, June 1, 2000.

——. Personal E-mails. Jan. 30, 2007.

Cott, Jonathon (*sic*). "Afternoon Tea with Ray Davies." *Rolling Stone*, Nov. 26, 1970: 30–1.

Cott, Jonathan (*sic*) and Sue Cox. "Rolling Stone Interview with Mick Jagger." *Rolling Stone*, Oct. 12, 1968: 14–18.

Crouse, Timothy. "The British Scourge." *Show Guide Magazine*, 1969. Rpt. on *Dave Emlen's Unofficial Kinks Web Site*, Jan. 21, 2007.

Daly, Mike. Rev. of *Arthur. Rolling Stone*, Nov. 1, 1969: 38–9.

"Dave Davies in Conversation with Bill Orton & Russell Smith." *Dave Davies, Unfinished Business: The Magazine*. Warwickshire, U.K.: Official Kinks Fan Club, 1998: n. pag.

Dave Emlen's Unofficial Kinks Web Site.<http://kinks.it.rit.edu>.

Davies, Dave. *Kink*. London: Boxtree, 1996.

Davies, Ray. *X-Ray: The Unauthorized Autobiography*. Woodstock: Overlook, 1994.

——. *Waterloo Sunset*. London: Viking, 1997.

——. *Waterloo Sunset*. New York: Hyperion, 2000.

——. "Guitars and Greasy Spoons." *Electronic Telegraph*, Feb. 22, 2001. Feb. 24, 2001 <www.telegraph.co.uk>.

——. "New Orleans—The Ideal Place to Get Shot." *Times Online* [London] Sept. 7, 2005. Sept. 8, 2005 <http:www.timesonline.co.uk>.

——. "Lazy, Sunny Afternoons at Highbury." *Times Online* [London], May 6, 2006. May 17, 2007 <http://www.timesonline.co.uk>.

——. "Ray Davies Reviews the Beatles LP." *Disc and Music Echo Magazine*, August 1967. Rpt. on *Dave Emlen's Unofficial Kinks Web Site*, Nov. 28, 2006.

Davis, Natalie Zemon. *Society and Culture in Early Modern France*. Stanford: Stanford University Press, 1975.

DeCurtis, Anthony. "Rocking My Life Away." *Rolling Stone.com*, Mar. 29, 2002. Apr. 10, 2002. <http://rollingstone.com/news/newarticle>.

Denselow, Robin. "London Calling." *Guardian*, Oct. 3, 2005. Oct. 13, 2005. <http://www.guardian.co.uk>.

di Perna, Alan. "A Kink's Kronikle." *Guitar World*, Jan. 1997: 54ff.

Edmands, Bob. "The Robert Oppenheimer of Beat Music." Rpt. in *Dave Davies, Unfinished Business: The Magazine*. n.d., n. pag.

Emerson, Ralph Waldo. *The Portable Emerson*, ed. Carl Bode. New York: Penguin, 1981.

Eskow, Gary. "Ray Davies: The Storyteller." *Mix*, Aug. 1998: 54–60.

Esslin, Martin. *The Theatre of the Absurd*. New York: Penguin, 1983.

Field, Elizabeth. "Skin and Bone, Tea and Scones: Food and Drink Imagery in the Kinks' Music, 1964–1994." Kitts and Kraus 61–7.

The Filth and the Fury. Dir. Julien Temple. Perf. Sex Pistols. FilmFour, 2000.

The 500 Greatest Albums of All Time. Rolling Stone Special Collectors Issue, Dec. 11, 2003.

Freeman, Alan. "Iron Man of the Kinks." *Rave*, Dec. 1964. Rpt. on *Dave Emlen's Unofficial Kinks Web Site*, Apr. 30, 1997.

Freeman, Paul. "Ray Davies, Always a Kink." Rpt. in *The Year in Review—1996*. Atherstone, UK: Official Kinks Fan Club, 1997: n. pag.

Garbarini, Vic. "Ray Davies: The Kinks' Innocent Abroad." *Musician*, Aug. 1983: 58–66.

Gendron, Bernard. "Theodore Adorno Meets the Cadillacs." *Studies in Entertainment: Critical Approaches to Mass Culture*, ed. Tania Modleski. Bloomington: Indiana University Press, 1986: 18–36.

George, Chis. "The Kitchen Sink Kink." *The Independent*, Aug. 27, 1994. Rpt on *Dave Emlen's Unofficial Kinks Web Site*, Mar. 13, 2006.

Gilbert, Jerry. "Ray Quits Kinks." Loose clipping, summer 1972.

Gilbert, Martin. *Winston S. Churchill: Road to Victory, 1941–1945*. Boston: Houghton Mifflin, 1986.

Greene, Andy. Rev. of *Ray Davies*. Bootleg, recorded at the Wiltern Theater, Los Angeles. *Rolling Stone*, Sept. 7, 2006: 108.

Guarino, Mark. "20th Century Man." *Daily Herald* [Arlington Heights, IL], Mar. 30, 2006, sec. 4: 1, 4.

Hale, William Harlan. *The World of Rodin, 1840–1917*. New York: Time-Life Books, 1973.

Hammer, Mike. "The Kinks Kronikled." *RockBill*, May 1988. Rpt. on *Dave Emlen's Unofficial Kinks Web Site*, Nov. 28, 2006.

Hasted, Nick. "Ready Steady Kinks!!!" *Uncut*, Sept. 2004: 46–66.

Heath, Chris. "God Save the Kink." *GQ*, Feb. 2006: 122ff.

Heatley, Michael. "Classic Career: Dave Davies." *Classic Rock*. n.d. Rpt. in the newsletter of the Official Kinks Fan Club, Jan. 2002: n. pag.

Heylin, Clinton. *Babylon's Burning: from Punk to Grunge*. Edinburgh: Canongate, 2007.

Hickey, Dave. Rev. of The Kinks: Felt Forum. *Rolling Stone*, Feb. 2, 1975: 78.

Hinman, Doug. *The Kinks Part One: You Really Got Me: An Illustrated World Discography of the Kinks*. Rumford, RI: Hinman, 1994.

——. *The Kinks: All Day and All of the Night*. San Francisco: Backbeat, 2004.

Hoeveler, Diane Long. *Romantic Androgyny: The Women Within*. University Park: Pennsylvania State University Press, 1990.

Holdship, Bill. "Ray Davies Unravels the Kinks." *Creem*, Dec. 1981: 40–2f.

Hollingworth, Roy. "Thank You for the Days, Ray." *Melody Maker*, July 21, 1973.

Hudd, Roy. *Music Hall*. London: Eyre Methuen, 1976.

"If It's Thursday, It Must Be Tea with the Queen." *Time*, July 19, 1999: 93.

I'm Not Like Everybody Else: The World of Ray Davies and The Kinks. Pro. and Dir. Vanessa Engle. BBC. 1995.

"Interview with John Dalton: Early Days." *John Dalton: Bass Lines*. Atherstone, UK: Official Kinks Fan Club, 1996: 3–21.

"An Interview with Mick Avory: Part Two." *Now & Then*. Official Kinks Fan Club, 2 (1991): 7–12.

Jahn, Mike. "The Kinks Draw an Unruly Crowd." *New York Times*, Apr. 1, 1971: 50.

James, Henry. "The Lesson of the Master." 1888. *Henry James: Representative Selections*. Ed. Lyon N. Richardson. Urbana: University of Illinois Press, 1966.

Jazz on a Summer's Day. Dir. Bret Stern. Perf. Louis Armstrong, Chuck Berry, Jimmy Giuffre, Gerry Mulligan, et al. New Yorker Video, 1958.

"John Dalton Takes Over from Quaife in Kinks." Clipping, c. spring 1969. Rpt. in *John Dalton: Bass Lines*. Atherstone, UK: Official Kinks Fan Club, 1996: 11.

"The John Gosling Interview: Part One." Rpt. in Rebecca Bailey, 114–19.

"The John Gosling Interview: Part Two." *Now & Then*. Official Kinks Fan Club, 6 (1993): 22–31.

"The John Gosling Interview: Part Three." *Now & Then*. Official Kinks Fan Club, 7 (1994): 16.

Joseph, Greg. "*80 Days*: If Play Seems Lavish, There's Good Reason." *Tribune* [San Diego], Sept. 6, 1988: D1, D3.

Kermode, Frank. Introduction. *English Pastoral Poetry: From the Beginnings to Marvel*, ed. Kermode. London: Harrap, 1952.

Kinks: Come Dancing. Electronic press kit. Dir. Ray Davies. Weird Films, 2000.

"Kinks 'Enormously Gratified' in US." *Rolling Stone*, Dec. 27, 1969: 12.

"Kinks: Now a Ray of Hope." *Melody Maker*, July 21, 1973: cover inset.

"Kinks Split—Says Pete Quaife." Clipping, c. spring 1969. Rpt. in *John Dalton: Bass Lines*. Atherstone, UK: Official Kinks Fan Club, 1996: 11.

The Kinks: Virgin Modern Icons. London: Virgin, 1997.

"Kinks Walk Out on ABC." Clipping, c. June 1971. Rpt. in *The Kinks on Tour*. Atherstone, UK: Official Kinks Fan Club, c. 2002: n. pag.

Kirby, Danny. "Peter Quaife: Interview Part One." *Now & Then*. Official Kinks Fan Club, 7 (1994): 4–6.

———. "Peter Quaife: Interview Part Two." *Now & Then*. Official Kinks Fan Club, 8 (1994): 9–11.

Kitts, Thomas M., and Michael J. Kraus, eds. *Living on a Thin Line: Crossing Aesthetic Borders with The Kinks*. Rumford, RI: Rock 'n' Roll Research Press, 2002.

Kitts, Thomas M., ed. *Popular Music and Society*. Special issue on the Kinks, 29.2 (2006): 139–284.

Kraus, Michael J. "A Conversation with Mick Avory." Kitts and Kraus 186–99.

———. "A Conversation with Bob Henrit." Kitts and Kraus 228–48.

———. "A Conversation with Ian Gibbons." Kitts and Kraus 219–27.

———. "A Conversation with John Dalton." Kitts and Kraus 200–13.

———. "A Conversation with John Gosling." Kitts and Kraus 214–18.

———. "The Greatest Rock Star of the 19th Century: Ray Davies, Romanticism, and the Art of Being English." Kitts 201–12.

Kreiswirth, Sandra. "Ray Davies Working Out the Kinks." *The Daily Breeze* [Torrance, CA], Aug. 26, 1988: E3, E16.

Levine, Robert. "Clive Davis: Greatest Hitmaker." *New York Magazine*, Dec. 20–7, 1999: 81.

"Lola Completely Banned." Rpt. in *The Kinks on Tour*. Atherstone, UK: Official Kinks Fan Club, c. 2002: n. pag.

"London Calling." *Guardian Unlimited*, Oct. 3, 2005. Oct. 13, 2005 <http://www.guardian.co.uk/arts/features/story/0,,1583362,00.html>.

Love, Courtney. "Courtney Love Does the Math." *Salon.com*, June 14, 2000. Nov. 8, 2005 <http://archive.salon.com>.

Mackie, Robin. "The Kinks: A Band to Preserve." *Record Mirror*, Jan. 13, 1973: n. pag. Rpt. in the newsletter of the Official Kinks Fan Club, Jan. 2000: n. pag.

Mander, John. *Great Britain or Little England?* Cambridge: Houghton Mifflin, 1964.

Marcus, Greil. Rev. of *Arthur*. *Rolling Stone*, Nov. 1, 1969: 39.

——. *Like a Rolling Stone: Bob Dylan at the Crossroads*. New York: Public Affairs, 2005.

Marotta, Joseph G. "The Loss of Identity and the Myth of Edenic Return in Ray Davies." Kitts and Kraus 68–77.

Marsh, Dave. *Louie Louie*. New York: Hyperion, 1993.

Marten, Neville and Jeffrey Hudson. *The Kinks: Well Respected Men*. Surrey: Castle, 1996.

Martens, James W. "And Still He Walks the Streets of the Big Black Smoke: Ray Davies's Working Class." Kitts and Kraus 38–43.

——. " 'Where Have All the Good Times Gone?': The Kinks, An Inquiry into the Debate on Taste." *Popular Music and Society*, 14.4 (1980): 77–88.

Martin, Alec. "Pop Star Attacks Air Hostess." *Truth* [Melbourne], June 5, 1971. Rpt. in *The Kinks on Tour*. Atherstone, UK: Official Kinks Fan Club, c. 2002: n. pag.

Martin, Gavin. "Ray's Back with a Bullet." *Mirror*, Feb. 10, 2006. Feb. 14, 2006 <http://www.mirror.co.uk>.

Marwick, Arthur. *British Society Since 1945*. London: Penguin, 1982.

Mehlman, Lisa. "Kinks at Carnegie Hall What a Performance." Clipping, c. March 1972. Rpt. in *The Kinks: A Live Experience*. Atherstone, UK: Official Kinks Fan Club, c. 2001: n. pag.

Meisel, Perry. *The Cowboy and the Dandy: Crossing over from Romanticism to Rock and Roll*. New York: Oxford University Press, 1999.

Mendelssohn, John. *The Kinks Kronikles*. New York: Quill, 1985.

Miller, Andy. *The Kinks Are the Village Green Preservation Society*. New York: Continuum, 2003.

Miller, James. *Flowers in the Dustbin: The Rise of Rock and Roll, 1947–1977*. New York: Simon and Schuster, 1999.

Miller, Stephen Paul. "Elevated Tracks: The Films of Ray Davies." Kitts and Kraus 143–6.

Mitchner, Stuart. "Put the Kettle On, Mate, and Have a Cuppa Ray Davies." Rev. of *Other People's Lives*. *Town Topics*, Mar. 1, 2006. Apr. 26, 2007 <http://www.towntopics.com>.

My Generation: The Kinks. Dir. John Pigee. Granada Television, 1995.

Nelson, Paul. "Ray Davies Gets His Kinks Out." *Rolling Stone*, Mar. 24, 1977: 11–15.

Norris, Chris. "One Kink's Story." Rpt. of clipping in *The Year in Review—1996*. Warwickshire, UK: Official Kinks Fan Club, 1997. Original publication not cited, n. pag.

O'Donoghue, Claire. "Ray Davies's Proustian 'Tea-ses' and 'Mad-e-lines.'" Kitts and Kraus 148–52.

Orwell, George. *The Lion and the Unicorn: Socialism and the English Genius*. 1941. Rpt. Harmondsworh: Penguin, 1982.

Osborne, John. *Look Back in Anger*. 1957. New York: Penguin, 1982.

Paglia, Camille. *Sex, Art, and American Culture*. New York: Vintage, 1992.

Palmer, Robert. "Kink in Manhattan: Ray Davies Loses His Innocence." *Rolling Stone*, Jan. 4, 1973: 14.

Partridge, Andy. "Andy Partridge of XTC on 'Autumn.' " Excerpted from Mac Randall, *Musician Magazine*, May 1997. Rpt. on *Dave Emlen's Unofficial Kinks Web Site*, Nov. 10, 2006.

Patterson, Rob. "Ray Davies: 'God Save the Kinks!' " *Fi*, Dec. 1998: 19–22. Rpt. in the newsletter of the Official Kinks Fan Club, Jan. 2000: 3–6.

Paytress, Mark. "Tales of Ordinary Madness." *Mojo*, Mar. 2006: 66–81.

Perkins, David. *The Quest for Permanence: The Symbolism of Wordsworth, Shelley and Keats*. Cambridge, MA: Harvard University Press, 1959.

Phipps, Keith. "Ray Davies." *The Onion A.V. Club*, Jan. 23, 2002. Jan. 24, 2004 <http://www.theonionavclub.com>.

Pitalo, Stephen. "Kink Think." *Flatiron*, summer 1996: 38–40.

"Pub is Honoured for Part in Kinks History." *Hornsey & Crouch End Journal*. Feb. 15, 2006. Feb. 22, 2006 <http://www.hornseyjournal.co.uk>.

Quaife, Peter. Personal Interviews. May 24–6, 1998.

——. Personal e-mails. May 16, 2006 through Jan. 12, 2007.

"Ray Article in German Mag. [*Der Spiegel*]." May 2006. Trans. RumbleDoll. *Ray Davies Website*, May 17, 2006. May 17, 2006 <http://raydavies.3.forumer.com>.

"Ray Davies Confirms Kinks Return." *Contactmusic.com*. May 30, 2006. June 2, 2006 <http://www.contactmusic.com>.

Ray Davies: Visions of England. Pro. and Dir. Ray Davies and Ron Trickett. Anglia Programme, 1998.

Ray Davies: The World from My Window. Dir. Matthew Longfellow. Isis Productions, 2003.

Rayes, Ken. "The *Village Green* and *The Great Gatsby*: Two Views of Preservation." Kitts and Kraus 153–64.

"Razorlight Team up with the Kinks." *NME* [*New Musical Express*] *News*. June 8, 2006. Sept. 15, 2006 <http://www.nme.com/news/kinks/.23272>.

Robinson, Lisa. "Raymond Douglas Davies: 'Some People Like to Live with Dreams.' " *New York Daily News*, c. late Nov. 1974. Rpt. in the newsletter of the Official Kinks Fan Club, April 1999: n. pag.

——. *The Kinks: A Mental Institution*. London: Proteus, 1984.

Rogan, Johnny. *The Complete Guide to the Music of The Kinks*. London: Omnibus, 1998.

Rooke, Margaret and Ruby Wellington. "First Person." *Telegraph Magazine*, c. early 1997. Rpt. on *Dave Emlen's Unofficial Kinks Web Site*, Apr. 30, 1997.

——. "Sunny Afternoons and Full Moons: Sunlight, Moonlight, and Stormy Skies in the Songs of The Kinks." Kitts and Kraus 54–60.

Ruocco, Olga. Personal E-Mail. May 12, 2006.

Russell, Rosalind. "Why You Just Can't Classify the Kinks." Clipping, c. early 1971. Rpt. in *The Kink: A Live Experience*. Atherstone, UK: Official Kinks Fan Club, c. 2001: n. pag.

Sanders, Gerald DeWitt, John Herbert Nelson, and M. L. Rosenthal, eds. *Chief Modern Poets of Britain and America*. New York: Macmillan, 1970.

Saunders, Mike. Rev. of *The Kink Kronikles*. *Rolling Stone*, May 25, 1972: 64.

Savage, Jon. *The Kinks: The Official Biography*. London: Faber and Faber, 1984.

Schact, Jane. "Ray Davies Unravels the Muswell Puzzle." *Circus*, Feb. 1972. Rpt. on *Dave Emlen's Unofficial Kinks Web Site*, Feb. 8, 2007.

Schruers, Fred. "The Once and Future Kinks." *Rolling Stone*, Nov. 7, 1978: 11–12.

Schwartz, Tony. "The Rock of Ages." *Newsweek*, June 26, 1978: 77–9.

Sharp, Ken. "A Conversation with Pete Townshend." *Goldmine*, Feb. 2, 2007: 16–19.

———. "He's Not Like Everybody Else: God Save Ray Davies." *Goldmine*, Mar. 1, 1996: 1–9.

———. "Working Out the Kinks: Dave Davies Comes into His Own." *Goldmine*, Nov. 21, 1997: 48–56.

Sillitoe, Alan. "Mr. Raynor the School Teacher." *The Loneliness of the Long-Distance Runner*. New York: Knopf, 1959.

Sims, Judy. "Kinks at Their Best, and Worst." c. Nov.–Dec. 1970. Rpt. in *The Kinks: A Live Experience*. Atherstone, UK: Official Kinks Fan Club, n.d: n. pag.

Skanse, Richard. "20th Century Man, Ray Davies Online Kinks Anthology Interview." *Rollingstone.com*, Dec. 11, 1998. Mar. 7, 2007 <http://www.rollingstone.com/news/story>.

Slick, Grace. *Somebody to Love? A Rock-and-Roll Memoir*. New York: Warner, 1998.

Smith, Dennis. "Knowing Your Place: Class Politics and Ethnicity in Chicago and Birmingham in 1890–1983." Thrift and Williams 276–305.

Smith, Harold L. *Britain in the Second World War: A Social History*. Manchester, UK: Manchester University Press, 1996.

Smith, John. *The General History of Virginia, New England, and the Summer Isles*. 1624. *The American Tradition in Literature*. Vol. 1, eds. George Perkins and Barbara Perkins. New York: McGraw-Hill, 2007: 36–48.

Smith, Russell. *The Songs I Sang for Auntie*. Warwickshire, UK: Official Kinks Fan Club, 1996.

Smith, Russell and Bill Orton. *The Official Kinks Fan Club Present Dogs, Squirrels and Black Crowes*. Warwickshire, UK: Official Kinks Fan Club, 1999.

Spera, Keith. "Singer for the Kinks Wounded in N.O." *Times-Picayune*, Jan. 6, 2004: clipping.

Stanislavski, Constantin. *An Actor's Handbook*. Ed. and trans. Elizabeth Reynolds Hapgood. New York: Theatre Arts Books, 1963.

Stephenson [no first name given]. "Ray is Still a Dedicated Follower of Fashion." British Press Association, c. spring 1997 <http://www.pa.press.net/spotlight/music_davies.html>.

Stevenson, Warren. *Romanticism and the Androgynous Sublime*. Madison, NJ: Fairleigh Dickinson University Press, 1996.

Strauss, Neil. "A Chance to Break the Pop Stranglehold." *New York Times*, May 9, 1999, sec. 2: 1f.

———. "The Pop Life." *New York Times*, Oct. 5, 1995: C22.

Stayton, Richard. "80 Days Is a Work of Years for McAnuff." *Herald Examiner* [Los Angeles], Aug. 21, 1988: E1–2.

Sullivan, Jim. " 'I'm a 20th Century Man . . . But I Don't Wanna Be Here.' " *Boston Globe*, Sept. 29, 1996: N1.

Tamarkin, Jeff. "The Kinks: Seventeen Year Itch." *Hit Parade*, Mar. 1982: 25–7.

Thierry, Lauren. Rev. of *X-Ray*. *New York Times Book Review*, Sept. 24, 1995: 24.

Thompson, Dave. "The Kinks: Thirty Years Gone." *Goldmine*, Aug. 19, 2005: 14–18.

Thrift, Nigel and Paul Williams, eds. *Class and Space: The Making of Urban Society*. London: Routledge and Kegan Paul, 1987.

Tolinski, Brad. "Woodshed: Sixty-Nine, Dude!" *Guitar World—1969: The Greatest Year in Rock*, June 1999: 22.

Toliver, Harold E. *Pastoral Forms and Attitudes*. Berkeley: University of California Press, 1971.

"Top 10 Rock Bands of the Century." *Rolling Stone*, Dec. 16–23, 1999: 256.

Townshend, Peter. "Meaty, Beaty, Big and Bouncy." *Rolling Stone*, Dec. 9, 1971: 36–8.

Tunis, Walter. "Kinks Leader Has His Own Story to Tell." *Lexington Herald-Leader on the Internet*, May 10, 1998. Excerpt rpt. in the newsletter of the Official Kinks Fan Club, July 8, 1998: n. pag.

Twelker, Uli. "The Kinks: Brit-Broadway Schoolboys in Commercial Disgrace." Kitts and Kraus 111–18.

Unterberger, Richie. "Interview with Shel Talmy: Part One." *Shel Talmy Productions*. 2000. May 26, 2006 <http://www.sheltalmy.com/links.htm>.

Vega, Carlos Garcia de la. "Ray in Madrid: The Press Conference." Newsletter of the Official Kinks Fan Club, July 2000: n. pag.

Vivinetto, Gina. "Business Puts a Kink in Music." *St. Petersburg Times* (Florida), Mar. 18, 2001: 9F.

Ward, Tom. "The Great Lost Kinks Movie." *Village Voice*, Oct. 1, 1985. Rpt. on *Dave Emlen's Unofficial Kinks Web Site*, Apr. 30, 1997.

Weinstein, Deena. "Relations in the Kinks—Familiar but not Fully Familial." *Popular Music and Society*, 29.2 (2006): 167–88.

Weird Nightmare: A Tribute to Charles Mingus. Dir. Ray Davies. Weird Films. 1993.

Wetzsteon, Ross. "Theater: Dedicated Follower." Rev. of *20th Century Man*. *Village Voice*, Feb. 27, 1996: 75.

White, Timothy. *The Nearest Faraway Place*. New York: Holt, 1994.

Wild, David. "The Brothers Grim." *Rolling Stone*, May 13, 1993: 24.

Williams, Paul. Rev. of *The Kinks Are the Village Green Preservation Society*. *Rolling Stone*, June 14, 1969: 35.

Williamson, Bill. *The Temper of the Times: British Society since World War II*. Oxford: Basil Blackwell, 1990.

Willman, Chris. "Return of the Kink." *EW.com*. Feb. 17, 2006. Mar. 26, 2007 <http://www.ew.com>.

Wolfson, Susan J. " 'Their She Condition': Cross Dressing and the Politics of Gender in *Don Juan*." *English Literary History*, 54 (1987): 585–618.

Wordsworth, Willliam. Preface to *Lyrical Ballads* (1800). *Bartleb.com: Great Books Online*. Jan. 23, 2007 <http://www.bartleby.com/39/36.html>.

Worrell, Brendan John. *Racing at Royal Ascot*. 2000. Jan. 22, 2007 <http://www.upnaway.com/~worrelle/rat.htm>.

Yeats, William Butler. "Anima Hominis" (1924). *Per Amica Silentia Lunae*. Feb. 22, 2007 <http://www.horrormasters.com/Text/a1989.pdf>.

INDEX

Note: Songs are shown in inverted commas, albums are shown in *italic* type.

155, 163, 164–8, 170, 175, 181, 211, 220, 229
"Ev'rybody's Gonna Be Happy" 51–2, 64, 79
"Expectations" 217

"A Face in the Crowd" 182, 183, 220
Face to Face 72–3, 75, 76, 82, 86
Faithfull, Marianne 4, 105, 257
"Fancy" 94, 163, 232
Fanfare for Europe concert series 167–8
Fantoni, Barry 69, 70
Far from the Madding Crowd (novel) 265
Farlow, Tal 18
"Fat Flabby Annie" 161
"Father Christmas" 79, 80, 180
Fellini, Federico 23
Felt Forum (New York) 152, 171, 191
"Fern Hill" (poem) 119, 121
Ferry, Brian 28
Field, Elizabeth 135
Fillmore East (New York) 105, 145, 146, 149
Fillmore West (San Francisco) 105, 148
Finkle, Julie 236
"Fire" 116
"The First Time We Fall in Love" 184, 202
Flaherty, Robert 23
"Flash's Dream" 173
The Flatlands 174, 247, 251
Fleming, Bruce 33
Flower Power 89, 104
Flynn, Errol 93, 160
Ford, Mary 18
Formby, George 19, 65, 141
Four More Respected Gentleman 112
Fowley, Kim 148
Frampton, Peter 108
Freddie & the Dreamers 31
Freeman, Alan 109
Freewheelin' Beatles (*Revolver*) 103
"From Me to You" 28
Frost, Robert 118
Fu Manchu 118
"Full Moon" 156, 187, 196–7
"Funny Face" 4
Fury, Billy 40

Gainsborough, Thomas 161
"A Gallon of Gas" 19

Garland, Judy 18
Geldof, Bob 85, 264
Gendron, Bernard 93
Genesis 43, 187
Gerry & the Pacemakers 31
"Get Back in Line" 155
"Get Up" 27, 192, 211
"The Getaway" 210, 249
Gibbons, Ian 54, 193, 199, 205
Ginsberg, Alan 85, 104
Give the People What They Want (album) 191, 197, 200–1, 203, 205, 211, 247
"Give the People What They Want" (song) 200–1, 247
Gladstone, William Ewart 231
Glamour 214
Glitter, Gary 99
"God's Children" 157
Gomelsky, Giorgio 28
"Good Day" 209, 211, 212, 213
"Good Day Sunshine" 104
Gosling, John 27, 149–50, 153, 157, 158, 161, 165, 170, 171, 173, 179, 180, 183, 184, 185, 191, 192, 193, 196
got Live if you want it! 84
"Got Love If You Want It" 31, 36, 39, 43
"Got My Feet on the Ground" 50
"Got to Be Free" 164, 220
"Gotta Get the First Plane Home" 72
Grace, Mark 71
Graham, Bill 105, 205
Graham, Bobby 42, 214, 260
Granada Television 126, 130, 144, 181
Grand Funk 226
The Great Lost Kinks Album 94, 99, 107, 112
Green Day 49
Greenslade, Arthur 261
Greenwich, Ellie 41
Grundy, Bill 187
Guiffre, Jimmy 22
Guitar World magazine 143
Gunner, Yvonne *see* Davies, Yvonne
Guns N' Roses 220
Gurvitz, Adrian 262
Gurvitz, Paul 262
Guthrie, Woody 50

Haggard, Merle 20, 152